**Glendale College
Library**

NUCLEAR WITNESSES
Insiders Speak Out

NUCLEAR WITNESSES
Insiders Speak Out

Leslie J. Freeman

W · W · NORTON & COMPANY · New York · London

363.179
N964

Library of Congress Cataloging in Publication Data
Main entry under title:

Nuclear witnesses.

   Bibliography: p.
   Includes index.
   Contents: Chronology of events in the history of
nuclear power—James Pires, pipefitter—Rosalie
Bertell, medical researcher—Ernest J. Sternglass,
physicist—[etc.]
   1. Atomic energy industries—United States.
2. Atomic workers—United States—Interviews.
3. Atomic workers—Diseases and hygiene—United
States. I. Freeman, Leslie, J.
TK9023.N83   1981   363.1′79   81–3951
ISBN 0-393-01456-8   AACR2

W. W. Norton & Company, Inc. 500 Fifth Avenue, New York, N. Y. 10110
W. W. Norton & Company Ltd. 25 New Street Square, London EC4A 3NT

1 2 3 4 5 6 7 8 9 0

*To all the children everywhere
for all time*

Contents

Author's Note   ix

Acknowledgments   xiii

Chronology of Events in the History of Nuclear Power   xv

Chapter 1 *James Pires,* PIPEFITTER   1

Chapter 2 *Rosalie Bertell,* MEDICAL RESEARCHER   22

Chapter 3 *Ernest J. Sternglass,* PHYSICIST   50

Chapter 4 *John W. Gofman,* MEDICAL PHYSICIST   78

Chapter 5 *John Everett,* CARPENTER   115

Chapter 6 *Kee Begay,* URANIUM MINER; *Pearl Nahkai,* WIDOW OF URA-
NIUM MINER; *Fannie Yazzie,* WIDOW OF URANIUM MINER;
Elsie Peshlakai, NAVAJO ORGANIZER   137

Chapter 7 *William H. Hodsden,* ATOMIC BOMB TEST VETERAN   171

Chapter 8 *David Pyles,* LAB TECHNICIAN   206

Chapter 9 *Tom Martin,* MILLWRIGHT; *Richard Ostrowski,* WELDER;
Dale G. Bridenbaugh, ENGINEER; *Gregory C. Minor,* ENGI-
NEER; *Richard B. Hubbard,* ENGINEER   245

Afterword by Helen Caldicott, M.D.   293

Bibliography   300

Index   321

Author's Note

Two things happened that led me to write this book. First, a doctor tried to convince me to take radioactive iodine for an overactive thyroid. I refused. Several months later John Gofman told me I was very fortunate. The radioactive iodine, he explained, would have increased the chance of my getting cancer by more than 100 percent.

The other thing that led me to write this book was the accident at Three Mile Island. Coincidentally, my thyroid condition had been diagnosed the same week that Three Mile Island vented radioactive gases into the atmosphere. I read everything I could lay my hands on, groping for the truth behind the evasive reports published by the Nuclear Regulatory Commission. I finally read verbatim transcripts of the Commissioners' meeting held the day after the accident. The words these men said to each other stunned me. They had no idea what was happening and no idea how to stop it. And meanwhile they were issuing reassuring reports to the public.

I wanted the truth. For the first time I felt my survival was at stake —nuclear power was not an abstract issue: it was a matter of life and death. I started to talk to people—scientists, doctors, nuclear workers.

I interviewed twenty-four people who have worked with or around nuclear materials. In nineteen cases I traveled to the person's home or place of work. Most interviews took between two and four hours and were followed up by phone interviews. I taped the in-person and telephone interviews and listened to them several times, taking notes. I then selected and transcribed those which I felt contained the clearest and most important information and were also the most fascinating as narratives. These were the transcripts from which I worked for the chapters of this book.

A word about the editing I did. In every case I tried to maintain the exact words, the exact flavor of the speech, and the exact meaning intended by the speaker. I have cut out sections that were redundant, irrelevant, unnecessary, or confusing. The repetitive "you know" or "like I said" was eliminated when it seemed too distracting—appropriate perhaps in conversation but not on the page.

Each chapter was returned to the narrator in draft form for comments, accuracy, and approval. In some cases a name was changed to protect an informant, an expression was changed, a statistic was corrected.

The final version of each chapter was then written—including an introductory section, footnotes, and a bibliography of sources relevant to the chapter. Each narrator was also asked for a photograph to include with his or her chapter.

The question that I asked initially in each interview was about personal background. This was followed by a series of questions about what experiences the person had which made him or her change or develop a point of view on nuclear power. I did not merely listen. When I did not understand, I asked questions. When I did not believe something, I said so. I asked for proof, for reasons, for the thoughts and feelings which made people act the way they did. I asked them to describe experiences in such a way that I could see what they saw and hear what people said and did. They described specific hearings and meetings. Again and again I asked to be told what went through their minds as they experienced the things they told me about. It was these personal moments that most brought me into their lives and that I have attempted to bring to the reader.

It is the premise of this book that if the American people knew the truth about radiation there would be no nuclear issue. The information speaks for itself. In this book people who have had direct personal experience with the nuclear establishment speak about what they learned. They did not necessarily start out as proponents or opponents of nuclear power; they are people who have in common a genuine respect for hard work. In almost every case they found their integrity as workers threatened by involvement with the nuclear establishment. When they mentioned that something was done sloppily, that some regulation was being violated, that something was dangerous, their concerns were ignored, trivialized, rationalized, or twisted. Some, unable to work under such conditions and feeling their sense of decency outraged and their survival in jeopardy, began to speak publicly. Then they found out what they were up against: it wasn't just their boss, it wasn't just their boss's boss: it was the union, the utility company, the military-industrial complex that were insisting on the myth that nuclear power was "safe." No one was permitted to challenge this myth and retain credibility. Nuclear energy existed for the "benefit" of the people and nuclear weapons were necessary for "national security."

The stories in this book are evidence that even in the face of intimidation, people still believe their own experience matters and that other people matter. They are concerned about the lives of their children and the continuation of the species. These people know that when people hear the truth, they listen.

Acknowledgments

A project of this kind involves the collaboration and assistance of many people. In particular I would like to thank Teri Phillips, who believed I could learn enough to write this book; Saul Newton, who shared his wisdom and heart when I most needed it; Helen Moses, whose critical reading sharpened my political awareness and always made me feel more hopeful; Janet Steele, whose research and friendship supported the project from beginning to end; Joan Harvey, whose commitment to life inspired me again and again and whose brilliant documentary film on the aftermath of the nuclear disaster at Three Mile Island, *We Are the Guinea Pigs* (Parallel Films, New York City), showed me what people can do when they get together; and the Fourth Wall Repertory Company, whose productions articulate the belief that together we can change the world.

The following people offered me encouragement and invaluable critical comments: Marilyn Aronson, Karin Batten, Bonnie Bean, Leslie Black, Joel Brodkin, Jody Carlson, John Cates, Elsie Chandler, Suzanne Clare, Carol Fassbender, Christina Franke, Joan Franklin, Libby Howell, the late Orville Kelly, Wanda Kelly, Jane Levitt, Audrey Mang, Charleen Martin, Anna Mayo, Gregory Minor, Gail McDaniel, Bonney McDowell, Stephanie Noland, Katherine Pettus, Richard Piccioni, Daniel Pisello, Kal Rabinowitz, Claudia Rosenhouse, Julie Schneider, Nancy Silver, Karen Spalding, and Aline Wolff.

I would also like to thank those who helped me contact the people who speak in this book: Brooke Audreyal, Tom Barry, Rosalie Bertell, Helen Caldicott, Scotty Embree, Peter Faulkner, John Gofman, Anna Mayo, Ronald Smothers, and Lynda Taylor. Because of the limitations of space a number of people who told me about their experiences with the nuclear industry could not be included in this book. I would like to thank Peter Faulkner, Victor Griffin, Edwin Hofstadter, Miriam Karkanen, Thomas Mancuso, Michael McGarry, George Robinson, Arthur Tamplin, Bonnie Tompkins, and William Winpisinger. There are numerous others whose help is much appreciated.

To my editors at W. W. Norton & Company, Edwin Barber, Olivia Pittet, and Josepha Gutelius, I extend my thanks.

Chronology of Events in the History of Nuclear Power[1]

1895   Wilhelm Roentgen discovers the X-ray. (Germany)

1896   Henri Becquerel discovers uranium has radioactive properties. (France)

1898   Marie and Pierre Curie discover radium. (France)

1905   Albert Einstein publishes the Theory of Relativity: all matter is a dormant form of energy.

1932   James Chadwick discovers the neutron. (England)

1934   Enrico Fermi uses the neutron to bombard uranium; misinterpreting the result, he reports a new element. (Italy)

        Ida Noddack suggests that Fermi has split the atom. Her interpretation, which is correct, is ignored.

1938   Otto Hahn and Fritz Strassmann split the atom, repeating Fermi's experiment; they report not a new element but several known ones in place of uranium.

1939   January 26. In Washington, D.C., Fermi announces that each splitting of the uranium atom releases a few neutrons; he foresees the possibility of a chain reaction.

        March 3. Leo Szilard and Walter Zinn prove possibility of chain reaction, performing experiment in Pupin Hall, Columbia University.

        March 16. Hitler annexes the last of Czechoslovakia, which is the richest known source of uranium.

        August 2. At urging of several scientists, Einstein signs a letter to President Roosevelt, alerting him to the feasibility of building an atomic bomb.

        October 21. The Uranium Committee, appointed by Roosevelt, holds first meeting to investigate the possibility of building an atom bomb.

1940   June. Hitler invades France.

        November 8. The first contract is signed with Columbia University to develop bomb material.

1. The main sources for the Chronology are listed in the Bibliography, p. 300.

1941   June. Hitler invades Russia.

December 6. An all-out push to build the atom bomb, approved by Roosevelt, is announced at a secret meeting of the Manhattan Project (Manhattan District Project, the code name for the A-bomb project, was first used on 17 June 1942.)

December 7. Japan attacks Pearl Harbor.

1943   Construction of the Hanford Engineer Works takes place at Richland, Washington, to produce plutonium (for the Nagasaki bomb). Du Pont directs the operation.

Construction of Clinton Engineer Works takes place at Oak Ridge, Tennessee, to produce enriched uranium—U-235 (for the Hiroshima bomb). Du Pont directs the operation with the assistance of the University of Chicago.

Construction of Los Alamos Scientific Laboratory takes place in New Mexico (where the atom bomb is secretly designed and assembled by a group of British and U.S. scientists).

May 11. U.S. government acquires land in the Colorado Plateau after signing contract with Union Mines, a subsidiary of Union Carbide, to mine uranium.

1945   March. Leo Szilard writes Roosevelt warning of arms race.

April 12. Roosevelt dies. Truman is sworn in as president.

May 8. Germany surrenders.

May 14. Plutonium is injected intravenously into a human subject of a plutonium experiment carried out by the Los Alamos Scientific Laboratory. Eighteen human subjects are injected with plutonium in 1945–1946.[2]

June 11. Franck Report: seven scientists who worked on the Manhattan Project warn that an unannounced bomb attack on Japan will lead to arms race.

July 16. First atom bomb is detonated at Alamogordo, New Mexico (200 miles from Los Alamos.)

August 6. U.S. drops A-bomb on Hiroshima (uranium bomb).

2. W. H. Langham, S. H. Bassett, P. S. Harris, and R. E. Carter, "Distribution and Excretion of Plutonium Administered Intravenously to Man," Los Alamos Scientific Laboratory Report LA-1151, September 1950, p. 16. See also C.R. Richmond, "Current Status of Information Obtained from Plutonium Contaminated People," in *Radiation Research*, Proceedings of the Fifth International Congress of Radiation Research (Seattle, Washington, 14–20 July 1974).

August 9. U.S. drops A-bomb on Nagasaki (plutonium bomb).

October. A struggle begins in U.S. Congress over whether civilian or military sector will control development of atomic energy.

Argonne National Laboratory begins experiments on effect of internal irradiation; bone deformities and malignancies develop in lab animals.

1946   August 1. Atomic Energy Act is passed: establishes civilian Atomic Energy Commission (AEC); gives AEC monopoly in atomic energy; establishes Joint Committee on Atomic Energy (JCAE).

U.S. starts nuclear bomb tests in the South Pacific.

1947   Effects of strontium and plutonium on fetal and infant dogs are reported from 1945–1946 in Argonne Laboratory study. (Not all information made public until 1969.)

October. Atomic espionage becomes public issue with growing fear that the Soviet Union will get A-bomb; Hollywood blacklistings begin as anticommunism sweeps across the country.

1948   AEC authorizes purchase of uranium to stockpile nuclear weapons; corporations start mining uranium on Indian reservations in Southwest.

1949   September 23. President Truman announces that USSR has tested A-bomb. U.S. monopoly on A-bomb ends.

October 29. AEC committee, headed by J. Robert Oppenheimer, votes against hydrogen bomb; Edward Teller urges construction of hydrogen bomb. (In 1953 Oppenheimer will lose security clearance and be declared a security risk.)

1950   January 21. President Truman orders construction of hydrogen bomb.

February 9. Senator Joseph McCarthy accuses State Department employees of membership in the Communist party, signaling the beginning of intense anti-Soviet sentiment in U.S. and justifying arms race.

June 24. Korean War begins.

August 17. Julius and Ethel Rosenberg are indicted in atom spy case. They are said to have given the Soviet Union the secret of the atom bomb.

December 20. First electricity is generated from atomic power at Idaho National Engineering Lab, Idaho Falls.

U.S. increases weapons testing.

Fallout shelters are built as part of major Civil Defense program.

1951   Rocky Flats Nuclear Weapons Facility is constructed 16 miles from Denver.

1952   October 3. Great Britain explodes its first atom bomb.

November 1. U.S. explodes first hydrogen bomb.

December 12. NRX Reactor at Chalk River, Canada, goes out of control; fortunately, a partial core meltdown is contained. Future President Jimmy Carter, a nuclear engineer in the U.S. Navy, is involved in the clean-up and receives a maximum dose of radiation.

Nuclear tests begin at the Nevada test site; between 1951 and 1963, 93 nuclear bombs are tested in the atmosphere over the Nevada desert.

1953   June 19. Their clemency appeal denied, the Rosenbergs are executed as Russian atom spies. Protest is sounded around the world; Rosenbergs die proclaiming their innocence.

August 12. USSR explodes its first hydrogen bomb.

December 8. President Eisenhower delivers his "Atoms for Peace" speech to the UN General Assembly, calling for agreements with other countries for technical assistance and introducing sale of uranium for "peaceful" purposes.

December 23. Oppenheimer is declared a security risk because of contact with Communists in the 1930s and opposition to development of H-bomb.

1954   Atomic Energy Act of 1954 is passed. This is a revision of 1946 act to permit private ownership of nuclear power.

Kerr-McGee opens uranium mines in Red Rock, Arizona, employing one hundred Navajos.

March 1. U.S. hydrogen bomb test over Bikini Atoll results in fallout over Marshall Islands 100 miles away, irradiating crew of twenty-three fishermen aboard the *Lucky Dragon.*

September 6. Ground broken for first commercial nuclear power plant, Shippingport Atomic Power Station, Pennsylvania.

1955   May 10. USSR proposes atmospheric test ban.

July 9. Albert Einstein and Bertrand Russell issue global antiwar statement.

August 8–20. Conference on the Peaceful Uses of Atomic Energy, 1st Geneva International.

1956   March. The Law Enforcement Intelligence Unit (LEIU), a national private police force, is organized, ostensibly to fight crime. The LEIU is known to keep intelligence files on political dissidents, including antinuclear activists.

June 6. AEC safety study warns against construction of the Enrico Fermi Atomic Power Plant, a fast breeder, near Detroit.

1957 May 15. First British hydrogen bomb destroys Christmas Island in South Pacific.

August 31. "Smoky," a nuclear bomb, is tested at the Nevada test site.

September 1. Eisenhower signs Price-Anderson Amendment to the Atomic Energy Act to induce utilities to invest in nuclear power. This amendment limits the liability of the nuclear industry in case of accident to $60 million and guarantees up to $500 million in federal coverage. This legislation makes the taxpayers responsible for any catastrophic nuclear accident, which, according to some estimates, would cost more than $7 billion.

September 11. One million dollar fire at Rocky Flats blows out filter and releases plutonium thousands of times in excess of allowable limits.

October 10. A fire in the Windscale Pile No. 1 reactor located on the northwestern English coast contaminates milk in a 200-mile radius with iodine-131. The contaminated milk is dumped into the Irish Sea.

1958 (Date uncertain) Nuclear wastes plant explodes in Ural Mountains in USSR, killing hundreds, destroying hundreds of square miles of land, and causing thousands to suffer radiation sickness. (Not reported until 1976.)

March 31. USSR announces unilateral suspension of nuclear bomb tests.

May 23. NRU experimental reactor at Chalk River, Canada, goes out of control, releasing large quantities of radiation. Reports claim no radioactivity reached the environment.

June. Alice Stewart, a British epidemiologist, publishes first major findings on carcinogenic effect of diagnostic radiation on children *(British Medical Journal)*.

August 11. UN Scientific Committee on the Effects of Atomic Radiation (UNSCEAR) reports that "even the smallest amounts of radiation are liable to cause deleterious genetic and perhaps also somatic effects. . . ."

August 22. U.S. and Great Britain announce one-year bomb test moratorium.

Construction begins on Commonwealth Edison's Dresden Nuclear Power Station, Unit 1, outside Chicago.

1959 February 17. Alarming levels of strontium-90 reported in U.S. milk and in children's bones.

The Tri-State Leukemia Survey is begun in New York, Minnesota, and Maryland.

1960   February 13. France explodes its first atomic bomb.

April 3. Waltz Mills, a test reactor outside Pittsburgh, Pennsylvania, has partial meltdown.

May 1. U-2 incident: U.S. reconnaissance plane is shot down over USSR.

Dresden-1 goes on line, first boiling water reactor manufactured by General Electric.

Yankee Nuclear Power Station goes on line in Rowe, Massachusetts.

1961   January 3. Idaho Falls SL-1 test reactor goes out of control; three maintenance men—McKinley, Legg, and Byrnes—are killed.

June. Walter Reuther releases study of forty atomic reactor accidents, arguing trade union opposition to construction of the untested Fermi fast breeder near Detroit.

June 12. With Justice Black and Justice Douglas dissenting, the U.S. Supreme Court gives the Fermi fast breeder a go-ahead.

September 1. USSR resumes nuclear testing.

September 12. Fifty thousand protest nuclear testing in Trafalgar Square, London; Bertrand Russell and thirty-two demonstrators are arrested.

September 15. U.S. resumes underground nuclear testing.

October 30. USSR explodes 50-megaton bomb.

1962   March 15. USSR proposes complete disarmament.

Indian Point Station, Unit 1 goes on line 26 miles north of New York City.

October 22. President J. F. Kennedy gives USSR ultimatum about nuclear missiles in Cuba.

1963   June 13. Construction begins at first commercial reprocessing facility, Western New York Nuclear Service Center, West Valley. (Nuclear Fuel Services, subsidiary of W.R. Grace-Davison.)

June 20. USSR and U.S. sign "hot line" agreement.

August 5. Partial Test Ban Agreement is signed on testing nuclear weapons in the atmosphere.

November 22. President Kennedy is assassinated.

1964   April 21. U.S. satellite disintegrates over Madagascar and releases plutonium into the atmosphere.

October 16. China explodes its first atom bomb.

1965   June. Thomas Mancuso begins study of Hanford nuclear workers for the AEC.

October 15. Hundreds of workers are exposed to plutonium in a fire at Rocky Flats.

1966   January 17. U.S. atom bomb is lost in air crash over Spain; finally it is recovered from 2,500-foot depth in ocean.

October 5. Fermi fast breeder outside Detroit suffers partial core meltdown.

West Valley reprocessing plant goes on line in New York.

1967   Project Ketch is proposed as part of the Plowshare Program to explode over 1,000 nuclear bombs to build underground gas storage cavities.

1968   November. A ship carrying 200 tons of bomb grade material vanishes. Israel is suspected of the theft.

1969   September. Ernest J. Sternglass publishes "The Death of All Children," contradicting the view that atomic fallout is harmless *(Esquire)*.

October. John Gofman and Arthur Tamplin, researching the effects of low-level radiation, report that there is no "safe" threshold.

Tarapur Atomic Power Station goes on line in India, built by General Electric.

Grace-Davison Chemical Company sells Nuclear Fuel Services to Getty Oil (includes West Valley reprocessing facility and uranium/plutonium processing plant in Erwin, Tennessee).

1970   June 5. Dresden-2 reactor near Chicago goes out of control and releases radioactive iodine.

June 6. Alice Stewart and George Kneale publish results of Oxford study of ten million children in England and Wales, showing obstetric X-rays significantly increase risk of cancer in children *(Lancet)*.

December 18. An underground nuclear blast at the Nevada test site results in escape of cloud of radioactivity; six hundred workers have to be evacuated.

1971   June 3. President Nixon asks Congress to appropriate funds for a fast-breeder nuclear reactor.

Pilgrim Station, Unit 1 goes on line in Plymouth, Massachusetts.

Gofman and Tamplin publish *Poisoned Power* (Rodale Press).

Shippingport reactor is reported to have "zero release" in radioactive emissions for 1971.

1972   March 8. President Nixon orders secrecy on nuclear information in the interest of "national security."

August 25. Plane crashes into Millstone nuclear complex in Connecticut. Sternglass publishes *Low-Level Radiation* (Ballantine Books). Reprocessing stops at West Valley; waste storage continues.

1973   June 8. Leakage of 115,000 gallons of liquid high-level waste is discovered at Hanford, Washington. (It has been leaking for 51 days.)

Fall. Yom Kippur War.

Oil embargo begins. Despite domestic coal reserves of 800 years and other known energy alternatives, the public is told of imminent energy "crisis." This "crisis" provides rationale for increased reliance on nuclear power.

David Rockefeller (chairman, Chase Manhattan Bank) and Zbigniew Brzezinski form the Trilateral Commission, composed of several hundred members of the ruling elite of North America, Western Europe, and Japan. (Members have included Jimmy Carter, Henry Kissinger, George Bush, Walter Mondale, John Anderson, Cyrus Vance, and others from international business, banking, academia, media, and labor.) The Trilateral Commission shapes political policy, safeguarding the interests of multinational banks and corporations and promoting the expansion of nuclear technology to the Third World.

1974   May 18. India explodes its first nuclear bomb.

August 9. Dresden-1 reactor releases radioactive water into Des Plaines River, Morris, Illinois.

August 20. Rasmussen Report (WASH-1400) is released, claiming possibility of death from nuclear reactor is as remote as being hit by a meteor.

September 26. Karen Silkwood testifies to the AEC on safety violations at Kerr-McGee nuclear facility, a plutonium processing plant in Oklahoma.

October 11. Energy Reorganization Act is signed: abolishes the AEC and establishes the Nuclear Regulatory Commission (NRC) and Energy Research and Development Administration (ERDA).

November 13. Karen Silkwood is killed in car crash on way to meet David Burnham, a *New York Times* reporter. The documents she was carrying are not found in the car.

Daniel F. Ford and Henry W. Kendall publish findings predicting emergency core cooling system in nuclear reactors may not work (Union of Concerned Scientists/Friends of the Earth).

1975   January. Virginia Electric and Power Company (VEPCO), a utility operating two nuclear reactors (Surry Power Station Units 1 and 2) and planning four more (North Anna Power Station Units 1,2,3, and 4), asks state legislature for right to establish a police force with power of arrest and investigatory functions.

January 30. NRC orders 23 nuclear reactors shut down because of cracking in the coolant pipes.

March 4. U.S. and Iran sign agreement for 8 nuclear reactors to be delivered in next ten years; cost: $7 billion.

March 22. Fire at Browns Ferry Nuclear Plant, a General Electric plant in Decatur, Alabama, almost uncovers the reactor core.

1976 January. NRC identifies possible nuclear energy centers in its 1975 Site Survey (NUREG-0001), i.e., nuclear parks with 10 to 40 nuclear reactors clustered together.

January 13. Robert Pollard, a safety systems engineer, submits his letter of resignation from the NRC, charging that the NRC is "blind" to unresolved safety problems.

February 2. Three high-level GE nuclear engineers resign—Dale G. Bridenbaugh, Gregory C. Minor, and Richard B. Hubbard—stating that nuclear reactors are too risky to operate.

February 6. Before leaving the NRC, Pollard submits a report on Indian Point, Units 2 and 3, concluding that there is no basis to assume a "very serious accident" will not result other than by "sheer good luck."

February 18. The three GE engineers and Pollard testify before the Joint Committee on Atomic Energy, U.S. Congress.

May 12. Westinghouse requests that nuclear reactor manufacturer's information should be kept secret.

August 22. One hundred seventy-nine demonstrators are arrested at antinuclear rally, Seabrook, New Hampshire.

August 30. Accident at Hanford, Washington, contaminates nine people.

November. NRC fines VEPCO $32,500 for making "material false statements" about an earthquake fault at the site of VEPCO's North Anna nuclear plants.

1977 September 9. Information is released about intelligence operations of Georgia Power Company against antinuclear activists.

October 1. Department of Energy (DOE) is created with James Schlesinger, former head of the Atomic Energy Commission, as its first director.

November 23. Two maintenance workers, James Pires and Ralph Fitts, enter wrong room at Pilgrim-1 nuclear plant; Fitts is overexposed, Pires probably is.

Exxon begins exploratory drilling for uranium mines in New Jersey.

Rosalie Bertell publishes "X-ray Exposure and Premature Aging" *(Journal of Surgical Oncology)*, claiming a correlation between irradiation and premature aging.

1978   January 4. Waste storage tanks at West Valley are discovered to have leaks.

January 24. Nuclear-powered Soviet satellite crashes in Canada, seriously contaminating a wide area.

April 1. The NRC grants operating license to North Anna reactors 1 and 2, despite evidence that the sites are unsafe.

April 30. Five thousand demonstrate at Rocky Flats nuclear weapons facility, seeking to shut it down.

1979   January 19. The NRC withdraws endorsement of 1974 Rasmussen Report.

March 28. Three Mile Island Nuclear Station, Unit 2 (TMI-2) near Harrisburg, Pennsylvania, almost completely melts down when safety systems fail and uncontrolled amounts of radioactivity are released to the environment.

March 31. Hydrogen gas bubble in reactor core of TMI is considered highly dangerous. (Over next few days it gradually decreases in size.)

April 9. Carl Johnson, an epidemiologist with the U.S. Public Health Service, reports higher cancer rates among Colorado residents living downwind of Rocky Flats, where plutonium triggers are assembled for bombs.

April 23. Washington State Senate approves a bill giving reactor owners the power to create police forces.

May 6. Between 75,000 and 125,000 march on Washington, D.C., in protest against nuclear power.

May 18. Silkwood family is awarded $10.5 million because of Kerr-McGee's negligence with radioactive materials.

June 3. Fifteen thousand participate in antinuclear protest at Shoreham, Long Island; more than six hundred are arrested.

July 16. In largest radioactive spill in history, tailings dam breaks at United Nuclear-Homestake uranium mill near Grants, New Mexico; 100 million gallons of radioactive water and 1,100 tons of radioactive tailings spill into the Rio Puerco, contaminating drinking water for 75 miles.

September 7. Senators Kennedy and Thurmond propose a new and repressive criminal code reform bill, S.1722, targeting antinuclear activists and defining as federal crimes: (1) the planning of any demonstration, e.g. an antinuclear demonstration, that *could* obstruct any federal function, and (2) the revealing of the identity of a former CIA agent. 1722 also would severely limit the right to strike and give a judge broad discretionary powers to deny bail and lock up accused persons *before* trial.

October 16. An attempt is made on the life of Rosalie Bertell, an expert on low-level radiation, on highway outside Rochester, New York.

November 9. False report of enemy missile attack results in U.S. fighters taking off before being recalled; the mistake is result of computer malfunction.

November 11. Heidelberg study concludes the NRC judgments on how much radioactivity crops pick up is "between 10 and 1,000 times too low."

December 4. Arizona Civil Liberties Union sues the state of Arizona after sheriff acknowledges a decade of surveillance of nuclear opponents.

December 4. Full Senate Judiciary Committee approves S. 1722, 14-1.

Standard Oil of Ohio (Sohio) begins surface exploration for uranium in New Jersey.

1980 January 24. Earthquake (5.5 on Richter Scale) rocks Livermore Valley, California, damaging the walls of the Lawrence Livermore National Laboratory where large quantities of nuclear materials are kept and causing leak of radioactive tritium.

January 28. President Carter's 1981 budget appropriates $1.26 billion for nuclear research (nonmilitary).

February. International Nuclear Fuel Cycle Evaluation report, prepared by 66 nations, claims that breeder reactors, which use a plutonium core, are cleaner and safer than reactors that use a uranium core.

February 21. CBS News reports that Israel detonated an atomic bomb off the coast of Africa (with assistance from South Africa) on 22 September 1979.

February 26. France plans additional fast breeder reactors by 1985.

February 27. France agrees to supply Iraq with weapons grade uranium and reactor.

March 3. U.S. Department of Transportation announces intention to ship radioactive wastes, including spent fuel, through cities, overturning local state and city health bans.

March 17. U.S. claims that Italy has supplied Iraq with nuclear bomb technology.

April. Two plutonium leaks reported at Livermore Laboratory due to unexplained failures in the ventilation system.

May. California's Department of Health Services reports Livermore Laboratory employees have fivefold higher rate of malignant melanoma than control group.

August 25. House of Representatives approves $20 billion commitment to nuclear fusion over next 20 years with $434.5 million authorization for 1981 fiscal year.

August 29. National Cancer Institute is reported in *Science* as saying that the cancer rate in the U.S. increased 25 percent from 1969 to 1976.

September 19. Titan II missile silo explodes in Damascus, Arkansas. A 9-megaton nuclear warhead is blown 200 yards away. More than twenty workers injured.

September 21. En route from Pennsylvania to Toronto, two canisters containing radioactive material fall off truck on New Jersey's Route 17. Truck driver does not discover missing cargo until he reaches Albany, New York, when he finds only one of three original canisters left on truck.

October 3. Water from Hudson River floods into the containment building of Indian Point-2. A warning light in the control room is ignored.

October 17. Con Edison discovers the water level inside Indian Point-2 has risen 91 inches and flooded the reactor pit. The NRC orders shutdown of Indian Point-2.

November 4. Ronald Reagan elected to presidency on strong pronuclear policy.

December 11. NRC reports that Con Edison was at fault for Indian Point-2 flooding and proposes fine of $210,000. Utility denies charge.

December 11. Reagan names Caspar Weinberger secretary of defense. Weinberger is vice-president of the Bechtel Power Corporation, the largest nuclear construction company in the United States.

1981   January. Senate Judiciary Committee, headed by Strom Thurmond

(R-South Carolina), forms new Subcommittee on Security and Terrorism. "Terrorists" may soon include antiwar and antinuclear groups.

February 25. Reagan Administration proposes elimination of the Council on Environmental Quality and an "easing" of the Clean Air Act to "facilitate energy development."

February 26. Reagan proposes $41.4 billion in budget cuts for fiscal year 1982. Social systems will be cut 25 percent.

March 8. Reagan's proposed budget for the development of nuclear fission is being raised 50 percent or more.

March 8. Defense Secretary Caspar Weinberger insists that the *MX* nuclear missile system must be built. Estimates of cost are between $35 and $100 *billion*. According to the *New York Times* the federal government is spending $4 million *a day* on the MX.

March 10. *Clinch River Breeder* (plutonium-fueled) *Reactor* in Oak Ridge, Tennessee, gets a green light from Reagan. President Carter had opposed the Clinch River project on the grounds that it would spur nuclear weapons proliferation.

March 10. The *New York Times* prints front-page article on new CIA intelligence plan to gather information on U.S. citizens by means of "searches, physical surveillance and the infiltration of domestic organizations." "Terrorists" is the new code word for political dissidents, including antiwar and antinuclear activists.

NUCLEAR WITNESSES
Insiders Speak Out

CHAPTER 1

James Pires, Pipefitter

29 August 1979, Brockton, Massachusetts. Early evening. We are inside a dining room filled with cardboard boxes. There are two small children and Pires's wife, dark-haired, attractive, in her late twenties. She tells me they are moving out of Brockton the following week. After a few minutes, she and the children go out, leaving us to talk in privacy.

Pires leans forward over the dining-room table, his face lit by an overhead hanging lamp. He is a powerfully built twenty-nine year old, with curly light brown hair. He has lived in Brockton all his life. His father was a superintendent of buildings: "He taught me how to fix things, how to put things together."

After completing high school, in 1971, Pires went to work in a nuclear power plant. At that time, Pilgrim Nuclear Power Station Unit I was under construction by the Bechtel Company in Plymouth, Massachusetts. "It was great. Times were good. Everyone worked all the time." Sometimes he took home five hundred a week with overtime. When the plant went on line in 1972, it was an impressive sight: "They had a grand tour showing everybody the whole situation."

But things changed. By 1977 Pires thought Pilgrim I had become so radioactive and the working conditions so unsafe[1] that he decided to quit. Early in November 1977 he made his announcement publicly and

---

1. "Boston Edison admits its Pilgrim I plant in Manomet exposed workers in 1976 and again in 1977 to more radiation than any other plant in the country. . . ." "Highest N-Radiation at Pilgrim 1 Admitted," *Brockton Enterprise*, 13 March 1979, p. 1.

James Pires

walked out. He quit at a time when the most highly radioactive jobs are usually done—when the plant is shut down for routine maintenance.

Three weeks later he received a phone call from the union official who arranges jobs for workers in the Plumbers and Pipefitters' Local. Could he come back for a job involving a possible pipe blockage? Pires figured the highly radioactive work had been done already, so he agreed to do the job.

On that day, 23 November 1977, he and another worker, Ralph Fitts, received an overdose of radiation. Companies consider a worker who has received an overdose of radiation to be a liability, and since that day he has not been able to get a full-time job. But Pires will not go back to any work that involves radiation. Other work is hard to find. Last year he made six thousand dollars, which is hard with a wife and two small children.

He is in the middle of a lawsuit against Boston Edison and Crouse Nuclear Energy Services, a subcontractor,—asking millions in damages. He will take his case "all the way" to the Supreme Court, if necessary. He wants people to know his story.

Orientation: 1971

Guys have questions when they're going down to Plymouth to get hired. They have this guy in there to give you orientation. And he says, "Now, you've got to pass this test before you get hired."

And as he's giving you the orientation, he says—this was all pre-arranged—"I'll be tapping on the desk when there's going to be something important."

Meaning that it was going to be a question on the test. So you were going to pass no matter what. Every time he came up to something, he'd rap on the desk and tell you to remember that point.

A part of the orientation was to convince you on how radiation isn't going to hurt you. "It's not going to bother you. It's only small levels. It's not even as dangerous as smoking cigarettes. You see people smoking cigarettes and living for years. It's the same type of thing."

One day I said, "Well, how much radiation have *you* received in the last year?"

He said he hadn't received anything.

"Oh, right," I said. "Don't you go in there?"

"No."

Here he is saying, "Oh, don't worry about it. It's not going to hurt you or anything else," but I asked him how much he's received and he did nothing but stay off-site and teach guys about working with radiation.

I was always the type of guy to be curious.

First Impression of Pilgrim I: 1971

I'd never seen such a big job in my life. There are miles and miles of piping, different turbine areas, reactor areas. If you've never been in there, you should go down.

It was hundreds and hundreds of men. You get lost in there. It wasn't just one wide open area when you walked in. It was all different rooms, compartments. There were quadrants—the southeast quadrant, northeast quadrant. These went down—oh, jeez—floors and floors and floors, down into the earth where there were miles of piping, say, one hundred fifty, two hundred feet—into the air. It's something incredible.

It was new to me. I wanted to learn all about it and become a good tradesman.

The Plant Goes into Operation: 1972

And that's what I did. I proved myself. I really got into the work I was doing, for a year and a half, two years, building the plant. It was good money, all overtime. A big contractor like Bechtel, money was no object to them.

When we first started, it wasn't too bad. They had federal limits on radiation. They used to cut you off around 1,700 to 2,000 milliroentgens,[2] but you didn't have to worry about it because the plant was new, and there was no buildup of contamination.

The first time, I only picked up 700 milliroentgens, which is nothing

2. *milliroentgen:* thousandths of roentgens, i.e., a common measurement of radiation dosage. Federal regulations require that nuclear workers receive no more than 3,000 milliroentgens over any three-month period.

in three months. You were allowed 3,000 over three months.[3] And I was working right in the reactor, in the steam tunnel all that time.

But as time went on, it got progressively worse. The equipment, the valves were starting to wear out. Radiation was circulating through the plant. It got to a point to where this incident happened to me in 1977, November 23. . . .

In the beginning you used to have to follow these procedures in breaking down[4] these massive valves in the reactor. There'd be QC men in there—quality control men—who made sure what you were doing. And if you were doing something wrong, they'd say, "Hey, no!"

But all of a sudden it's too hot. Now the Edison men and the QC men aren't in there. So they explain to you from the *outside.*

Oh, it's a joke! Last time I went in, it looked like a junk pile. They had parts from the other valves all mixed up.

The plant got so radiated that you would only last a week until you got close to the federal limits. Now the amount of time you were in there wasn't stretched out over three months. Now they had to use more men. And they were burning them out.[5] These guys were starting to wonder —Jeez, I'm really getting used here. They're stabbing me with three months' worth of radiation! And some of them were only lasting maximum a week, week and a half. Then they were laid off. "See you later."

This is the way the Edison operates.

These people are so shrewd. Let's say you started work in December. You're allowed 3,000 milliroentgens in three months. It should be counted from the day you get there, but Edison sets it by the calendar.

They schedule a breakdown[6] conveniently for them, at the end of December, say. They get everyone down there. Jam you with the quota just under the federal limits. Shut you off around 2,900. Okay, so you're here maybe one, two weeks, at the end of December, and you got 2,900

---

3. The Nuclear Regulatory Commission recommends five rems (equivalent to 5,000 milliroentgens) a year but permits nuclear workers to receive three rems in three months. Ralph Nader's Health Research Group alleges that the NRC is permitting overexposure of workers by "30 times higher than recommended by the National Academy of Sciences." "Highest N-Radiation at Pilgrim I Admitted," p. 1.

4. *breaking down:* maintenance repair of major equipment.

5. *burning them out:* using up their full quota of radiation exposure, in this case, 3,000 milliroentgens.

6. *breakdown:* a plant shut-down for routine maintenance work and/or refueling.

already accumulated.

Now January comes along. New quarter. Now you're allowed to get a whole other 2,900 or 3,000. Now you work another week and a half, maybe two weeks. So in two weeks you get maybe 5 rems.[7] You get double the dose![8]

I didn't know much, but I got friendly with a lot of the health physics people. They were into monitoring workers like myself, you know, and I didn't talk to many Edison people because they wouldn't tell you anything. But these health physics kids went to school and studied radiation. And they were my age, some of them, traveling around from different plants.

I used to ask them about chromosome damage and what the levels of radiation were and the measurements. And they'd go over the measurements and everything else. Like signs and horn noises—a warble, a siren, and alarms in case of emergency—one was in case something in the plant was airborne with radiation, one certain sound. And another sound was to evacuate the building completely.

I asked them about this certain thing where we were getting jammed with all this radiation and actually they were going by the calendar date.

I said, "Would *you* take five rems in two weeks?"

And some of them said, "No," they wouldn't.

7. *rem:* rem stands for "roentgen equivalent man." This is a measure of the amount of damage a certain quantity of radiation does to human cells and tissues. One rem = 1,000 millirems, often equivalent to 1,000 milliroentgens.

8. *double the dose:* It is technically legal for workers to receive three rems in any three-month period. But when the utility uses the calendar to define "three-month period," the worker can receive up to six rems in as little as a particular three- to four-week period, which is actually double the dose, or twice the intended limit of federal regulations. This increases the potential radiation damage to the worker.

For the utility, this practice minimizes the number of workers required to complete the repair work involving substantial radiation exposure. It also minimizes the time the plant is shut down because there are fewer workers to train to perform complex jobs. When a plant is shut down, it costs the utility from $200,000 to $300,000 a day to purchase the equivalent electrical power from other sources.

Getting Burned Out

This last time I was on a breakdown. Everyone was down there getting burnt out. Well, what I did, I went down there. I said, "I want to get laid off. I don't want to receive any more radiation. I want my lay-off papers."

Everyone looked at me, said, "What the hell you quitting for?"

I said, "I don't want any more of this. I don't want to take any more radiation. They're burning guys out. I ain't going to last much longer. They'll gimme another dose." But most of them thought I was crazy. Giving up this job and the money.

So my business agent (union man) called me to come back to work on November 23, 1977.

"Jimmy, it's just start-up,"[9] he says.

I was supposed to go in there "just in case," you know, they needed a quick job done. So I had figured at this point only me and this other guy (Ralph Fitts), who also had quit, had radiation left to take. So we went.

I figured, well, my business agent called me and said it was only start-up. So I figured it wasn't going to be in any "hot" areas. All the work has been done—they were just keeping us there, in case something happened.

Well, something did happen.

We—me and Ralph Fitts—were supposed to go into a room down in the rad-waste area.[10] I was supposed to go in there and look inside a valve and see if there was a blockage. This is what my instructions were.

So we got all suited up in cloth suits. You have rubber booties, rubber gloves, masks—your whole body covered. It isn't shielding radiation from going *through* you; it's shielding contamination. So, say some rust here was contaminated. Sure, it isn't on your body. So it's on the suit, you see what I mean? The radiation is still penetrating through you.

They said, "Jimmy, where you guys are going to go in, there'll be two

---

9. *start-up:* when the plant is at a low power level and less radioactive.

10. *rad-waste area:* that part of the plant where the contaminated gases, liquids, solids, and clothing materials, such as gloves and boots, are stored and treated for release or shipment off-site. Pires expected to work in the "clean" rad-waste area, where there is relatively little radiation.

tanks. The pipe is running over the two tanks."

The tanks were like twenty feet in height, probably fifteen feet in diameter.

"There's going to be a ladder and a catwalk between these two tanks," they said. "Watch out when you go in there. It's going to be dark. The tanks will be dome-shaped, and they're going to have hatches on them. It's going to be open, so watch out not to fall down into the tanks."

I didn't know what was in the tanks. They just said watch out.

The pipe we were supposed to work on was running right over these tanks.

They said, "Okay. Take this drop light with you because it's dark in there."

I said, "Well, where's the plug receptacles?"

I wanted to know where the light plug receptacles were, because they have blueprints of everything.

They said it would be over by a ladder.

We went in this gate. They unlocked this gate for us. This door, now, *they* unlocked.

They said, "You're going in here." They tied it back. "Go through the pump room. You'll see a couple of pumps. Go over to this ladder."

Which was a ladder on a concrete wall like a regular horse-shoed ladder going off the side of a boat—just a walk ladder—and they said, "Go over by the ladder. There should be a plug receptacle to the left of the ladder."

Which there wasn't.

So I came out the first time and said, "There's no plug receptacles where you say there's supposed to be one. You sure you got me in the right room?"

They said, "Yeah, yeah. You went by the pumps?"

"Yeah, we went by some pumps."

So we went back into the room, around the pumps to the ladder in the back left corner. We climbed up this steel ladder and then onto a step of a concrete archway where there was a heavy wire-mesh gate going three-quarters up to the top of the archway. The gate was locked.

Then I went out there and told them that the plug receptacle wasn't there.

I said, "There's a gate there. There's another locked gate."

So they gave us a key.

They said, "Don't get it contaminated."

So now this is the second time I've been out there. They said, "Don't get it contaminated. Put it in the bucket."

You know, they gave us a bucket to take in there. Just throw it in the bucket after we were through.

So I went in again. The key didn't work.

But you could reach the other side of the lock without even standing on your tiptoes. So Ralph, who was working—I was doing all the running back and forth, letting these guys know I didn't think I was in the right room, and that these things weren't jibing with what they were telling me—and Ralph tried the key and it didn't work. So he reached over and opened up the gate.

He started going in when I said, "Ralph, *don't* go in. I'm going out and tell them that the key doesn't fit and that you could reach over and unlock the door."

Back out I went. "Hey, that key doesn't fit. I think you got us in the wrong spot. I don't think we're in the right room. But we see a couple of tanks in there."

Two gigantic tanks with a ladder right through the middle like they explained and a catwalk on the top.

They said, "Yeah, you're in the right room."

I said, "But the key doesn't fit. Ralphie opened the gate by reaching over. Should we go in?"

They said, "Yeah, go ahead in there."

So I went back and up the ladders to the catwalk. But I found the plug receptacle on the other side of this gate. I plugged the light in there and we climbed to the top of the tanks. They weren't dome-shaped!

They were flat. There were no hatches on them!

So I said to Ralphie, "Let's get the hell out of here. I know they've got us in the wrong room!"

Ralphie's saying, "Slow down, slow down."

I said, "Slow down nothing! I'm getting the hell out of here!"

So I went out there. "I know you people got me in the wrong room."

Here's the Edison man, my foreman, the health physics guy. They're just standing there. These guys are giving me keys and telling me to go in and whatever, do this, do that. So finally I said, "Hey, the tanks in there, they don't have any domes, and there's no hatches on the top of them. You got me in the wrong room."

"Are you sure?"

"Yes, I'm sure," I said.

They said, "Why don't you go back in there and just check again."
At this time the health physics took my dosimeter.

We have pencil dosimeters which are fairly accurate, but not as accurate as a film badge. You can monitor yourself, how much radiation you're getting. There's a high dosimeter which goes up to three [rems] which is just high range. They don't usually budge in a lot of the areas. And then there's a low range that only goes to like five hundred milli-roentgens. So we had two of them.

This time when he says to go back in to check, the health physics said to me, "Jimmy, let me see your dosimeter."

He took out my pencil dosimeters.

The needles were buried! They were *gone* off both of them!

So he screamed, "GET THE HELL OUT OF THERE!"

I came out faster than Ralphie, and when I heard the health physics say, "The needle's buried," I said, "You gotta be shitting me! You guys don't even know—you own this plant, and you don't even know where the hell you're sending me!"

And from that point on, it was just a big screw up. They had sent me in the sludge tank room where the radiation—all the radioactive waste —is kept.

No one's ever been in there.[11]

They sent an HP (health physics person) in—not into the room where I went—but around there with a long ten-foot probe and measured— he wasn't even *near* the tanks I was climbing on which were holding the waste—he was just measuring the field. The force field in there was reading 300 R, which is 300,000 milliroentgens per hour! I was getting one roentgen per minute. I was only in there three minutes, and the job was supposed to take anywhere from twenty minutes to a half hour.

If I was in there fifteen minutes, I would've passed out.

They would've thought we were working on the valve, and we would've been dead. So many things were wrong and they were going to send me back in there. The first thing—the missing plug receptacle —should've told them that they didn't have us in the right room. Here's these engineers, the people that own the plant. The second thing was the key that didn't fit the gate. The third was when I told them the tanks weren't what they were supposed to have been! And then they were going to send me back in for the fourth time!

11. See p. 18 for a map of the rad-waste area.

So, right after that I got upset. I wanted to find out how much I racked up because it was feeding off so much radiation I didn't know how many thousands of milliroentgens I had. They rushed us into one of the offices and they got our testimony. They got my boss's testimony. Now he was really upset to hear this. My boss—he's out of *my* local, he's a brother in *my* local, but now he's getting his instructions from Edison personnel, and he feels that he almost killed two of his men by listening to their instructions.

But it's such a thing down there, where they have so much power, a lot of people don't think to question these people. They think they're so intelligent, so smart. You're just a worker. They own this nuclear power plant, and who's going to question them?

We got rushed to the TLD reading room[12] where they read my badge. There are four little chips in a badge. They read two chips on the badge. I asked them, "How come you're not reading the other two chips?"

This guy Bob McCarthy said to me, "There are only two chips we're interested in." He says, "This one and this one. If these two chips are over" (which they were: one was 3.181, one was 3.029). "your final reading is between them two chips."

"So I'm overexposed?"

I wrote down both.

"Yeah," he says, "you're overexposed."

And Ralphie who was in there a little longer than me because I kept running out and relaying all these messages, his was a little bit higher than mine.

"Is this the final reading?" I asked.

He said, "Yes. Your final reading is going to be between them two figures, and they're both over 3,000."[13]

I said okay, and wrote it down.

Then they put us over in the pipe shop out of the plant, so we wouldn't pick up any more radiation.

Now we get a call over to this Butler Building which is main offices. A secretary hands me a piece of paper. She'd got this big shot on the phone from the power plant. He's saying, "Have them read this and sign it."

12. *TLD reading room:* a room with special equipment for reading the total exposure measured on thermoluminescent detector devices (TLD).

13. milliroentgens.

I started reading it. I read around a paragraph and said, "You got to be shitting me!"

This started to say: *"We have two pipefitters, James Pires and Ralph Fitts, unfamiliar with power plant, wandered into wrong room."*

This is what they wanted me to sign!

So I said to them, "We're not signing this!"

And she said on the phone, "They're not going to sign this."

"Send them over to me, in the office," he says. "I want to talk to them. One at a time."

Ralphie went over first. I started to go with him.

She says, "He wants to see only one at a time."

So Ralphie went over, and the guy said, "Why ain't you going to sign this?" (This is what Ralphie told me.) And he just said he's not signing it. It's all slanderous. It's not the way this happened. You sent us into this room. It's you people overexposed us. We weren't wandering around the plant and unfamiliar with it and wandered into this wrong room.

The hell with this, I thought, I ain't going to see this goofball.

But I did go down to their doctors. They gave us blood tests and a physical. I had refused at first and called my lawyer, but he said it was okay and I should see the doctor.

This doctor works for the Edison. He does all the blood tests. So, this guy says to me—it's *their* doctor—"You don't have to worry about a thing, Jim. I'm going to explain to you. It's like taking, oh, a couple of X-rays, chest X-rays."

What I'd taken is like the radiation from two to three hundred X-rays at one shot. It's like lying on the table and letting him keep clicking.

I said to him, "You're taking my blood. I want an accident report."

He says, "Accident report? There's been no accident, Jim. You haven't fallen down, broken your leg or anything."

I said, "Well, why are you taking blood from me?"

No one else ever had to have blood taken from him when he got laid off.

I said, "My lawyer told me to ask for an accident report because it was a radiation accident. I was overexposed."

He wouldn't give me one.

The big shot came over to the pipe shop.

"Well, what's the story now?" I asked. "What's going to happen to us guys? You gave us three months of radiation. It seems ridiculous. I

James Pires, Pipefitter   13

was supposed to have been here for some time, a little bit of time anyways. I'm here for one day."

"Well, we're sorry, Jim. It happened. This unfortunate thing that happened. But there's nothing that we can do about it. We're going to have to lay you off."

I said, "There's nothing you can do? You can't give us—keep us on for a while? We'll work in the pipe shop."

"No. There's nothing we can do. It's unfortunate that this happened, but we're sorry."

I says, "You're sorry?"

He says, "That's all we can say."

And that was it.

Let me tell you, the Edison is so powerful.

They read my badges the next day and said, "Jimmy, you are underexposed. One of your chips was 2,910. So you are underexposed."

I said, "What do you mean I'm underexposed? Bob McCarthy gave me the readings. I wrote them down."

"Well," they said, "three of your chips were over. One of them was under."

I called the Nuclear Regulatory Commission right after, the same day, and told them there's been an overexposure.

Edison hadn't let them know yet. See, they held off.

The Nuclear Regulatory Commission said, "What gives you people the right to say because one chip was under and three are over, he's underexposed?"

The NRC flew out to my house to get the story within a few days. They wanted to make sure I wasn't lying because this is serious business.

Eventually, they interviewed all these other people, and the stories matched to a T. So now, as much as the NRC wanted to let Edison off the hook, there was too much, too many people's stories matched.

And I also told them how I had seen my badges read, and how they told me I was overexposed by these two readings.[14] I confronted the

14. According to the NRC, there were four readings on Pires, three exceeding the NRC radiation limit, one just under. There "appeared to be no sound technical basis for supporting the [Boston Edison] contention that the Card G-7, Chip 2 [the only one registering under three rems] provides the best measurement of an individual's whole body dose." U.S. Nuclear Regulatory Commission, Office of Inspection and Enforcement, Region I, Report No. 50-293/77-31, Docket No. 50-293, "Event Description," p. 7.

NRC. I thought the Edison was tampering with my levels. I didn't trust them at all.

The NRC had no alternative but to fine Edison for negligence, for not protecting us from high levels of radiation, exposing us beyond federal limits.

They fined Edison sixteen thousand dollars.[15] But what good does that do me? I'm the innocent bystander that got overexposed. They slapped the Edison on the hand. Sixteen thousand is nothing. They paid the fine and admitted to guilt.

So in my case the *negligence* part has all been proved. They've been found guilty. They didn't contest it. They paid the fine. Now it's just the *damages* that we're going after. We have to prove damages.

I fear my life being shortened. I don't know if I'm going to come down with leukemia. I know I don't want any more kids. There's no way that my wife's going to have a kid after I've been—

How would you like to have a husband, and all of a sudden you get pregnant? Would you feel comfortable carrying the baby, not knowing whether it's going to be deformed or not? How would you feel?

My insurance companies don't feel that they're liable to me to pay for all these doctors I got to see. They don't want to cover.

These things Edison inflicted on me, and they don't want to make any recourse of action on it. They haven't ever gotten in touch with me to see how I was doing.[16] This is the whole situation with them. The Edison is for the Edison only. Their object is to make money, and that's that.

15. The NRC report listed Boston Edison's "46 items of noncompliance" with NRC safety regulations over an eighteen-month period. "The chronic and repetitive nature of the items of noncompliance at this plant [Pilgrim I] demonstrates a lack of effective radiation controls." U.S. Nuclear Regulatory Commission, Office of Inspection and Enforcement, to Boston Edison Company, Docket No. 50-293, 8 March 1978. See also Appendix C: "Boston Edison Company Enforcement History Relating to Radiation Protection 5-12-76 to 11-30-77: Noncompliance Items."

16. "Ralph E. Lapp, a nuclear physicist, is a consultant for Edison and seven other nuclear plants on management problems and radiation exposure. . . . When Edison was asked if it intended to follow up studies on Fitts or other nuclear workers to determine what effect radiation might have on them, Lapp said such a study would be meaningless because there are not enough people involved, even nationally, to get a valid scientific conclusion." Robert J. Rosenthal, "His Massive Dose Called 'Time Bomb' by Wife," *Boston Globe*, 30 April 1979, p. 8.

They're a sophisticated company. They make sure that everything they do with the guys, they're written off. If you're working in radiation, you've signed, believe me, you've signed your life right off to them, right off the hook. Anything happens to you after that, you've signed for it. But they went over federal limits with me, and that's the only battle I've got.

Otherwise I'd be just like the rest of these guys in the future—who knows?

One guy in my local already has leukemia. When he worked down there, his blood was fine. But he signed to work down there. He's trying to fight it in court, but he doesn't have a leg to stand on. They didn't break any federal limits. Now the man's dying. What's he going to do?

We're the records of the future. All these guys in the service are just coming up now.[17] A lot of them, they don't even have names. They didn't follow up. They were ignorant of the facts of nuclear exposure and radiation. But we have records of guys working there, how much exposure they got. In the future we're going to see how these guys do. We'll know what the low levels of radiation are doing to them. If they drop off with cancer, you'll have the records. . . .

When I first started going to lawyers, they were promising me the world. "They can't do this to you, Jimmy. There's no way. We'll sue them for this, and this."

But lawyers are foxy. These guys thought they were going to get 45 percent, a third plus 10 percent for expenses. Then, all of a sudden, I'd get a call a week or two later.

"Well, Jim. We're sorry. We can't handle the case."

What they were doing, they were trying to find previous cases. Well, there aren't any previous cases. There's *no* precedent.

So now the lawyer's saying, "Jeez, there's no case I can follow. Nothing's been precedented. Now, am I going to take this case on a contingency basis and do all this work, and maybe Edison gets found innocent, and I do all this work and get paid for nothing?"

Lawyers are like vultures. They want cut and dried cases.

They were saying, "Well, Jim, as soon as you get more medical records, or if you come down with cancer, we'll take your case."

This is what I was being put up with—trying to get some justice

17. See Chapter 8.

against these people. So I was getting frustrated.

And then finally I went to these lawyers, union lawyers, and they really believed that Edison couldn't get away with this. They took the case. "We'll take it," they said, "and we're going to shoot for the moon with it."

I've been going to see doctors, professional people, psychologists, psychiatrists, regular doctors for blood tests to see how it's affected me. It's been a big burden. I haven't been the same person. I've been laid off. You know, I get irritable. It's a lot on my mind. It really is, and on my wife's mind. In two years it's changed my life, believe me. And it's going to be tough sailing against a big outfit like this.

The only reason I'm giving this story to you is I figure people should know what is going on with us guys.

And when it goes in front of a jury—I believe on the day of reckoning —we're going to have twelve people—just like reporters that never heard this—and they're going to say, "This kid really got screwed." Which I did.

There's a lot of things been on my mind. I think about it. I think, Am I ever going to get justice for this? Am I just going to be pushed aside as a serial number? Hey, they're so powerful. I drive in my car. Believe me, I look in my rear-view mirror wondering, What if an accident happened to me? They could have someone knock me off. They'll do anything. . . .

Lots of nights I can't sleep thinking about dying at an early age. The possibility is there. How would you feel? I don't want any more kids. That's another thing. I wanted more kids and now I'm not going to have any. I'm all done.

I won't go back to Plymouth again. No way. And I feel sorry for these other guys that are really being sucked in, and that's what it is, being sucked in, to work down in places like that. There's going to be more accidents. It's so "hot" now, you can't ever go in there.

Now Ralphie, he never had white hair. Since this happened, his hair turned white. He's got sores that don't heal right, that are taking months to heal.[18]

18. *Ralph Fitts:* forty-seven years old, received, according to Edison and NRC officials, 3.561 rems of radiation. Within three months (February 1978) Fitts became ill and lost weight (from 142 to 124 pounds). He developed skin irritations and his hair turned white. Rosenthal, "His Massive Dose of Radiation Called 'Time Bomb' by Wife," p. 8. See also Chapter 2 for a discussion on how radiation causes premature aging.

James Pires and his children

I asked for a trial by a twelve-man jury. I don't want one judge's decision. They can get to judges. Judges are paid off every day, whether you want to believe it or you don't. But they're not going to pay off a full jury.

I'm going to let people know. I went on TV. I wouldn't give any talks, which they wanted me to give, out in an open area like in the Boston Common. There's no way I go out on any platform and let anyone take a pot shot at me. But news media, I let them all know. Because I think the people should know what the heck they're getting into, what they're voting for, what they're letting them do.

The Edison labels me a troublemaker.

When I go to the news media, this is like a stake through their heart, because it hurts the Edison for people to know the truth.

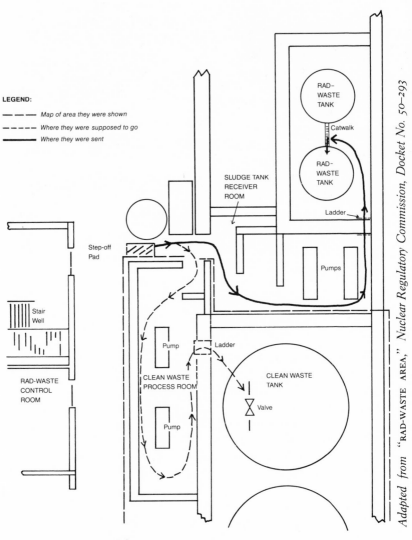

Adapted from "RAD-WASTE AREA," *Nuclear Regulatory Commission, Docket No. 50–293*

RAD-WASTE FLOOR, Pilgrim-1

Author's Note

It is worth noting the Nuclear Regulatory Commission's records of safety violations at Boston Edison's Pilgrim I Nuclear Power Station. The NRC inspected Pilgrim I several times during the eighteen months (May 1976 through November 1977) prior to Pires's accident. [19] *They found forty-six "items of noncompliance," including chronic and repetitive overexposure of workers, failure to post radiation and high-radiation areas, failure to control access to high-radiation areas, failure to properly instruct workers about the level of radiation in the work area, failure to monitor the level of radiation in the air, and failure to survey the work area before sending workers in to perform a job. These violations are listed in Appendices A–C of the report of the NRC Office of Inspection and Enforcement. They were brought to the attention of the Boston Edison Company prior to the accident which took place on 23 November 1977.*

Subsequently, the NRC reported that radiation levels in the room that Pires and Fitts entered on 23 November 1977 were "as high as 200 rems per hour." (Federal regulations limit a worker to a maximum dose of three rems over a three-month period.)

In the NRC report there is also mention of the "survey map" that Pires and Fitts were shown before they went into the sludge tank room. The map did not cover the entire area. It was a partial map, showing only the clean waste room and totally neglecting the adjacent sludge tank room. Nothing was labeled. This made it impossible for Pires and Fitts to be aware of the presence of the dangerous sludge tank room and its location relative to the clean waste room.

The Boston Edison personnel had to use a map because none of them knew where the valve was that the pipefitters were supposed to fix. They had to get the "Rad Waste Coordinator" to give them directions. Using the map, the coordinator explained the whereabouts of the valve, the plug receptacles, and the tanks. He did not, however, make clear that there was a dangerous room adjacent to the clean waste room. Then he "left the area." Since the doors of the two rooms were not distinct in any way, and since no one who was left there knew anything about the

---

19. All the information in the Author's Note is taken from NRC Docket No. 50-293. All quoted material comes from the "Event Description" and "Boston Edison Company Enforcement History Relating to Radiation Protection 5-12-76 to 11-30-77" contained in Docket No. 50-293.

*area they were directing the workers into, the personnel of the Edison
Company "apparently assumed that door "A" (Figure 1) was the access
to the Clean Waste Process Room, since it was the most visible . . ."
(NRC Docket No. 50-293).*
   *The map is on p. 18. Pires and Fitts were shown only the part of the
map that is in the lower right-hand corner, within the dotted line.*

Boston Edison Comments on the Pires and Fitts Case

PAUL McGUIRE, MANAGER OF PILGRIM I:

*"The point is this. They [Pires and Fitts] violated procedures. We
spent a day instructing them on procedures of the plant. They went in
there and jumped over a gate. Now if that's not going out of your way
to get yourself into trouble, I don't know what is."*

> —Quoted in Rosenthal, "His Massive
> Dose of Radiation Called 'Time Bomb'
> by Wife," p. 8.

FRAN WEIDENMANN, DIRECTOR OF NUCLEAR INFORMATION, BOSTON
EDISON:

*"I think what we had was a breakdown of communications between
the people who were on the scene at the time. . . ."*

> —Quoted in Martha Raber, "Pilgrim I
> Accident 'Coverup' Charged," *Brock-
> ton Enterprise,* 30 March 1978, p. B-1.

CARL ANDOGNINI, EDISON MANAGER OF NUCLEAR OPERATIONS:

*"He (Fitts) was exposed to 3.5 rems. Right now I can go down
anywhere and, according to NRC regulations, on March 31, get exposed
to three rems and on April 1 get three more. So I'd have a total of six,
and he got 3.5."*
   (Andognini was asked if he'd want to do that.)
   "Sure I would."

> —Quoted in Rosenthal, "His Massive
> Dose of Radiation Called 'Time Bomb'
> by Wife," p. 8.

"Your Radiation Protection, Safety and Security at Pilgrim"
—Edison pamphlet:

"To exceed Pilgrim quarterly and weekly guide values, you must have written permission of Pilgrim Health Physics Engineer. To exceed Quarterly Guide Value (1.250 rem) you must also have written permission of Pilgrim Station Manager."

> —Quoted in Rosenthal, "His Massive Dose of Radiation Called 'Time Bomb' by Wife," p. 8. (This pamphlet, given to workers at Pilgrim-I, suggests that Pilgrim exposure limits are lower than NRC regulations call for. The NRC limit is three rems per quarter.)

Unidentified Boston Edison spokesman:

"An unidentified Boston Edison spokesman credited a period of instruction on safety methods in the plant with giving the men enough information for them to realize 'almost immediately' that they were in the wrong place."

> —Quoted in Raber, "Pilgrim I Accident 'Coverup' Charged," p. B-1.

CHAPTER 2

Rosalie Bertell, Mathematician
and Medical Researcher

*A rainy afternoon, late in August 1979. We are in the basement of
a conference center in Stony Point, New York. From the next room
come muffled voices and occasional laughter. It is close to the end of
a Conference on Global Dimensions of Justice Issues. A few workshops
are still in progress.*

*Dr. Bertell is here to lead one of the workshops. She lives in Buffalo
with the Order of the Grey Nuns of the Sacred Heart. She has been a
nun since 1951. She is also a mathematician and an expert on the
relationship between low-level radiation and public health.*

*She is fifty years old, a small woman, with short, graying hair, dressed
simply, without makeup or jewelry. She does not wear a nun's habit. Her
speech is thoughtful and slow, until she talks about how data from health
studies has been suppressed: "There's been a campaign since 1951 to
convince the public that low-level radiation is harmless." She leans
forward, indignant. "People have a right to know what's happening to
human health."*

*Dr. Bertell once worked for Bell Aircraft, interpreting data from tests
of guided missile systems. Now she is labeled by many as an enemy of
the nuclear industry. "The patriotic thing to do is to get it all out into
the open. Let people know what's happening." She sometimes fears for
her own safety but feels she has no choice: "I can't go on with business
as usual with what I've seen and with what I know." She remembers
when she began to speak out: "I was very naive. Very dumb. I had no*

Dr. Rosalie Bertell

idea what I was walking into. There was a whole evolution to my understanding."

Growing Up: Guided Missiles and Becoming a Nun

Dr. Bertell was born in 1929 in Buffalo, New York, and grew up there. Her father was "a self-made man who hadn't even finished high school but had taught himself very complicated math, physics, and optics." He had designed the submarine periscope systems used in World War II and gone on to become the president of a corporation, the Standard Mirror Company of Buffalo. Because of her interest in math, Bertell used to help her father by doing ten-year financial projections for his company. "I worked with him and learned a lot about the corporate business world."

Her grandmother lived with the family. "She was paralyzed from the waist down. My mother kept her at home, and we took care of her until she died at age eighty-seven." When Bertell completed high school, she won two scholarships, one in mathematics from a local college in Buffalo, and the other in music from a college in Rochester. "I decided to take the scholarship in Buffalo and give up music as a career because I wanted to stay home and help my mother care for my grandmother."

In college she majored in mathematics. She held many elected offices in clubs, working on state and national levels, and was always in the front line of everything. But she did not feel happy. "Somehow or other I had the feeling that I needed to pull away, that I was so engrossed in activity that I was not understanding what was going on. It seemed right that I enter a Carmelite monastery. They're one of the most withdrawn of Catholic religious communities. You go in and your whole life is encompassed within their walls. Usually people don't ever come out for the rest of their lives."

Not long after she finished college, she made the decision to enter the Carmelite monastery to be more in touch with herself, with "inward spaces." She needed two thousand dollars, "the dowry you are asked to bring in order to enter—a great deal of money to me in 1951. I did not ask my father. Part of our upbringing was to always pay our own way." So to earn the money and because she thought it would be a challenge, she took a job with Bell Aircraft and found herself involved in the basic research on guided missile systems.

"I had FBI security clearance, working in an office where armed people walked up and down between the desks. If you left your place during the day, you had to lock your papers in the desk drawer—even to go to the ladies' room. Our thermos bottles were examined at night when we left work, to see if we were carrying any papers out.

"These guided missiles were going to be the most wonderful weapons of the future, whereby you could target military objectives only, and never again hit hospitals or schools. It would revolutionize war. You were made to feel that you were doing a fine thing for humanity by inventing these bombs. And I believed all that."

Bertell found working at Bell Aircraft a tremendous intellectual challenge. "The job used my brain in a nice way. I remember being very excited one time when a missile was shot off and they couldn't tell whether or not it had turned upside down during the test. If it had turned upside down, all the instruments were recording opposite to the usual orientation." She took that problem on as a special project and saved their doing one missile shot over again. "Everyone praised me, and it was exciting."

While she worked at Bell Aircraft, Bertell did not question the purpose of these missile tests. "We were pretty well satisfied that everybody was a good guy and that this work wouldn't be used for a bad purpose." Her work seemed important, patriotic—a benefit to humankind.

One thing Bertell particularly noticed at Bell Aircraft was their technique of having people work only on their own small section of the weapons program. She realized that no one person was supposed to see the whole picture. "This was deliberately designed in for national security reasons. In fact, even today, our whole weapons production is designed not only so that no one person works on all parts, but also to be spread throughout the country." Uranium is mined in the Southwest, enriched at Oak Ridge, Tennessee, shipped out to Rocky Flats, Denver, where the nuclear triggers are fabricated, and then to Pantex, in Amarillo, Texas, where the nuclear bombs are assembled.

After working on guided missile systems, Bertell entered the Carmelite monastery. Her whole lifestyle changed. "We used to dig four-foot ditches and lay pipes to run our own irrigation system. I learned how to thread pipes and put them together and lay cement walks. I learned plumbing and basic electricity. I found out that women could be pretty

self-sufficient." *She learned how to paint doors and grain wood, how to*
make sandals out of hemp, and while she worked, she had time to think.
  What had she been doing at Bell Aircraft? What were the bombs
being made for? What was war all about? Did people have to live in
constant preparation for destruction? Maybe it was possible for people
to live nonviolently. . . .
  Bertell lived with the Carmelites for five years, and then left the
monastery and entered an order in the Church which does teaching and
social work. She also went back to graduate school and got a master's
degree in mathematics in 1959.
  In 1963 she was offered a National Institute of Health grant to get
her Ph.D. in mathematics. At the time there was a national program to
shift mathematicians out of physics and chemistry and into biology and
biological applications. "I became interested in taking what I already
knew and moving it into understanding living systems."

Learning about Low-Level Radiation: The Tri-State Leukemia Survey

  I worked on things like the kidney filter which screens out materials
in the body, on how the body maintains a constant temperature and a
constant level of blood sugar. All these can be modeled mathematically
so as to predict what's going to happen when you perturb the system
by introducing something foreign.
  I finished the program and received the doctorate in 1966. I continued teaching in a junior college north of Philadelphia, Sacred Heart
Junior College, during the regular academic year. We also have a college
in Buffalo where I taught in the summers.
  Then I received a postdoctoral grant from New York State to work
at a National Cancer Research Center in Buffalo, Roswell Park Memorial Institute. This was originally a summer job. I started working at the
research center in 1969, using the math to try to evaluate a very big
statistical study that had been done.
  It's called the Tri-State Leukemia Survey, and it was initiated because
of an increase of leukemia at that time. Researchers had followed sixteen
million people over three years between '59 and '62 in three states: New
York, Maryland, and Minnesota. Those states have tumor registries, and

they have a law on the books requiring a doctor to report as soon as he diagnoses leukemia. This meant these people could then be interviewed for the study.

We had about two thousand leukemias. We also had a random sample of controls, ways of learning the background of those who didn't have leukemia. We had detailed information on everybody—on family background, what parents and grandparents had died of, their own health history, any sicknesses they'd had, surgery, medicines they'd taken, their complete occupational history, residential history, whether they'd been exposed to farm animals or not, whether they had pets, whether they had sick pets—just about everything you could think of.

Included among our pieces of information was each individual's medical X-ray history. That was taken orally, and then checked by researchers at the source—the hospital, doctor's office, or dentist's office—who got verified signed reports of exactly what had been X-rayed and how many X-rays were taken.

When I was hired at Roswell Park the data had been collected and computerized but evaluation was just beginning. What was I looking for? Whatever it was seemed smaller than a needle in a haystack. But I spent the whole summer on it and got very interested, very involved in solving the puzzle.

The Biostat Department people liked me and I liked them, so I stayed beyond the summer, still teaching at the college in Buffalo but working one or two days a week at the research center on this survey. Eventually I stopped teaching and moved full time into research.

In all, I spent ten years on the analysis of this data.

At first I did all the general things, like examine occupations and socioeconomic status. We wanted to identify what it was that was increasing leukemia in this population. After about four years it became obvious to me and everyone else on the team that the really strong effect —leukemia effect—was coming from diagnostic medical X-rays.

That's when I became interested in radiation problems. For decades we had been told that these very low levels of radiation were harmless!

Leukemia and Premature Aging: Health Effects of Low-Level Radiation

What I discovered is really very simple, looking back. But it took me a long time to get to it because I wasn't thinking that way.

Low-level radiation, the level of ordinary chest X-rays, or dental X-rays, accelerates the aging process. The increase in leukemia that we were seeing was really nothing more than premature aging. People were getting leukemia that they might not have gotten until they were much older. Or they might have died before they got it. By using X-rays we were increasing leukemia by accelerating body breakdown, aging. The person could no longer fight it off.

The leukemia rate is high at both ends of the age scale. Very young children, whose immune system is not yet operating fully, are vulnerable to it, as are the elderly. Leukemia rate reaches a low point at age fifteen and then it gradually goes up for the rest of life.

No one in medical research was talking about premature aging, but I found it mathematically. I found that the rate of leukemia went up like compound interest about 5.3 percent per year, just by living. It also went up at a rate of about 4 to 5 percent for trunk X-rays. You could see the leukemia rate go up with each chest or spinal X-ray.

I decided I would try to measure radiation differently. I would see whether I could quantify this aging process.

You know, if you ask the right question, you start getting different answers. The question I asked was: If leukemia rate goes up with age, how much radiation would be equivalent to one year of aging for increasing the rate? In other words, I used natural aging as the measuring rod, and I said: How much radiation causes damage equivalent to the damage which occurs gradually with a year's aging and catches up with us eventually, even though we don't feel it happen?

What I found out was startling. An X-ray in the abdominal area, where it really hits the major blood-forming organs of the pelvic arch, ages us at the rate of about one rad, one year. One spinal X-ray is about one rad, and that's equivalent to one-year natural aging for increasing your leukemia rate. If the radiation is chest area or even upper thigh, one rad is about six-tenths of a year. You're not hitting as much of the bone marrow, apparently.

Then I learned that if you had dental X-rays, and X-rays of arms and legs, which are again less bone marrow exposure, one rad was equivalent to about a quarter of a year.

This was a measurable health effect.

Then I started finding other things. Radiation effects are more pronounced when people who show signs of premature aging—like those with heart disease, diabetes, or signs of inability to cope with the environment, such as asthmas and allergies—are exposed. You can account this way for something like 70 to 80 percent of these leukemias that occur before age fifty. These are the young adults who die of it—70 to 80 percent are young adults who show inability to cope with the environment through some chronic disease five or more years before they are diagnosed with leukemia. Their death is hastened by X-ray exposure.

The combination of radiation exposure and natural aging tips the balance.

This is now documented.[1]

I'm using this information to try to develop something for those who work with radioactive materials, so that by recognizing these signs of incompatibility with the environment, they'll know to get out of the business of handling radioactive materials.

Premature Aging and the Workers at Erwin, Tennessee

I had done all this research theoretically, but in 1979, when I went down to talk to the workers[2] in Tennessee, who were out on strike, the theory suddenly came alive in people.

What the workers were telling me was really shocking. The union's basic negotiating point was retirement at age fifty-five. The workers told me they're not going to "make it to age sixty-five." These were men who

1. See Rosalie Bertell, "X-ray Exposure and Premature Aging," *Journal of Surgical Oncology* 9 (1977) 379–391; idem, "Measurable Health Effects of Diagnostic X-ray Exposure," in *Effect of Radiation on Human Health: Radiation Health Effects of Medical and Diagnostic X-Rays*, vol. 2, hearings before the Subcommittee on Health and the Environment of the Committee on Interstate and Foreign Commerce of the U.S. House of Representatives, serial no. 95-180 (Washington, D.C., 11, 12, 13, and 14 July 1978), pp. 80–139.

2. *workers:* workers who process plutonium for nuclear submarine fuel rods. Erwin, Tennessee, is operated by Nuclear Fuel Services, the same company that operates West Valley (see Chapter 8) where plutonium is reprocessed.

have worked eighteen to twenty years making plutonium fuel rods for navy submarines. They've been working with radioactive materials for a longer time than those in commercial industry.

I met a man there twenty-nine years old. I would've sworn he was sixty. He had pure white hair.

I spoke with about a hundred men. Twelve of them have had spinal surgery for what the doctors are calling "degenerative spine and premature aging."

Finally some of the workers asked me what it meant when you saw blood in the urine.

"Is this something that you can *see,*" I said, "or is this something the doctor detected with microscopic techniques?"

They said, "Oh, no! You can see it."

Out of a hundred workers, a hundred had experienced gross blood in the urine.

That means they were breathing in radioactive material—uranium and/or plutonium—and probably the body's water system was washing it through the kidneys and doing gross damage to tissues.

This radioactive material is doing tissue damage in very fine internal organs like the kidneys or bladder, producing gross blood in the urine. You know, the men were right: they're not going to make it to sixty-five.

And yet the social pressures on them right now are great, because they're being accused of being "unpatriotic." They're striking against the navy, and the navy needs fuel rods. Because they're asking for retirement at age fifty-five, it seems unreasonable to the ordinary American worker.

On the other hand, because of the men having eighteen to twenty years working with radioactive material, they can't get another job. No other employer wants to assume liability for a worker who has worked that long with radioactive materials. They can't retire under the present system, and they're not physically able to continue what they're doing. As you can imagine, this is heavy. This whole thing is heavy.

That is only one story among many.

A LETTER TO H. DAVID MAILLIE, DIRECTOR OF HEALTH PHYSICS, UNIVERSITY OF ROCHESTER MEDICAL SCHOOL, 3 APRIL 1980

I believe the problems at the Erwin N.F.S. plant are serious. I attempted to set up chromosome breakage and chromatid sister exchange tests for a few employees, so that we might have some idea of chemical and/or radiological damage to bone marrow. The men agreed, but the union doctors in Washington, D.C., failed to fulfill their function with respect to drawing blood and expressing it by air to Buffalo for analysis at Roswell. After this the union leaders were jailed and the men forced back to work. They have not responded to my follow-up letter, and I was told by others they were afraid of losing their jobs.

The Erwin plant has more recently been closed by the N.R.C. because of unexplained loss of plutonium. The former workers are apparently dispersed—trying to get other employment and silent about their experience. Other dialogue I have had with workers at the Rocky Flats, Colorado, plutonium plant and the enrichment plant in Paducah, Kentucky, convince me that there are real worker problems. However, unless the workers are free to cooperate with a serious study, I am at a loss as to how to proceed. In trying to do worker follow-up at the West Valley plant, I ran into legal blockades and finally a "reorganization" of the Erie County Departments with dissolution of the Environmental Health section and firing of the official who was supportive of the study.

. . . The public should be made aware of the blatant non-collection of data responsible for the exorbitant claims of the nuclear industry. . . .

Sincerely,

Rosalie Bertell, PhD, GNSH

Radiation Standards for Workers and the Public

I had been measuring the health effects of one, two, three, four, and five chest X-rays. Then I found that the federal government allows the general public to receive up to five hundred millirems per year. That is equivalent in bone marrow dose to one hundred chest X-rays per year. That really was shocking!

Moreover, I learned that nuclear workers are allowed to receive up to five rems—which is the bone marrow equivalent of one *thousand* chest X-rays per year! These are the federal regulation protection standards! When you approach it from that direction, from low to high, instead of coming down to the standards from the atomic bomb casualties where people died immediately from high levels of radiation, the impact is different.

Federal standards derive from research on high exposures in a bomb situation. Those who determined the standards reduced the exposure level to one where you didn't see anybody drop dead.[3] It looked like a "safe" amount. But it isn't.

Understanding this standard is crucial right now with respect to the Three Mile Island accident, because the NRC has declared it "not an extraordinary event." And their criterion for declaring something an "extraordinary event" is that somebody off-site, a member of the general public, received an exposure of twenty rems or more.

That's the equivalent of *four thousand* chest X-rays![4]

There are no legal steps to protect or compensate the public until someone receives the equivalent of four thousand chest X-rays. That's an "extraordinary event."[5]

Most people have no idea of this definition and its implications for public health.

The criteria were established when no one was watching this industry. All of these definitions went through democratic processes, but nobody was paying any attention to it. And now they're all in law. This is the law.

3. The most important radiation standards are not laws; they are merely recommendations of the International Commission on Radiological Protection, the National Academy of Sciences, the National Council on Radiation Protection and Measurements, and National Research Council. Several government agencies also set, interpret, and enforce radiation limits, such as the Nuclear Regulatory Commission, the Public Health Service, the Department of Energy, and the Environmental Protection Agency. An excellent discussion of the problems of radiation protection standards can be found in *Radiation Standards and Public Health,* proceedings of a second Congressional seminar on low-level ionizing radiation (Washington, D.C.: Congressional Research Service, Library of Congress, 10 February 1978), particularly pp. 8–18.

4. There is a move to increase the amount of radiation nuclear workers are permitted to receive. Dr. Karl Z. Morgan, professor of Health Physics at the Georgia Institute of Technology and a pioneer in radiation protection, believes that the International Commission on Radiological Protection report (ICRP No. 26) will lead to "large increases in the present ICRP values for maximum permissible concentration or permissible dose limits. . . ." *Radiation Standards and Public Health,* pp. 12–13.

5. *Report to the Nuclear Regulatory Commission from the Staff Panel on the Commission's Determination of an Extraordinary Nuclear Occurrence,* NUREG-0637 (Washington, D.C.: U.S. Government Printing Office, January 1980).

Killing the Proposed Nuclear Power Station at Barker, New York

I thought I just had an argument on my hands with the medical profession. I thought the task was convincing them that medical X-rays were causing health problems. I saw it as a limited problem.

Then a citizens' group telephoned the hospital to say there would be a public hearing near Buffalo in Niagara County, on a proposed nuclear power plant.[6] The group wanted somebody to come and talk on the health effects of low-level radiation, and the hospital contacted me.

I knew nothing about nuclear power plants, but I said I would tell them what I knew about radiation. The forum had been managed and organized by the utility company, who wanted to push the benefits of nuclear power, and advocated a generator in the community. That was my first experience of a public forum run by the utility companies, and it was an eye-opener.

The meeting was held at a local community college. The county legislators were there, and between two and three hundred citizens.

When we went in the back door of the auditorium, we were handed a piece of paper. It contained questions that the county legislators had asked and that we were supposed to answer. It seems the utility company had had the questions for two weeks. And they handed them to us as we walked in the back door that night. That was the first problem.

I had prepared a statement, and it was hard at the last moment, when the forum was about to start, to focus on the questions from the legislators. So I tried mentally to put the questions into the context of what I had prepared. Perhaps I could cover what they were asking.

Then we were handed programs, printed by the utility company. They had five speakers of their own, and they gave the speaker's name and expertise, books they'd written, that sort of thing. Below was a blank space marked "Citizens' Energy Committee," that was the four of us. Our names were not listed, and of course none of our credentials were given.

Next I discovered that they had only enough chairs on the stage for the men from the utility company. We were asked to sit in the audience.

When I asked for an overhead projector—this *was* a community

6. The Barker plant was proposed by New York State Electric & Gas Company. This public hearing was held in 1974.

college—I was told they didn't have one. But I kept insisting until I got an overhead projector. That one I won!

The five men representing the utility spoke first. Each took fifteen minutes to deliver a very tight speech, careful wording, and to show high-powered movies of nice, clean-looking nuclear power plants, everything done by remote-control equipment, people behind leaded glass looking in. You know, it was really impressive.

But then I listened to what they said about the health hazards, and I knew that they were not telling the truth. They were giving the impression that there was no problem at all. Everything was under control and radiation wasn't harmful at these low levels.

As I listened, the audience around me sat there, not moving. There was no clapping. No audience response. They were mostly overwhelmed by the jargon, the physics, the movies, all the nuclear terms, the whole slickness of it.

I was called as the first speaker for the citizens' group after this performance, and when I went up on stage I was mad.

"Now that you're all finished," I said over the microphone, "maybe you'll get up and give your seats to the citizens' group."

They had to do that. Everybody in the hall had heard it.

It caused a little stir in the crowd, too.

As the men left the stage and the citizens' group replaced them, I realized the citizens' group was all women and the other group all men. I hadn't thought it out, but I just looked around and saw the women and said, "It's too bad that we have split this way on the issue. Maybe it is concern for life."

I got a standing ovation from the audience. The bottled-up emotion that people had, sitting there listening to all this stuff, was released. After that, anything we said got all kinds of audience response. It just broke the ice. Of course, the legislators reacted to the audience more than the information. They know where their votes are coming from.

I went into what happened when people were exposed to radiation, what low-level radiation did, what I had discovered about medical X-rays, and how this nuclear situation was comparable.

I told them about Dr. Gerald Drake in Big Rock, Charlevoix County, Michigan. He was a general practitioner up there and had known the families for years. Big Rock was one of the first commercial nuclear power plants. I told them how he started noting changes in the health of his community, an increase in leukemia and cancers. He started noting this and reporting it and he was being told that it wasn't due to the power plant. It was the socioeconomic status of the women up there that had changed. Well, he had lived there all his life, and the problems came up after the nuclear plant moved in. I knew him and I had looked at his data.

But what really came out in the discussion and what really tipped the balance on the issue was that next to this power plant [Barker] was the Cornucopia Farms where they grow Gerber's baby food.

I think that convinced the audience.

The Niagara County legislature voted the first moratorium in the United States against nuclear power not long after this. The moratorium still holds. They have since built a small, fairly clean coal-fired power plant, and there's no talk in that whole area about ever putting in a nuclear power plant. They just killed it in one fell swoop.

So I started out with a victory.

Nothing of this had been in the Buffalo newspaper, even though about a million people lived in Buffalo, within thirty miles of the plant! It was discussed in Lockport, a little town nearby. Just a very small notice to rate-payers: "We are considering building a new plant." These plans are usually kept quiet. That was '73 or '74. The nuclear power plants would move into a location very quietly. Most people didn't even know one was being proposed or constructed.

Retaliation: The Nuclear Industry Declares War

I think I caused the nuclear industry a lot of damage that night at the public hearing in the Niagara Community College, but their retaliation was even more surprising to me than the meeting had been. They managed to enlist somebody at the cancer hospital where I worked, a person who lived in Barker, who wrote a really strong letter to the Niagara County legislature and leaked it to the press. Following that, there was a big story in the Lockport press with the headline: ROSWELL DISAVOWS SCIENTIST.

This article implied that my science wasn't representative of the institute. They used the term "representative" so the ordinary person would think it meant my science wasn't any good, but it was used in a

technical sense, meaning that I was not representing the institute's
official position on nuclear power.

It was a very nasty article and another eye-opener. I hadn't expected
that kind of thing. My department chairman wrote a letter to the
newspaper, and the newspaper was pretty good about retracting the
original article.

Then I got an invitation to speak on a local television talk show. It
was just a daytime talk show, and I had not accepted, but I had mentioned at work that I had been invited to speak.

That's when I got a telephone call asking me to come to the office
of the director of the scientific staff at Roswell Park. I asked what the
purpose of this meeting was. I requested to have it put in writing, but
they refused and told me they were just going to talk to me about the
policy of speaking on TV, that the institute had a policy. They wanted
to explain it to me.

Well, I got suspicious, and I don't know why except that I had asked
them to put it in writing, and they hadn't.

So I went to my supervisor [Dr. Irwin Bross]. He thought I was being
paranoid, but he agreed to come because he thought it would make me
feel better.

When we got downstairs and he saw six or seven top men at the
institute going into the room, he really thought twice about having
doubted my fears. Later he said he was very glad he had come. *I* was
glad, because he was my only witness.

This meeting had been called very hastily, in violation of one of the
written agreements with employees. If you call an employee on the
carpet, you have to notify her supervisor, but they didn't notify Dr.
Bross. It was very definitely an intimidation session.

In any case, they brought in—without telling me the purpose of the
meeting—both a cassette tape of what I had said at the meeting in
Niagara Community College and a written transcription of it. Apparently the utility company had taped and transcribed what I'd said.

Their claim was this: when I introduced myself—and remember, my
name was not on the program, nor any of my affiliations—and said that
I worked at Roswell Park Memorial Institute, I had seemed to be
speaking for the institute, for their policy, which is a very delicate
question in an institute.

When I asked them to play the tape over, there was some static on it at the crucial point. They were guessing at what I had said during the static. They had no evidence at all.

The meeting went on for an hour. They were really uptight, especially the assistant director of the institute, who spoke for about five minutes straight about how terrible it was to cause trouble in the local community and speak in the name of the hospital.

When he finished, I asked him if he was trying to tell me that when I do research at public expense, and then go to a public meeting, I shouldn't tell the public what I've found out.

This question so frustrated him that he walked out of the room, slammed the door, and never said another word.

Later I received a carefully worded letter changing the accusation. They were originally accusing me of saying I "represented" Roswell Park Memorial Institute. The rewording of the letter said I had spoken in such a way that some people in the audience might have thought that I was representing Roswell Park Memorial Institute.

So I wrote back and said I was glad to see they had changed the charge, and actually I had rights for a grievance procedure, and I would think about it. I let it go at that, and the institute let it drop too. I went on with my research.

The Barker experience made me suspicious. If it had not occurred, maybe something else would have made me suspicious, but it was this overreaction that led me to find out more about what was going on in the nuclear power industry. I had a very uneasy feeling. They were working too hard to keep me quiet.

So I began to study the history of the federal regulations. I started investigating it on my own and reading everything I could find. I started looking at where the utility companies were getting the information they were giving people on the radiation questions. I found out it was pretty much coming from the American military experience at Hiroshima and Nagasaki.

I found that in September 1945, shortly after the bomb was dropped, the Americans set up the Atomic Bomb Casualty Commission in both Hiroshima and Nagasaki, and that the government has kept total control of the information on radiation effects ever since. The data base is not released to the scientific community. Research papers are released, but not the key information on doses for people, which would allow independent research on health effects.

Author's Note

One of the major problems with this data is that both the test group —A-bomb survivors—and the control group—people living in the suburbs of Hiroshima and Nagasaki at the time—were irradiated—the survivors, from the initial bomb blast, and the people in the suburbs, from radioactive fallout. Initially, the control group was comprised of people who had received less than fifty rads exposure, and these people were compared to people who had received more than fifty rads. Obviously, this would obscure the observable differences between an irradiated and non-irradiated population and imply there was less an increase in the incidence of leukemia and cancer caused by radiation.

Later studies used a control population that had received less than ten rads and then used the general Japanese population, all of whom were exposed to radiation. Each time the control group's radiation exposure was decreased, the comparison rate of health effects increased.

Radiation standards in the United States are derived from the data of the Atomic Bomb Casualty Commission, and according to many scientists permit both nuclear workers and the general population to be exposed to unsafe levels of radiation.[7]

Congress Joins the Attack: The Joint Committee on Atomic Energy

The more Bertell spoke out, the more she realized that radiation exposure levels were just one aspect of the nuclear problem. She began to write about her findings. One of her first articles, "Nuclear Suicide," published in America *in 1974, led to nasty letters written in to the editor.* America *would print neither a follow-up article nor Bertell's responses.*

7. See J. Rotblat, "The Puzzle of Absent Effects," *New Scientist* 75 (1975): 475 and *Effect of Radiation on Human Health: Health Effects of Ionizing Radiation,* vol. 1, hearings before the Subcommittee on Health and the Environment of the Committee on Interstate and Foreign Commerce of the U.S. House of Representatives, serial no. 95-179. (Washington, D.C., 24, 24, 26 January and 8, 9, 14, 28 February 1978), pp. 1082–1086. The Atomic Bomb Casualty Commission is now called the Radiation Effects Research Foundation (RERF).

"Somehow news of me filtered through to Congress. Senator Pastore, head of the Joint Committee on Atomic Energy, had worked with ERDA.[8] So he asked them to look into what I was saying, and James Liverman, head of ERDA,[9] wrote me a letter, asking me to send some of my written works. Naively, I thought they were really interested."

On 1 July 1975 Bertell sent them copies of her research articles, including an unfinished paper. She received a thank-you letter back and a request that she keep them on her mailing list. Nothing more.

"Then I got a letter from a man—I won't tell you his name—who worked for Union Carbide in Oak Ridge." He warned her that Union Carbide had begun to critique her scientific works. Union Carbide, one of the companies most heavily invested in the nuclear industry, would not critique Bertell's work objectively. She wrote the man from Union Carbide back, but never heard from him again. *"He might have lost his job over it."*

Then in September 1975 Bertell received a letter from a woman in Rhode Island who sent a packet containing a twenty-one page booklet critiquing Bertell's work. It was unsigned, and there was no indication of its source. The woman had received it from Senator Pastore.

The questions raised in the critique were designed to suggest that medical X-rays could not be causing the increased incidence of leukemia the Tri-State Study was investigating. *"For example, they suggested that I hadn't considered medical X-rays being taken to diagnose the leukemia and that was why leukemia patients had received more X-rays. But I had eliminated any X-rays for the whole year prior to the diagnosis just to avoid that problem. I counted only those from one to twenty years prior to the diagnosis. They could have answered this question by a telephone call. It immediately put the reader in the frame of mind—'Oh, this person wasn't very thorough. After all, she didn't think of all these things.' It included anything they could find wrong with my work, even typographical errors. Other paragraphs were marked 'No comment' when they were important concepts. One thing that really got me—they*

8. The Atomic Energy Commission was dissolved and split into two agencies in 1974 —the Nuclear Regulatory Commission (NRC) with regulatory functions, and the Energy Research and Development Association (ERDA), which handles research.

9. James Liverman was director of the Division of Biomedical and Environmental Research. He requested Dr. Bertell's published reports on health hazards on behalf of the Joint Committee on Atomic Energy in a letter dated 24 June 1975.

always referred to me as sister, never doctor.
"This critique was being sent out by members of Congress to their constituents."[10] *It was one of the turning points for Bertell. "I realized that this fight must be pretty important if government agencies would use this kind of low tactic."*[11]

The Funding of the Tri-State Leukemia Study Gets Cut

We were asking for a renewal of the grant in order to repunch our data. Our questions on low-level radiation could be answered with no more than a repunching of the data we already have in the Tri-State Leukemia Survey. This would save the government a lot of money—if they really want to know the answers.

Much more research is possible with this data. For example, the computer codes are now crude: upper-trunk, lower-trunk X-rays, limbs, arms and legs, head and neck, dental. I would have wanted to go back to the original folders which have detailed information and code directly a spinal X-ray, a barium enema, a pyelogram, etc. One could focus on the individual diagnostic procedure.

This Union Carbide critique of my work involved Sidney Marks, who worked for ERDA under James Liverman, and was apparently the man who hired Union Carbide to get these booklets together, and then provide them for Congress.[12] He worked sometimes at Battelle North-

10. For example, Senator John O. Pastore, chairman of the Joint Committee on Atomic Energy, sent Emma Sacco, a concerned constituent from Rhode Island, Dr. Liverman's report on Dr. Bertell's publications, claiming that ERDA "had considerable difficulty obtaining the publications by Sister Bertelle [sic]," despite the fact that she had mailed her publications to Liverman within a week of the time he had requested them. Pastore to Sacco, 22 September 1975.

11. According to Dr. Irwin D. J. Bross, ERDA wasn't interested in reporting on the scientific value of Dr. Bertell's work but in "a hatchet job" (from his letter to Senator John O. Pastore, chairman JCAE, 6 October 1975.)

In a letter from James Liverman to Mr. George F. Murphy, Jr., executive director of the Joint Committee on Atomic Energy, 17 September 1975, Liverman acknowledges that the critique of Dr. Bertell's work was carried out by Union Carbide's statisticians from Oak Ridge and his staff at ERDA. Liverman himself critiques "possible flaws" in Bertell's leukemia study, concluding that the "results of Sister Bertell's research activity are not relevant to the nuclear power issue in an important way."

12. According to James Liverman, "In October 1975, Dr. S. Marks of my staff requested

west[13] and sometimes at ERDA.

He's the one who managed to have the ERDA grant taken away from Mancuso[14] and the one who went out to Denver when they found the

---

Drs. J. Storer and D. Gardiner, Oak Ridge National Laboratory, to undertake an analysis of Dr. R. Bertell's publication. . . . A report on the analysis of her findings was sent to the JCAE [Joint Committee on Atomic Energy, U.S. Congress] on November 14, 1975." James Liverman to Senator John Durkin, U.S. Senate, 20 March 1978.

Senator John Durkin had written James R. Schlesinger, secretary of the Department of Energy, that he was "deeply concerned that actions by your department appear to have had the effect of discouraging research into the health effects of low-level radiation. . . . The Tri-State Leukemia survey . . . and research conducted by Dr. Thomas Mancuso . . . have indicated that cancer may be caused by exposure to low-level radiation. "This research is of major importance to the country. . . ."

Durkin expressed "dismay" at the "pattern of DOE interference with these essential independent studies" and stated that "Dr. Bertell's funding was recently cut off by the National Cancer Institute after unsigned critiques of her work were circulated, apparently by Dr. James Liverman, the acting assistant secretary for environment at DOE. Dr. Liverman did not see fit to send copies of the critiques to Dr. Bertell, although they challenge her professional competence. Dr. Liverman was also the official who relied on the phantom retirement plans of Dr. Mancuso to stop his research, a fact which raises questions about his commitment to learning the true dangers of low-level radiation." Durkin to Schlesinger, 27 January 1978.

13. Battelle-Pacific Northwest Laboratories is a private research organization funded by the federal government and noted for doing research in support of the nuclear industry. Dr. Sidney Marks worked for Battelle after working for the Atomic Energy Commission and ERDA. Congressman Tim Lee Carter, serving on the subcommittee which held hearings on the effects of ionizing radiation in 1978, commented that "it was an unusual situation in that $58 million and Dr. Marks went to Battelle about the same time." *Effect of Radiation on Human Health,* vol. 1, pp. 697, 725, 748–749.

14. Dr. Marks acknowledged that the decision to terminate the control with Dr. Mancuso was "my decision arrived at jointly with the staff. The matter was referred to Dr. Liverman. . . ." *Effect of Radiation on Human Health,* vol. 1, p. 697.

Dr. Mancuso was the principal researcher in a study of nuclear workers at the Hanford nuclear facility in Richland, Washington. Begun in 1965, the study was originally funded by the AEC, then ERDA, and then, when it appeared that the results would show a definite correlation between low-level radiation and cancer, ERDA transferred the project out of Mancuso's control to the pronuclear Oak Ridge Lab (run by Union Carbide) and Battelle Northwest (which handled research for the Department of Energy). Mancuso's funding was cut in July 1977 after Liverman's staff reviewed the study. Initially, Liverman explained the decision to cut Mancuso's funding as due to Mancuso's "imminent retirement." In a letter to Senator John Durkin, Liverman admitted his "use of the phrase 'imminent retirement' was unfortunate and in error" and that "other factors were overriding in importance in my decision" to cancel Mancuso's contract and transfer the program to Oak Ridge. Liverman to Durkin, 20 March 1978.

plutonium[15] and told them not to worry, the government would do a study of their health. And the government has never done it. I mean, there's a whole story about Sidney Marks and ERDA relative to assurance of the public that low-level radiation posed no problem.[16]

A site team from the National Cancer Institute then came to make a recommendation on our grant. Dr. Seymour Jablon, head of the Atomic Bomb Casualty Commission, which provided the information to back the present radiation standards,[17] was part of the site visit team.

Congressman Paul Rogers had this to say: "Well, it looks like this to me, Dr. Liverman. First of all, you give retirement as the excuse, and now you say that was wrong. That is not what was meant. You never provided the doctor with his peer reviews so he could answer criticisms. Now you are claiming that the peer reviews were all negative, and they are not at all. The consensus was positive." *Effect of Radiation on Human Health*, vol. 1, p. 719.

The reviewers of Mancuso's study recommended that the study be continued and that the University of Pittsburgh should continue as the contractor. But "contracts are being shifted here," Rogers noted, concluding, "It doesn't look very good, Dr. Liverman, I must say." Ibid., p. 722.

15. Plutonium has escaped from the Rocky Flats Nuclear Weapons Facility outside Denver, Colorado through several fires, leaking barrels of radioactive materials, and emissions to the atmosphere from the smokestack of the plant. In June 1976 four hundred cubic yards of radioactive dirt contaminated by plutonium had to be removed. It had been contaminated in 1968 when fifty-five-gallon metal drums in a storage area leaked. Anna Gyorgy and Friends, *No Nukes: Everyone's Guide to Nuclear Power* (Boston: South End Press, 1979), p. 64. Rocky Flats, managed by Rockwell International, manufactures nuclear weapon components out of plutonium.

16. According to Dr. Bertell, Dr. Sidney Marks produced a scathing critique of Dr. Mancuso, Dr. Stewart, and Mr. George Kneale's study. Dr. Mancuso had to invoke the Freedom of Information Act to get a copy of the critique. After criticizing Dr. Mancuso for the Department of Energy, Dr. Marks went out to Battelle-Northwest and accepted a DOE contract to reanalyze Mancuso's data. Now he claims he needs at least twenty more years to get conclusive results. R. Bertell, "The Nuclear Crossroads" (La Veta, Colorado: Environmental Action Reprint Service). See also *Effect of Radiation on Human Health*, vol. 1, pp. 72, 714–727, 964–965 for a discussion of Dr. Liverman and Dr. Marks, and the way in which research on the effects of low-level radiation is suppressed.

17. Seymour Jablon served on the review panel of the Tri-State grant. He had studied the effects of the Hiroshima/Nagasaki bomb survivors, comparing radiation doses of one to two hundred rads with a nine-rad control standard. This study used a control group which had been exposed to nine rads of radiation, a level that the U.S. regards as causative of cancer. In congressional hearings, Jablon admitted, "We would have been better off not to have used persons with any measurable dose at all as controls. . . ." *Effect of Radiation on Human Health*, vol. 1, p. 1085.

He's now with the National Academy of Science. As far as I can tell, Jablon had never before gone out representing the National Cancer Institute. In any case, I think he was one of the ones who wrote a negative critique of the grant proposal, saying something like the research "flies in the face of all known facts."

This implied that one only does research on what is already known! That's not a very good reason for turning down a grant proposal. Finally, the National Cancer Institute denied the renewal of the grant.[18]

So many other things happened at the same time that it is hard to sort them out. The American College of Radiology was promoting their mammography screening program—mammography for breast cancer. They were going to set up satellite cancer detection places all over the country, and I think it was a million and a half dollars they were getting to set up the mammography program.

Anyway, their arithmetic was wrong, and if they had gone through with the original program, they probably would have caused four to twelve breast cancers for every cancer they picked up, because of the radiation dose they were giving to women who had no symptoms.

Dr. Bross, my department chairman at Roswell,[19] went in rather strongly with other scientists and scuttled the mammography program. It is no longer discussed. But the radiologists lost all this money, and their satellite stations too.

Our grant proposal came up just afterward. We had the radiologists mad at us as well as the nuclear industry and I guess it wasn't too hard to get a few people to write negative reports on the funding.

At the bottom of the grant proposal it said:*If you would like to change your line of research, you could submit a new request for funds. We would be very happy to consider it.*

18. Irwin D. J. Bross, "A Report on the Action of the Two Federal Agencies, ERDA and NCI, in Terminating Funding for Two Major Studies of the Health Hazards Produced by Low Levels of Ionizing Radiation," 5 July 1977, in *Effect of Radiation on Human Health*, vol. 1, pp. 951–976.

19. Irwin D. J. Bross, "Major Strategic Mistakes in the Management of the Conquest of Cancer Program by the NCI," testimony to the Subcommittee on Intergovernmental Relations and Human Resources of the Committee on Government Operations of the U.S. House of Representatives, 14 June 1977. Dr. Bross testified that mammography would cause five times as many breast cancers as it detected. Dr. Bross's cancer study grant from NCI was cut soon afterward.

I felt it was outrageous. The research team—then down to nine professionals—had to disperse and find new jobs. We were out of money. We couldn't do computer work. We had no clerical assistance. One couldn't have access to the basic data.

Since I was not about to go into another research area—no way—I decided to strike out on my own. I wanted to ease the radiological burden on the public.

I resigned at the end of May 1978, with no definite future plans.

After Leaving the New York State Department of Health

Without the research job at Roswell Park, Bertell had no source of income. "It was rather scary. I not only have to eat and support myself, but we take care of our elderly retired Sisters and their medical bills, food and clothing, and also our young Sisters who are studying." By September 1978 Bertell had organized the Ministry of Concern for Public Health, a nonprofit association, and had begun acting as a radiation health consultant. Then, in December 1979, she asked the Board of Trustees of Global Education Associates to accept what she was doing as an International Task Force under their auspices, dealing with questions of energy and health. This gave the Ministry of Concern for Public Health nonprofit corporation status and nongovernmental organization status at the United Nations.

In organizing the Ministry of Concern for Public Health, Bertell intended to lend professional support to the individual researcher. She knew how powerless the lone scientist could feel against the entire nuclear industry.

"I'm trying to surround these researchers with other researchers, provide them with friendly reviews of their works and friendly criticism so as to help them do a better job. We are trying to be precise, honest, and unbiased. We have no vested interests, and even stand to lose funding and reputation because of our determination to protect the public health rather than military and economic policy."

Bertell considers genetic damage, i.e., damage done to the sperm or ovum, the most urgent problem facing us. When she speaks of genetic damage, she distinguishes between severe and mild damage. Severe damage could result in spontaneous abortions, neo-natal deaths, death in early childhood, or institutionalization, with the person having no offspring, and thus not further propagating the damage. Those with mild damage, such as asthmas and severe allergies, on the other hand, often live to thirty-five or fifty. "These are the ones I am concerned about, because they do have children, and they produce children with the same defects they have."

The problem is escalating dangerously. *"Increasing radiation in our environment is producing more of these mild mutations, people who are already genetically damaged when they're born and less physically able to cope with a radiation environment. Now you can't continue to increase the number of people in a population with mild mutations at the same time as you increase radiation pollution that they are not able to handle. As far as I am concerned, this is a death process in the human species."*[20]

Bertell fears that by the time people realize what is happening, there will be so much radiation in the environment that it will be too late. In addition to the normal radioactive emissions from nuclear plant operations, the *"military is setting off two to three bombs a week in Nevada,* blasting an incredible amount of radioactivity into the desert floor and venting some radioactive gases to the atmosphere." People are unaware of the increasing danger to their health. *"They don't even know what to look for, if exposed. All they know is that they might die of cancer, but what they're experiencing is acceleration of the aging process. They have no idea that when they get heart disease, that it's at a younger age than they would've gotten it had they not been exposed to radiation."*

Furthermore, people have no idea of the effect of radiation on children. *"Take, for example, a nuclear worker who has a child with dysentery. He doesn't know that that sickness may be connected to his work. He just thinks it's something unfortunate. People don't realize that the effects of radiation in children can be increases in asthmas, allergies, rheumatic fever, pneumonia, dysentery, besides the leukemias and cancer, and any chronic diseases with a genetic component."*

With what she has seen and what she knows, Bertell cannot be silent. *"We are in a crisis,"* she says, *"a big crisis."*

---

20. See R. Bertell, "Radiation Exposure and Human Species Survival," *Issue Papers: Working Documents of 10 March 1980 Public Meeting*, vol. 1 (Bethesda, Maryland: Committee on Federal Research into the Biological Effects of Ionizing Radiation, National Institutes of Health, 1980).

Deciding to Take On the Whole Thing

It got to me for a while. Four years ago I went to Barre, Vermont, and I stayed at a Carmelite monastery for a year (1975–1976) because I had to work it out within myself. I didn't know how to handle it. I was beginning to realize what an incredible hoax was being promoted, but I spent a year in Barre before I felt free enough to confront death and accept it, free enough to give myself to this work, to care nothing about money or status, or what people think, or what "a Sister ought to be doing," or whether I ought to be teaching school someplace, or what the bishop thought, or all the rest of these encumbrances we have hanging on us. These we must set aside.

You have to become free, and to believe it possible to accomplish something. I think only God gives you that sense of hope. I had to feel the earth suffering, and I had to know that it didn't have to suffer. I had to know that we can live in harmony with the earth, that this is crazy —this production of nuclear bombs, just for the sake of blowing one another off the face of the earth.

This is no way to live. It's totally unnecessary, and nobody wants it. The Soviets don't want it any more than we do. They want to live. They're people. They have families. They have children. They don't want this kind of thing. Nobody does.

The sadness gets to me when I see kids, young kids, and I wonder what their future's going to be.

No matter what anybody does, nobody can take my past away. I'm fifty. I've had a good life. But what will life hold for those now being born?

What Can Be Done?

We need to start documenting changes in human health through the Public Health Service, preparing evidence for courts of law, and getting a mechanism in place which makes companies accountable for the damage they do. We need written documentation, constant monitoring of community health.

We need to stop the total preoccupation of Public Health departments with infectious diseases and convince them to collect the information needed to document environmental diseases. That's a big shift in public health policy.

We're legally helpless now. Take the Three Mile Island accident. The public does not have a piece of paper saying what their health characteristics were before the accident, so how can they prove there's been a change?

The most responsive organizations right now are out in British Columbia. Two full-time workers hired by the B.C. Medical Association have collected millions of pieces of information, and entered it into the computer in the University of Vancouver. They're getting an idea of the health of the British Columbia population, and if uranium mining moves in, as threatened, they're going to hold the mining companies responsible for whatever happens to public health as a result.

Once you get all the machinery in place and you're watching what's being done, the companies are going to be one hundred times more careful!

The worst straitjacket, however, is one we created for ourselves by dropping the atomic bombs. Thereby we did away with the time lag between attack and mobilization for war. Once you move into the nuclear age, you must be able to react to attack in less than a half-hour or you are wiped out.

This requires constant alert. We have been on military alert since 1945. ~~It's causing inflation, unemployment, and it's causing great tension in the country~~.

It's draining money out of the domestic economy into the war machine. Government labs all over the country are brain drains for our finest young men and women. Oak Ridge, Brookhaven, Argonne, Lawrence Livermore, Los Alamos, all of these big expenditures for government laboratories are really dedicated to the weapons industry.

We could do without the Department of Energy. The Department of Energy has a mandate from Congress to develop weapons systems. They have three programs for energy: the nuclear, which is a front for the atomic bomb; fusion,[21] which is a front for the hydrogen bomb; and

21. The House of Representatives approved overwhelmingly a twenty-billion-dollar commitment to nuclear fusion research over the next twenty years. "20 Billion Voted for Nuclear Fusion," *New York Times*, 26 August 1980, p. C-1.

the new solar-powered satellites;[22] which are a front for the particle beam, laser, and microwave weapons of the future.

The 1980 budget of DOE contains more than 39 percent for weapons production. The proposed 1981 budget is over 41 percent weapons-production oriented. Energy is only a front at the Department of Energy. Unless we remove from DOE the mandate to develop weapons systems and change its pseudo-military character and eliminate the secrecy under which DOE operates in the name of defense and national security, we're not going to solve the energy crisis.

It is possible and necessary. We can do it together. People who care must turn in the same direction. I wouldn't be putting effort into resolving this crisis if I didn't think we could make it. But time is running out.

Postscript: 4 October 1979

I was driving home after speaking by invitation to a group of doctors at Grand Rounds at Highland Medical Center in Rochester, New York. My remarks were primarily on the effect of radiation exposure from medical X-rays, but I did extend them to the nuclear power problem, since there is a nuclear power plant in Rochester.

Route 490 is three lanes each way, and I was in the middle lane, in fast rush-hour traffic. I became conscious of a white car in the left lane. It was too close to my car, so I pulled back, and when I did, the driver

22. Dr. Bertell learned about the solar-powered satellite system because she was on the review committee for the Citizens' Energy Project. The Department of Energy circulated the proposal for comment. (U.S. Department of Energy, DOE/NASA Satellite Power System and Evaluation Program, "Some Questions and Answers about the Satellite Power System," DOE/ER-0049/1, Washington, D.C., January 1980.)

"Sixty space stations are planned in this solar-powered satellite system (SPS), each of which is estimated to cost one trillion dollars. The SPS would work by concentrating the sun's rays, using laser and microwaves, down to a rectenna (a receiving antenna) on earth. The rectenna would convert solar energy to electricity. The SPS is also capable of wiping out all communications systems in a city, including computer memories, and can destroy ballistic missiles in air. It is an incendiary weapon and an antipersonnel weapon. The microwave can kill people and save buildings."—Bertell.

See Ron Brownstein, "A $1,000,000,000 Energy Boondoggle," *Critical Mass Journal*, June 1980, pp. 4–5. Additional information about the SPS system can be obtained from the Citizen's Energy Project (1110 6th Street, N.W., Washington, D.C. 20001).

maneuvered into my lane directly in front of me and dropped a very heavy sharp object—metal, I think—out of the car, in line with my front left tire. I saw it coming, but I couldn't move out of the way. I tried to straddle it, but it caught the inside of the tire and totally blew it. It cut a deep slit in the tire about three inches long and put a lip in the metal rim. It must have been a very heavy object.

I think if I had hit it head on, it could have turned the car over because I was in a small Toyota.

The driver in the left lane must have seen what happened because he let me through, and I got onto the median strip, stopped, and got out to assess the damage.

A few minutes later a brown car marked "Sheriff" pulled over next to me. There were two people in it. I didn't see the driver. The passenger did not have a uniform on. He asked what happened and when I told him, he wanted to know if I had either the license number of the car or the piece of metal itself. I said no to both questions.

Then he told me that this wasn't their jurisdiction, but they had radioed the local Rochester police who would be there any minute. Then they took off down the highway.

I was there over an hour and no police came.

Later, when I contacted the sheriff of Monroe County, his office verified that the second car was not a sheriff's car. Monroe County doesn't have any cars of that description. Their men are told to stay with someone in distress even if it's not their jurisdiction.

The Monroe County sheriff's office combed all the written reports which had been broadcast on the police radios for the local cities, towns, county and state police. Nothing made reference to the incident.

The second car apparently was connected to the first one and had followed after to see what had happened.

CHAPTER 3

Ernest J. Sternglass, Physicist

"*Back in 1947 they knew. The data had been gathered at Argonne National Laboratory.[1] They knew that the newborn puppies, whose mothers had been fed small amounts of radioactive strontium-90, were dying of underdevelopment and serious birth defects. The government knew, and decided to keep it secret. The government set up the study. The government knew the results. And the government kept those results from the American people. Why?*"

We are at the University of Pittsburgh Medical School in the office of the director of the Department of Radiological Physics, Dr. Ernest Sternglass. He is sitting in a swivel chair in his tiny, cramped office. He is a man in his late fifties, balding, with glasses. He came to the United States from Nazi Germany when he was fourteen, in 1938. He leans forward, gesturing with his hands. "I know how a government can be totally destructive of its own people, how people in the highest level of

1. The study referred to here was performed under the auspices of the Atomic Energy Commission in 1945 and 1946. Reports were printed by the AEC in 1947 (USAEC Report CH-3843, Argonne National Laboratory, 1947) and 1948 (USAEC Report ANL-4227, pp. 71–82, Argonne National Laboratory, 1948) but the complete results were not made public until 1969. See Miriam P. Finkel and Birute O. Biskis, "Pathologic Consequences of Radiostrontium Administered to Fetal and Infant Dogs" in *Radiation Biology of the Fetal and Juvenile Mammal, Proceedings of the Ninth Annual Hanford Biology Symposium at Richland, Washington, 5–8 May 1969*, ed. Melvin R. Sikov and D. Dennis Mahlum, CONF-69050 (Springfield, Virginia: Clearinghouse for Federal Scientific and Technical Information, 1969), pp. 543–564.

Dr. Ernest J. Sternglass

government can use lies to achieve their political purposes."

Dr. Sternglass has been working for almost twenty years to publicize the dangers of low-level radiation. His article on the increased incidence of leukemia from fallout was published in Science in the spring of 1963. The Atomic Energy Commission "pooh-poohed the whole thing." They said his statistics "weren't good enough." His findings threatened the nuclear establishment. The government and the nuclear industry tried to discredit his evidence by making Dr. Sternglass out to be a "kook." It took courage to continue to speak out.

"I was giving a paper at a health physics meeting here in Pittsburgh. I figured, at least here there would be some newspaper reporters. Someone told me, go, talk to one of the reporters in the newsroom. So I did. I gave him a rundown of the significance of my findings. He took notes and said he'd do a story. That story never got out on the wires. Some time later I told someone at the AP office in Pittsburgh about my findings. 'Dr. Sternglass, how come you didn't give us this story before?' I said, 'I did give it to you. There was a stringer.' And I gave him his name. He said, 'I'll look it up.' And he called me up and said, 'There is no such individual working for Associated Press.' Who had I spoken to? I never found out."

After World War II the U.S. military was intent upon building up its weapons arsenal. But Americans were sick of war. The military figured that the way to get their weapons program funded was to make the bomb look "peaceful and happy," to take away the spectre of war and transform atomic energy into a "promise for peace." The "peaceful atom" was a cover for the continued proliferation of weapons development. It was an elaborate lie. Dr. Sternglass gradually realized how far-reaching the lie had been. "The military was behind everything. "

Growing Up: Germany, X-rays, and War

Ernest Sternglass was born in 1923 in Berlin, Germany. Both his parents were physicians. His mother, a pediatrician and obstetrician, had an office in their home. His father's dermatology office was in another part of Berlin, and for some reason he had a number of fetuses in bottles high on a shelf, fetuses at every stage of development. He also had X-ray equipment and ultraviolet machines which he used in treating skin cancers and other conditions. Sternglass's parents frequently discussed their cases at the dinner table. "I remember them talking about patients who had been given excessive amounts of radiation for acne or ringworm of the scalp, patients who then came to my father for treatment."[2]

When Hitler came to power, the Sternglass family knew they would have to leave Germany eventually. Sternglass was ten years old, old enough to understand the growing danger. "We had a little house in the country, and there were days, sometimes nights when people came to throw rocks, trying to break our windows. I lived in fear of my father being arrested at any time." The Sternglass family finally left Germany in 1938, when Ernest was fourteen, and by the time they came to the United States, Sternglass was "very appreciative of what this country meant."

The family was in difficult financial straits when they arrived in New York City. While Sternglass's father learned English and struggled to pass his Licensing Board Examinations, his mother supported the family by giving health massages and working as a doctor in summer camps. Sternglass did household chores to help out.

When Sternglass completed high school at the age of sixteen, war had broken out in Europe, and while he did not know what would happen, he decided he would go to college. Although his heart was in physics, in basic research, his mother persuaded him in another direction.

"You aren't going to have a job to support yourself and your family if you are only a physicist," she warned her son. "You need something like engineering—something practical to keep you going. Later on, if you want, you can always turn to physics."

So when Sternglass entered Cornell, he registered for an engineering program. His family was still deep in financial trouble, and he had to leave school for a year to help support the family. When he returned to Cornell, the United States had already entered the war, and Sternglass learned that people were wanted in radar and electronics. Since he had had some engineering training and had studied electronics, he volunteered for the navy.

"I was about to be shipped out with the invasion fleet to Japan, when the atomic bomb was detonated over Hiroshima. When the announce-

2. In the 1920s and 1930s it was common practice to treat skin disorders, such as acne and ringworm of the scalp, with X-ray treatments.

*ment came about this bomb that had suddenly ended the whole war,
I was very relieved. I didn't have to be shipped out. Only later did I
understand what had happened, what the bomb meant."*

After the war, Sternglass married and moved to Washington, D.C.,
where he worked as a civilian employee at the Naval Ordnance Laboratory, which researched military weapons such as mines, torpedoes, and
guiding systems for underwater missiles. Sternglass began investigating
imaging devices that would enable a soldier to see the enemy at night.
He found the work fascinating. *"I wanted to understand the interaction
of electrons with matter, the penetration of electrons into solids, and the
scattering of radiation by solids."* Sternglass's work involved radiation,
an interest dating back to his childhood. He began to explore a theory
of electron emission from solids, related to the photoelectric effect, for
which Einstein had won the Nobel Prize.

The year 1947 was a turning point for Sternglass. Not only did his
wife give birth to their first son, but Sternglass had the opportunity to
meet Einstein in person.

Meeting Albert Einstein: 1947

Let me explain what Einstein had done many years ago. In 1905 he
discovered that light behaves like a particle. Instead of acting like a wave
that spreads out all over, light waves—or photons—hang together like
little balls, little bunches of radiation. When they hit a metal plate, they
knock out an electron, a single electron, right out of the plate. Light hits
a metal, and if there is enough energy in the light, it will overcome the
force that binds the electron in the metal. For this discovery Einstein
received the Nobel Prize.

My ideas about this phenomenon were somewhat different, and I
wrote to Einstein about them. Three days later I received a letter asking
me to come visit him. I was all shaken up. After all, I was just a young
kid who hadn't even finished graduate school. I was only taking one or
two courses at George Washington University in the evenings.

I remember arriving in Princeton and walking from the station over
to Einstein's house. It was a beautiful day in April, but I was shaking
all over inside. I didn't know if I would be able to talk to him at all. God,
he must get thousands of letters.

I walked up to this beautiful little white frame-house on Mercer Street, and knocked on the door. One of his secretaries came and ushered me in.

"Here. You sit here and wait."

I waited in the dining room, which had icons all around it. I was really amazed looking at them. Why would he have icons in his dining room? Then I saw him coming down the hall, shuffling in his slippers, wearing his baggy gray pants, and the white hair, exactly the way all the pictures looked. He was close to seventy at the time.

He looked at me and said, "Well, young man, the weather is nice outside. Let's go and sit on the back porch."

So we went through to the back of the house and sat down. He lit one of these long clay pipes he had and said, "First of all, tell me about your ideas."

And so I started talking, but he stopped me.

"Tell me, do you still speak German?" he said.

"Yes." I still had rather a heavy accent.

"Well, then," he said, "let's talk in German. It's easier. So tell me about your ideas."

He listened very carefully. I explained how I believed one cannot treat the metal as if there were only one electron per atom, but one had to look at the whole structure of the atom deeply.

And he nodded. "That sounds pretty reasonable to me."

When I got through, he said, "I think you're on the right track. Keep this up. I think that's the right direction."

Oh, I felt very pleased.

"Now let's talk about some interesting things," he said, *"really* interesting things. Tell me your ideas about particle physics."

"Well," I said, "people have been trying to come to grips with this particle concept for years—"

And he said, "Yes, I know, I know. . . ."

I told him that I felt that of all the particles that had ever been discovered, only one we've seen so far does not disintegrate, can never be smashed up, which seems to be the ultimate smallest charge. And that's the electron.

He said, "Yes. . . ."

And I said, "No one has ever seen an electron and positron annihilating without any ashes left over. They become pure energy. They form two gamma rays, two light waves."

And he said, "That's certainly true."

And I said, "It seems to me that we should look at the electron as a source of an electric field, and forget any idea that there's a little hard core of matter inside the electron."

And he said, "Mmmm . . . I thought about this at some time myself."

Then I said, "Well, I believe that's the only way we can make any progress, because there's no point worrying about what holds the electron together at this time, if we have absolutely no way of knowing that the electron ever disintegrates. Why not assume that the total mass of the electron is simply due to the pure energy in its field?"

And he said, "Well, that's possible. But we don't have any solid knowledge about this. . . . I've thought about this."

I reminded him of things that he had said at various times in his life about the electron. At times he had talked about it as being like a little hard ball of matter and having some charge around it, and at other times he had talked about it as being a pure field entity.

He said, "Well, you know, I made many mistakes in my life, and you're right, you have to keep trying. Let's talk some more. What about light waves? How do you explain the fact that the photon hangs together?"

And I said, "I really don't have any adequate model for it yet, but—"

"Well," he said, "that will take a long time to discover, but you might follow up this business of the electron being just a pure charge." He put down his pipe. "Why don't we go for a little walk here in the garden?"

As we started walking, he said, "You see that tree over there? Now turn around. Now that you don't see the tree, is it still there?"

And so we got to talking about fundamental problems of quantum theory. And after we had discussed philosophy for a long time, a secretary came out and said, "Dr. Einstein, there is someone waiting for you. You have another appointment."

He turned to me, "You be quiet and sit here. I'll get rid of him quickly!"

I sat there and said to myself, My God, it's strange that he should have an interest in continuing to talk to me, an absolute nobody.

He returned in a few minutes. "Tell me," he said, "Are you planning to go back to school?"

"Yes, I'm thinking about it."

"Don't go back to school. They will try to crush every bit of originality out of you. Don't go back to graduate school."

"Well, I—"

"Be careful. There will be enormous pressures to conform."

And then he told me about his own life and the mistakes he had made. "Don't do what I've done," he said. "Always have a cobbler's job. Always have a job where you can get up in the morning, face yourself, that you're doing something useful for humanity. Because nobody can be a genius every day. Don't make that kind of mistake. You know, when I accepted a job at the University of Berlin, I had no duties really. Nothing to do except wake up and solve all the problems of the universe every morning. Nobody can do that. Don't make that mistake."

And then we talked a good deal more about his attempts to formulate a unified theory.

"Look," he said, "come upstairs." So he took me upstairs to his study. "You see these papers here?" They were full of the equations of the unified field theory that he'd been working on for years. "You see all this? I will never know whether any of this has any meaning whatsoever."

And so we talked for five hours. All afternoon. Among the things we talked about was the atomic bomb. This came up because he was terribly depressed about the fact that the bomb was going to be used again, that the nations of the world had not managed to find some international way of controlling it. He and many other concerned scientists at Los Alamos were in the midst of a campaign to mobilize the scientific community and educate the public. The bomb was not just another weapon. The use of this bomb could lead to the destruction of mankind.

His sense of guilt was enormous—the sense of having made so many mistakes, of having allowed himself to be used in the business of getting the first bomb built. Even though he hadn't worked on the bomb himself, he had written a letter to Roosevelt, telling him about the discovery of fission. The Manhattan Project had followed.[3] I could see

3. *Manhattan Project:* a top-secret wartime project to develop the A-bomb. It was established ostensibly because of fear that the Germans were working on the bomb. In fact, the Germans weren't even close to building the A-bomb. The scientists who convinced Einstein to write Roosevelt in 1939 were Leo Szilard, Eugene Wigner, and Edward Teller. See Walter and Miriam Schneir, *Invitation to an Inquest: Reopening the Rosenberg "Atom Spy" Case* (Baltimore: Penguin Books, 1973), pp. 14–19.

Einstein felt tremendously unhappy about this. Not only because of Hiroshima and Nagasaki, but because more bombs were being created. He was concerned that Russia would soon have the bomb. This would surely lead to an arms race that would fill the world with atomic bombs, and sooner or later someone would use them.

"That, by far, is the most terrible problem confronting all of us." The man was crushed by this thought. I could see it in his eyes. He had wanted his discoveries to benefit man. His real ambition, his real hope, had been to find the secret of the universe, to understand what makes it all tick and cohere.

I learned a great lesson from Einstein: that no one can control the direction in which his research is used, for evil or for good; and I came back from Princeton a different person. I knew it would always be part of my life to prevent the use of this weapon again—in any form—and that the biggest job was to try to warn the public, show people that this was not just another weapon, that there was immense danger in atomic bombs—far beyond what anyone comprehended.

That same year Sternglass began to notice that something strange was happening to his baby. "When he tried to sit up, he wasn't able to keep his balance. I saw him fall over, again and again, hitting his head. He was a beautiful child. There was nothing amiss physically that I could see. . . ."

But by the time the baby was six months old, it was apparent that there was some serious problem. They sought help from specialists, but no one could diagnose the difficulty. For Sternglass, it was a terrible time, a nightmare. "The baby had to be cared for every minute. One thought did occur to me. My father had worked very heavily with radiation. He had used X-rays before I was born, and he had hardly ever worn a lead apron. He could have overexposed himself through carelessness or lack of knowledge. He could have damaged a gene. That gene could be showing up now in my baby."

Eventually the baby was diagnosed correctly at Buffalo's Children's Hospital as having Tay Sachs disease. Tay Sachs is an inherited metabolic disturbance, genetic in origin, and prevalent among Jewish people. It leads to the complete deterioration of the brain.

Sternglass was beside himself, watching his child lose one function after another. Finally he and his wife decided they could not continue to care for the child and they had him institutionalized. The baby died at the age of two and a half.

"Sometimes it gives me a chill when I think of it now. My father didn't take even simple safety precautions. And though Tay Sachs disease is common among Jewish people, still there are so many conditions —hundreds, thousands of different genetic diseases—connected to radiation.[4] It could have been a factor. I'll never know for sure."

Westinghouse: 1952–1967

In 1952, a year before he completed his Ph.D. in engineering physics at Cornell University, Sternglass was offered a job with Westinghouse in Pittsburgh. The Westinghouse Research Laboratory was involved in fluoroscopy. "Fluoroscopes are these screens that you stand in front of —X-ray machines—so the doctor can look at your insides." Fluoroscopy exposes an individual to a considerable dose of radiation, and Westinghouse was trying to develop a way to use X-rays at lower doses. Sternglass knew what overexposure to X-rays could do.

He helped develop a new kind of electronic tube that could be used in fluoroscopy, and he found the work fascinating. "There were all these facilities I could use, the biggest playground in the world. Next, I worked on a new kind of television tube for satellites to take pictures of the universe. When NASA launched a satellite and my device was in there, it was exciting." Eventually Sternglass was placed in charge of the Westinghouse Lunar Station program.

Throughout the time he worked for Westinghouse, Sternglass was surrounded by people who had worked on the nuclear submarine engine at Bettis Laboratory,[5] and he reported to the man who directed research and development on the first nuclear submarine, the Nautilus. All Sternglass's work at Westinghouse from 1952 to 1967 involved nuclear instrumentation.

4. The researchers on the Tri-State Leukemia Survey concluded that "it does not take a very great amount of X-ray to produce the kind of genetic damage that will eventually lead to leukemia or other diseases." *Effect of Radiation on Human Health,* vol. 1, pp. 940–941. See also Chapter 2, p. 28.

5. *Bettis Laboratory:* a nuclear research laboratory operated by Westinghouse and located in Pittsburgh, Pennsylvania.

In 1958 I went to Paris for the International Exhibition of the Peaceful Atom for Westinghouse to try to get ideas for future company projects. Like other physicists, I was optimistic about nuclear fission and the "peaceful atom." I believed nuclear fission could be enormously beneficial.

But then, quite suddenly, emphasis changed. There was talk of atomic war—and, to go along with it, of fallout shelters. I started reading up on both subjects—war and fallout shelters.

My wife was concerned too.[6] We were even thinking of putting a fallout shelter in the new home we were building in 1962. I remember thinking, Should I or shouldn't I? It would've been easy. And then I said to myself, It's crazy. There's no way to survive an atomic war. What am I going to do even if I get out of my fallout shelter alive? I would have to live in a world filled with huge amounts of radioactive fallout. But I left out the windows in the basement. That was my compromise, just in case. A brick wall is better than a thin window.

And then I ran across the work of Dr. Alice Stewart.[7] She had discovered that a small amount of radiation to an unborn child—even a single diagnostic X-ray—could double the child's chances for leukemia and cancer. When I saw her figures and then compared them to what one megaton bomb could do, I realized that a nuclear war could destroy the next generation.

It was madness. There was no way that one could really protect one's family, when all the food, the water, the milk, everything would be contaminated. Even if by some miracle someone should survive, still there would be no chance babies would survive.[8]

I was very upset by all these people minimizing the dangers of atomic war. One scientist working for the military, Herman Kahn, wrote a book about how the nation could survive a nuclear war.[9] And Kissinger wrote a book about small tactical nuclear wars as an instrument of policy,

6. This was Sternglass's second marriage. The trip to Paris in 1958 was his second honeymoon.

7. *Dr. Alice Stewart:* head of the Department of Preventive Medicine of Oxford University and a world-famous epidemiologist responsible for a pioneering study on the effects of low-level radiation in England, then later for her work with Dr. Thomas Mancuso on a study of nuclear workers and health effects at Hanford, Washington.

8. Young babies and fetuses are much more susceptible to radiation than adults are.

9. Herman Kahn, *On Thermonuclear War* (Princeton, New Jersey: Princeton University Press, 1960).

telling the military and political leaders not to be afraid to use nuclear bombs.[10]

But I'd worked on radiation, and I realized that nobody had really thought about the aftermath, about what would happen to people. Nobody wanted to look at it, even though people like Linus Pauling[11] had been warning people all through the fifties that we were bound to produce more genetic damage, that there was no safe threshold of radiation.

But the military keep assuring us, "Yes, there's evidence of a safe threshold of radiation below which nothing will happen. And therefore you can have a nuclear war."

My long involvement with radiation, from the time I was a child, made me very sensitive about this issue. Other scientists were more concerned about fire damage and blast damage and medical care. I decided to look at what would happen to the babies born after a nuclear war.

For the next eight years Dr. Sternglass studied the effect of nuclear fallout on infants and children. He studied populations in areas where fallout had rained down from recent atmospheric testing. He found not only an increase in leukemia and cancer, but also a significant increase in infant mortality—infants who are born alive but die before the age of one—and fetal deaths—infants who die before birth or who are stillborn. "Each nuclear test meant a loss of thousands of babies. . . ."

The Decision to Leave Westinghouse

Between 1958 and 1966, while Sternglass researched the effects of atomic fallout, he did not experience a conflict between this research and his work at Westinghouse, one of the major suppliers of nuclear technology in the United States. Then, after developing a new type of thyroid scanner, he was invited to participate in a symposium at the University of Pittsburgh Medical School. At the end of his talk, the head of the Department of Radiology asked him to consider leaving Westinghouse to work at the medical school.

Sternglass did not give this proposal serious consideration until later

10. Henry Kissinger, *Nuclear Weapons and Foreign Policy* (New York: Harper & Brothers, 1957).

11. Dr. Linus Pauling: twice a Nobel prize winner, for chemistry and for peace.

that year when he was at Stanford University working on theoretical physics.

While I was at Stanford, an article came to me from Yale University. It was a U.S. government-funded study of the survivors of Hiroshima and Nagasaki.[12] The study concerned leukemia in children born to parents who had gotten a big dose of radiation from the brief flash of the bomb in the cities. The study compared them to the children of parents who had been outside the cities, in the suburbs, and supposedly not affected much by the bomb flash. They had found no more leukemia, or other health effects for that matter, in the children of parents who had had the higher doses. Therefore, the study tended to support the idea that radiation was not that dangerous.

But they had neglected something. They had completely ignored the heavy fallout that had come down in the suburbs of Hiroshima and Nagasaki.[13]

I began to suspect that this whole study of survivors had been designed to avoid fallout—never to take into account the possibility that their control group was also exposed to heavy radiation.[14] If radiation from the fallout in the suburbs had been as significant as radiation from the intense flash of the bomb, then the lack of difference between the two populations wouldn't prove a damn thing.[15]

12. Dr. S. Finch et al., *Preliminary Findings* (New Haven: Yale University Study, 1966) sponsored by the Atomic Bomb Casualty Commission. They compared 17,000 children whose parents were within 2,000 meters of the bomb to children whose parents were in the suburbs farther than 2,500 or 3,500 meters from the explosion. See Ernest J. Sternglass, *Low Level Radiation* (New York; Ballantine Books, 1972), p. 63.

13. *Fallout in the suburbs:* "Fallout was probably slight and can be neglected as a major source of contaminating radiation." J. W. Hollingsworth, "Delayed Effects in Survivors of the Atomic Bombings: A Summary of the Findings of the Atomic Bomb Casualty Commission, 1947–1959," *New England Journal of Medicine* 263 (September 1960): 481–487. See also E. T. Arakawa, "Radiation Dosimetry in Hiroshima and Nagasaki Atomic-Bomb Survivors," *New England Journal of Medicine* 263 (September 1960): 488–493.

14. The Atomic Bomb Casualty Commission study was set up in cooperation with the Atomic Energy Commission and the National Academy of Science.

15. The problem was that health effects were measured by comparing an irradiated population with another irradiated population, which obviously obscured the differences between them. A real control population would have been a nonexposed population.

See p. 37 in Rosalie Bertell's discussion of the Atomic Bomb Casualty Commission. This study provided the basis for determining safety standards on radiation exposure.

I had come to Stanford to work at the high-energy physics lab. But I began to think I would have to leave Westinghouse and change my life. Here I was, sitting on top of knowledge that the public was being deceived about the true effects of radiation and fallout. And I was trying to go back to my ivory tower, back to things the physics community accepted, where I felt comfortable. I thought about giving all this up, devoting myself entirely to getting to the root of all this. Down deep I knew exposing the facts about radiation from fallout would get me into a lot of trouble.

I talked to my wife: "I think I'm going to have to work on the effects of radiation on the fetus. I'm going to accept that job at the Pittsburgh Medical School and abandon my position at Westinghouse."

She agreed. I would be in a better position to talk freely and investigate the medical effects of radiation. I had to follow up on what I had begun to believe was a very important problem.

The "Peaceful" Atom Bomb: Project Ketch

In 1967 my hopes were still alive for the "peaceful atom." But in December of that year, when I was lying at home in bed with bronchial pneumonia, I got a call from my friend John Lofton, an editor with the *Pittsburgh Post Gazette.* He had sent me a report which I hadn't yet read, about something called Project Ketch.

"Ernest," he said, "we're asked to take a position on this. Would you please take a look at it?"

"What is it?"

"Somebody wants to build an underground gas storage cavity in central Pennsylvania by exploding an atomic bomb."

"Are you kidding?" I couldn't believe it.

"No. It's true. They want to set off a Hiroshima-sized bomb in central Pennsylvania[16] to create a storage space for underground gas. They haven't got enough gas here in the winter, and they want to pump it

16. The proposal for Project Ketch called for detonation of a twenty-four kiloton explosive three thousand feet deep near Renovo, Pennsylvania. The feasibility study was done by Columbia Gas System of New York with the Atomic Energy Commission and the Department of the Interior and submitted to the AEC on 28 August 1967. See *Nuclear Explosives in Peacetime* (Denver, Colorado: Scientists' Institute for Public Information, 1977), p. 8.

up in the summer, then store it underground. Somebody here has persuaded the Columbia Gas Company to take a nuclear bomb, drill a hole
somewhere in a state park in central Pennsylvania, about forty miles
north of State College, and explode it. You know, they think it would
be a great way to use nuclear energy for peaceful purposes."

Pennsylvania, already blessed with the first nuclear reactor,[17] was now
to have the first peaceful nuclear explosion on the East Coast.

Well, I looked at the report briefly, but I was sick and not an expert
on nuclear bombs, so I put it away. Then Lofton called me again. He
needed the help, and since I had nothing else to do I really looked at
it hard. My eyes popped out when I saw that any possible accident might
release as much as four million curies of radioactive iodine into central
Pennsylvania, actually not very far from where a big release happened
later at Three Mile Island, maybe a hundred miles away.

"These people are crazy," I told Lofton. "This is the heart of dairy
country. Millions of curies of radioactive iodine would poison the milk
all the way up to New England, all the way to New York, Washington,
down to Philadelphia. This is madness. How can anyone—"

He interrupted me. "Ernest, look. Write me a little editorial. I'll
publish it."

So I made some calculations and wrote an editorial saying that the
price for the underground storage project could be an immense disaster,
and could result in a huge increase in leukemia and cancer all over the
eastern United States.

It appeared two or three days later, and all hell broke loose. I got
dozens of phone calls. One of them was relayed to me by my wife.

"Ernest, tonight there is supposed to be a conference at Carnegie-
Mellon University promoting Project Ketch. They've flown in people
from the Lawrence Livermore Laboratory in California,[18] from all over
the country, to try to sell this project to the engineering community of
Pittsburgh, and your editorial has exploded right under them. People
want to know if you are going to be there."

17. Shippingport Atomic Power Station, Shippingport, Pennsylvania, was started up in
1957. It was a Westinghouse reactor.

18. *Lawrence Livermore Laboratory:* the government's Lawrence Radiation Laboratory
at Livermore, California, is a weapons laboratory, then under the Atomic Energy Commission. See Chapter 4.

I had no intention of going. I hadn't even known of this meeting. "Well, I suppose I'll go," I said. "I ought to go."

That meeting was not "open" at all. It was an attempt to suppress information. When I arrived, there were little cards lying on every seat. It seemed they were only going to have written questions, and no embarrassing ones.

Hank Pierce had also just come in. Hank Pierce, a science reporter I had known for years, had written about my scientific work at Westinghouse. He knew my work, and he'd seen my editorial that day.

"What's going on here tonight?" he asked me.

"Hank, I think there's dirty business afloat. I think they're not going to allow any questions about health effects—about leukemia and things like that from this project." He said he would write my question down with his name on it and pass it in for me.

It was a big hall at Carnegie-Mellon University. Maybe two, three hundred people packed in. Up there on the stage was a combination of colonels—the military—and scientists who thought they had a nice gadget. They showed slides, and they had people talk about the great economic advantages of Project Ketch, how there was no danger. They would explode thousands of these nuclear bombs, and it would be an economic boon to Pennsylvania to have all this underground storage for the East Coast. They needed it—and on and on. It was an enormous sales pitch to make the bomb look peaceful and happy.

Everyone on the panel was lying about the true danger of what was really going to be done to the people of Pennsylvania and the entire East Coast. No one was mentioning potential side effects—if there would be an accident or anything went wrong. I decided to raise a fuss. I wouldn't let this happen.

My weapon was Hank Pierce, because I knew the panel was afraid of an editorial the next day in the *Post Gazette*, one that charged this meeting with an attempt to suppress information about the potential health threat. The plan was, if they did not get to my question Hank Pierce would get up and start to walk out, and that's exactly what happened. My question was obviously not going to be chosen. So, Hank Pierce stood up slowly and started out, and at that moment they pulled out the question he had written.

When they called him, Hank seized the opportunity. Would they allow Dr. Sternglass, if he was in the audience, to explain the concern that he had expressed in the morning's editorial of the *Pittsburgh Gazette?* And I just happened to be there.

I blew the meeting sky high. I told of a series of nuclear explosions in Nevada and New Mexico[19] that had already vented large amounts of radioactivity into the air. I pointed out that these would be equivalent to many, many diagnostic medical X-rays to pregnant women all over Pennsylvania. I spelled out how many infants might conceivably be affected, and that we were talking about tens of thousands, hundreds of thousands of people being affected by a single accident.

It caused an uproar. There were questions from the audience, and more debate, and the other newspaper reporters wrote this down. And it just blew the idea that there was no danger in Project Ketch. This elaborately staged selling campaign was ruined.

Enormous things followed. It was the first citizens rebellion of the nuclear age in this part of the world. They had one hearing after another. People came and found out more about Project Ketch. And I testified. The movement grew—conservationists, local citizens, local concerned

---

19. *nuclear explosions in Nevada and New Mexico:* The Nevada test site was the most extensively used location for underground bomb testing. It is located in Nye County, Nevada, about sixty-five miles from Las Vegas. Most tests before 1968 were less than four kilotons. One of them, "Palanquin" (April 1965), at a depth of 380 feet, resulted in an explosion which burst out through the hole that had been drilled for the bomb. It created a volcaniclike crater and released "most of its radioactivity." See *Nuclear Explosives in Peacetime,* p. 11.

Another test in New Mexico, Project Gasbuggy, also released a large amount of radioactivity into the atmosphere. Project Gasbuggy, a twenty-six-kiloton explosion 4,240 feet underground in the San Juan Basin of northwestern New Mexico, was the first test designed to obtain natural gas. This project, on 10 December 1967, used a so-called clean bomb of the Plowshare Program, the kind of bomb planned for in Project Ketch. The gas created by this underground explosion was far too radioactive for use. Gas was burned in the open in the hope that once the upper level of radioactive gas was vented, the gas underneath it might be usable. "Hundreds of millions of cubic feet of gas" were vented, but the level of radioactivity was not reduced "to acceptable levels." Radioactive krypton-85 was released into the atmosphere. Even Fred Holzer, of the Atomic Energy Commission's Lawrence Livermore Laboratory, said, "It is pretty clear . . . that these concentrations, especially the tritium, need to be reduced." Radioactivity was discovered downwind of the test in the air and in plants. "The amount of radioactivity due to tritium inside those plants has been raised ten times." Once absorbed in the food chain in this way, radioactivity finds its way into milk and beef, and eventually into the tissues of human beings. See *Nuclear Explosives in Peacetime,* pp. 4–5.

scientists at Penn State, many people came to realize that this thing was another attempt on the part of Livermore Weapons Lab to make these people guinea pigs. And they demanded cancellation of the project.

Most disturbingly the governor had already signed the papers to okay the blast! Preliminary holes had been drilled, and they were beginning to remove the trees. All approvals had been obtained from the various state health authorities. The whole thing was ready to go! They were really going to do it.

I think a lot of people who had worked on the nuclear weapons system —especially Edward Teller—felt desperate about these weapons. Nobody wants to build a gadget that is never used. They were always looking for ways to put the atom to "peaceful" uses.

So they created a large and varied program called Plowshare, basically designed to use nuclear bombs like dynamite. If dynamite can be used to kill people, it can also be used to make tunnels, to move rocks. Nuclear explosives could build a new sea-level Panama Canal[20] right smack across the isthmus of Panama. And believe me they had it all worked out through preliminary bomb experiments in Nevada. They were going to take maybe a hundred megaton worth of nuclear bombs, maybe two hundred megaton, and set them off in a string to dig this new canal. This kind of mad scheme was active in 1966 and 1967.

The military was encouraging them, trying to make the bomb look "peaceful" with the motto, "Beating swords into plowshares." As long as you can convey the idea that setting off bombs in people's backyards is no threat, you can use these bombs to fight nuclear wars. If it's okay to dig a canal this way, and the radioactivity from that fallout isn't going to hurt anybody, then setting off nuclear weapons in Europe to defend ourselves isn't going to hurt anybody either. That's what I found out, beginning at that meeting on Project Ketch.

---

20. Several sea-level canal routes were under consideration. Some would cut across more than sixty miles of Panama. This part of the Plowshare Program was developed by the Atomic Energy Commission in conjunction with the Army Corps of Engineers. One plan to cut through the continental divide would require three 25-megaton and one 50-megaton bomb set off together—an explosion of 125 megatons. Areas which would receive significant fallout could extend throughout South America and other areas as well.

A Note about the Plowshare Program

Devised in the 1950s and 1960s the Plowshare Program was the brainchild of the Atomic Energy Commission. It was an elaborate attempt to convince the public that underground bomb-testing could benefit energy-hungry Americans.[21] *The AEC claimed that huge quantities of natural gas would be created by detonating nuclear bombs under New Mexico, Utah, Colorado, and Wyoming—areas known to possess a lot of natural gas underground in shale. Other sites, such as Pennsylvania, were selected as underground gas storage cavities. These cavities were going to hold vast amounts of gas for use in the eastern states.*

The AEC projected that "nuclear stimulation"—exploding bombs underground in these areas—would create as much as three trillion cubic feet of gas. To achieve this end by the year 2060, fifty-six hundred wells, each created by four to six nuclear bombs—would be needed. A total of thirty thousand nuclear bombs were earmarked for this program.

In 1967 the AEC exploded a twenty-nine-kiloton nuclear bomb underground in New Mexico. Project Gasbuggy produced a good deal of natural gas, all radioactive and unusable. Nevertheless, another explosion was planned for 1969, a mile underground in Colorado's Rocky Mountains. This was Project Rulison. This plan elicited some protest from local residents, mostly women. Around thirty people staged a demonstration near the blast site. The test proceeded on schedule, throwing some of the demonstrators up into the air. Project Rulison produced a shock wave that damaged the foundations of buildings, irrigation lines, mines, and an industrial plant. While Rulison did produce some recoverable gas, city councils in Aspen and Glenwood Springs voted that none of this gas would be used unless the citizens voted approval through balloting. In 1973 the AEC planned another underground explosion in western Colorado, Project Rio Blanco. Eight thousand signatures were obtained in the campaign to stop this explosion. The blast went off on schedule. No gas was recovered from Rio Blanco, but it cost $11 million of public money. Before 1970 a total of $138 million was spent by the

---

21. Most of the information in this section is contained in James Robertson and John Lewallen, eds., *The Grass Roots Primer* (San Francisco: Sierra Book Club, 1975), pp. 125–135.

federal government on the Plowshare Program. The chairman of the AEC, Glenn Seaborg, defended the Program: "Large nuclear explosives give us, for the first time, the capability to remedy nature's oversights."[22]

Nuclear Reactors Must Be Safe At Least

While I was opposed to bomb testing and concerned about the misuse of medical X-rays, I still believed that you could keep radioactivity inside a nuclear reactor. All you had to do was make it airtight. I believed we could have thousands of nuclear reactors without danger of radiation. Certainly we could keep the stuff inside a reactor, as we had done in submarines.[23] If the radiation was getting out, the men would be dead —they were living twenty, thirty feet from an enormously powerful source of radiation inside that submarine. Engineering know-how was the answer. Radiation could be contained in a reactor. I just believed it. I wanted to believe it.

I myself had worked on a project at Westinghouse, a gas-cooled nuclear reactor which would generate electricity by heating up a stream of gas. I had been excited about it, never thinking that reactors were a problem. But in 1970 my view changed.

Early in May 1970 I gave a talk at a meeting of physicists in Wisconsin. At that meeting I secured a report put out by the Bureau of Radiological Health about radioactive releases from nuclear power reactors. On the plane home, I opened this thing, and there I saw that

22. Glenn T. Seaborg and William R. Corliss, *Man and Atom: Building a New World through Nuclear Technology* (New York: Dutton & Company, 1971), p. 188.

23. Dr. Thomas Najarian conducted a study of submarine workers at the Portsmouth Naval Shipyard, where the *Nautilus* and *Tullabee*, the first U.S. nuclear-powered submarines, were overhauled in the late 1950s and early 1960s. Najarian examined 100,000 death certificates, including 1,752 from Portsmouth shipyard workers. He discovered that the cancer rate among the shipyard workers who had worked with nuclear-related projects was much higher than those who had not worked on projects with the risk of radiation. The national mortality rate from cancer was 18 percent, and of shipyard workers who had worked on nuclear projects, 38 percent. See Thomas Najarian and Theodore Colton, "Mortality from Leukemia and Cancer in Shipyard Nuclear Workers," *Lancet* (1978): 1018–1020. See also "The Danger of Radiation at Portsmouth Shipyard," *Boston Globe,* 19 February 1978, p. 1.

instead of .001 or .0001 curies[24] coming out of nuclear reactors, as I had been told about Shippingport,[25] some reactors were discharging hundreds of thousands of curies—millions, hundreds of millions times more than what I had been led to believe.[26] It was all in the official tables.[27]

I was shaken up, and I said to a group of my medical students at Pittsburgh, "What do we do now? If I'm right about fallout, and these figures are right about radioactive releases, then there must be increases in infant mortality around every nuclear reactor in the United States."

So the students went to the library. I told them to take a look at the Dresden reactor near Chicago.[28] And what we found was exactly what we expected—the closer you got to the reactor, the more babies were dying. When radioactive releases went up, so did infant mortality; when they went back down, so did infant mortality. Babies were dying of respiratory failure, of all sorts of ordinary conditions normally associated with prematurity.

Some would say, "Well, the baby was premature. That's why it died."

But when we looked at the statistics we found that prematurity grew 140 percent in the county when the radioactive releases went up and declined again when the leaky fuel rods were replaced. I got a friend of mine, Dr. Morris DeGroot, head of the Statistics Department at Carne-

24. *curies:* a single curie of iodine-131 "could make 10 billion quarts of milk unfit for continuous consumption according to the existing guidelines" of the government. Sternglass, *Low-Level Radiation,* p. 160.

25. *Shippingport:* the first commercial nuclear power plant in the United States. It is located about thirty miles from Pittsburgh, Pennsylvania. It went on line in 1957. "Zero releases" were claimed for Shippingport in 1971. See Joel Griffiths, "Backgrounding the Controversy," *Beaver County (Pa.) Times,* 7 June 1974, p. A-7.

26. Dr. Sternglass had read the report of the U.S. Public Health Service, March 1970. According to Charles Weaver, director of the Division of Environmental Radiation of the Bureau of Radiological Health, the Shippingport reactor had emitted a total of 0.001 curies into the air in 1968, or "240 million times less than was released the same year by the Dresden reactor near Chicago." Sternglass, *Low-Level Radiation,* p. 161.

27. In the published record of the *Environmental Effects of Producing Electric Power,* hearings before the Joint Committee on Atomic Energy, 91st Congress, part 1, October-November 1969, Sternglass read of two nuclear reactors which in 1967 had discharged "as much as 700,000 curies." This was the first time Sternglass had evidence that nuclear reactors released enormous quantities of radioactivity routinely. See Sternglass, *Low-Level Radiation,* pp. 160–161.

28. *Dresden:* Dresden Nuclear Power Station, Unit 1, Morris, Illinois, went on line in 1959. It was the first commercial boiling water reactor in the United States.

gie-Mellon University, to look at some of these things. He did his own study, using a different technique, and he found definite, positive relations between releases of radioactivity and infant mortality.[29] But for Shippingport he couldn't find a positive correlation. Only later did I learn why.

It was during the hearings on Beaver Valley—a new reactor Westinghouse planned near Shippingport—that I got a call from someone who worked at Shippingport.

"Dr. Sternglass," he said, "you're onto something, but you don't know the whole story. Would you like me to tell you the whole story?"

And he did. He told me that some years ago a friend of his at Shippingport had noticed fewer and fewer entries for air releases—radioactive releases—which have to be logged into a book. His friend became suspicious, so he walked out in the yard, and he noticed that some of the gas tanks, where they stored the radioactive gases until they could be released,[30] had broken seals on them—locks that had been broken, and valves that had corroded and not been fixed.

So he asked his supervisor about it, and the supervisor said, "Don't worry about it. It's not your business."

Well, his friend went back again, and when he was alone on the shift he took a dish of soap, and with a brush he painted soap around the valves. When you paint a film of soap around a leaky valve and air is coming out, it makes soap bubbles. And this man found big bubbles of radioactive gases coming out. He could see them leaking out! No wonder there weren't any entries in the logbook for radioactive venting. It was happening all the time! This sort of dumping allowed Shippingport to go before the AEC and claim zero-release, as indeed they did in 1971.

Westinghouse used it in a big advertising campaign. "WESTINGHOUSE CAN BUILD ZERO-RELEASE REACTORS." I have the news clippings. Westinghouse invited people from all over the world to come and see and buy the miracle at Shippingport. "ZERO RELEASE. NO MORE RADIOACTIVITY IN THE ENVIRONMENT."

29. Morris H. DeGroot, "Statistical Studies of the Effect of Low-Level Radiation from Nuclear Reactors on Human Health," in *proceedings of Sixth Berkeley Symposium on Mathematical Statistics and Probability*, J. Neyman, ed. (Berkeley: University of California Press, 1971).

30. Radioactive gases can be released after a certain amount of time, after they become less radioactive and meet federal regulations.

When we put the operators from Shippingport on the witness stand, one of them testified that large quantities of radioactive gases were deliberately allowed to leak out, so they would not have to report anything in the log.

That's all in the sworn testimony of the Beaver Valley-1 operating licensing hearings.[31]

So much for the reason behind Dr. DeGroot's failure to find any correlation between the officially announced radioactive releases and the changes in infant mortality in Beaver Valley.

A Note About Shippingport

In 1971 the Duquesne Light Company, responsible for the Shippingport plant, hired Nuclear Utilities Services Corporation (NUS) of Rockville, Maryland, to conduct a survey of radioactivity in the general area where they were constructing a new nuclear plant, Beaver Valley-1. New government regulations required measuring the precise level of radioactivity in the general area before a new nuclear plant went on line. Although Shippingport had its own radiation monitoring program, it was not considered sufficient since "Shippingport's personnel had done relatively little monitoring beyond the plant's own grounds."[32] However, this inhouse monitoring program had made Shippingport a showcase: the plant's releases of radioactivity were known to be "the lowest of any commercial nuclear reactor in the country."[33] In 1971 the Shippingport monitoring program made Shippingport appear to be "the first

31. Dr. Karl Morgan of Georgia Institute of Technology and former director of Health Physics at the AEC's Oak Ridge stated that based on "the recent testimony of one of Shippingport's own reactor operators . . . there certainly were undetected and unreported releases from Shippingport." And Dr. Morris DeGroot, professor of mathematical statistics and chairman of the Statistics Department at Carnegie-Mellon University, Pittsburgh, said that the radiation monitoring program at Shippingport was "inadequate" and that "radioactivity levels measured in 1971 by NUS were ignored by the Duquesne Light Company, the AEC and the relevant health agencies until Dr. Sternglass blew the whistle. There was dereliction of duty, I think." Dr. Morgan agreed: "Then, when they did get some detailed environmental data from NUS showing high levels, they sat on it." Joel Griffiths, "State Panel Questions Radiation Safety," *Beaver County (Pa.) Times,* 7 June 1974, p. A-7.

32. Griffiths, "Backgrounding the Controversy," p. A-7.

33. Ibid.

commercial plant in the world to release no radioactivity whatsoever out its stack for an entire year."[34]

NUS scientists measured levels of radioactivity in milk, drinking water, soil, and air from January 1971 to March 1972 and sent their reports to the Duquesne Light Company. In December 1972 Dr. Sternglass examined the NUS reports and found that "during the spring and summer of 1971 there had been high radioactivity levels all over Beaver Valley, in many instances 20 or more times higher than normal."[35] Radioactivity had been detected "just about everywhere they looked."[36] During the spring and summer of 1971 NUS had measured high levels of strontium-90 in soil around Shippingport and in milk from "six local dairies."[37] Iodine-131 levels in this milk were 21 percent over maximum permissible limits. This data was collected in 1971, the same year that Shippingport had claimed "zero releases" out its stack.

When Dr. Sternglass made the NUS report public, the AEC responded by attributing the high levels of radioactivity not to Shippingport but to fallout from Chinese bomb-testing. However, after an investigation, the AEC conceded that it was "highly unlikely" that the radioactivity was from Chinese tests. "Most likely it was either of local origin or the result of inadequate sampling procedures."[38]

In February 1973 NUS was asked by the AEC to make a search for its original soil samples to prove that the radioactivity had really been there. But NUS could not locate any. This was not unusual since it was company policy to dispose of soil samples within a year. Nevertheless, in June 1973, after the AEC suggested that NUS was incompetent and an investigation would "certainly turn up gross calculation errors or even that some doctoring of the numbers had occurred,"[39] NUS suddenly found its original soil samples and retested them. No radioactivity could be detected. Everybody was relieved—the AEC, NUS, Duquesne, and

34. Ibid.
35. Ibid.
36. Ibid.
37. Richard Pollock, "Business as Usual in Pennsylvania: 1971 Radiation Scare Fails to Bring Action," *Critical Mass Journal,* December 1979, p. 7.
38. Griffiths, "Backgrounding the Controversy," p. A-7. " 'Local origin' was a euphemism for Shippingport, since there was nothing else in the vicinity that could have produced that amount of radioactivity"—Griffiths.
39. Ibid.

the residents of Beaver Valley.

But nine miles east and downwind of the Shippingport plant in Aliquippa, Pennsylvania, Dr. Sternglass found that infant mortality had risen to a twenty-year high for the years 1970 and 1971, "more than double the overall state rates" and that Aliquippa had the state's third highest leukemia rate.[40]

The Larger Picture

After that, I started to look into the figures for infant mortality in the area around Pittsburgh. I knew there had been a release of radioactivity right in Pittsburgh from the Waltz Mills reactor in 1960.[41] It had happened when I was working for Westinghouse. A big cloud of radioactive gases had escaped from the Westinghouse testing reactor—one of Waltz Mills's big fuel elements had partially melted down. Just like Three Mile Island. Many of my friends had been involved in the cleanup. They had had to find ways to cart the radioactive stuff away. Not knowing what to do with all that radioactive liquid, they had discharged it gradually, over a period of time. And a lot of it had been stored.

I had heard about it. But, like everyone else, I didn't pay much attention. Okay, there was an accident. So there was some escape of radioactivity. But I had no inkling that Waltz Mills could have produced any change in infant mortality.

Then I looked at the health statistics downstream of the reactor on the Youghiogheny River, and I found an increase in infant mortality in the people drinking the water from the Youghiogheny. Nobody had been told how much radioactivity had washed through there. All the people were drinking the water. I felt desperate—because it was happen-

---

40. Pollock, "Business as Usual in Pennsylvania," p. 7.

41. *Waltz Mills:* On 3 April 1960 a fuel element meltdown occurred in the materials testing reactor operated by Westinghouse at Waltz Mills, near Yukon, Pennsylvania, some twenty miles upstream from the city of McKeesport along the Youghiogheny River, from which McKeesport gets its drinking water. This is close to Pittsburgh as well. A sharp increase in infant mortality was detected in areas of western Pennsylvania within a year following the accidental releases. See Sternglass, "Infant Mortality Changes Associated with Nuclear Waste Discharges from Research Reactors into the Upper Ohio Watershed," AEC Rulemaking Hearings on proposed amendments to 10CFR50, Washington, D.C., 15 February 1972.

ing right here in my own home town. I read studies that showed significant quantities of strontium-90 in the neighborhood, that the fish were highly radioactive, that the soil was contaminated, that the area around the Shippingport reactor had been poisoned by years of releases from the old Shippingport plant. Since the Shippingport reactor went on line in 1957, my friends at Westinghouse had not been telling me the truth about what was going on—about how much radioactivity was really being released into the environment. Most likely they did not know about this themselves. Right here we had been poisoning our own water supply. I had been drinking that water. . . .

Until 1970 or so I had really believed that one could trust our scientists and engineers to be honest. I really believed that our bureaucrats in Washington were honest people. And some of them were. They had written a report telling about the large leaks of radioactivity coming out of nuclear reactors.[42]

Little did I know that soon those honest people would be fired, stripped of their power to do any further detailed investigations of nuclear reactors. Their authority would be transferred from the Environmental Protection Agency to the newly created Nuclear Regulatory Commission—really just a bunch of AEC boys that would be moved over.

Nixon did this. I think he got a big payoff from the utilities, the oil companies, the banks, and all the other big corporations that had a heavy investment in uranium. The facts were devastating. The big corporations that were violating environmental laws and worker safety laws made payoffs so that the Nixon administration would go easy on enforcement. And Nixon promised the big energy companies, "No more regulation. We're going to hold the regulators down."

All attempts to enforce tighter regulations were turned aside and sabotaged, so that nuclear reactors were able to release the highest amounts of radioactivity ever recorded in the history of nuclear energy in 1974 and 1975 at the Millstone plant.[43] Two million nine hundred and seventy thousand curies of radioactive gases were discharged. One

42. U.S. Department of Health, Education, and Welfare, Bureau of Radiological Health, "Radioactive Waste Discharges to the Environment from Nuclear Power Facilities," BRH-DER 70-2, Rockville, Maryland, March 1970.

43. *Millstone Nuclear Power Station:* Waterford, Connecticut. See Sternglass, "Strontium-90 Levels in the Milk and Diet near Connecticut Nuclear Power Plants," Report to Congressman C. J. Dodd and Representative John Anderson, 27 October 1977.

curie represents as many disintegrations per second as a whole gram of radium. The entire world's supply of radium in hospitals before the bomb was a few dozen grams. And they were releasing millions of curies of radioactive gases into the air of Rhode Island and Connecticut, not giving a damn. Except how much "on time"[44] the reactor would have, how efficient it would look, and how many more reactors they would sell, based on their excellent operating record.

When I turned against nuclear reactors—as contrasted to just attacking bomb testing—the Health Department of the state of New York, the Health Department of Pennsylvania, Governor Shapp's Commission, the Atomic Energy Commission, and the Environmental Protection Agency all issued statements saying that there was no truth, no credibility in anything I had found. And I lost almost all my friends who had stuck by me when I was only attacking bomb fallout—because in effect I was saying that they were not only unwitting baby killers during the time of the bomb testing, but they were baby killers whenever they ran a nuclear reactor, whether it was at Waltz Mills, Shippingport, Millstone—or anywhere.

But I could not remain quiet about nuclear reactors. If I had, it would have been criminal on my part. Secrecy is the one way an open society can be controlled—namely by keeping things from the public.

The military supports secrecy, and the military is behind the entire nuclear reactor program, and behind the entire Plowshare Program. It's behind everything connected with nuclear energy—even artificial hearts powered with plutonium pacemakers. The military feels that they need to use nuclear weapons in order to protect this nation. You have to be willing to use the weapons. If you yourself are suspected of believing that the weapons are too poisonous to use, then they lose their value as a military deterrent. But, if we're going to get our people to fund these weapons and our soldiers to use them, they can't be told that the fallout will go back and kill their babies. Say you're a soldier, and someone hands you a gun and says, "I want you to go out now. And I've got a little gadget here that is guaranteed to really keep the Russians away. It's got two barrels on it. Now you worry about this one barrel. Let's point it at the Russians. I want you to pull that trigger when I tell you to."

---

44. *"on time":* refers to how much time a reactor can operate without having to be shut down for mantenance and/or refueling.

And you say, "What's the other barrel for?"

He says, "Well, the other barrel is aimed at your baby at home."

Would you pull that trigger?

So they tell you there's only one barrel to the gun. Otherwise they couldn't get decent, patriotic people, willing to defend their families from being taken over by the Commies, to use those weapons and pull the triggers whenever they want them to.

That is the entire rationale behind the avid support of nuclear energy versus coal, versus solar, versus every other aspect of energy generation. Because only nuclear energy makes bombs. The military-industrial complex could not sell nuclear energy if the public knew that the use of nuclear weapons would destroy the very thing we are trying to protect, the very thing that in the past we have asked soldiers to go out into the field and give their lives for—namely the survival of their way of life, of their children, and their children's children, for which people are willing to give their lives. But to ask people to go and use a weapon whose poisonous gases would cripple the minds of their children and destroy their bodies for generations to come—could you sell that as a weapon? To Congress? Or to the soldiers who were going to be asked to die in the battlefield under the nuclear mushrooms of Europe?

CHAPTER 4

John W. Gofman, Medical Physicist

A cool, crisp morning, late in August 1979. From inside a meticulously furnished living room in the quaint house, built high on a hill overlooking the city of San Francisco, you can see the city, orange and white, glittering in the distance.

John Gofman sits across from me on a wooden bench-sofa built into the corner of the living room. He lights a pipe and crosses his legs. On the verge of sixty, he is surprisingly youthful. His oval-shaped face is framed with a thick snow-white beard. His skin is ruddy and smooth, his eyes quick, piercingly alive.

As usual, I begin the interview by explaining what led me to write this book. I tell him about discovering I had an overactive thyroid and the thyroid specialist who recommended radioactive iodine as a cure. Gofman's eyes narrow. He leans forward. "Did you take the radio-iodine?" I shake my head no and explain, "I was afraid of it."

"Let me tell you what that would have done to you," he says. His voice rises in anger as he explains that the dose the specialist said he wanted to give me would have increased my chances of developing cancer by "50 to 100 percent—which is a massive increase!" Gofman sits back and relights his pipe. Then he continues, warming to the subject: "The logical question is: if what I say is true, then how come the medical profession doesn't know it? Well, there are many reasons, some of which don't even surface. For example, hundreds of thousands, perhaps a few million people have been given radio-iodine treatments already. Think of how hard it is for the physician to think that his

Dr. John Gofman

profession can have endangered the lives of five hundred thousand to a million people. So psychologically he has a wall that says, 'No, this cannot be harmful. I personally have not seen a single cancer from it.' Which of course is a ridiculous way to look at it.

"The Public Health Service sponsored a follow-up study of some 30,000 people who had received radio-iodine. Came to the conclusion that it didn't appear that cancer was seriously increased. Absolutely rotten, miserable, stupid, unscientific study. Published in a quality medical journal—but that didn't in any way prevent it from being all those things—unscientific, miserable, and stupid. What was wrong with that study? First of all, we know that very few cancers surface before ten years after the radiation. Then they get more and more frequent. In the study, the average person was followed up only nine years. In other words, they were studying the people in the period when you don't expect *cancers to occur!*

"Also, the number of radiation-induced cancers goes up in proportion to how frequent that particular cancer type is anyway. Breast cancer is 20 percent of all cancer in women. So after you have treated women of twenty-five or so with radio-iodine, you should look in the fifty-year age bracket, when breast cancer becomes a common disease. So the whole damn study, averaging nine years of follow-up, is at the wrong time and is giving a false impression of security that's going to kill more and more people.

"The epidemic of doctor-induced cancer from radio-iodine is ahead of us yet!

"You would think that medicine would have become wiser from the experience with asbestos, with vinyl chloride, with radiation. But they don't seem to learn from such experience. They seem to think that radio-iodine is something special. The next thing will be radio-strontium is something special. Then plutonium is special.

"I'll sit here and confidently say into your recorder—and if you hold the tape for another ten years, I will still be confirmed. I don't say many things positively. A lot of things I'll tell you I don't know—we're uncertain, more work needs to be done. But on this one I don't put any of those qualifiers in. It is going to occur. The dose to the body from radio-iodine at therapeutic levels is such that it's going to produce many, many cancers. Then it's going to be: 'Oh, we must not use radio-iodine any more. At the time we did it, it was the best medical practice.'

"See, that's the out. If the whole profession was idiotic in a given time and agreed to the idiot position, that's regarded as the 'best medical practice of the time.' That's the story."

Gofman sits back. It is the attempt to deceive the public that makes him so angry. His reaction was the same when he learned how the Atomic Energy Commission was deceiving the public about the effects of low-level radiation. When the AEC tried to censor his findings about radiation-induced cancers, Gofman reached his turning point. To him, censorship is "the descent of darkness."

"I'm not interested in being a crusader," Gofman says, "but somebody had to say something about this issue, so why not me?"

The Beginning: Uranium-233

Born in Ohio, John Gofman grew up in Cleveland and attended Oberlin College, with a major in chemistry. He thought he might like to do medical research, so in his junior and senior years he took courses to qualify him for medical school. After graduating from Oberlin in 1939 with an A.B. in chemistry, Gofman entered Western Reserve University Medical School. Although he enjoyed learning medicine and did quite well his first year there, he realized he was not getting the sound scientific background in physical sciences that he would need for medical research. In 1940 Gofman took a leave of absence from medical school and enrolled at the University of California at Berkeley as a Ph.D. candidate in chemistry. "The first thing you did when you came to Berkeley as a Ph.D. candidate was to choose a research field. I looked around and there was a young professor there by the name of Glenn Seaborg, who was working in artificial radioactivity."[1] Glenn Seaborg was the scientist who discovered plutonium,[2] the man-made radioactive element that would be used five years later in the atomic bomb dropped on Nagasaki (9 August 1945).

1. *artificial radioactivity:* radioactivity was discovered in uranium in 1896 by Becquerel. All substances that are found naturally and are radioactive are "naturally radioactive." When man bombards an element to convert it to a new radioactive element, as Madame Curie's daughter did in the mid 1930s, this new radioactive element is referred to as "artificially radioactive."

2. *Glenn Seaborg* received the Nobel Prize for chemistry in 1951 and became chairman of the Atomic Energy Commission in 1961. He remained in that position for ten years.

I thought, probably all kinds of biochemical problems in medicine are going to be solved by the application of radioactive tracers.[3] How better could I prepare myself for a future medical career than to work on a problem involving artificial radioactivity?

So I elected to work with Glenn Seaborg. He assigned me a problem —there was a possibility from thorium you might be able to make a substance called uranium-233, provided it existed, and we didn't know whether it would exist or not.

He said, "Why don't you see if you can find out whether it exists or not?"

It was just an interesting problem in nuclear physical chemistry—an unknown part of a whole systematics of the heavy elements. So I started to look, and the work went quite well, and in about a year and a half I had discovered uranium-233.

We used the Berkeley cyclotron—an accelerator machine—to develop very high energy particles, and from this to develop neutrons with which we could bombard natural thorium. By a complex series of chemical steps I was able to isolate and prove the existence of uranium-233 at a time when I had four one-millionths of a gram. This was not an amount I ever saw—you traced it around by its alpha particle radioactivity. So all the chemistry I was doing, I could never see the material I was working with; I was only tracing it. I had to measure the amount I had by its radioactivity—instead of a scale that uses gravity, you're using radioactivity to weigh things.

By then, things had shaped up to the point that it appeared possible America would enter the war and that the discovery of nuclear fission might mean that nuclear bombs were possible. Scientists in this country voluntarily stopped talking about their work in public. It was an informal agreement.

It was possible that uranium-233, which I had discovered, might be one of the substances used to make a bomb. It depended on whether it fissioned more easily or less easily than plutonium, which had been discovered by Seaborg, or than uranium-235, which exists naturally. These were the three candidates to make a bomb, and certain physics

3. *radioactive tracer:* use of a radioactive substance to trace the behavior of an element in the body. Radioactive potassium-40, for example, traces the movement of potassium through the body.

measurements on the fissionability would determine which was the best. So I started to work on trying to find out if uranium-233 was fissionable, and I proved that it was, using what's called both slow- and fast-moving neutrons. In fact, I proved that it was even better in many respects than plutonium for this purpose.[4] All that was connected with my Ph.D. thesis which I finished in 1942.[5]

The Manhattan Project: Building the A-Bomb

I was all in favor of making a bomb. And I want you to know that I have no guilt about it. I would do it again, and for this reason: as I appraised the situation at that time, there was not for a long time in history any worse aberration of human conduct and human monstrosity than the Nazi regime in Germany. And the idea of an atomic bomb that could win the war against Germany was highly attractive to me. While nothing required me to work more than eight hours a day, I spent at least sixteen in the average day on the bomb project. I was very highly motivated simply because I thought it was important to win the war against Germany.

By this time the Manhattan Project had started, and the government was backing it. They hadn't backed any of our work before. We were working for peanuts in terms of money. Seaborg's group became one of the integral parts of the bomb project, and then Seaborg left to go to Chicago to the headquarters where the Fermi reactor—the first one— had run. They were definitely going to go ahead and attempt to make a bomb out of plutonium.

I stayed behind in Berkeley and became the leader of the residual Berkeley group that Seaborg had had before. Seaborg and a fellow by the name of Arthur Wahl were the first two people in the world to work with plutonium, and I became the third.

4. U-233 can be made from natural thorium. Thorium does not chain react by itself. Another element that makes the thorium chain react was necessary—uranium-235 or plutonium. Then the thorium continued to chain react and could produce U-233. However, at the time there was not enough U-235 or plutonium around to use for converting the thorium to U-233.

5. Ph.D in Nuclear/Physical Chemistry from the University of California at Berkeley, 1943. Dissertation: The discovery of Pa-232, U-232, Pa-233, and U-233. The slow and fast neutron fissionability of U-233.

In order to make a bomb out of plutonium, we had to learn a hell of a lot of chemistry of plutonium, at a time when practically no plutonium was available. We had never even seen it. We were tracing its radioactivity around by its alpha radioactivity.

But we learned quite a bit about the chemistry of plutonium in the year that followed. About that time, J. Robert Oppenheimer[6] took a large group down to form the Los Alamos Laboratory in New Mexico, which was to be a secret isolated lab, to go on with the bomb work. The other labs—in Berkeley, Chicago, and Columbia—were feeders to that project.

Very shortly thereafter, Oppenheimer came up to see me and said, "We have a very desperate problem. We need to have half a milligram of plutonium."

That was something like ten times what had ever been available before.

"You're going to have grams of it in a year," I said, "when the Oak Ridge reactor runs. Why do you need half a milligram now when you're going to have two thousand times that in a year?"

"We need that measurement," Oppenheimer said. "We need it badly because it will alter the whole way the Project goes."

"Well, what do you want?"

"Well," he said, "I talked to Ernest Lawrence"—who was head of the Lawrence Laboratories—"and he has agreed to give up the cyclotron for as long as it will take to have you make some plutonium. We figured out," he said, "that you could make half a milligram if we bombarded a ton of uranium for maybe a month or two."

So after a few hours of thinking about it I finally agreed to do it, to place a ton of uranium nitrate—that's two thousand pounds—and then go through an intricate and complicated series of steps to purify the plutonium from all that uranium. We were going to make half a milligram, less than a needle in a haystack.

It was a big, dirty job, and dangerous, because uranium gets hot as a firecracker with radioactivity from all the fission products that accumulate—all the strontium-90 and all the cesium-137 and the radio-iodine,

6. *J. Robert Oppenheimer:* a nuclear physicist involved in the Manhattan Project, and selected to head the Los Alamos Scientific Laboratory to lead the race for the atomic bomb. A respected scientist, he was later accused, in 1954, of being a Soviet agent.

and everything else. I didn't know enough to have good sense, but I knew that it was dangerous.

To make a long story short, we bombarded the uranium night and day for six or seven weeks. I set up a small factory and built it on the Berkeley campus. In three weeks we isolated what turned out to be not half a milligram, but 1.2 milligrams of plutonium. Pure. In about a quarter of a teaspoon of liquid, out of this ton. I gave it to the Los Alamos Lab.

So I was the first chemist in the world to isolate milligram quantities of plutonium, and the third chemist in the world to work with it. We knew nothing of its biological problems.

I got a good radiation dose in doing that work. I feel that since that time, with each year that's passed, I consider myself among the lucky, because some of the people who worked closely with me in the Lawrence Radiation Lab died quite prematurely of leukemia and cancer. I'm still at a very high risk, compared to other people because of the dose I got. I probably got a hundred, hundred and fifty rems in all my work. That's a lot of radiation. And damn stupid, but nobody was thinking about biology and medicine at that point. We were thinking of the war. So we did it.

For the next few years Gofman continued working to develop processes for separating plutonium. "It was already clear that we were going to have big reactors running at Hanford, Washington, to try to make enough pounds of plutonium to make a bomb, and they'd need to be able to separate it." The process Gofman had worked out in Berkeley to separate one milligram of plutonium was a candidate process. After working intensively on the project, Gofman decided in 1944 that he was no longer needed. "I felt that from here on out it was strictly engineering work. We didn't know if the war would last one year or ten. I didn't want to do engineering work—not that I was against the bomb or anything—I just felt the project didn't need my kind of talent any more."

Gofman applied to the second-year class at the University of California Medical School and was accepted in their accelerated program. He was still a medical student when the bombs were dropped on Hiroshima and Nagasaki. "When I heard the announcement of the explosion of an atomic bomb, I knew they'd completed the project. That was my only reaction." He finished medical school in 1946 and did his internship in internal medicine at the University of California Hospital in San Francisco. Then in 1947 he was offered an assistant professorship at the University of California, Berkeley, which he accepted.

Gofman remained in that position, teaching and doing research from 1948 to about 1961. He made a number of major discoveries working with cholesterol and lipoproteins.[7] By 1954 he had moved up to a full professorship and had become internationally known as a result of numerous publications on coronary heart disease. Then something happened which altered the course of things for him.

Early in the 1950s a controversial decision had been made to set up a second weapons laboratory in the United States.[8] The first weapons laboratory was at Los Alamos, New Mexico, where the atomic bomb had first been designed and tested. The second, the Lawrence Livermore National Lab, was set up at Livermore, fifty miles east of the University of California at Berkeley, under the aegis of the university's Lawrence Radiation Laboratory, of which Gofman was a member. Much of Gofman's funding at the Lawrence Radiation Lab came from the Atomic Energy Commission, although at the time Gofman was not doing any radiation work himself. With the decision to set up a new weapons laboratory, there were two parts to the Lawrence Lab—one at Berkeley and one at Livermore.

Ernest Lawrence called me in one day. We were good personal friends. "I'm worried about the guys out at Livermore," he said. "I think they may do some things to harm themselves. You're the only person who knows the chemistry and the medicine and the lab structure. Could you do me a favor and go out there a day or two a week and just roam around and see what the hell they're doing, and see that they do it safely? If you don't like anything they're doing, you can tell them that your word is my word, that either they change, or they can leave the lab."

So I decided to do it.

While I was out there—to have something to do between times of

7. *lipoproteins:* all the fatty materials in the body that are not soluable in water, such as fat and cholesterol, are not transported by themselves in the blood, but combine with certain proteins. These proteins are called lipoproteins.

8. J. Robert Oppenheimer opposed this second weapons laboratory. Edward Teller, a nuclear physicist involved in the Manhattan Project and credited with being "the father of the H-bomb," strongly supported the new lab. Teller won.

roaming around—I organized a Medical Department at the Livermore Lab. It was then a lab of about fifteen hundred people. It's now about seven thousand. I organized the Medical Department and served as the medical director. But I was there only a day or two a week. The rest of the time I was in Berkeley teaching.

In the course of my wandering around I got to know all the weaponeers who were working there. I worked with them, helped them with some of their calculations on health effects and problems of nuclear war, and so forth. They were making bombs, new bombs, hydrogen bombs, designing all the bombs within the nuclear subs, for missiles and so forth.

I stayed out there until, one day, in 1957, I thought, I've done this long enough. Besides, one of my former students, Dr. Max Biggs, had come back as assistant director of the Medical Department. It was time for me to go back to Berkeley, to teach and also return to my research.

By about 1960 I decided that, although there was still a lot left to do in heart disease, the excitement of my early discoveries, the night and day work, wasn't there any more. I'm not very good at dotting I's and crossing T's. If it's not something really new and unknown, it's not something I want to do.

By then, two of my students were on the faculty and were doing very nice work. So I said, "I'm going to get out of the heart disease work totally. You take over." They did, and they're still there, doing fine work. I shifted my major emphasis to the study of trace elements in biology and worked hard on that from about 1959 to 1962.

In 1962 I got a call from John Foster, who was by then the director of the Lawrence Livermore Lab.

He said, "I'd like to have you come out." I'd met with him and worked with him during the years that I'd been at Livermore. He said, "We had a very interesting approach from the Atomic Energy Commission. They're on the hot seat because of this 1960s series of tests which clobbered the Utah milkshed[9] with radio-iodine. And they've been getting a lot of flak. They think that maybe if we had a biology group working with the weaponeers at Livermore, such things could be averted

9. *milkshed:* an area where dairy cattle graze and provide milk. The 1961–1962 series of atomic tests resulted in radioactive fallout being carried to Utah. Between 1958 and 1961 Eisenhower and Khruschev had informally stopped testing. Testing resumed in 1961 and was finally banned in the atmosphere in 1963.

in some way—like you'd advise us not to do this or to do this differently."

And I said, "So?"

He said, "They're willing to set up something very nice—like a biology and medicine lab at Livermore, with a very adequate budget, starting at three to three and a half million dollars a year. You know, we've got the best computer facilities in the country. We've got engineering talent coming out of our ears, and electronic and mechanical engineering. So you'd have support. What do you think of coming out here and setting that up?"

"That's crazy," I said. "I'm perfectly happy in Berkeley. I've got my research. I'm up to my neck in my trace element research. I've gone down from having to supervise fifty people in my heart disease project to where I now have three people working with me. And it's just the way I like to work. I can be in the lab, and I don't have to think about administrative details. And now you're telling me to come out and head a division and be back in the administrative field. I'll be out of the lab—"

"Oh, no, no, you won't be out of the lab. Just organize it. And after a year or two you can get back in the lab full time, but under circumstances that are much better than you'd ever have."

"Well, I can tell you one thing," I said. "I wouldn't consider giving up my professorship to take this thing, because I don't trust the Atomic Energy Commission."

He didn't seem surprised at that.

I said, "I don't think they really want to know the hazards of radiation. I think it's important to know, but I don't think *they* want to know."[10]

I kicked around the idea of going back to Livermore for a while. Sometimes you have a lapse of cerebration, and in one of those weaker moments I finally agreed that I would go to Livermore and do that job, because Johnny Foster said, "Listen, the AEC can't fight the University

10. The Atomic Energy Commission "had tried to ridicule Linus Pauling's calculations about strontium-90 and carbon-14 in the late fifties—for which Pauling got the Nobel Peace Prize. They said his calculations were wrong. I even got caught up in that mythology —thinking that Pauling might be wrong about the low-radiation doses causing all these diseases. I took the wrong position in 1957 on Pauling's work, saying, 'Since we don't know the answer for sure, we should not impede progress' "—John Gofman.

of California, the Regents, and this lab. And I can tell you one thing, if they try to prevent you from telling the truth about what you find about radiation, we'll back you and the Regents will back you, and they'll just have to eat it."

Well, those were nice words. I didn't completely believe them. But the Regents wrote me. The president of the university wrote me a letter of terms, stating that if for whatever reason I was unhappy about the Livermore set-up, or the AEC's behavior, I could return full time to my teaching with no further explanation.

So I cut my teaching down to 10 percent, and took two posts at Livermore—one as head of a new bio-medical division, the exact mission of which was to calculate and do the experimentation needed to evaluate the health effects of radiation and radionuclide release from weapons testing, nuclear war, radioactivity in medicine, nuclear power, etc.—all of the atomic energy programs. And I was given a three million dollar budget to start. I pulled in ultimately about thirty-five scientists—some who'd worked with me before at the university, some from outside—and finally built up a division which was one hundred and fifty people total, with engineers, technicians, and so forth, including the thirty-five senior scientists. I also became an associate director of the entire laboratory. There were nine associate directors and a director. Anything in biology or medicine was my general area. As an associate director, once a week I was at directors' meetings that concerned all lab matters. So I was involved in the bomb testing and everything else.

A Visit to the Washington Office of the Atomic Energy Commission

A couple of disturbing things happened. Within a few weeks after I'd gone out to Livermore, I had a call from an Atomic Energy Commission official, who said, "You've got to come into Washington next week."

"What for?"

"I can't tell you over the telephone."

"Sure, I'll come."

I got there. There were five other guys from AEC-supported labs around the country assembled in a room, and this AEC official.

"The reason I called you together," he said, "is we have a problem.

We've got a man in the bio-medical division in the Washington AEC office by the name of Dr. Harold Knapp who has made some calculations of the true dose that the people of Utah got from the radio-iodine from the bomb tests in 1962. And he says that the doses were something like one hundred times higher than we've publicly announced."

So this group of six people, of which I was one, said, "What do you want us to do?"

"We must stop that publication," he said. "If we don't stop that publication, the credibility of the AEC will just disappear, because it will be stated that we've been lying."[11]

I said, "Well, what can we do? What do you want us to do? If Knapp has that evidence, then he ought to publish it."

"We can't afford to have him publish that evidence," he said.

"But if it's right, we can't stop him. It's not our job to stop him."

He said, "Well, will you do this? Talk to him. Look at the data, and see if you can convince him that it would be better not to publish it."

So he brought Knapp in the room and he left. Knapp was surly, and properly so. Because here was a guy that did a straightforward scientific job, and he had this evidence, and he wanted to write it up.

And he said to the group, "What's wrong with what I've done?"

We hadn't even seen his data yet.

He gave us his data and said, "Do you think I'm too high? Or do you think I'm right? Or too low?"

We looked at the data, and as a matter of fact, there were a few minor technical questions the people had to ask him, and then we concluded that the guy had a very good scientific story and it ought to be published. So we told Knapp he could leave, and the AEC person came back in.

"Did you get anywhere?" he asked.

"Yeah," we said, "we think Knapp ought to publish his data and you face the music."

11. "When I told them in '62 how high the dosage levels were, the deputy director of the Division of Operational Safety had this pitch: 'Well, look, we've told these people all along that it's safe and we can't change our story now, we'll be in trouble.' And I told him, 'Well, I know you guys have been telling them that, but I haven't, and I'm supposed to be studying fallout. So don't tell me what answers I have to get'—Dr. Harold Knapp, former member of AEC fallout studies branch. In Anne Fadiman, "The Downwind People: A Thousand Americans Sue for Damage Brought on by Atomic Fallout," *Life*, June 1980, p. 39.

He was very disappointed. But since the committee wasn't going to do anything—this is a matter of record now—do anything to help the AEC try to suppress scientific truth, Knapp did publish. And the sky didn't fall. Unfortunately, in this society it takes a hell of a lot more than revealing some awful things for the sky to fall.

But it taught me something that was very, very different from what Glenn Seaborg had told me. (By now my former professor was chairman of the Atomic Energy Commission) When we had signed the contract for the Livermore work, I told him, "You know, Glenn, you ought to think twice about my being the head of this thing. Because I don't really give a damn about the AEC programs, and if our research shows that certain things are hazardous, we're going to say so. And so why don't you think twice about me taking this job?"

"Oh, Jack," he said, "all we want is the truth."

And here within a matter of a few weeks one of his chief men at the AEC is asking us to help suppress the truth. So I came back to the lab and I told Johnny Foster, "Well, the first encounter with Washington was to help with a coverup."

And he said, "Well, how did you handle it?"

"We told them to go to hell."

He said, "That's fine. That's fine."

So there was no further flap from that. But it taught me something about the Washington office—that they would lie, coverup, minimize hazards. My worst suspicions were confirmed.

Plowshare: A Minor Disagreement[12]

There was a project called "Plowshare"—peaceful uses of nuclear bombs. Big project. They wanted to dig a new Panama Canal with 315 megatons of hydrogen bombs. The current Panama Canal is not too good for large ships, and they were thinking of digging a deeper canal. They were going to implant hydrogen bombs and blow a big hole in the ground. Two places were being considered—Panama and Colombia— and negotiations were under way with those countries. They would place more bombs and blow them up, and finally dig this whole trench with

12. See Chapter 3, pp. 68–69.

bombs. But all the radioactivity would spew into the atmosphere and over the countryside.

One of my first assignments was to figure the biological hazard of that, and I concluded by 1965 that the project was biological insanity. Just an awful thing for the biosphere. Kill a lot of people from radiation, from cancer eventually. Project Plowshare. Turning our swords into plowshares.

Even with the fragmentary knowledge we had then, I opposed the project—which did not earn me a lot of favor with the Atomic Energy Commission. They thought I was being obstructionist. But my objections didn't stop it at all.

What stopped it were U.S. efforts to negotiate a test-ban treaty. And the ability to have a test-ban treaty with ongoing shots for so-called peaceful nuclear explosives could always be shots that were really for military purposes. So they elected to stop that project temporarily. It was really nothing to do with the biological hazard that made them quit. It was because of these political negotiations to keep other countries who didn't yet have bombs from developing them. As though the ones that do have them can be trusted for anything.

In any case, in 1965 the bio-medical division got known in the lab as "the enemy within" because we opposed things like Plowshare. But it was really fairly good-natured. In no way did it interfere with my status in the lab. I did give up the headship of the department after two and a half years. I appointed one of my junior associates as chairman of the division so I could go back into the lab. I had a new project by then, on cancer and chromosomes and radiation. It was an area I was very interested in, and a new one for me.

Things went quietly until 1969.

Sternglass Challenges the AEC

By 1969 Johnny Foster had gone on to head the Defense Department Research and Engineering, under McNamara, secretary of defense, and he was no longer head of the lab.

That year a man by the name of Dr. Ernest Sternglass, who had been studying infant mortality, published some papers saying that something on the order of four hundred thousand children might have died from radioactive fallout from the bomb testing. And *Esquire* published an article called "The Death of all Children" based on Sternglass's work.[13]

The AEC was desperately worried about this because they were just then trying to get the antiballistic missile through Congress, and they thought if Sternglass's work was accepted, it might kill the ABM in the Senate. So they sent Sternglass's paper to all the labs. I got it, looked at it quickly, and wasn't sure what to make of it.

But Arthur Tamplin, one of my colleagues, was much more into that thing than I was. And I said to him, "Art, would you look at this?"

He came back about three weeks later and said, "I think Sternglass is wrong. His interpretation of that curve is not right."[14]

I'll say today—ten years later—the new evidence coming out suggests to me that Sternglass may have been right. But Tamplin's argument seemed good to me at the time. I felt he should write it up as a report. And he did, as an article to be published in the *Bulletin of the Atomic Scientists*, stating that he thought Sternglass was wrong, and since people had raised the question, he estimated how many deaths had been caused by fallout. His estimate was four thousand, not four hundred thousand.

At Livermore, Tamplin became the "hero of the lab." He had countered this man who was saying that something was going to hurt the ABM program, which the lab was heavily involved in. So Tamplin was an absolute hero, even to someone like Edward Teller, who all through that period was also an associate director of the Livermore Lab.[15]

Tamplin wrote the paper and submitted it through the lab, to tell Washington what he thought of the Sternglass thing.

I saw one of the top lab officials with whom I got along very well, and he said, "Something's wrong. I don't know what's going on, but Washington AEC has called me up. They're very disturbed about Tamplin's paper and don't want him to publish it the way it is."

13. See Chapter 3, p. 61.

14. The curve showed that infant mortality in the United States had been steadily declining, and that the decline had leveled off right after the atomic bomb testing. Dr. Sternglass's interpretation of this leveling off was that it was a result of more babies dying from radioactive fallout from atmospheric bomb testing. (See Sternglass, *Low-Level Radiation*.)

15. "In truth, Edward Teller ran the Livermore Lab, but for public purposes he liked it better to be known as only an associate director"—John Gofman.

"*Disturbed* about Tamplin's paper!" I said. "He's the hero of the day. He saved their neck on the ABM program. What in the world can they be disturbed about?"

"Look, Jack," he said, "I don't know what they're disturbed about. It's not my area. Would you do me a favor and call this fellow at the AEC?"

So I called the AEC and told Arthur Tamplin, "You better be on the other line. Just in case. It's your work they're concerned about."

On the phone I said, "What's on your mind about Tamplin's study?"

"Oh," the AEC official said, "we like Tamplin's study."

I said, "Gee, I heard you were terribly disturbed about Tamplin."

"No, no. We like Tamplin's study. *Very* well."

"So what's the problem?" I said.

"Well, Tamplin has proved that Sternglass is wrong, and that four hundred thousand children did not die from the fallout. But he's decided to put in that paper that four thousand did die. And we think that his refutation of Sternglass ought to be in one article—like the *Bulletin of the Atomic Scientists,* which is widely read—and that his four thousand estimate ought to be in a much more sophisticated journal."

"Well," I said, "I've talked to Arthur about this, and he says that doesn't make sense, because if you publish an article saying Sternglass is wrong, the first thing anyone will ask you is what do you think the *right* number is?"

"No, the two things are just separate," he said.

Arthur Tamplin was on the phone. I said, "Art, I don't think it makes sense."

"No, it doesn't make sense to me."

I said, "What in the world is the sense in separating these two things?"

And this AEC fellow said, "Well, one ought to be in a scientific journal."

I said, "What you're fundamentally asking for is a whitewash. And for my money, you can go to hell."

That's where we ended the conversation.

So I saw my friend at the lab, and he said, "Did you call Washington?"

And I said, "Yeah."

"What was it?"

"They wanted a whitewash of Tamplin's four thousand number." I

explained it to him.
  He said, "What did you tell them?"
  "I told them to go to hell."
  And he said, "Fine."
  That was April 1969. And I never heard a word more about it.
Tamplin published that paper.

The Harassment Starts: Low-Level Radiation

*During the 1950s and 1960s the Atomic Energy Commission main-
tained there was a "safe threshold" of radiation below which no health
effects could be detected. This so-called safe threshold provided the
justification for exposing American servicemen to atomic bomb tests, for
permitting workers in nuclear plants to receive a yearly dose of radiation,
and for operating nuclear power plants which released radioactivity to
the environment and exposed the general population even during normal operation. But in the 1960s evidence began to come in from around
the world—from the atomic bomb survivors,[16] from some people in
Britain who had received medical radiation[17]—with estimates of the
numbers of cancers occurring per unit of radiation. Gofman and Tamplin assembled these figures and concluded that there was no evidence
for the AEC's so-called safe threshold of radiation. In fact, they estimated that the cancer risk of radiation was roughly twenty times as bad
as the most pessimistic estimate previously made.*

  *When Gofman was invited to be a featured speaker at the Institute
for Electrical, Electronic Engineers meeting (IEEE) in October 1969,
he and Tamplin decided to present a paper on the true effects of
radiation. "So we gave this paper,[18] and said two things. One, there
would be twenty times as many cancers per unit of radiation as anyone*

  16. See Chapter 2, p. 38 and Chapter 3, p. 62.
  17. Dr. Alice Stewart's epidemiological study showed that pregnant women receiving
diagnostic X-rays had children with a higher risk of leukemia and cancer. See Alice
Stewart, Josefine Webb, and David Hewitt, "A Survey of Childhood Malignancies,"
British Medical Journal (1958): 1495–1508, and Alice Stewart and George Kneale, "Radiation Dose Effects in Relation to Obstetric X-rays and Childhood Cancers," *Lancet*
(1970): 1185–1188.
  18. Gofman, "Low Dose Radiation, Chromosomes and Cancer," presented at the
Institute for Electrical Electronic Engineers (IEEE) Nuclear Science Symposium, San
Francisco, 29 October 1969, pp. 640–652.

had predicted before, and two, we could find no evidence of a safe amount of radiation—you should assume it's proportional to dose all the way up and down the dose scale." The paper did not attract much public attention, only a small article in the San Francisco Chronicle *and nothing in the national press. Senator Muskie was holding hearings on nuclear energy at that time[19] and invited Gofman to address the Senate Committee on Public Works. Muskie did not know about the paper given before the IEEE but invited Gofman because of his position as associate director of the Lawrence Livermore Laboratory. Gofman gave an amplification of the paper he and Tamplin had presented at the IEEE meeting entitled, "Federal Radiation Guidelines: Protection or Disaster?" This was picked up by the Washington press.*

Within two weeks I began to hear all kinds of nasty rumblings that we were ridiculous, we were incompetent.

Here I'd been getting a budget of three to three and a half million dollars a year for seven years, and suddenly I'm hearing rumors out of Washington that my work is incompetent. That wasn't a criticism of me. That was a criticism of them. If they give someone three million a year for seven years and in two weeks they suddenly decide he's incompetent, what's wrong with them for seven years?

It was obviously related to what we'd said.

A guy from Newhouse News Service phoned me and said, "I have a statement from a high official on the Atomic Energy Commission, and I asked him about your cancer calculations, and he said that you don't care about cancer at all. All you're trying to do is undermine the national defense."

I said, "Me, undermine the national defense?"

He said, "What do you have to say about that?"

"Nothing."

"You're not going to deny it?"

I said, "Do you think I would lower myself to deny a statement like that?"

He said, "You wouldn't be considering a lawsuit for libel if I publish that statement?

19. Gofman, "Federal Radiation Council Guidelines for Radiation Exposure of the Population at Large: Protection or Disaster?" presented to the Senate Committee on Public Works, 18 November 1969, in *Environmental Effects of Producing Electric Power*, pp. 695–706.

"What I consider doing is my business," I said. "You're a journalist. You've got a story. If you'd like to publish that story, you go ahead and you take your chances, but I'm not going to tell you whether I have in mind a libel suit or anything else. You just do what you want with it."

"You're not going to deny the story?"

"No. I'm not even going to comment on something that low."

He never published the story.

The next thing we experienced was this. I'd had an invitation about four months before, to come and give a talk in late December '69. It was to be a symposium on nuclear power and all the questions about it. And I'd said to the person inviting me, "You know, the kinds of things you want from me are much better handled by Arthur Tamplin, because that's been the area he's worked on. Instead of me, could he give the talk?"

"Oh, that's just fine," they said. "We wanted to be sure to have one of your representatives there."

So he was scheduled to give the talk on December 28.

Well, this friend of mine at the lab asked to talk to me right after the Muskie hearing. And he said, "Jack, I have a problem. The AEC has contacted me, and they're very disturbed about your IEEE talk and your Muskie testimony."

"What are they disturbed about? I've sent them the paper, sent it out to a hundred scientists. If they're disturbed, they can tell me what's wrong with it."

"No, no. They're not saying that," he said. "What they're saying is that it's just embarrassing to them to have these things given at a meeting and then in testimony before they've had a chance to review it. If you would just in the future do me one favor, send them your papers —your testimony—before you give it, I think the whole problem would be solved. They just don't want to be caught unawares."

"Well," I said, "that's very reasonable. Sometimes we have a scientific paper ready, sometimes we don't, to give it to them three weeks in advance or so. But we'll try."

I talked to Arthur Tamplin. He said, "Sure, what do I care. They can have it."

His paper was about a month from delivery before the American Association for the Advancement of Science. So I said, "Would you give me a copy of it for the lab to send to the AEC so they can scan it?"

So he did. Three days later Tamplin came into my office mad as hell, and threw this thing down on my desk.

Apparently someone in the lab had done some editing on it, and the editing was such that all that was left was the prepositions and conjunctions. All the meat was gone. This hadn't even gone to Washington. It was our *own* laboratory that had censored it! My own colleagues who were going to *protect* us from censorship.

I went over to my friend and said, "What the hell is going on? When you asked me if we'd give the papers to the AEC in advance, I told you I wouldn't tolerate any censorship. And you said, 'Jack, do you think *I* would tolerate any censorship?' "

He said, "Jack, be realistic."

"I'm very realistic, "I said. "We're just not going to tolerate any form of censorship."

"You're overwrought."

"Listen, you know what I'm going to do? I'm calling up the guy from that meeting from the American Association. I'm going to tell him what has been told to Tamplin—that if he gives the paper unaltered, he cannot say he's a member of the Livermore Lab, he must pay his own travel expenses, and cannot use a lab secretary to type the paper."

That's what the lab had told him!

I said, "I'm going to call the AAAS[20] and tell them I'll send a letter instead of Tamplin going to the meeting. In the letter I'm going to say that the Livermore Laboratory is a scientific whorehouse and anything coming out of the Livermore Lab is not to be trusted."

"Jack, you're just excited," he said. "Go home. Think it over. Let's talk tomorrow."

I said, "I'm really very cool, but if you want to talk about it tomorrow, that's okay. You know what I'm going to do."

The next day he came over to my office. "Well, did you get some sleep and think it over?"

"Sure, I got some sleep, and I've thought it over. And I also took care of what I told you I would."

He said, "What do you mean?"

"I called the guy from AAAS and told him what I was going to do, that I was going to submit this letter to be read before the assembled public meeting, that the Livermore Lab is a scientific whorehouse and

20. *AAAS:* American Association for the Advancement of Science.

practices censorship."

He turned all colors and just stormed out of my office.

Well, the upshot was the lab backed off on virtually everything—Tamplin could have lab funds and so forth. A couple of minor modifications to the paper, which Tamplin agreed to—and they removed the censorship. So my statement was never read and Tamplin did go to the meeting.

The Decision to Fight: January 1970

Gofman had resigned from his position as associate director of the laboratory six months prior to this episode with Tamplin, although he remained in the Livermore Laboratory as a research associate. "The resignation of my associate directorship had nothing to do with politics. I just thought it was time to go back to teaching."

Gofman was now teaching part-time at Berkeley and spending half of his time at Livermore doing research. In January 1970 he learned that Tamplin had been stripped of twelve of his thirteen staff people.

I went back to my friend at the lab, and said, "You son of a bitch! What you're doing is so obviously just harassment to please the Atomic Energy Commission. I didn't think you could stoop this low."

"Jack, it's not that," he said. "Tamplin didn't want those people."

"Don't tell me Tamplin didn't want those people. I know what Tamplin wants. And he didn't want to lose any of them. He's got a lot of work to do, and so do I on the radiation hazard question. You've looked at our calculations. What the hell are you harassing Tamplin for?"

"It's not harassment," he said. "It's just that the laboratory budget was cut."

"The laboratory budget was cut 5 percent and Tamplin was cut 95 percent. That doesn't make any sense."

But it stuck. I wasn't able to undo it. I wrote a letter of complaint to Glenn Seaborg, and he said, "I can't interfere with lab management." Which was bullshit too.

Then I started hearing that there were a lot of people from the electric utility industry who were insulting us and our work. They were saying our cancer calculations from radiation were ridiculous, that they were poorly based scientifically, that there was plenty of evidence that we were wrong. Things like that. So I wondered what was going on there. At that point—January 1970—I hadn't said anything about nuclear power itself. In fact, I hadn't even thought about it. It was stupid not to have thought about it. I just wondered, Why is the electric utility industry attacking us?

I began to look at all the ads that I had just cursorily seen in *Newsweek* and *Time* and *Life,* two-page spreads from the utilities, talking about their wonderful nuclear power program. And it was all going to be done "safely," because they were never going to give radiation above the safe threshold.

And I realized that the entire nuclear power program was based on a fraud—namely, that there was a "safe" amount of radiation, a permissible dose that wouldn't hurt anybody. I talked to Art Tamplin. "They have to destroy us, Art. Because they can't live with our argument that there's no safe threshold."

He said, "Yeah, I gathered that."

"So," I said, "we have a couple of choices. We can back off, which I'm not interested in doing and you're not interested in doing, or we can leave the lab and I go back to my professorship and you get a job elsewhere, or we can fight them. My choice is to fight them."

He said, "I agree."

Congress Hears the Evidence

The system used to discredit scientists like us is usually to call you before the Joint Committee on Atomic Energy—it's a Congressional committee—and they let you present your evidence, and then they get all their lackey scientists, the ones who are heavily supported, to come in and say why you're wrong.

So I got the call just like I expected to from the Joint Committee. Would I come in on January 28, 1970 to testify?

I said, "Art, just as expected, they're ready to slice our throats at a Congressional hearing. We've got a lot more evidence that's sort of undigested than we had when you gave your paper and we gave the one at the Muskie hearings."

In about three weeks we wrote fourteen scientific papers. I'd never done anything like that in my life. And we learned new things. Stuff was falling together. We took on the radium workers. We took some data on breast cancer. There was a whole study of radium workers and their deaths. A guy at MIT had said they wouldn't get cancer below the safe threshold. We pointed out his papers were wrong. There were the uranium miners, who were getting lung cancer. And we analysed that and showed how it also supported the idea that there was no safe dose. We studied the dog data. Studies were being done at the Utah laboratory and sponsored by the AEC—they were irradiating dogs and studying how many cancers appeared. We took a whole bunch of new human and animal data and wrote fourteen additional papers that buttressed our position, that indicated, as a matter of fact, that we'd underestimated the hazard of radiation when we'd given the Muskie testimony.

We were going to take all this as evidence before the Joint Committee. But I wanted to be sure that our material got out to about a hundred key scientists in the country in case the AEC tried to prevent us access via the journals.

—That's always something you have to worry about. The journals can easily not publish what you want to say. It's a simple technique. If the journals have editors and staffs supported by an industry or government agency, you can be blocked from getting your things published.

So to be sure that people knew what we were saying, we sent our material around to about a hundred separate scientists to let them know what we were doing.

I went to the lab and said, "I want 400 copies Xeroxed." We had put together 178 pages.

The dwarves who occupy such positions of course immediately ran to the master and said, "Gofman wants 400 copies of this! Do we have to do it?"

And so he came to me. "What's this 400 copies of 178 pages?"

"Well, the chairman of the Joint Committee on Atomic Energy has requested that we testify. We need 200 copies to send them, and I need 200 copies for other distribution. If you prefer, I'll call up Mr. Holifield, the chairman of the Joint Committee, and tell him the laboratory even wants to censor things from Congress."

"Oh, no, no. Don't do that!" he said. We'll do the papers. I just wanted to know what you needed them for."

So we shipped off our 200 copies to the Joint Committee. Their purpose was, of course, to distribute the papers to the people that they were going to get to come in and attack us.

January 28 was the day. I presented the evidence based on these fourteen additional papers.

At the end of the testimony, Mr. Holifield said, "Now I certainly appreciate your presenting this material, Dr. Gofman. You realize that with 178 pages of testimony we haven't had all the time it would take to digest it in detail, but we'll invite you back sometime."

They didn't have any answers. Their people were just caught flat-footed, and meanwhile we'd gotten things out to a lot of people—a much stronger story. Their little escapade failed.

One of the guys we had mailed the papers to called me up. He was in the Public Health Service, in a division separate from AEC. It was on a weekend.

"I've got something disturbing to tell you," he said, "but if I tell you and you ever want to use it legally, I'll deny that I told you."

"That sounds like terribly useful information," I said. "I can't use it, but you think I ought to know it. Well, go ahead."

"Someone from the AEC came to my house last weekend," he said. "He lives near me. And he said, 'We need you to help destroy Gofman and Tamplin.' And I told him you'd sent me a copy of your paper, and I didn't necessarily agree with every number you'd put in, but I didn't have any major difficulties with it either. It looked like sound science. And—you won't believe this—but do you know what he said to me? He said, 'I don't care whether Gofman and Tamplin are *right* or not, scientifically. It's necessary to destroy them. The reason is,' he said, 'by the time those people get the cancer and the leukemia, you'll be retired and I'll be retired, so what the hell difference does it make *right now?* We need our nuclear power program, and unless we destroy Gofman and Tamplin, the nuclear power program is in real hazard from what they say.' And I told him no. I refused. I just want you to know if you ever mention this, I'll deny it. I'll deny that I ever told you this, and I'll deny that he said it to me."

"Well," I said, "it's nice to know. We realized that we were in a war to the death, and that there was no honor, no honesty in the whole thing, but that's the way it is. You're not going to stand behind what you found out. That's okay with me too."

Abolishing the Atomic Energy Commission

By now I was convinced that nuclear power was absurd and fraudulent, that there was no safe level of radiation. Tamplin and I were writing and giving talks against nuclear power. In June 1970 I gave testimony at the Pennsylvania state legislature, recommending that all new construction of nuclear power plants cease—at least for five years—till the whole problem was sorted out. Our stock at the Livermore Lab was zero.

But we couldn't get them to fire us. They wouldn't do that. If they fired us, it would be an admission that they couldn't tolerate the truth. We put out more and more reports that were scientifically damaging to the atomic energy program. Meanwhile our Muskie testimony[21] had gotten very wide notice in the press, and Ralph Nader had entered the action and was asking Muskie what he was going to do about this testimony if it was so damaging to the nuclear power program. Muskie contacted Robert Finch, secretary of HEW, and said, "What are you going to do about this study of Gofman and Tamplin's?"

So Finch went to the National Academy of Sciences and said, "I call for a study of whether Gofman and Tamplin are right," and awarded the National Academy three million dollars to do a study. Some sixty scientists were invited to participate.

At no time did the National Academy of Sciences invite either Tamplin or me to be on this committee or contact us—from 1970 to today. But in 1972 the National Academy of Sciences published a report called the BEIR Report—Biological Effects of Ionizing Radiation—a long, thick report, in which they walked around the problem as best they could, and finally concluded that we were too high between four and ten times. But if you read the fine print, they were admitting that we might just be right.[22]

When that came out, everybody realized that the AEC was not worth a damn. By then the AEC had gotten themselves into another flap. Henry Kendall and Dan Ford of the Union of Concerned Scientists

21. Hearings on nuclear energy were held in 1969 by Senator Muskie. Dr. Gofman delivered a paper entitled, "Federal Radiation Guidelines: Protection or Disaster?" which was an amplification of the talk given at the IEEE meeting three weeks before.
22. National Academy of Sciences, "The Effects on Populations of Exposure to Low Levels of Ionizing Radiation," report of the Advisory Committee on the Biological Effects of Radiation (BEIR Report), November 1972.

showed that the AEC didn't know whether the Emergency Core Cooling System would ever work or wouldn't.[23] The Emergency Core Cooling System was the last barrier of safety in a major nuclear accident. This further damaged the credibility of the AEC.

Those two events—the conflict with Ford and Kendall and the conflict with us—finally led them to realize they could no longer use the words "Atomic Energy Commission," and so the government abolished the AEC.

"We are now solving the problem," they said. "We'll create two new agencies—ERDA (Energy Research and Development Agency) and NRC (Nuclear Regulatory Commission)."

ERDA was supposed to promote the development of atomic energy, and NRC was supposed to concern itself with public safety. The idea was that it was the promotion of nuclear energy that made the AEC's safety work so poor. The new NRC was only supposed to involve itself in safety—no promotion.

Which turned out to be one of the greatest lies in history.

Resigning from Lawrence Livermore

Meanwhile I continued my work on cancer and chromosomes in the Livermore Laboratory. We continued to put out reports on the radiation hazard problem. In 1972 one of the people at the lab came to me.

"We have a problem," he said. "Now you may not believe this, John, but last year the AEC came to me and said, 'We need to take Gofman's money away that he has for his cancer chromosome work' [which was $250,000 a year] and we told the AEC that while we disagreed with your position on nuclear power, we thought your cancer chromosome work was first-class science, and we were not going to remove your funds. And they let it go. But this time they've come back and said, 'If you don't remove Gofman's funds, then we will remove $250,000 from the lab budget. You can fire other people if you insist on keeping Gofman's program.' So what do you want us to do?"

"Under no circumstances can anybody lose their funding because of

23. Daniel F. Ford and Henry W Kendall, *An Assessment of the Emergency Core Cooling Systems Rulemaking Hearings* (San Francisco: Friends of the Earth/Union of Concerned Scientists, 1974.)

my problem," I said. "I'll tell you what I'll do. I'll go back to the National Cancer Institute and see if I can get $250,000 to move my program to Berkeley with my professorship, and then I'll resign from the lab if I can."

So I went and saw the head of the National Cancer Institute. We talked about three hours.

I said, "You know all about the conflict with AEC?"

"I know all about the conflict," he said. "We like your program. We need it. It might take me three or four weeks to arrange it, but I think I can get you the money."

So I went back and told the lab it looked good.

Three or four weeks passed, and I didn't hear anything. Six weeks passed, and I didn't hear. So I dropped the head of the National Cancer Institute a note. I didn't want to press him because those things can take longer.

Then the strangest thing happened. I got back a letter from one of his third-echelon deputies, saying, "Thank you very much for your inquiry. Your work on cancer and chromosomes is not a mainline interest of the National Cancer Institute. We cannot fund it under any circumstances. But don't be discouraged about further applications at some later time on some other programs to the National Cancer Institute. Sincerely yours."

So I realized what must have happened. The head of NCI had probably talked to some other people in the government and gotten the word back. "This guy has just created nothing but havoc for the AEC, and now you're going to take him on to do the same thing for the National Cancer Institute? You need to support Gofman like a hole in the head!"

I went to my contact in the lab and said, "I've failed. I know of no other source to accumulate $250,000 a year. So tomorrow I'll let all the people know that the program has ended. You can reassign them to other work."

As long as they weren't working with me, it was fine with the AEC. So the AEC won. They managed to destroy my cancer research program.

He said, "What are you going to do personally?"

"Well, I have a few more things I'd like to write up," I said. "But let's figure about six months, and then I'll resign from the lab."

"You know," he said, "you don't have to resign."

"Yeah, I know. But that's what I choose to do, and I'll go back to Berkeley full time, without the research. I'd like to keep my secretary and one assistant for the six months."

"Oh," he said, "that's just fine." It was really funny—he said, "Gee, you're driving out here fifty miles a day. Couldn't we make the last six months a little more comfortable for you? You know, we could get you space in the Berkeley division of the Lawrence Lab and you wouldn't have to drive out here."

"Well, that's very nice," I said. "As a matter of fact, I'll take you up on it."

So they arranged space for me in one of the buildings of the Berkeley Lawrence Lab, and I spent the last six months there, except for my teaching, which I was already doing half time.

And on February 1, 1973 I resigned formally and became a full-time professor.

I had made one mistake. If the Department of Energy or the AEC gives you money on a sensitive subject, they don't mean for you to take the job seriously. They need you—with your scientific prestige—so they can point to you. "We have so and so studying the problem." Studying the problem is marvelous. But if you want the money and the continued support, you should go fishing or play golf. My mistake was I discovered something.

After Resigning from Lawrence Livermore

Tamplin stayed on about another year and a half in the lab as, in his words, a "non-person." He had no staff, he worked alone. Then he joined the Natural Resources Defense Council as a senior scientist.

When I got back to my own lab in Berkeley, I thought, Well, the National Cancer Institute wouldn't give me the $250,000, but surely I can get a small grant to continue the kind of calculations we've been making on cancer, particularly since in a major symposium at Berkeley, Dr. David Levin got up and added further shock to the AEC by stating —and it's on record in that publication—We in the National Cancer Institute have checked out the Gofman calculations by a totally separate method and have come up with the same answers.

So I applied for a grant from NCI for $30,000 to continue my calculations on cancer and radiation. It was a good application. I figured, Gee, a $30,000 grant they're not going to refuse me. I got a letter back from them saying the grant's refused on the basis that this sort of work is better done by a committee than by an individual. It was a revelation to me.

It seemed to me that I must be on a list of "enemies of the state." I never saw a list, but you know it was the Nixon administration, and Richard Nixon was said to have such a list, so I concluded that very likely I couldn't get any money from federal sources at all.

"The AEC Made a Mistake Not to Get Rid of Me"

It's a hazardous occupation, you ought to understand, to take the position that we ought to cancel the whole nuclear power program. It would probably have been wise for them to get rid of us—physically—in the early seventies.

Today I don't think it matters what they do to us because hundreds of thousands of people know about nuclear energy and its deficiencies. But at that time it was a very small group of people, and Tamplin and I were among the leading individuals giving the AEC trouble. Physically eliminating us from the scene would have been a useful thing to do. I don't know why they didn't. Of course there's always a hazard—you don't want to make martyrs. But you can have people have accidents on the highways and things like that. I sometimes wondered when I started my car whether it was going to explode. . . .

Funny thing—when the fire occurred in 1973, at the height of the period when we were really giving nuclear energy the most trouble, my friends said, "I heard the AEC burned your house down."

So I said, "That's crazy. It couldn't have been the AEC. Listen, the house next *door* caught on fire, and ours caught fire from *it.*"

They said, "Do you think they'd start a fire *in* your house?"[24]

24. Gofman's sister-in-law was in his house. She was the only one there at the time. She got out safely. The house burned to the ground. Gofman says, "I have no evidence that the AEC had anything whatsoever to do with it."

Researching Plutonium: The Cancer Hazard

After leaving the Livermore Laboratory and finding that he could not get government funding for his research, Gofman was not sure what to do with his life. "Personally I am not cut out for the social scene. You know, I'm most comfortable in a laboratory, working with instruments and materials, and not seeing people. I don't like going to public things. People can change, but if you've been doing something you like to do for something like thirty years, to try to develop a new format of things you prefer is difficult."

Gofman decided to take an early retirement at the age of fifty-five, so he gave up his position at the university in 1975 and became professor emeritus. Although no longer engaged in active teaching, Gofman did not give up research. In the next years he discovered that plutonium was even more hazardous than he had thought. "Plutonium is so hazardous that if you had a fully developed nuclear economy with breeder reactors fueled with plutonium, and you managed to contain the plutonium 99.99 percent perfectly, it would still cause somewhere between 140,000 and 500,000 extra lung-cancer fatalities each year."

There are no commercial breeder reactors operating at this time (1981) in the United States. However, breeder reactors are planned, are even now prefabricated, waiting in storage for a go-ahead on construction. The Clinch River reactor, for example, is a fast breeder proposed for a site in Oak Ridge, Tennessee. All the components have been built by Westinghouse and are now stockpiled in warehouses. Every year the U.S. Congress appropriates millions of dollars for the Clinch River project and advanced breeder technology research.

Breeder reactors have a plutonium core surrounded by a blanket of U-238, a nonfissionable isotope of uranium. When the plutonium fissions, it gives off fast neutrons that hit the U-238 atoms, converting the uranium blanket to plutonium. Thus the breeder reactor produces, or "breeds," more plutonium than it starts with. Plutonium is the ingredient essential for producing nuclear weapons.

As the nuclear industry readies itself for full-scale breeder development, reports on the carcinogenic nature of uranium are suddenly receiving widespread coverage in the press. The San Francisco Chronicle, *for example, reports that the "breeder reactor would likely reduce the number of occupational deaths associated with the nuclear industry, since it largely operates on plutonium and thus would reduce the need for the uranium that fuels existing atomic power plants."*[25] *It also quotes a U.S. official as stating that "the dominant factor by at least a factor of 100 in real fatalities is in uranium mining." There is a cruel irony in admitting the danger of uranium mining only to seduce the American public into accepting an even more treacherous plutonium technology.*

Breeder reactors will lead to a nightmare "epidemic of lung cancer in this country,"[26] *and widespread weapons proliferation. In themselves, breeder reactors are extremely dangerous. They use liquid sodium as coolant, which ignites and violently explodes on contact with air. The plutonium fuel, if ignited, can produce a nuclear explosion equivalent to an atomic bomb, which would rupture the reactor's containment building and release enough deadly radioactivity to kill millions of people.*

The requirement for controlling plutonium in a nuclear economy built on breeder reactors would be to lose no more than one millionth or ten millionth of all the plutonium that is handled into the environment where it could get to people. Which brings up a fundamental thing in nuclear energy—there are some engineers, scientists, who are not merely fraudulent sycophants of the system. They're really out of touch with reality.

I was once on an airplane with a strong pronuclear engineer. I said, "I've done some new work on plutonium. I think it's a lot more toxic than had been thought before. At what toxicity would you give up nuclear power?"

He said, "What are you talking about?"

"If I told you that you had to control your plutonium losses at *all* steps along the way—burps, spills, puffs, accidents, leaks, everything—that you can't afford to lose even a millionth of it, would that cause you to give up nuclear power?"

"Oh, I understand your point now, John," he said. "Now, you tell me

---

25. "Fast-Breeder Reactor Backed—Jolt for U.S.," *San Francisco Chronicle,* 26 February 1980, p. 5. The uranium hazard arises from the exposure to radon gases in the uranium mines.

26. John W. Gofman, *"Irrevy," An Irreverent, Illustrated View of Nuclear Power.* (San Francisco: Committee for Nuclear Responsibility, 1979), p. 105.

—we look to biologists like you to tell us how well we need to do. If you say I've got to control it to one part in ten million, we'll do it. If you say it's got to be one in a billion or ten billion, we'll do it. You tell us what we have to engineer for, and we'll do it."

I said, "My friend, you've lost touch with reality completely. I've worked in chemistry laboratories all my life, and to think you can control plutonium to one in a million is absolutely absurd. If you were a patient of mine who came in to see me, I'd refer you to a psychiatrist."

"Well, John, engineering is my field. And we believe we can do anything that's needed."

Engineers do believe that. That's the arrogance of engineers—they think they can do anything. Now their mistakes catch up with them, as you see from the DC-10s and the Tacoma Narrows Bridge that fell down, and the Teton Dam and the most recent episode, Three Mile Island—where the unthinkable, the impossible, did happen.

Nuclear Power: A Simple Question

Many people think nuclear power is so complicated it requires discussion at a high level of technicality. That's pure nonsense. Because the issue is simple and straightforward.

There are only two things about nuclear power that you need to know. One, why do you want nuclear power? So you can boil water. That's all it does. It boils water. And any way of boiling water will give you steam to turn turbines. That's the useful part.

The other thing to know is, it creates a mountain of radioactivity, and I mean a *mountain:* astronomical quantities of strontium-90 and cesium-137 and plutonium—toxic substances that will last—strontium-90 and cesium for 300 to 600 years, plutonium for 250,000 to 500,000 years—and still be deadly toxic. And the whole thing about nuclear power is this simple: can you or can't you keep it all contained? If you can't, then you're creating a human disaster.

You not only need to control it from the public, you also need to control it from the workers. Because the dose that federal regulations allow workers to get is sufficient to create a genetic hazard to the whole human species. You see, those workers are allowed to procreate, and if you damage their genes by radiation, and they intermarry with the rest of the population, for genetic purposes it's just the same as if you irradiate the population directly.[27]

So I find nuclear power this simple: do you believe they're going to do the miracle of containment that they predict? The answer is they're not going to accomplish it. It's outside the realm of human prospects.

You don't need to discuss each valve and each transportation cask and each burial site. The point is, if you lose a little bit of it—a terribly little bit of it—you're going to contaminate the earth, and people are going to suffer for thousands of generations. You have two choices: either you believe that engineers are going to achieve a perfection that's never been achieved, and you go ahead; or you believe with common sense that such a containment is never going to be achieved, and you give it up.

If people really understood how simple a problem it is—that they've got to accomplish a miracle—no puffs like Three Mile Island—can't afford those puffs of radioactivity, or the squirts and the spills that they always tell you won't harm the public—if people understood that, they'd say, "This is ridiculous. You don't create this astronomical quantity of garbage and pray that somehow a miracle will happen to contain it. You just don't do such stupid things!"

Licensing Murder

Licensing a nuclear power plant is in my view, licensing random premeditated murder. First of all, when you license a plant, you know what you're doing—so it's premeditated. You can't say, "I didn't know." Second, the evidence on radiation-producing cancer is beyond doubt. I've worked fifteen years on it, and so have many others. It is not a question any more: radiation produces cancer, and the evidence is good all the way down to the lowest doses.

The only way you could license nuclear power plants and not have murder is if you could guarantee perfect containment. But they admit that they're not going to contain it perfectly. They allow workers to get irradiated, and they have an allowable dose for the population.[28] So in essence I can figure out from their allowable amounts how many they are willing to kill per year.

27. See Chapter 2, p. 45.
28. See Chapter 2, p. 31 on health effects of current allowable radiation doses.

I view this as a disgrace, as a public health disgrace. The idea of anyone saying that it's all right to murder so many in exchange for profits from electricity—or what they call "benefits" from electricity—the idea that it's all right to do that is a new advance in depravity, particularly since it will affect future generations.

You must decide what your views are on this: is it all right to murder people knowingly? If so, why do you worry about homicide? But if you say, "The number won't be too large. We might only kill fifty thousand —and that's like automobiles"—is that all right?

People have told me they agree with my calculations. One of the associate directors at Livermore actually said to me, "Jack, you have a right to calculate that thirty-two thousand people would die from the standards we have in force. What I don't understand is why you think thirty-two thousand a year is too many."

"Look," I said, "if I didn't think thirty-two thousand were too many, I'd give up my medical diploma saying I didn't deserve it."

He didn't understand that.

People like myself and a lot of the atomic energy scientists in the late fifties deserve Nuremberg trials. At Nuremberg we said those who participate in human experimentation are committing a crime. Scientists like myself who said in 1957, "Maybe Linus Pauling is right about radiation causing cancer, but we don't really know, and therefore we shouldn't stop progress," were saying in essence that it's all right to experiment. Since we don't know, let's go ahead. So we were experimenting on humans, weren't we? But once you know that your nuclear power plants are going to release radioactivity and kill a certain number of people, you are no longer committing the crime of experimentation —you are committing a higher crime. Scientists who support these nuclear plants—*knowing* the effects of radiation—don't deserve trials for experimentation; they deserve trials for murder.

First Strike Capability: "The Power Disease"

In the six years that I was on the Board of Directors at the bomb laboratory, I became more and more worried about nuclear weapons. One day, after a couple of years at Livermore, I said at a lab meeting, "Do you know, every week we get together and talk about the next bomb thing. This whole business of trying to solve any problems with nuclear weapons is ridiculous. We ought to be having our discussions about the sociopolitical aspects of missilery and nuclear weapons, not just about bomb design."

I was told, "You're wrong, John."

"What do you mean, I'm wrong?"

"Look, we're scientists. Our job is to design the best bombs we can. It's for statesmen and the politicians to figure out what ought to be done about it."

That bothered me a great deal. My thoughts were these: everybody thinks nuclear weapons are a way of deterring war. That's not true. Nuclear weapons are going to *lead* to war. I'll tell you why. If you're a weaponeer in the United States, what do you have to think about? Since you don't know the facts, you must assume that the Soviet weaponeers are trying to get in a position where they can either hand you an ultimatum or bomb you out of existence if they think they have what's called a "first strike capability"—namely, the ability to bomb you out of existence without you retaliating. The only reason there hasn't been a nuclear war yet is that both sides realize that they haven't been in that technical position of being able to get away with it without too severe losses on their side.

Now some people say, "You don't need to worry. If one side gets a first-strike capability, the other side will get it too." That's not true. Scientific and technological advances are such that one side *might* get there six months early or a year earlier. Then they would be in a position to say, "Now we have the other side so they can't retaliate."

What would happen under those circumstances? Suppose the United States made the breakthrough.[29] "We've just figured out a way we can destroy the Soviet Union and not get any significant damage in return. We can either not use it, or we can use it."

Now why should we *not* use it? You say to yourself, "What if the

---

29. The U.S. has more than thirty thousand nuclear bombs in its weapons arsenal at the present time and is capable of destroying the Soviet Union dozens of times over. The development of a whole new generation of weapons—cruise missiles, the MX missile, and Trident missiles—suggests that the policy of "deterrence" is really a cover for the development of a "first-strike capability"—that the U.S. is actually planning for a nuclear war. See Robert Thaxton, "Directive Fifty-nine: Carter's New 'Deterrence' Doctrine Moves Us Closer to the Holocaust," *Progressive*, October 1980, pp. 36–37.

tables were turned and *they* were the ones that reached this point? Would they also not use it?" I think there's a high chance that if one side gets that advantage, they'll use it. The only solution is, you must stop *all* efforts to develop first-strike force solutions everywhere—whether they be nuclear or other—and move toward a more just society.

Even if you made an agreement to abolish all nuclear weapons, but you left established power structure in the U.S. and the USSR, they'd go on to research mind control or some chemical or biological thing. My view is, there exists a group of people in the world that have a disease. I call it the "power disease." They want to rule and control other people. They are a more important plague than cancer, pneumonia, bubonic plague, tuberculosis, and heart disease put together. They can only think how to obliterate, control, and use each other. They use people as nothing more than instruments to cast aside when they don't need them any more. There are fifty million people a year being consumed in a nutritional holocaust around the world; nobody gives a damn about starvation. If fifty million white Westerners were dying, affluent Western society would worry, but as long as it's fifty million Third World people dying every year, it doesn't matter.

In my opinion, what we need is to move toward being nauseated by people who want to be at the top, in power. Can you think of anything more ridiculous than that the Chinese, Russian, and American people let their governments play with superlethal toys and subject all of us to these hazards? The solution is not to replace one leader with another or to have more government. Society has to reorganize itself. The structure we have now is, the sicker you are socially, the more likely it is that you'll come out at the top of the heap.

CHAPTER 5

John Everett, Carpenter

The living room of John Everett, Yaphank, Long Island. A bitterly cold December evening. In the corner of the room, an old wrought-iron wood-burning stove. Everett gets up every now and then and puts wood in the stove.

He is tall, extremely thin, bearded, twenty-eight years old. He wears a brightly patterned shirt, tight-fitting blue-jeans.

From 1973 to 1976 Everett worked as a carpenter on the construction of Shoreham nuclear power plant. The plant, being built by the Long Island Lighting Company (LILCO), is scheduled to go on line in 1983. Everett walked off the job in 1976. "I just saw too many defects." The more he learned about Shoreham and nuclear power, the more convinced he became that the plant should never have been built. "My life is at stake if Shoreham goes into operation."

On 3 June 1979 Everett decided to go over the fence at Shoreham in an act of civil disobedience at a mass demonstration. "You're not going to solve anything by breaking the law," his father said. His father, James Everett, is the business agent of the Suffolk County District Council of Carpenters. "My father's the man who hands out the union jobs," Everett says. "And the union is pronuclear. Very pronuclear."

The night before he was scheduled to testify on behalf of one of the Shoreham demonstrators, Everett says he got a call from his father, who

John Everett

threatened him with loss of his union job (shop steward) if he testified.[1]
*Everett chose to go ahead and testify. He lost his union job, and a week
later was laid off his construction job.*

*Everett responded by bringing charges against the union, LILCO,
and the construction company for conspiring to block his speaking up
publicly about construction defects at Shoreham nuclear power plant.*

*His attorney, Arthur Schwartz, says LILCO is putting pressure on the
union because it "hopes to chill the rights and desires of others working
at the plant to speak out about shoddy workmanship and poor safety
standards."*[2]

*"Who's kidding who?" Everett says. "They're making money off of
us. We're the ones who are paying higher and higher rates, and we're
the ones who are going to die because of this plant. Why should we have
to die because of it?"*

*Everett's experience with the nuclear industry cannot be separated
from his experience with the union. Over the last ten years the Shoreham nuclear power plant has been "the only major source of work on
Long Island for certain construction unions. These unions have been
among the staunchest supporters of the nuclear plant. . . ."*[3] *Workers
who challenge the nuclear industry also find themselves running up
against the union. "Anyone who talks and gets found out by the union
or the contractor will never work in the Northeast again."*[4]

1. Frances Cerra, "L. I. Union Agent Ousts Son Over Atom Plant Testimony," *New York Times,* 7 December 1979, p. B-1. "The business agent for the union, James Everett, John Everett's father, confirmed in a telephone interview that he had warned his son last night that if he went ahead with his testimony he would be replaced as shop steward. This morning, that action was taken, he said." The elder Everett has denied that he threatened to fire his son if he testified and claimed his son quit "voluntarily." Steve Wick, "Fail-Safe Improved at N-Plant: LILCO," *Newsday,* 8 December 1979, p. 6. See also Susan Jaffe, "Repression: The New Nuclear Danger," *Village Voice,* 31 March 1980, p. 26. "Frances Cerra was subpoenaed and, armed with two *Times* lawyers, verified under oath that James Everett told her he fired his son."

2. Robert Lane, "Sues Dad Over N-Plant 'Blackball,' " *Daily News,* 28 December 1979.

3. Cerra, "L.I. Union Agent Ousts Son Over Atom Plant Testimony," p. B-1.

4. Gloria Jacobs, "Inside the Nuclear Industry's Heart: Construction Workers Talk about the Monster They're Building at Shoreham," *Seven Days,* 26 October 1979, pp. 7–10. Also see Chapter 9, pp. 245–253.

The Union

In Suffolk County my father is Number Two. They've got one man over him, George Babcock,[5] and that's it in the carpenter's union. My father's the business agent,[6] the man who controls the jobs.[7]

When I joined the union, I didn't want to tell anybody who my father was because I didn't want the foreman running around and telling everybody, "You gotta take care of him. He's Jimmy Everett's son." But I had to give my name to the shop steward. Then, when he brought me down to the crew I was going to work with, he introduced me to the foreman and told the foreman my name. So right away they knew who I was. I ended up doing twice as much work as most of the men on the job, only because I didn't want them to say, "Well, he's the business agent's son. He doesn't have to work." I busted my ass every time I was there—every day I was on the job.

But in 1973 Everett had an argument with his father over doing non-union work. That was on a weekend.

I went back on the job Monday morning, and the superintendent came over to me. "I don't know what's going on," he said, "but I got this call from your father to lay you off at eight o'clock this morning." And he handed me my paycheck.

I was out of work for six months. I couldn't find a job, non-union or union. I couldn't even get a job in a delicatessen. I believe my father let the word out that I was not to go to work. It wasn't until I went over to his house to tell him I was getting married that he said, "Well, if you're gonna get married, you need a job." He called me up on the weeked. "Go to Shoreham Monday morning," he said. "You're going to start work."

I thought, Great. I got a job that's going to last me a good long time instead of these jobs that only last a month or a week. I was very happy

---

5. Babcock is president of Local 1222, secretary, treasurer, and general business agent of the District Council.

6. *business agent:* an extremely powerful position in the union. The business agent is in charge of putting union members to work.

7. "The carpenters' union is more like a labor contractor than a labor union. It puts members on jobs at high union wages and can also put members out of work." Jaffe, "Repression: The New Nuclear Danger," p. 27.

about going to Shoreham nuclear power plant because a lot of people I knew were working there.

Working at Shoreham

Monday morning I went to work. There were about fifty other guys hired the same day I was hired. The big push was on to get this nuclear plant built. There were about three hundred carpenters on the job already, and five hundred laborers. They had about two thousand employees in all.

When you come on the job in the morning, they're handing out leaflets telling you how safe nuclear power is, and what they're doing, and how far advanced the company is, compared to the first nuclear power plants.

There was this big hole in the ground we started working from—one hole with a big concrete slab in it, where we were going to build a reactor. I was told I was going to go to work in the reactor building, putting the pedestal walls—the primary containment walls—in the reactor. I worked for a year doing that.

The wintertime was very cold, with the wind blowing off of that water. And in the summertime it got real hot working out on top of that concrete. If you've ever been out on the beach—that's what it's like being out on the concrete all day long. Just sweating up a storm.

The only thing about Shoreham that was different compared to other jobs I'd worked on was the fact that 75 percent of the time you stood around and did nothing because they didn't have anything for you to do.

See, the contractor has to pay a certain wage to each worker. The contractor charges LILCO—the lighting company—more than it costs them. So the more men the contractor has on the job, the more money he's going to make.[8] So it paid to have more men on the job. And nobody seemed to care whether you stood around all day or what. The contractor was happy if you just stood around. Then he could say, "We need more carpenters. The work's not getting done. We need more laborers. We need more welders." The more money that's spent, the

8. "The contractor was padding the payroll," another construction worker at Shoreham said, "and we had more guys than we needed." Jacobs, "Inside the Nuclear Industry's Heart," p. 8.

more money the contractor is going to make.

But you always had to look busy. Which is one of the hardest jobs to do—to look busy and not have anything to do. You stand there and nail a couple of two-by-fours together, and then you stand there and pull the nails out, and turn the two-by-fours around and put the nails in the other way. There were guys who walked around the job with the same two-by-fours on their shoulder all day long. Walked from one end of the job to the other and then back again.[9]

Every now and then someone would come over to you and tell you to make a cabinet or a picnic table—all sorts of things. So you would, if you had nothing else to do. And these cabinets and picnic tables were taken off the job. You wouldn't know where they were going or who had ordered them.

It's hard to imagine. I've worked on a lot of construction sites, and you'd never see anything like that going on. Most construction jobs, everybody's out there working hard seven hours a day.

The funny part of it was they would want you to do overtime at night. You wouldn't do anything for seven hours all day long, and then they'd tell you you were going to work three hours that night—which is double pay. And then they'd tell you you're working Saturday and Sundays. You come in on Saturday or Sunday, you get double time. Sometimes they had work for you. Other times they had nothing.

Another big thing that went on at Shoreham was drugs. I knew particular guys that would be able to push twenty-five pounds of pot in a week on that one job. That was just selling ounces. They were doing a great business—their own salary plus what they were making pushing drugs. I could never smoke or do drugs like these guys, while I was working. You couldn't function properly—especially working on a girder a hundred and eighty feet up in the air.

I started noticing a lot of things that didn't seem right. I was working on the pedestal walls of the reactor—the walls that hold up this vessel that sits inside the reactor with the uranium in it. It's big—like the size of this house. It had to be around fifty feet long and twenty feet across, and it was shaped like a medicine capsule. I saw that when they were

9. "A 1978 audit by the State Public Service Commission said that craft workers, including steamfitters, electrical workers, iron workers, laborers and carpenters were involved in 'direct work' only 21 per cent of their work day. In contrast, they spent 42 per cent of their day just 'waiting.'" Robert Fresco, "Shoreham: Delays and Rising Costs," *Newsday*, 4 April 1979, p. B-2.

pouring the concrete, this guy would stand there with a vibrator, and he would push it down in the concrete, and then, instead of pushing it down a couple of times to make sure the air bubbles came out and moving over only a foot at a time, he would do it once and move over four feet at a time. And as the guys poured the concrete, people would say, "He's using a vibrator. It's okay. That's all he has to do."[10]

So when the concrete hardened, it left honeycombs—air pockets and bubbles. Someone would come in and patch over the holes so the inspectors wouldn't see them.

I thought, This thing is going to hold up this tremendous vessel. How come they're allowing these guys to get away with these mistakes? Why don't they say something about it and have them correct the mistakes instead of just covering them up?

I asked my foreman why they weren't properly taking care of the honeycombs. And he said, "We'll take care of it." It was sort of "move along, sonny. Go back and do your work and keep your mouth shut." And it just kept going on.

In May 1979 a carton of "dump documents" was discovered in the Southold town landfill twenty-five miles from Shoreham.[11] The contents of the carton included about one thousand reports describing construction problems and nuclear safety–related problems at the nuclear plant. The papers revealed flaws in the welding of pressure piping. Such flaws could lead to breaks in the pipe and, depending on where the pipe is in the plant, a major loss of coolant accident (LOCA), which could uncover the core and lead to a disastrous core meltdown. There were reports in these papers of reinforcement bars (which keep the concrete of the containment dome under proper pressure) being severed accidentally. In case after case, problems were identified in the construction, and then solutions were suggested which eliminated the need to replace the faulty weld, anchor bolt, stiffeners, etc. The reports read like this: "Problem: The hangar installed on the wrong side of Col. 4, and 2 in. low for reactor controls. Construction requests that the hangar be

10. Everett testified at the trial of Matthew Chachere that the primary containment wall at the core of the reactor building was also flawed with cracks. Lane, "Sues Dad Over N-Plant 'Blackball.'"

11. See Steve Lawrence, "Shoreham: The First $2 Billion Plant?" *Daily News*, 12 February 1980.

left as installed. This nonconformance is documented on attached. Problem Solution: Approved."[12]

The NRC has conceded that there are 17,000 to 18,000 reports of Shoreham plant safety–related problems, but LILCO maintains that these are routine and no cause for concern.[13]

"We're delighted that the NRC inspectors are coming out because we are sure that [they] will substantiate the fact that we are building the plant [Shoreham] safely and properly. All our concrete meets with standards agreeable to the NRC."

> —LILCO spokeswoman, June Bruce. Quoted in Robert Fresco, "NRC Probes Shoreham Construction,"*Newsday,*15 December 1979, p. 7.

I don't think my foreman knew how to read blueprints. Several times he gave me measurements, and I would check them out, and they wouldn't fit. So one time I went back and looked at the blueprints myself, and I realized he didn't know how to read them. Every time he gave someone something to do, he messed it up. It got to the point where he would ask me to read them for him.

You start with a hole in the ground. You put up two plywood panels —called forms—and you pour concrete in between them. These are your walls. You put threaded rods through the concrete and the wood to hold the walls together, so the concrete can't push them apart. You put what's called a shear-bolt on either end of the rod to hold it there.

12. See Karl Grossman, "Shoring Up Shoreham: Long Island's Nuclear Interlock Has Big Plans, Leaky Pipes," *Seven Days,* 26 October 1979, pp. 5–6.

13. "William Museler, assistant project manager of the Long Island Lighting Co., said that NRC inspectors found a defect in one weld in pipes within the reactor area, the most critical section of the $1.58-billion plant, which is scheduled to go on line in 1981. [Current estimate is 1983.] He said that the utility's quality assurance team found three other defects in piping in the reactor area. Museler said that six more pipes within the reactor area were found to be in violation of industry specifications." Wick, "Fail-Safe Improved at N-Plant: LILCO," p. 6.

In January 1978 inspections of 408 welds on "crucial plant safety systems revealed 82 that were 'unacceptable.'" Lawrence, "Shoreham: The First $2 Billion Plant?", p. 31.

The plywood holds the concrete until the concrete gets hard enough to hold itself up alone. Then you take the shear-bolts out and pull the wood forms off. That's basically what a carpenter does on construction sites in the early stages of a building.

A lot of times at Shoreham when we unscrewed the shear-bolts, we would unscrew the threaded rods right out of the concrete. These threaded rods were roughly five-eighths of an inch in diameter, and they would leave these holes going right through the concrete. This was the pedestal wall.

I notified the foreman. "We just pulled the threaded rod out of the wall."

And he said, "I'll send a laborer over to patch over the hole. Nobody will see it."

What could you say? You're brushed off again. "Somebody will take care of it. Go away, sonny. We'll have someone take care of it. You don't know what you're talking about anyway."

When you've worked in construction long enough, you know those threaded rods shouldn't come out of the wall. They're supposed to stay there. But nobody wanted to get in trouble, so nobody would say anything. Rather than report it to somebody, everybody would just cover it up. "Oh, yeah. Everything's going fine."

I'm not a physicist or anything, but I have learned that holes like that can really cause problems. The wall is structurally sound for any downward pressure, but for any pressure going against it horizontally, the wall is weaker. It was explained to me by a reactor physicist, that when there's a gas blow-out and the reactor core actually gets exposed, all this high-pressure steam comes out. And this steam comes down and across all in one shot. This wall wouldn't hold these pressures.

I saw so many mistakes made, even in the primary containment walls —honeycombs[14] and cracks that ran all the way up the whole wall.

---

14. Complaints about shoddy construction of nuclear facilities are not uncommon. Honeycombing in the containment wall of the Marble Hill nuclear power plant in Indiana resulted in the Nuclear Regulatory Commission ordering a complete halt on construction of that facility. At the nearby Zimmer Nuclear Power Station in Moscow, Ohio, workers have testified that there are serious defects in the plant's concrete, welding, cable trays, and control rods, among other problems. See "PSI Explains Its Side of Marble Hill Dispute," *Cincinnati Enquirer,* 20 July 1979, p. B-2, and Jim Greenfield, " 'Cutting Corners' Called Top Concern at Zimmer," *Cincinnati Enquirer,* 20 June 1979, p. C-1. See also Chapter 9, Tom Martin, pp. 251–253.

I would say, "Hey, the wall's cracked!"

I was told, "You can't tell the difference between a surface crack and a through-wall crack."

No, you can't. But when you tell somebody the wall's cracked, and they say, "It's only a surface crack. Don't worry about it," how do *they* know it's only a surface crack? I mean, this is the containment wall.

At the beginning, working at Shoreham was just another job. But after about a year—maybe even less than a year—I started doing some research on my own. I'm a nosy person. I have to find out how things work. I'm not satisfied with a radio because it's a radio. I have to know why the radio works. So I started getting books from the library and sending away for research magazines and papers from the government about how nuclear reactors work. I wasn't looking for something *wrong* with them, I just wanted to find out how they worked.

I started questioning inspectors on the job, too. "How much pressure does this have to withstand? What's going to be held in this room? How long is this plant going to be operating? How long does it have to operate?" And they couldn't come up with answers. They weren't interested in finding out answers either. Even the people who were supposed to know what was going on didn't know what was going on.

Like the temperature of the water that was going to be pumped out into Long Island Sound. A lot of people were saying, "Yeah, it's going to be great for the fishing because this is going to keep the fish here all the time." You know, because the water is going to be warmer.

You got to be kidding. You're pumping radioactive water into the Sound. The fish are going to die. Sure, the water's going to be warmer, but fish can't live in that type of water. I said, "This water's going to kill the fish."

"Oh no, no. When the water goes down in there, it's going to be purer than the water that's in the Sound now." This is what the people on the job were told. "You can drink this water when it comes out of here. It's going to be so pure. It's going to be better than the drinking water that you drink now."

So I said, "How do you get the radiation out of the water?"

"The water's boiled and boiled and boiled."

And I said, "The water's already boiled in the reactor. That's how the reactor generates steam. There's radioactive particles in the water."

"Oh, yeah," they said, "but it's no more than what you get in a chest X-ray or when you go to the dentist to get a tooth X-rayed."

"Well, that means that you can't be in the water for any more than a second at a time," I said. "You're in the water any longer than that, you're getting too much X-ray. It's like standing under an X-ray machine for two hours."

They'd shake their heads. "You don't know what you're talking about."

But I had read about it. They don't boil the water to get radiation out of it. They use chemicals. These guys knew nothing about what was going on.

A nuclear plant requires huge quantities of water to cool the reactor core. This water is heated as it travels through the core, and becomes intensely radioactive. According to the Nuclear Regulatory Commission, coolant water is not returned to the environment until it falls within federal guidelines on permissible radioactivity. It is generally recognized both inside and outside the nuclear industry, however, that there can be no absolutely safe level of radiation. Federal guidelines are "not a dividing line between safe and unsafe," but are based on the pragmatic principle of ALARA—"as low as reasonably achievable."[15]
"Reasonable" is interpreted by the regulatory agencies according to what the nuclear industry needs to maintain its operations. The NRC acknowledges that radioactivity cannot be completely cleaned out of coolant water. This radioactivity finds its way into algae, which is eaten by fish. Radiation accumulates in the fatty tissue of fish in concentrations millions of times higher than in the algae. This is one way that radioactivity finds its way into the food chain and into the bones and tissues of human beings.

Thermal pollution also results from the dumping of this heated water into oceans, rivers, lakes, and streams. When the water temperature changes, certain species of fish cannot survive. Fish exposed to sudden changes in temperature die from "thermal shock." In January 1972 a huge school of fish attracted to the warmer waters in the vicinity of Oyster Creek nuclear power plant, New Jersey, did not migrate south as usual. When the plant shut down for routine maintenance that

15. *Radiation Standards and Public Health*, pp. 10–11, 17.

month, the temperature of the water dropped sharply. Some two hundred fifty thousand fish died as a result.[16]

It was unbelievable. I read material that was antinuclear and pronuclear, and I noticed the pronuclear was not saying that the antinuclear was wrong. It was just saying, "That's a chance you have to take." And that started to scare me. They're testing these things, and they're taking chances with our lives. We're the ones who are going to lose. In a matter of minutes, you're talking about three hundred thousand people dying. It's worse than World War I, the amount of people that would die in a few minutes.

I started getting worried about all these defects. There were so many air bubbles and air pockets in the concrete, so many cracks in the walls, and so many improper welds made—pipe welds, mixed instrumentation welds—everything. If something happened and one of these critical pipes broke, and severed the instrumentation lines, you could lose all your valves. The cables that control the valves run through these pipes. You could have a pretty serious accident. . . .

A Note about the Risks

If Shoreham had a Class-9 accident, or core meltdown, the results would be devastating. A "worst possible accident," where 50 percent of the core melts, could kill forty-five thousand people, injure one hundred thousand, and cause seventeen billion dollars worth of damage. Radiation would contaminate an area the size of Pennsylvania downwind of the reactor.[17] *Metropolitan New York, Long Island, Westchester County, New Jersey, and Connecticut would be uninhabitable for hundreds of years.*

Jeff Booboor, a LILCO engineer, claims that LILCO has a plan under which approximately ten thousand people living within two miles of the plant could be evacuated, should an accident take place at Shoreham.

16. Gyorgy, *No Nukes*, p. 121.

17. This estimate comes from an AEC commissioned report in 1964. The AEC considered the report so shocking that it was not made public until 1973. In fact, the AEC denied the existence of the report. See Gyorgy, *No Nukes*, p. 114.

No plan exists for the one hundred fifty thousand Long Islanders who live within ten miles of the plant.[18]
    The nuclear industry maintains that the chance of a core meltdown is extremely remote. The Rasmussen Report, funded by the AEC, states that "the likelihood of being killed in any one year in a reactor accident is one chance in 300,000,000."[19] *Playing a probability game with statistics, the report concluded that the chance of one thousand people or more being killed from a reactor accident is about as remote as it is for one thousand people to be killed by a meteor shower. The risks of nuclear power are termed "negligible."*[20]
    Those who have worked in the nuclear industry, however, tell a different story. "Maybe it's time the AEC told the public that if people want to turn the lights on they are going to have to expect to lose a reactor now and then, and possibly suffer great dislocations and property losses as well," said one reactor safety engineer from the National Reactor Testing Station at Idaho Falls, Idaho.[21] *Keith Miller, a consultant to the NRC's Advanced Code Group, wrote a letter to Stan Fabic of the NRC in May 1976, saying that the Rasmussen Report "will come to be viewed as a severe blow to the scientific credibility of the NRC. There already exist devastating criticisms of its methodology, conclusions, and misleading summary. . . ."*[22]
    In January 1979 the NRC repudiated the Rasmussen Report, admitting that the report "greatly understated" the risk of a nuclear accident.[23]

Another thing. I did welding for almost two years at Shoreham, even though I failed the welder's test seven times, so I wasn't certified to weld.

18. See Fresco, "Shoreham: Delays and Rising Costs," p. B-2.
19. The Rasmussen Report took two years to complete and cost three million dollars. U.S. Atomic Energy Commission, "Reactor Safety Study: An Assessment of Accident Risks in U.S. Commercial Nuclear Power Plants" (WASH-1400), Summary Report, Washington, D.C., August 1974.
20. Gyorgy, *No Nukes,* p. 114.
21. Quoted in Robert Gillette, "Nuclear Safety (I): The Roots of Dissent," *Science,* September 1972, p. 771.
22. Professor Keith Miller, consultant, Advanced Code Review Group to Stan Fabic of NRC, Washington, D.C., 7 May 1976, in Gyorgy, *No Nukes,* pp. 116–117.
23. Gofman, *"Irrevy": An Irreverent, Illustrated View of Nuclear Power,* pp. 57–59.

I could do an overhead weld, a vertical weld, a horizontal weld, but I couldn't do a flat weld—welding something that is lying flat in front of you. When it was overhead, I could hold the rod steady. Vertical I could hold it. But when it was down straight underneath me, my hands couldn't hold the weld rod steady. So I failed the test for flat welding. There were times they didn't have anybody available and they wanted something done, so they told me to do it. The majority of welding I did was flat welding.

I wasn't the only one. I know of three others. I can't tell you their names or anything. It was brought up in testimony. They wanted the names of the other people who weren't certified and were welding. I couldn't—wouldn't—give them. Those welders wouldn't testify in court because they were afraid that their jobs were going to be taken away from them.

LILCO pulled all the cards on welders and couldn't find any card that said I was a welder there or that I did any welding. I told them that there wouldn't be any cards or records because I had failed the test seven times and wasn't supposed to weld.

The Reactor Design

This plant at Shoreham is only going to last for maybe twenty, thirty years, and then they're going to have to shut it down.[24] Here they are, building this tremendous thing costing more than a billion dollars,[25] and it's only going to last a little longer than it takes them to build it.

Then I found out that the reactor that they were using in Shoreham was outdated when they bought it. General Electric had discontinued these reactors—this particular model—because there were too many things wrong with the ones they'd already sold. The Shoreham reactor had actually been *scrapped*. LILCO got this good deal on it—bought it at a very cheap price.

24. Thirty-five years is typically the economic lifetime of a nuclear reactor. Decommissioning a nuclear reactor can take seventy-five to one hundred years.
25. When LILCO first announced the Shoreham project in 1968, the estimated cost was $271 million. Since then, estimates have risen to $2.2 billion, which makes Shoreham the world's most expensive reactor to date. See Lawrence, "Shoreham: The First $2 Billion Plant?".

The Shoreham reactor was originally designed by General Electric for the New York State Gas & Electric Company (NYSEG) in the mid-sixties to be used at another site. When community opposition forced NYSEG to put up a coal-fired plant instead, GE offered the 800-megawatt reactor to LILCO. The Shoreham plant had actually been designed to house a smaller nuclear reactor and thus all specifications had to be modified.[26]

The GE reactor sold to LILCO was an old design and not up-to-date with present standards. The reactor uses a containment called the MARK II, which has not been completely tested and is "a highly questionable design," according to Dale Bridenbaugh, a former nuclear engineer at GE who was involved in evaluating its safety and design. Gregory Minor, another former GE nuclear engineer, describes the Shoreham reactor as having "all the drawbacks of the older models. If you went to the NRC today with an application for licensing this reactor, you'd probably get turned down."[27]

Quitting Shoreham and Going Over the Fence

The more information I received the clearer it got that the people at Shoreham just didn't want to give you any answers. The only answers I kept coming up with were antinuclear. I believed antinuclear was telling more of the truth than LILCO was or that people who worked for LILCO were. No matter how much complaining I did, the reaction I got was "If you don't like it here, then leave."

One of the things that really put a clincher on everything in my leaving was some of the research I did on solar energy. I found out that for what it's costing to build the Shoreham nuclear plant, you could put

26. See Jacobs, "Inside the Nuclear Industry's Heart," pp. 7–8 for a discussion of the "bargain-basement reactor core" LILCO purchased for its Shoreham nuclear plant.

27. Phone conversation with Gregory Minor, July 1980. See also the testimony of the three General Electric nuclear engineers before the Joint Committee on Atomic Energy for a discussion of defects in certain General Electric nuclear reactors. Dale G. Bridenbaugh, Richard B. Hubbard, and Gregory C. Minor, "Testimony," in *Investigation of Charges Related to Nuclear Reactor Safety*, hearings of the Joint Committee on Atomic Energy, U.S. Congress, Washington, D.C., 18 February 1976.

solar panels on every house in Suffolk County and still have money left over. I mean, who's kidding who? They're making money off of us. We could be building solar powered houses and heat our houses by the sun. They won't do that because no one can make money off of the sun. Nobody can stand there and say, "Well, you're going to get eight hours of sun today. You got to pay me a dollar for every hour you get off of the sun. Otherwise we're going to put a dome over your house so you can't see the sun."

It got to a point where everything going on in Shoreham was totally against what I believed in. I just couldn't see staying there. You know, I couldn't take it any more. Couldn't take the standing around doing nothing, the fact that mistakes were being made, the fact that nobody wanted to know about them.

One day in May 1976 I didn't go to work. I didn't tell anybody. I just didn't go. My father, who's business agent in the carpenters' union, called me up in June. The shop steward had reported to him that I'd been out of work a couple of weeks.

"How come you're not going to work?"

I told him that I didn't feel I should work at Shoreham.

"What do you mean?"

"I just can't work there with all of the mistakes that are being made and the lackadaisical attitude that people have there."

"I think you're being very stupid," he said.

A few months after I quit, my father asked me if I wanted to go back to work at Shoreham. If I played my cards right and kept my mouth shut, I could retire early out of there.

"Well, I don't really want to go back," I said.

"Those are the only jobs available right now," my father said.

Finally, he got me this construction job over at Parr Meadows, a race track. I worked a couple of other construction sites after that. Then in 1977 I got a job as shop steward in the union. I was working as a shop steward for the Austin Company—Peerless Photo Products—when I heard about a demonstration coming up at Shoreham.

I had gone to quite a few of the rallies against nuclear energy. I'd gone to Washington, D.C., when they'd had the big rally down there. After seeing how many people were there, I thought, This many people actually *came*. There's got to be ten times this amount of people who know what's going on and are just sitting back, and hundreds of times this amount of people who don't know what's going on. If they knew what was going on, they would be here too.

So when it came down to the rally at Shoreham, I decided to be one of the people who went over the fence.

Both my brothers got together with me. We were all sitting in my house and talking.

"Did you hear about the Shoreham demonstration?"

"Yeah."

"Are you going to go?"

"Yeah, let's go."

We knew there was trespassing involved, and that we might get arrested. This would give us a chance to go to court and get the facts out. We got hold of the SHAD Alliance. They came to my house and ran a nonviolence workshop. Fifteen people came from all different places. They told us, "Don't run. Don't make any moves after dark." If we were arrested, they told us how to let our family know. You know, the do's and don't's of a nonviolent demonstration. It took about five hours.

My brothers and I stayed very close together when we went over the fence. We stayed together throughout the whole thing. Even when we were arrested, we made sure we went in the same bus together.

Six hundred of us went over the fence in Shoreham and got arrested. Which was not enough people. I would have liked to see six thousand go over that fence. If there had been the amount of people that were in Washington, D.C., all go over that fence, they would each have been able to take a piece of concrete home as their reminder of what Shoreham Nuclear Power Station used to look like. And there would've been no one there to stop us. There would be no way they could control one hundred twenty-five thousand people walking onto that site.

After being arrested in Shoreham on June 3, I spent a few hours in jail. I decided not to take the offer of six months' probation. The way it was explained to me was, if you don't do anything wrong, you could be released with no record or anything. But I knew about Shoreham. I knew about the defects. I knew they were building the equivalent of a nuclear bomb, something nobody can control if it goes off. If it does ever blow up, where're you going to go?

If they were going to put me on the witness stand and try me for trespassing, I was at least going to be able to say, "Well, this is what's going on there." And they were going to have to listen. Somebody was going to have to listen. I thought, if somebody doesn't speak up, sooner or later they're going to turn this plant on, and we are all going to die.

Brookhaven National Laboratory

The Shoreham trespassing trial was set for late in the fall of 1979. On 2 July 1979 Everett got a job as shop steward working at the Brookhaven National Laboratory.

When I first heard about a job at Brookhaven, I thought, Oh, great. This is what I want—to work on something that's solar, to find out how it works. I thought Brookhaven was only a solar energy plant—a test facility. When I found out exactly what Brookhaven was, I'd already been there a couple of weeks.

How I found out is, one day we were working this job, and I moved around to the other side of the building to check something out. I saw all these signs that said, "Radiation Area. Keep Out."

So I started asking questions: "What's in this area?"

You really can't find out too much because nobody really wants to say. Most people don't know. I did find out that they had a reactor there that's been operating for twenty years, and that they've buried some waste there. They've dumped radioactive materials right there in the woods. There's an area where it's completely barren. Nothing grows.

There have been instances where the Conservation Department found mutated deer. You can see a lot of that in the wildlife around the area. I saw deer that had antlers that go straight up in the air, instead of curving and pointing forward, like most deer's antlers do. I've never seen deer like that before, and I do quite a bit of deer hunting.

I talked to a biologist who'd worked there at Brookhaven, and he said, "Yes, there's hot rabbits, hot deer, hot birds."[28] And he wouldn't eat any of them that came out of that area, because radiation wastes have been dumped in the woods.

I heard another thing too. Some people from the town of Brookhaven snuck down to the headwaters of the Peconic River and took pictures

28. *hot:* radioactive.

and test samples of the water. They found the radiation levels coming out of Brookhaven Lab were above what they should have been—quite a bit above. The headwaters of the river were completely destroyed. That's where the river first began. And that river goes right out the middle of the fork of the island, right out into the Peconic Bay.

I never went back up in that area again, except to steal one of the signs. I put it up on the front gate going into the site, just to let people coming in know that there was radiation in the area. It was eventually taken down, just before I left. They said that the danger of radiation was not there any longer, and that they had checked it out.

Everett worked at the Brookhaven National Laboratory from 2 July 1979 until December of that year, believing that his union position as shop steward made it possible for him to supervise the construction work and make sure everything was "done right, that the concrete was poured right and everything. I could oversee everything."

Testifying Against Shoreham

The trial for trespassing at Shoreham was coming up in December. Matthew Chachere, one of the people who had gone over the fence, asked me to testify on his behalf. He was my friend. I spoke to his attorney and told him that I could lose my job and never work again in Suffolk County, but I felt it was important to the case. I had to do what I could.

The newspaper came out Wednesday, and it had my name in it and that I was going to be one of the construction workers who was going to testify. Somebody powerful read that newspaper and had a talk with my father.

My father called me the night before the trial.[29] He told me that if I testified, I would be replaced as shop steward. I could call him in the morning and tell him whether I was going to testify or not. In other words, I had the night to think about it. I had thought about it. The next morning I called him and told him I was going to testify.

He said, "Okay. Then you are no longer shop steward on the job.

29. See Cerra, "L.I. Union Agent Ousts Son Over Atom Plant Testimony," p. B-1.

You're being replaced. It's not a shop steward's job to testify against construction defects."[30]

Now they have full right to replace me at any time. But they said—and they've been quoted in the newspapers—that the reason why I was being replaced was because I was going to testify.

See, the union is very much in favor of nuclear power.[31] They felt that to testify against nuclear power could mean the jobs of a hundred and thirty carpenters or so who were working at Shoreham, that my testimony could close down Shoreham. Which is a joke. The union feels that it's not right for a carpenter to testify against a place he works in. Even if it's not safe.

So I was removed as shop steward before I testified. I was told that I could work at Brookhaven, but there would be a new steward on the job. Then a week later my boss came up to me on a Friday, handed me my paycheck, and said, "I have to lay you off today."

And he didn't give any reason why. Just reduction in force. The following Monday they hired another man to replace me.

They were trying to violate my freedom of speech with a threat. That's what I'm going after them for now—taking the union into federal court—for the fact that they tried to mess around with my freedom of speech.

People I thought would be against what I had done surprised me. Like this one guy, Richie. He really surprised me, saying, "Well, you know, there are a lot of things wrong at Shoreham. I wish I could stand up and say something too."

And I received a letter from Pete Seeger, the folk singer, saying, "Dear John Everett, Congragulations for standing firm. Hope you keep on working as a carpenter for woods renewable, as I hope we all will be moved. Sincerely, Pete Seeger."

I talked to the attorney for Matthew Chachere. I told him what had happened to me and he said, "Well, listen. I'll get you an attorney." And

30. The elder Everett has denied this. See Wick, "Fail-Safe Improved at N-Plant: LILCO," p. 6.

31. According to Susan Jaffe, Babcock openly states this pronuclear position at union meetings, and the union's pronuclear position is reflected in its investments. The union holds several hundred thousand shares in utilities owning nuclear power plants and hundreds of shares in reactor manufacturers such as General Electric. See Jaffe, "Repression: The New Nuclear Danger," p. 27.

he did. While I was waiting to meet with my attorney, I received about a dozen calls from attorneys all over the country who wanted to handle the case. Paul Levy, who was one of the attorneys for Ralph Nader's group, called, and quite a few others.

The hearing was set for January 9. The union was making deals, bargaining. Someone told me the lawyer for the District Council had made a comment to my attorney that he was going to make it very difficult for me here in Suffolk County. He came out and made that statement. One of the people that we had subpoenaed was told by the District Council to leave town. "Don't answer the subpoena." The guy told me now that the hearing's over.

The hearing lasted three days—January 9 through 11. The judge said he couldn't really make a ruling on it, because he couldn't separate where union business—business agent (my father) talking to shop steward (me)—and a father-son relationship came in. We have a deposition for court set for March 15.

I'm bringing charges against the union[32] because I want to let other people know they can stand up and say what they want to say without the union telling them, "Well, you can say that, but you're not going to have a job." If I win the case, it'll show that there is some good to the law, after all. If I lose the case, it'll just show that even the law won't back you up.

I know that after I get done testifying against the union there won't be any work left on Long Island for me. I've seen what the union can do to people. They can have you blacklisted to the point where you can end up starving. I'll go someplace else. No matter where I go, I'll survive.

MHB Technical Associates, Preliminary Report:

In a preliminary report submitted by MHB Technical Associates (Dale Bridenbaugh, Gregory Minor, and Richard Hubbard—see Chapter 9) on the Shoreham nuclear power plant for the licensing proceedings, the following problems were discussed: (1) the design of the containment (which houses the Shoreham nuclear reactor) was discontinued by the manufacturer (General Electric) before LILCO

32. Everett is charging the union, LILCO, and the construction company, Hempstead Concrete, with conspiracy.

purchased it and has not been adequately tested; (2) various valves, seals, pumps, and monitoring instruments are questionable; (3) the turbine generator is improperly positioned, thereby increasing the chance of reactor damage in the event of turbine failure; (4) the control rod drive mechanism is faulty; (5) there are various LILCO quality control and quality assurance violations; and (6) no design changes have been made to prevent an accident similar to the Browns Ferry fire, which occurred at another General Electric power plant. (See Chapter 9, pp. 275–277.)

After MHB's preliminary report was released, LILCO is alleged to have waged a vigorous lobbying campaign to influence the Suffolk County legislature to deny funding to MHB. MHB's funding was cut in the spring of 1978 by a narrow ten to eight vote of the Suffolk County legislature. [33]

KARL ABRAHAM, NRC SPOKESMAN:

"We don't see anything in this [investigation] that should have any impact on the licensing process."

—Quoted in Fresco, "NRC Probes Shoreham Construction," p. 7.

KARL GROSSMAN, "SHORING UP SHOREHAM:"

"[The Shoreham nuclear reactor] represents more than just Long Island's first nuclear power plant: It's supposed to be the start of the plan to turn Long Island into the Northeast's nuclear center." [34]

33. Barbara Selvin, "Nuke Consultants Defend Role to Be Played," *Suffolk Life, 3 September 1980, p. 1.*

34. A nuclear energy center is defined in the Nuclear Regulatory Commission's 1975 Site Survey as "any site, including a site not restricted to land, large enough to support utility operations, or other elements of the total nuclear fuel cycle, or both if appropriate, nuclear fuel reprocessing facilities, nuclear fuel fabrication plants, retrievable nuclear waste storage facilities, and uranium enrichment facilities." The Executive Summary of the 1975 Site Survey, addressed to the Honorable Nelson A. Rockefeller, 19 January 1976, concludes that "depending on location, it can be feasible and practical to construct power plant centers of up to 20 nuclear power reactors. . . ." Simply stated, this means twenty *nuclear reactors* would be placed in a single location. See Leslie Freeman and Daniel Pisello, "Big Money—Nuclear Plans Behind Squeeze at Mohawk Nation," *Akwesasne Notes*, Summer 1980, pp. 10–11.

CHAPTER 6

Kee Begay, Uranium Miner
Pearl Nahkai,
Widow of Uranium Miner
Fannie Yazzie,
Widow of Uranium Miner
Elsie Peshlakai, Navajo Organizer

> "I feel this way. I speak for my mother, my father, my children, my sheep. Let's not give in to white corporate people. Money is gone or can be increased. If you sell the land away, you sell something that cannot be returned."
>
> —Widow of Navajo uranium miner, National Citizens' Hearings for Radiation Victims, Workshop on Uranium Mining

The Uranium Miners and Their Widows

The Navajo uranium miners and some of their widows have traveled by bus for three days and three nights from New Mexico. They have come to Washington, D.C., to tell people at the National Citizens' Hearings on Radiation Victims (12 April 1980) what is happening to them and to their land.

Most of them do not speak English. During the hearings they remain in the back of the large hall, quiet and observant. When it is their turn to speak, they climb the stairs to the stage in single file and stand facing a hushed crowd. They do not tell their stories easily. At several points they stop, and tears run down their cheeks.

The story emerges slowly. Since the early 1940s Navajo land has been

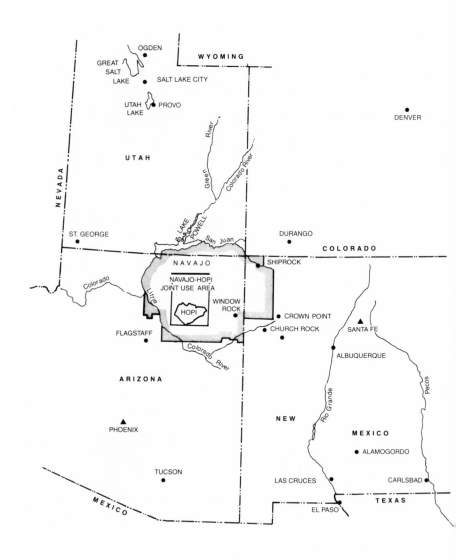

Four Corners Area

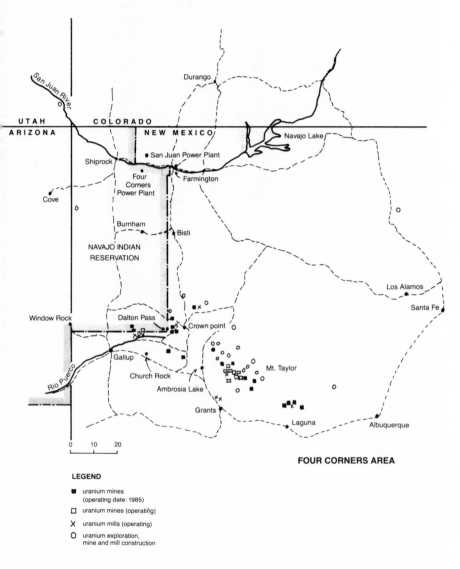

Uranium development in the San Juan Basin region (1979) *Janet Steele*

mined for uranium. It is here that the United States government found some of the richest uranium deposits in the nation—uranium that could be used for nuclear weapons. During the early part of the Second World War the government allowed some uranium to be extracted from this land for the secret Manhattan Project—the building of the first atomic bomb. Then, when the Atomic Energy Commission was created in 1946, Congress passed the Atomic Energy Act, authorizing the AEC to regulate nuclear research and development. The AEC was given power over the licensing of "source materials" containing uranium. However, the power of the AEC was limited "to source materials after removal from its place of deposit in nature."[1] The AEC interpreted this to mean that it did not have to regulate underground mining of uranium. The AEC did nothing to ensure safe mining conditions. In fact, it was not until 1972 that federal radiation-level standards were adopted.

Uranium is necessary for the production of nuclear power and nuclear weapons. In the Southwest, uranium is generally found underground in the same stratum of the earth where water is found. When uranium is extracted, water must also be pumped out of the mines. In New Mexico and the Southwest—where water is scarce and extremely valuable— water is pumped out of the mines at the rate of thousands of gallons per minute. This water is not drinkable or usable for irrigation because uranium mining contaminates it with radionuclides.

The uranium that comes out of the ground is mixed with rock and earth and must be refined. The raw uranium ore (rock that contains between .4 and 3 percent uranium) is crushed and ground into a fine, sandy substance at uranium mills generally located near the mines. The resulting mixture is known as "yellowcake." Only about four pounds of this valuable yellowcake can be extracted from two thousand pounds of uranium ore. The remaining materials—known as uranium tailings— contain dangerously radioactive radium, radon gases, and "radon daughters"—short-lived radionuclides produced as the radon in the ore decays into lead. "Radon daughters" are dangerous because they attach themselves to dust particles which can be inhaled. Once lodged in the lung tissue, these particles emit intense alpha radiation, which can damage the surrounding cells and eventually cause lung cancer and other respira-

---

1. Chris Shuey, "The Widows of Red Rock," *Scottsdale Daily Progress, Saturday Magazine,* Part I, 2 June 1979, p. 4.

tory diseases. Uranium tailings retain 85 percent of their original radioactivity for thousands of years. About seventy million tons of these radioactive tailings are lying uncovered in huge piles in New Mexico. Wind and rain blow these tailings all over the Southwest, contaminating air, water, and food. A 1975 Environmental Protection Agency statement reported that a good deal of the water from Grants, New Mexico —a major uranium mining area—was contaminated with radium and uranium.

When the big corporations came to Indian lands, there were no taxes and there was no regulation. There was a supply of cheap labor, and there was a great source of profit readily available. Mobil, Conoco, Kerr-McGee, United Nuclear, Anaconda, Vanadium, Utah International, and other energy corporations employed Navajos in the excavation of uranium.

According to La Verne Husen, director of the Public Health Service in Shiprock, New Mexico, the mines in the early days "had 100 times the level of radioactivity allowed today." They were "just holes and tunnels dug outside into the cliffs. Inside, the mines were like radiation chambers. . . ."[2]

Before 1965 the Navajos were remarkably free of lung cancer. But in 1965 2 Navajo uranium miners died of lung cancer. By 1970 8 Navajo miners had died of lung cancer. By 1979 25 had died. There are approximately 45 more who are still alive who have radiation-induced lung cancer.[3] Dr. Victor Archer, a physician and researcher from the National Institute of Occupational Safety and Health [NIOSH], studied 700 uranium miners in the Southwest and found a tenfold increase in the risk of cancer among uranium miners.[4] Many of the miners Archer studied were Navajos.

The nuclear industry has conducted studies which blame these deaths on smoking, not radiation. "I'm personally convinced that smoking is either helping [cause cancer] or is the main cause," says Dr. Robert W. Buechley, director of the industry-funded study. He claims that so far

2. Tom Barry, "Bury My Lungs at Red Rock: Uranium Mining Brings a New Peril to the Reservation," *Progressive*, February 1979, p. 27.

3. Michael Garrity, "The Pending Energy Wars: America's Final Act of Genocide, Part II," *Akwesasne Notes*, Early Spring 1980, p. 9.

4. Shuey, "The Widows of Red Rock, Part I," p. 5.

researchers have found no excess cancers in New Mexico Navajos.[5] *Union Carbide's Bob Beverly, coordinator of environmental control, is quoted in the* Denver Post *as saying that if "uranium miners had never smoked, we would never have known there was a problem."*

But a study by Doctors Victor Archer and Joseph Wagoner shows different results. The Archer-Wagoner study indicates that nonsmokers also face an increased risk of lung cancer.[6] *Wagoner told an audience in Albuquerque that he was "shocked to learn from uranium miners that they are told in their education courses that if they do not smoke, they will not develop lung cancer from exposure to radiation in the mines. This is not true. . . ."*[7]

Kerr-McGee owns the nation's largest underground uranium mine, near Grants, New Mexico. Seven hundred miners are employed there. Two of the widows at the radiation hearings today had husbands who worked in this mine. Kerr-McGee denies responsibility for these deaths. One Kerr-McGee representative, Bill Phillips, is quoted as telling a Washington *reporter: "I couldn't tell you what happened at some small mines on an Indian Reservation. We have uranium interests all over the world."*[8]

KEE BEGAY, URANIUM MINER

(Translated from Navajo by his son, Eugene)

My name is Kee Begay. I was a uranium miner for twenty-seven years, starting from the year 1942 to 1969. At that time we were not issued protective clothing. We were not even given safety precautions. We

5. Jack Cox, "Studies Show Radon Guidelines May be Weak," *Denver Post,* 4 September 1979, p. 1.

6. "Of 703 Indian uranium miners in the Southwest 11 died of lung cancer." The expected number for this group was 2.58. See Denise Tessier, "Uranium Mine Gas Causes Lung Cancer, UNM Group Told," *Albuquerque Journal,* 11 March 1980, p. A-14.

7. Joseph Wagoner, "Uranium Mining and Milling: The Human Costs," written text of a presentation at the University of New Mexico Medical School, Albuquerque, 10 March 1980.

8. Garrity, "The Pending Energy Wars, Part II," p. 10.

Ted Davis, M.D.

Kee Begay and his son at the National Citizens' Hearings
for Radiation Victims, Washington, D.C., 1980

were never told of any radiation effect. The mines were poor and unsafe
and not fit for human beings to work in. There was no ventilation inside
these mines. I think we actually breathed a lot more uranium dust than
any person on earth. . . .

The radiation affected my body—caused spasms. I coughed a lot, and
now I have difficulty breathing quite a few times a day. It has affected
my thyroids and given me pains in them. My legs are affected also.
. . . My lung condition was determined by a doctor from the Shiprock
Public Health Service. . . . He has said lung cancer.

I also lost a son, in 1961. He was one of the many children that used
to play in the uranium piles during those years. We had a lot of uranium

piles near our homes—just about fifty or a hundred feet away or so—
a lot of tailings. Can you imagine? Kids go out and play in those piles!

We had a lot of shortage of water too. Wherever we had water, they
would dig beside those wells. And at that time we did not know that
our water for drinking and preparing food was contaminated. . . .

I retired in 1969 when they found lung cancer. Now I ask the United
States government for compensation for the men who dug out the
uranium for our national *defense!*

This is all I have to say right now. Thank you for your attention.

Dr. Victor Archer, a NIOSH physician at the Western Area Occupa-
tional Health Laboratory, estimates that of the original 6,000 uranium
miners who worked in the region (western slope of the Rocky Moun-
tains), 1,000 will eventually die of lung cancer. [9]

PEARL NAHKAI, NAVAJO WIDOW OF URANIUM MINER

A small woman with skin sun-baked the color of clay, she wears a long
flowing skirt of coral silk, gathered at the waist. Her long black hair is
beginning to gray.

Although she cannot speak English very well, she chooses not to use
an interpreter.

My name is Pearl Nahkai. I am a Navajo widow. My husband, John
Smith Nahkai, was born in Red Rock, Arizona, on April 15, 1916. He
worked in uranium mine for twenty-one years in Arizona, Utah, and
Colorado for VCA, Kerr-McGee, and Climax Uranium. My husband
died of lung and stomach cancer in 1974. I was left with six children
to raise and support. It is very hard to be a mother and father. The

9. Shuey, "The Widows of Red Rock, Part I," p. 4.

Pearl Nahkai at the National Citizens' Hearings for Radiation Victims, Washington, D.C., 1980

Ted Davis, M.D.

money I get from Social Security is two hundred fifty dollars and eighty
cents each month.

My husband went to World War II in 1942 and came back in 1946
and there was no job for him, only the uranium mine. It was the only
job the people of Arizona work on. The company did not warn us it was
a dangerous thing to work on.

When he worked in the mine, we lived in a one-room house. There is our bed, there is our food, there is our dishes, and there is our stove. There he comes home. He didn't wash his hands real hard—just to eat in the afternoon. There he comes home with his dusty clothes and muddy clothes, and we just hang them right there, behind the stove, and it just dries out in there, and then he would be sleeping there.

He was just fine. But in 1972 all of a sudden he was short of breath. When he did something—like chopping wood—he just stands there . . . just holding onto something, and his breath is so . . . gone. That was the time I noticed something was wrong. I took him to the hospital to find out what's wrong with him. And then they told him that he had this stomach trouble. So they operate on him, and then after the operation the doctor said, "It's only six more weeks he's going to live." That's what he said. "He has cancer in his lung, in his liver, and his stomach."

The company never warned us. We wish they did! They never told us radiation can kill . . . like it killed my husband. They just want to get more, haul more in the truck, and always they want more more more! They chase them in the mine to get more. There was the dust and they eat in there . . . in the mine. When it's a long way to go in the afternoon, sometime he doesn't come home. He has to eat out there. And the dripping water in the mine they drink—with uranium in the water. It was no good.

The company left tailings in a pile across the street. We didn't even know about that. And the children play in there—play on it. We didn't know!

Around about two months ago one of my brothers passed away. Again, the same thing, from that mine. And the holes are still open out there. I wish they close it.

I want people to know I am a Navajo miner's widow, and I'm having a hard time with my six children. Everything is higher and very expensive for clothes, food, gasoline to take the children to school. It is a long ways to take my children to school every day, every morning. And school out, I bring them home. That's how I take care of my children. Me . . . a mother and a father.

I have come a long way to tell you that we need help with housing, running water, and compensation for our families. Many widows like me back home are suffering too. We want the government and the companies to pay us back. Thank you for listening to me. I want you to know that my husband never smoked.

".. . our breath would send a Geiger counter off scale after a shift underground."
".. . we had no protection at all. I quit working in the mines after three years, otherwise I most probably would not be here."

—Pratt Seegmiller, quoted in Reed Madsden, "Cancer Deaths Linked to Uranium Mining," *Deseret News*, 4 June 1979, p. 2B.

FANNIE YAZZIE, WIDOW OF CLIFFORD YAZZIE, URANIUM MINER

(Translated from Navajo)

My name is Fannie Yazzie. I am from a part of Red Valley Chapter House and I now live in Oak Springs, Arizona. I am the widow of Clifford Yazzie. At the time he went to work in the uranium mine, my husband did not know and I myself did not know there was any hazard in working in the mine. Before he worked there, he was in good health. He worked in the mine for twenty-five years and then he retired. Four years later he started showing all these symptoms and he visited a hospital in Gallup and he had surgery done on his lungs. Then he couldn't walk any more. So I took him to a VA hospital in Albuquerque to have more surgery done on him. Those people said it was incurable and to go home for a while to see if he could get better from the surgery. So I took him home for a week, but he was in pain, so they took him back to the hospital. After about a week he died.

The company told us that after the mining they would reclaim the land. To this day no reclaiming has been started. They ought to come in and plug up those uranium mine openings. A full-grown cow or horse

Ted Davis, M.D.

Fannie Yazzie

can fall in. You can have any sort of livestock fall in, and they can be lost, completely lost. . . .

I am scared that one of these days one of the children or myself will fall in. These openings are huge and sometimes they are covered with snow, and you can't see where they are. I don't let my sheep graze there. I herd the sheep myself. I sit between the openings and prevent the sheep from wandering over in those areas. I have been a sheepherder fifty-one years. I started taking care of sheep when I was seven years old. That was the only way the Navajos had back then. Like the buffalo to the Plains Indians, the sheep were to us. We make money from the sheep in our weaving and by selling wool.

I have gone out to my corral and found a dead sheep or goat, and I did not know the cause. Usually when this happens, my children go ahead and butcher it, but now my kids tell me I shouldn't do this because it may be related to those uranium tailings around here. I don't know why they are dying. No one has come to investigate it.

I dream of being compensated for my losses. Since my husband died I have been supporting eight kids. I have difficulty feeding them and clothing them. It cost seven thousand dollars to help my husband when he had lung cancer. Only this year (1980) I finished paying for my husband's funeral in 1972.

It is Kerr-McGee's responsibility. They didn't tell the people that working in the mine is dangerous. They didn't tell my husband anything. So Kerr-McGee should compensate me in some way. And also the Department of Defense, which needed the uranium for nuclear weapons. They are also responsible for what has happened to me and the other widows.

Ever since my husband died, I have been taking this to lawyers. I have traveled throughout the Four Corners area and spoken to lawyers in Shiprock, Albuquerque, Gallup . . . and all these lawyers have come up with nothing. I am wondering why that is—why the lawyers aren't coming up with anything, because I know I have a strong case.

But I am not educated. I really can't voice my opinions or grievances through an interpreter. There are words you cannot translate. Due to my illiteracy I cannot say exactly how I feel. I am defeated right away. I am up against a wall with nowhere to turn.

For almost forty years uranium has been mined in the western and southwestern United States. In New Mexico, Colorado, Arizona, Utah, Wyoming, and South Dakota, there are areas so badly contaminated by uranium mining that the federal government has suggested designating them "National Sacrifice Areas."[10]

---

10. "The Four Corners Today, The Black Hills Tomorrow?" *Black Hills Paha Sapa Report*, August 1979, p. 3.

ELSIE PESHLAKAI, NAVAJO ORGANIZER

Like the Navajo miners and their widows, Elsie Peshlakai has come to Washington to publicize what is happening to her people. Unlike most of the Navajos, Elsie speaks excellent English. She is wearing a startlingly beautiful velvet dress with heavy turquoise beaded necklaces and bracelets. She left the Navajo reservation when she was a child and was educated in southern Utah. A young, attractive woman with a roundish face and dark vibrant eyes, she works with a legal service group called DNA (Dinebeïina Nahiilna Be Agaditahe—Navajo for "economic revitalization of the people"). She is concerned about what is happening to the Navajos, and she is angry: "We need Navajos to speak for us. People who know where they're from. Not these white lawyers

Elsie Peshlakai

Leslie J. Freeman

*who don't do anything. We need people who make decisions that reflect
on how they want their young to be taken care of, so it really hits home.
Navajos who mean it. But we have people in office who don't have the
interests of the Navajo people at heart. . . ."*

*She returned to the reservation in 1976 and gradually realized that
people were dying. And she discovered that a mine was planned 800 feet
from her home. . . .*

Growing Up: Leaving the Reservation

I was born in Crown Point and raised in the little village of Church
Rock, about seven miles east of Gallup, New Mexico, in 1952. I went
to the public school with black children and Chinese and white and
other Indians. We were very poor. Our village was off the reservation,
but it was still considered reservation. There were eight of us children.
My father worked for the government at the army depot where they
store some kind of weapons. We were always short of money. But I
didn't feel bad about not having clothes and things because all the other
kids were like that too. We didn't have a TV, we didn't have electricity,
we didn't have running water. We hauled water in buckets from a well
in Church Rock.

My mom was very ill after my little sister was born, so I had to do
most of the babysitting and most of the work around the house. I used
to iron workshirts for my father in the morning, using those heavy irons
you set on the stove and they get real hot.

In the summer when I was about five or six I stayed with my paternal
grandparents and herded sheep. They prayed every sunrise. I used to run
about a mile every morning, and drink warm goat's milk, and my grandfather would sing to me and teach me, and it was beautiful to be with
them in the summers.

And my grandfather taught me. He taught me that this is the fourth
and the last world. We just came from the third world, and it was a
natural element that almost put an end to the human race, and that we
came out of water. And before that it was fire. But this time he told me
it was going to be air.

I heard that prophecy when I was five. My grandfather would say that
we have to take care of this land.

I left the reservation when I was about ten, and it was through this lady missionary from Hawaii. She was young—twenty or twenty-one—and tall, with brown skin. She told me about the Mormon church, and everything she said went hand in hand with my religion—the Indian religion.

When I went to other churches—Catholic, Baptist, Pentecostal—they always made us kneel: "Repent, you sinners!"

I mean, little children! What do five-year-olds know about sin? They would scare me to pieces. But this lady made me proud of who I was —proud to be an Indian. She told me I was as good as anybody else. She just sort of swooped me up and loved me.

She told me about Utah and that I could go there. And then other missionaries told me that too. There would be good schools in Utah. I would have "parents" there too. I'd always heard our leaders say, "Go to school and then come back and help. Go to school!" That's all you'd hear. I knew our school wasn't all that good because these white people came in and tested us every year. I could hear them talking about how bad this school was.

My grandfathers were both medicine men, and they endorsed my going away to school in Utah. But my parents didn't take it seriously. They signed the application the first time I tried to leave, but they made sure I wasn't there when the missionaries came. They sent me to Dalton Pass to visit my grandmother. When I came back, I found out the missionaries had already left. . . .

But the next year I knew I was going. I just did the application all by myself—signed my parents' name myself—and took out a little teeny suitcase and put my clothes in. I didn't know what to pack. I took underwear. I took one slip, some blouses, two skirts, and a suit. And tennis shoes. I forgot to bring socks.

I waited at the edge of this little dirt road, and they came in a Jeep. The Jeep took me to Gallup where they had three Trailways buses. We traveled all night and to Provo, Utah. I remember Provo because I saw the big "Y" whitewashed on the mountain.

Then I met my new "mother." She was very pretty. Her hair was just going gray, and it was set perfect. "Well, we'll have to give you a bath before you go to sleep," she said. She guided me to the bathroom. I couldn't say no or yes. As she ran the water, she said, "I've never seen skin so dark before. It makes me think that I should try to scrub it clean."

This little voice in me said, "You've got to go through with it. You've got to do it." But I didn't say anything. I didn't know if you could cry. I wanted to go home, but I couldn't. I just absolutely couldn't. I didn't cry for three weeks.

I watched and kept it all in. Then one day I went up on a hill of rocks and I cried my heart out. Maybe I had just taken on too much. Maybe I couldn't do it. But I didn't want to give up either. If I went back home, the kids would laugh at me like I couldn't handle it. If I left, people in Utah would always say I had to go home, that I just couldn't do it.

So I stayed. They raised me in Utah. I had a "sister" and two "brothers." It was much better than having to be at a boarding school. They treated me like I was their real daughter. I mean, you can't pay people in the social services enough money to give that kind of attention to young people. . . .

I went to grammar school in southern Utah, and then to Brigham Young University and Utah Technical College. I had fantasies of taking home about two or three diplomas—bachelor's and master's degree.

In the summers I came back to the reservation and worked. I saw occasional drillers on the land, but that was nothing to worry about—because at the same time at the local level[11] there was a resolution in to get a new water and sewer system for the community. So I thought —we all thought—the drillers were looking for water. People thought they were drilling for water, so they left them alone.

Many of my people didn't speak English, or read or write, so no one knew about a lot of the issues that were coming forth, and it didn't seem to be a problem. My mom and dad had an inkling that something was happening, but not all that much. My father speaks a little bit of English. My mother doesn't speak it at all. There were some drillers, but nobody was being impacted, so everything was quiet for a time.

Back to the Reservation: Something is Happening

I got to Utah in 1960 and didn't come back to the reservation to live until 1976 when I lost my foster mother. When I'd first come to Utah I'd made a vow that no one would ever take the place of my real mother

11. *the local level:* the lowest form of government of the Navajo tribe is the Chapter level. The highest form of government is located in Window Rock.

and father. But I had been wrong. I came to love my foster mother very much—just like my real mother. And then my foster mother died in January 1976. . . .

It was just—I couldn't do it—couldn't go on by myself. I met this guy from Gallup I'd known since I was very young. He took me to the funeral, and it was . . . I didn't break down. I held it all in. You know how you see clearly, but yet things keep happening like you're in a daze? That's how it was. I never had had anybody that I really loved that had died. I'd never experienced death before. I guess he knew I couldn't go through a day by myself—I was missing two or three hours. I just couldn't remember things. . . . So he took care of me. And then, when I came out of it, he was there, taking care of me. I just sort of stepped into marriage, and then six months later, when I found out I was pregnant, he brought me back home.

We lived in Gallup first. Then we moved to Fort Defiance by Window Rock. I was busy being newly-wed and trying to see about raising a family and if I could get back to school. While I was married I used to go over to my mother's house in Crown Point and spend time there. . . . Every now and then I'd see the drillers. People talked about them, but they didn't make a whole lot of fuss about the drilling because they didn't really know what to do.

I'd hear them talking:

"Those drillers are driving too fast on the road. . . . Who do they think they are? This is a dirt road. This is *our* road."

"Well, who authorized these people to come onto the reservation anyway?"

"Are they going to stay here for long? I mean, are they going to replant?"

"They just dynamited—they just set off some dynamites behind the hill."

"And did you see it yesterday? You know, the ground kind of shook. . . ."

"And Dewey Vallo was driving up and his whole front window cracked, and it burst open because of the blasting. . . ."

". . . shouldn't we do something about it?"

We lost a lot of sheep in the pits—sheep and horses and goats. The companies in our valley were drilling all over.

One day when I was at the house in Crown Point my father walked in and said, "We just had a hard day. We were herding up sheep, and we came across this mud pit, and we had to pull out a goat, but it was too late . . . it died."

My mom said, "Where?"

"Over there."

"Oh, we should say something about it."

"We did. They told us—they want us to go to Grants somewhere. They didn't give us an address. Their headquarters is in Grants, and their boss is in Denver, or way where the sun comes up—" that means way back East. And then he said, "And we're having trouble trying to communicate too. That driller doesn't understand enough English, and we can't speak Spanish. He only speaks Spanish, and we only speak Navajo, so how do we communicate?"

It went on like that for a long time.

Questioning

The first time that this thing ever sunk into my head was when United Nuclear Corporation set up a public hearing for their Draft Environmental Impact Statement, in Crown Point, New Mexico.[12] They had it over in Crown Point when they should have had it in Dalton Pass— because it was a Dalton Pass project. It was only 800 feet from our house! They were going to put a uranium mine there.

So my half-brother—he works at BIA (Bureau of Indian Affairs)—he told my dad to attend this hearing. My father went to the hearing, and then he came to me and said, "Elsie"—he's talking in Navajo—"do you know what uranium is?"

And I said, "No."

"Can you find out for me?"

"Okay. Who do I have to call?"

"Why don't you call BIA."

So I got on the phone. I thought it was just something that would take me maybe two or three minutes. I asked for the superintendant's office. I got the secretary.

"Do you know anything about a Dalton Pass mine that's going on?" I said.

She goes, "No, I'm sorry. You'll have to call Realty. Or BLO or

12. The public hearing was held in January 1978.

BLM[13] Operations."

"Okay," I said, "switch me over."

So I call them and they don't know. Then I called Realty, and they didn't know, and then I went over and had a meeting with the assistant to the assistant to the superintendant. All I wanted to know were the common things—the natural things you'd want to know if it was under your land. I wanted to know, what is this mine? Where's it going to be? What's it going to be used for? Who agreed to it? Lease? What lease? What contract? Is there one?

I went to Window Rock, and I went to BIA, went to Window Rock again. The chairman's office is in the West-East Building. I went to every single one of those offices—and there were a lot, maybe twenty offices up and down the hall. There was Tom Lynch[14] who was supposed to be in charge of the minerals department—minerals technician. He wasn't in. I left my number. I kept calling him. I never got him.

What I finally got out of the BIA superintendant's office—not the superintendant himself—was: "It's too late. It's already going on." They confused me with a coal gasification plant that was proposed for the Bisti area—that's between Farmington and Crown Point. I didn't know what coal gasification was.[15]

They said, "It's already approved over there too, and there's nothing anybody can do about it. Also in the Burnham area"—which is a little bit west of Bisti—"the companies want to strip coal. You know, Utah International[16] and all those consolidated companies—they're extracting coal."

I got all mixed up and then I had to go back to square one. But I was getting involved in this issue—so involved that it was interfering with my marriage. My marriage just wasn't working, so I moved back to my parents' house.

---

13. *BLO* is the Bureau of Land Operations and *BLM* is the Bureau of Land Management.

14. *Tom Lynch:* director of the Minerals Division in Window Rock, Arizona.

15. *coal gasification:* a process of gasifying coal with either air or oxygen as the oxidant to produce gas. This has application for the generation of electric power.

16. *Utah International:* a subsidiary owned by General Electric.

The Impact

Then the United Nuclear Corporation people started coming over to the Chapter House. The local form of government is called the Chapter House, and we belong to it. I met a lawyer called Joe Gmuca, who showed me a copy of the lease—the United Nuclear Corporation uranium lease negotiating the right to mine and mill and explore the land. I was—I was shocked!

It had been approved in 1971! I couldn't believe it. How come the Chapter officers didn't know about it? We had a Chapter secretary that had been in office for twenty years and the other two had been in office for twelve years! Why didn't they know? And then the councilman—our representative over in Window Rock—why didn't he know? How come nobody knew about it?

The tribal government over in Window Rock wouldn't tell anybody. But they had to know! They must want the money to get used there. They must be getting something for it—but the people, no! That money sure wasn't going to the people. . . .

Thirty-three thousand dollars for 2,500 acres. One dollar for an acre! For rent for one year. And four dollars minimum royalty. I mean, that's nothing! Thirty-three thousand—that isn't enough for 180,000 Navajos within the reservation—that's how many people we have. . . .

I started to talk to people—to doctors and lawyers. I found out that the companies had just walked onto the land and started drilling. They hadn't really asked anybody's permission.

On allotted land[17] the Bureau of Indian Affairs had someone who spoke Navajo, and they'd tell all of the allottees to meet at a certain place on a certain day if they wanted money for their land. All they had to do was sign this paper. They'd give them these slips of paper with these account numbers on them. "Check and see if you have money over in this place in the Bureau of Indian Affairs," they'd say. And they did and no one ever knew what they signed. They never saw the cover of the leases. They just saw the back page where they signed.

17. *allotted land:* one hundred sixty acres of land held in trust for the allottee by the Bureau of Indian Affairs. The allotments were set up between 1910 and 1930, when Indian land was reduced from twenty-four million acres to two and a half million acres. See Loretta Schwartz, "Uranium Deaths at Crown Point," *Ms.*, October 1979, p. 81.

Like Hah-nah-bah Charley. She signed away her surface rights. She gave them permission to drill for uranium. A man said, "You can sign here if you want money for your land." So she put her thumbprint on a piece of paper and gave the oil company the right to 160 acres of her land. That's it. She signed not knowing what she signed. She found out when the company started drilling on her land. She went to the Bureau of Indian Affairs.

"How come these guys are here? How come they're drilling? They're killing my sheep! This bentonite[18] water is running all over the place. My whole land's become like cement flooring."

But BIA said, "It's too late. You already signed it."

She kept pestering them and they got tired of her. "It's too late," they said. "You should have known."

And she wasn't the only one. There were a lot of people.

There are countless numbers of cases in which crucial information about a nuclear project has not been made accessible to the public until after the project has received approval, even though it may affect many people's lives. In the 1950s American servicemen were exposed to atomic bomb testing without being given essential information about the dangers of radiation known to the Atomic Energy Commission. (See Chapter 7.) Project Ketch, part of the "Atoms for Peace" program, was approved prior to a public hearing on the possible health effects of exploding atomic bombs underground in Pennsylvania dairy country. (See Chapter 3.) News about the Barker Nuclear Power Station, which was to have been built next door to the Gerber Baby Food factory by the Niagara Mohawk Power Company, appeared only in a small local newspaper, not the newspaper most people read. (See Chapter 2.)

This policy of giving information after the fact typifies the workings of the nuclear industry and federal agencies. Most people do not know, for example, that in order to be compensated under the Price Anderson Act, a nuclear accident must be termed an "extraordinary" event. The accident at Three Mile Island does not qualify as an "extraordinary" event. Five or more people would have had to die right away or be

---

18. *bentonite:* the substance used to fill the pits after holes are drilled. Similar to cement, it is nonetheless classified as clay.

hospitalized with serious injuries, there would have had to be $1 million worth of property damage, and some member of the general population would have had to receive twenty-five rem or more (which is the equivalent of five thousand chest X-rays) off-site before the accident could have been considered "extraordinary."[19]

    Another example. Residents of West Milford and Jefferson townships in New Jersey did not know that Exxon Minerals and Standard Oil of Ohio (Sohio) had been acquiring mineral rights and quietly searching for uranium in New Jersey, until the summer of 1980, more than one year after Sohio had begun surface exploration and three years after Exxon had begun exploratory drilling. John Andes, a public affairs specialist for Sohio, was questioned about the secrecy with which his company had proceeded. "This is a very competitive business and you don't want to tip your hand before you have to," he said.[20]

    The reason Sohio and Exxon did not publicize their plan to mine uranium in New Jersey and the reason that United Nuclear Corporation and other energy corporations do not publicize their plans for nuclear projects probably has less to do with fear of competition than it has to do with another fear: they know that when people gain enough information to understand that their lives are in danger, they act.[21] The big corporations are afraid of a popular movement that will paralyze energy projects from which they hope to make a great deal of profit.

    I started brushing up on my chemistry. Most people I talked to didn't tell me uranium was good or bad. But I learned the basic chemistry of what uranium is—of how you get "yellowcake," and what they do at a nuclear power plant—and that sort of thing. People didn't say, "This radon gas—you know, you breathe it and it's going to mutate the cells, and every step of the fuel cycle is dangerous." No, none of that. Nothing of the sort. But I got enough information that I could go ask Paul

19. See "Report to the NRC from the Staff Panel on the Commission's Determination of an Extraordinary Nuclear Occurrence," NUREG-0637 (Washington, D.C.: U.S. Government Printing Office, 1980).

20. E. R. Shipp, "Hunt for Uranium Upsets 2 Rustic Towns in Jersey," *New York Times*, 23 August 1980, pp. 25–26.

21. Public pressure has put a halt to many energy projects, such as the Barker nuclear power plant (Chapter 2) and Project Ketch (Chapter 3).

Robinson—an environmentalist with Southwest Research—and he gave me books to read. They were so technical that it was staggering at first.

I would tell my father all this, and we were amazed as we kept finding out more and more things. And all this time United Nuclear kept coming to the local Chapter House and saying how great this mining was. It would create jobs for us. Indians would have first preference. They would only hire qualified Navajos. . . .

But it's not creating jobs. Not really. Maybe for Anglo miners or people coming in from outside. The Navajos get jobs at first, and then the employers don't understand that the men have to be off for certain days to attend religious ceremonies. Or somebody's sick and they have to go get a medicine man. The employers misunderstand. And the Navajo employees don't really know how to speak up for themselves, so they get fired.

We met with the United Nuclear people four or five times. They were around all the time. There was already a mine going at Gallup—at Church Rock. And they were doing all this damage.

I am becoming more and more amazed. I'm telling my dad everything. By this time my mother doesn't understand anything any more. At the beginning she did, but now, no. . . . There are a lot of rumors at the Chapter level:

"We're going to have to move. . . ."

". . . they're going to pay us millions. . . ."

". . . they're not going to give us a penny!"

". . . what if they reduce our stock?"

"What if they contaminate our water?"

"Contaminate us?"

"Where are we going to live?"

We went through this horrible thing about the drillers because we have mesas, and all along the sides of the mesas they drilled as they went. They made roads on the sides of the mesas, which gave people access to the wood on top. We've seen white drillers hauling wood out—white people going in pickup trucks and hauling our wood out. They sell it in Albuquerque for forty dollars a cord. That's the wood we depend on, because we have wood-burning stoves. We don't mostly depend on electricity. A lot of us don't have electricity.

So we saw that. You must understand, we revere the earth as our mother. It's like a temple. One of the places where we worship—individually and together—they took a bulldozer on top of that mesa, and they just cleared the whole area that was deeply sacred to us. . . . They were bulldozing so they could drill in those areas. They drilled all along that mesa. Seeing that really did something. It's like turning a knife in your stomach.

You should see their Environmental Impact Statement.[22] They talk like nobody's living there. The impact that it would make on our culture is one little paragraph that doesn't amount to anything. Just saying, "Oh, these native people—these Navajos—seem to have some kind of special relationship with the earth." Something crummy like that.

When they drill, they have to clear an eight-by-ten-foot pad, and then on the sides they mix bentonite. The companies in our valley have drilled all over. In 2,500 acres they drilled over 3,000 holes. So there were a lot of these pits open to mix bentonite. Bentonite is the closest thing you can get to cement—but it still is mud, and it hardens very terribly. If you get it on vehicles or on sheep—when it gets on the wool, you can't wash it off. It does not wash off with water at all. They use bentonite to fill the drill hole after they've taken a core sample. After they get done, then they fill the hole up with this mud. It's supposed to harden, and then you should be able to reclaim the land. But a lot of these pits—these bentonite pits, these mud pits—aren't fenced, so we lose a lot of animals. They fall in, and you can't tell. They sink right down. But if it solidifies, you know . . . you can see arms and legs sticking out. It's gross!

And a lot of sheep have died. A lot of horses. Cattle have died. I have seen them. I have talked to all these people that have had their stock die. Just two families I know of have got anything back. One of them got two thousand dollars back for a rodeo horse that won trophies . . . and another family got something. . . . They lost a lot of horses, sheep, cattle, and a lot of goats. . . .

---

22. *Environmental Impact Statement:* required by law under the National Environmental Policy Act (NEPA) of 1969, the environmental impact of a project must be evaluated before going ahead with the project.

And the Water . . .

We have had wells go dry from their exploration. The majority of us get our water from Crown Point. Five hundred gallons at a time—we get it by truck from the well there in a big barrel. Ninety percent of the Navajos in that area get their water this way. And last month[23] Conoco started sinking a mine shaft there—in Crown Point.[24]

Conoco, Philips Petroleum, and Mobil have joined to try to find water in the chimney formation down below the west water canyon, which is 2,500 feet. So they would have to go down 3,500 feet to see if there's water there.

At the Chapter House, just recently, Milton Head, who is project manager, said, "We can guarantee that we will find you water within a year."

And I said, "And all the time you're going to be drilling?"

"Yes. Because you won't feel the impact of drilling this shaft until a year from now."

"Well, I don't think the people want that," I said. "I think they want to be sure that that water's going to be okay *now*—*before* you start drilling."

"Well," he said, "all we can do is take this up to the corporate heads and then we're handed down decisions."

I don't like their way of decision making. They're going to take their request and give it to some god in the big Conoco world, and then have this decision brought down. Why, if these people that came to the Chapter House aren't decision makers, why don't the corporate heads come down, and we can negotiate with them? This is the biggest insult.

They have a mining plan that they submitted to the United States Geological Survey. I asked them, "Are you going to follow this plan?"

"Yes," they said, "we'll follow the mining plan."

But that's just words. There isn't anybody that can make them follow

23. March 1980.
24. Crown Point is in danger of losing its only water supply. In a working paper entitled, "Impacts of the Uranium Industry on Water Quality," J. L. Kunkler of the United States Geological Survey put it this way: "Groundwater resources are being depleted by underground mining and, as a consequence, wells that yield water from the aquifers (natural underground water reservoirs) being mined will yield less water and may ultimately yield none." In Schwartz, "Uranium Deaths at Crown Point," p. 59.

that mining plan. See, when they were on federal allotments, they had to submit a mining plan. But now they've moved it over. They said they were far behind schedule—and now they're drilling on *private* land. That means it doesn't require federal action, so they don't have to submit a mining plan.

A mining plan says this is where the mine is going to be. This is where the shaft will be. The mill tailings will be in this area. The water will be coming from this point. The water for you will be sufficient. The runoff can travel to the next point and then it will be released. . . .

The government says they have to follow this plan. But now that they have moved onto private land, nobody can force them to follow any mining plan. In 1969 the National Environmental Policy Act (NEPA) was passed. That's a public law that says the company has to study how its project is going to affect the water and the air and the land and the people who live here. They have to do an Environmental Impact Study before, during, and after. But they're avoiding it by mining on private land. They say the only reason they're doing it on private land is so they won't fall behind schedule. That may be true, but they're also slipping right through the law, right by the impact statement.

"RADIATION FOUND IN COLORADO WATER SUPPLY"

Denver, July 13—Water supplies of hundreds of communities in 15 western states may be dangerous for long-term use because of low-level radiation from uranium, according to federal officials here.

The contamination, formerly believed to be harmless, has increased so dramatically in recent years that the Environmental Protection Agency estimates some residents here could be getting as much as 60 times the yearly amount of alpha radiation—a low-level variety that occurs naturally in food and water. The agency's review of a small community's water here could lead to establishment, for the first time, of a standard for radiation pollution of drinking water.

"It is of national significance," said Paul B. Smith, EPA's regional director of radiation programs in Denver. "You're dealing with the generic question of radiation in drinking water in the whole West."

The agency recommended "prompt control measures" to reduce alpha radiation levels in the Denver-area water, and Smith said that similar pollution was likely in other western communities, too.

He recommended an extensive re-evaluation of uranium radiation in drinking water in 15 western states. If the informal guidelines advised for the Denver water are applied elsewhere, he said, "some supplies could be rendered undrinkable"—Peggy Strain, *Washington Post,* 14 July 1979.

What Now?

This uranium mining has got to be stopped. We have all this waste everywhere—all these tailings.[25] I know it has gone into streams. It cannot just sit there in barrels of lead. It has gone into fish, and people have fished, and people have eaten it. . . .

But if you really like money and you like power, you aren't going to stop at anything. If I was a corporate head—if I was up there and I needed money, I would probably just coldly go in and mine. I'd do away with people—not purposely to do away with them, but they're in the way. You have to.

I don't think they do it to kill people. I think they do it to make money for the time being. I mean, the business of making money has become an art. . . . Some people are ignorant, but some people are not. These corporate people intend to do what they do. They do it on purpose to make more money because money has become a god. I don't know if they would have the nerve to go in there and kill somebody with a gun. But they can decide to have somebody else do it. What they have done to the Indian people is a kind of murder. They decide to have uranium mined and not worry about the people. Just to make money.

And these same people—they're "good" fathers, they're "good" hus-

25. *tailings:* According to *Science* magazine, with the rapid pace "at which the uranium industry is now expanding to meet its contracts with electric utilities, there could be a billion tons by the year 2000." The largest pile of tailings in the U.S. is maintained by Kerr-McGee Nuclear Corporation at its big mill near Grants, New Mexico, "where 7000 tons of ore are processed daily. Containing 23 million tons of tailings, it covers 265 acres and rises to 100 feet at its highest point." Luther J. Carter, "Uranium Mill Tailings: Congress Addresses a Long-Neglected Problem," *Science,* 13 October 1978, p. 191.

These tailings retain 85 percent of their original radioactivity and will remain radioactive for hundreds of thousands of years. They emit dangerous radon gases into the atmosphere, contaminating air and drinking water. They are dispersed over large areas by wind and rain. Radioactive tailings have also been mixed with sand for building materials and have been used in approximately 200,000 homes in the Southwest. Schwartz, "Uranium Deaths at Crown Point," pp. 59 and 81.

bands, philanthropists. They pay their taxes. They'll claim all that, and from all aspects they'll even look that way. . . . It's sad. I know those kind of people really do exist.

The companies that are mining now are United Nuclear at Dalton Pass . . . Pioneer still has a lease, Mobil still has a lease—it's doing a project right now—Conoco has a lease, Phillips has a lease, Western Nuclear has a lease, Grace Nuclear too. Gulf Minerals, at Mariana Lake, is going. Anaconda, at Grants, is going. United Nuclear, Church Rock, is going. Kerr-McGee at Church Rock is going. . . .

These companies leave their tailings behind. Sixty million tons of tailings are already lying around in New Mexico. The companies also leave a bad impression of white people. The drillers and the Indians have taken out guns and put holes all over each other's trucks. . . . You don't see the fights much, but on Friday and Saturday nights, you go to a bar, and it happens. . . .

People have told me that they've been stoned by little white kids—Indians have been, because they're wearing skirts like the kind I'm wearing. You know, the white kids think the Indians are different, and they throw pebbles and rocks at them. . . .

The Navajo tribe could do so much, but the General Council is made up of white men—lawyers. When they approve a lease for mining, those lawyers always know that *they* can leave the reservation and move somewhere else where it's better. I think we have too many people in office who are making the decisions without having the interest of the Navajo people at heart.

I have gone through being pressured by the Council men of the tribe —a lot of us have—the Council men trying to slow us down and shut us up. But I'm just not afraid of them any more. I want to tell people. I want people to hear the voices of the Navajo people.

All these people—even the private landowners, the white landowners —are becoming Indians too, because if a nuclear company wants to go in and mine on their property, no matter how rich they are, no matter how strong ties they have politically with the White House, they can still get stepped on. They are feeling what we've been going through for years and years. That's why white people and Indian people and Chicano people are coming together. It's good. The government's got to admit it and say, "We did wrong." And the first most important thing I think they should do is compensate the widows and the miners.

If they just open the door a little bit, I would like to swing that door open wide.

On 16 July 1979 one hundred million gallons of radioactive water and eleven hundred tons of uranium tailings spilled from the United Nuclear Corporation's waste storage pool at the mining facility in Church Rock, New Mexico. When the dam broke, radioactive debris poured into the Rio Puerco, the river that supplies drinking water to residents of Gallup, Lupton, and Sanders, New Mexico, and a great many people on the Navajo reservation. The riverbed was contaminated as was the soil adjacent to the river banks, and radioactive material was carried eighty miles downriver into Arizona. [25]

"Samples taken fifteen miles downstream from Church Rock, thirty to forty feet deep, show 'growing contamination,' indicating widespread seepage. . . ." reports Paul Robinson of the Southwest Research and Information Center. [26] *Residents were advised "not to drink from, swim in or otherwise touch the river water and not to let their livestock drink from it."* [27]

Although the spill was termed "the worst radiation accident in history," [28] *the* New York Times *did not report the incident until twelve days later.* [29] *There was a clear effort to make the real devastation caused by this accident seem negligible. "Both Government and corporate officials emphasize that there is no immediate health hazard from the spill," reports the* New York Times, *even though in the same article the* Times *admits that the first day the gross alpha count was measured in the river as "100,000 picocuries per liter" and "safe drinking water limit is 15 picocuries per liter."* [30]

Despite the obvious health hazard, the "New Mexico Environmental Improvement Division (EID) has not made an official statement about

25. Molly Ivins, "Dam Break Investigated; Radiation of Spill Easing," *New York Times,* 28 July 1979, p. 6. The Rio Puerco feeds eventually into the Colorado River.

26. Mark Alan Pinsky, "New Mexico Spill Ruins a River: The Worst Radiation Accident in History Gets Little Attention," *Critical Mass Journal,* December 1979, p. 5.

27. Ivins, "Dam Break Investigated," p. 6.

28. Pinsky, "New Mexico Spill Ruins a River," p. 5.

29. Ivins, "Dam Break Investigated," p. 6. Ivins's *New York Times* article termed the 16 July 1979 spill "the largest in this country involving radioactive wastes."

30. Ibid., p. 6.

the environmental impact of the contamination of the Rio Puerco, but New Mexico and Arizona officials demanded UNC (United Nuclear Corporation) post warning signs along the river. When the signs were posted, one Navajo Indian complained, 'Our sheep don't read.' "31

On 13 August 1980 one hundred Navajo families filed suit against United Nuclear Corporation for damages from the July 1979 spill.32 The Navajos claim that they can't use the river for drinking and many of their animals have died from drinking contaminated water and eating contaminated grass. In addition to demanding that United Nuclear pay damages, the Navajos want a fence built along the river to keep the animals out of it.

"The old ladies are always to be seen now running up and down both sides of the wash [river], trying to keep the sheep out of it. . . ."33

"Despite the fact that this is the seventh such spill of a tailings pond, its owner, United Nuclear, has already applied for permission to reopen the dam."34

Postscript

Some of the uranium for the first atomic weapons came from the small mines at Red Rock and Cove and the San Juan Mountains of southwestern Colorado. A number of studies were done to determine the effects of radiation in the early 1950s. Carried out by expert panels, such as the National Commission on Radiological Protection and the International Commission on Radiological Protection, these studies led to maximum permissible radiation levels being set for nuclear workers in the mid-1950s. The Atomic Energy Commission did not adopt radiation-level standards for uranium miners until 1972.35

31. Pinsky, "New Mexico Spill Ruins a River," p. 5.

32. Molly Ivins, "100 Navajo Families Sue on Radioactive Waste Spill," *New York Times*, 15 August 1980, p. A-12.

33. Ibid., p. A-12.

34. "The Native American Connection," *Up Against the Wall Street Journal*, 29 October 1979, p. 26.

35. See Shuey, "Widows of Red Rock, Part I," p. 4.

"The U.S. Public Health Service has called the lung cancer rate among uranium miners an epidemic."

> —quoted in Jack Cox, "Casualties Mounting from U-Rush of '49," Denver Post, 2 September 1979, p. 1.

"Those mines are . . . nothing but cancer factories. . . ."

> —Tony Mazzocchi, director of Health and Safety for Denver-based Oil, Chemical, and Atomic Workers Union (OCAW), quoted in Cox, "Casualties Mounting from U-Rush of '49," p. 1.

A Tennessee Valley Authority official spoke to the people of Crown Point to reassure them about uranium mining being proposed there. "I can't guarantee there will be no effect to you or your offspring," he said. "But then I can't one hundred percent guarantee you won't fall down in your bathtub tonight either."

> —quote from Schwartz, "Uranium Deaths at Crown Point," p. 81.

Author's Note

What happened to the uranium miners, the residents of Utah, and the American servicemen in the 1940s and 1950s is no different from what will happen to today's nuclear workers, the people of Harrisburg, and what could happen to all of us.

The uranium miners who worked in unventilated radioactive mines in the late forties and early fifties trusted the mining companies when they said the mines were safe. Today many of those miners are dying of lung cancer. The Atomic Energy Commission had studied the effects of radiation as far back as 1945 and 1946 at Los Alamos and at the Argonne National Laboratory. The studies showed that radiation was harmful, even at relatively small doses. Rather than sharing the results

of this research, the AEC suppressed the studies and denied their existence.[36]

Neither did the AEC inform the people of Saint George, Utah, in
the 1950s that radiation was known to be harmful when it was predicted
that winds would carry radioactive fallout from atomic testing directly
over their homes. Instead, the AEC published statements reassuring
Utah residents that atomic testing was safe and that radiation levels were
being carefully monitored. No effort was made to evacuate these people;
those who happened to have their radios on heard the announcement
to go indoors and shut their windows. Health studies carried out under
the auspices of the AEC were classified when they revealed that atomic
tests had dumped harmful amounts of radiation into the Utah milkshed.
Today these people are suing the federal government in a class-action
suit. They are frightened and angered by the excessive cancer, leukemia,
and birth defects they see in their communities.

American servicemen in the 1940s and 1950s trusted the military and
the AEC when they were told that observing atomic tests at close-range
was safe. Even those who developed radiation sickness were assured that
there would be no long-lasting effects from overexposure. Now, more
than twenty years later, veterans like William H. Hodsden, who tells his
story in the next chapter, are showing the effects of radiation exposure
from weapons testing in the fifties. Another of these veterans, the late
Orville Kelly, organized the National Association of Atomic Veterans,
so that servicemen who had been exposed to radiation could help each
other, since they were unable to get compensation or even information
from the Veterans Administration or the federal government.

What is happening now to atomic veterans like William Hodsden is
what James Pires, David Pyles, Richard Ostrowski, Ralph Fitts, and
their fellow workers may find happening to them ten or twenty years
from now, when they, or perhaps their children, become seriously ill.
Since the nuclear industry and governmental agencies keep imperfect
records and deny negligence and culpability, it will be virtually impossible for these workers to get compensation unless we have a radical shift
in legislative policy. As the next chapter indicates, however, there is
no evidence to suggest that the attitude of the government or of the
nuclear industry is any different today than it was in the early days

36. See Nuclear Chronology, p. xvii; Chapter 3, p. 50; and Chapter 4, p. 90.

of nuclear testing.

For example, when the 28 March 1979 accident occurred at Three Mile Island, people from nearby Harrisburg were not evacuated from their homes, even though at least one commissioner of the NRC thought such evacuation urgent. Instead, they were told there was nothing to worry about—just stay indoors and shut the windows. When evidence turned up to suggest that infant mortality downwind of the TMI reactor had increased during the year following the accident, the health authorities tried to discredit the scientists publicizing this data. [37]

The government and the nuclear industry allege that the radiation we receive from normal operation of nuclear reactors is no worse than smoking a cigarette or flying in an airplane. But the cancer rate is rising, due in part to the increasing levels of radiation around us. One out of four of us will contract cancer during our lifetime. Like the atomic veterans, we are being put in danger, and the people who have information about our health and safety seem intent upon keeping it from us. [38]

37. Anna Mayo, "The Nuclear State in Ascendency," *Village Voice*, 22–28 October 1980, pp. 17–21, 40.

38. "Up until very recently, I did not think there was any coverup. I felt that what had been done in the past was done through ignorance. . . . But now there is no doubt in my mind that unfortunately there was some deliberate coverup of concerns that were expressed in closed meetings of the Atomic Energy Commission back in the 1950s."— Senator Jake Garn (R-Utah), quoted in Fadiman, "The Downwind People," *Life*, June 1980, p. 40.

CHAPTER 7

William H. Hodsden, Atomic Veteran

Washington, D.C., 12 April 1980. Early evening. The National Citizens' Hearings on Radiation Victims have just ended. We are standing around a photograph of GIs observing an atomic explosion in the Nevada Desert, 1957. In the distance the huge mushroom cloud is rising, swirling. The servicemen in the foreground of the picture are lit up, as in an X-ray. "That's me," someone says. I turn around to see a tall, powerfully built black man pointing at one of the GIs in the photograph. "That's me," he says again, "second from the left. The army says I wasn't there, but I seen that. That's something you don't forget."

He is William H. Hodsden, a man who has come to the Citizens' Hearings because he hopes to find people who remember him at the blast site of "Smoky" on 31 August 1957 so he can prove he was there. This is crucial if he is to establish that his current health problems result from radiation exposure. Only then can he hope for compensation from the Veterans Administration.

Born 1935 in Washington, D.C., and brought up in New York City, Hodsden was deeply impressed by the military. In high school he joined the naval reserve: "I seen myself as the black John Wayne," he says, laughing. "I guess it was all them war flicks." In 1955, when Hodsden enlisted in the United States Army at the age of nineteen, he did not know that the military was involved in a full-scale effort to determine

William H. Hodsden as a young man

the effects of radiation on human beings,[1] and that thousands of American troops had already witnessed nuclear explosions.

After World War II the U.S. government began atmospheric weapons testing in the South Pacific. About seventy-five atomic tests were conducted in the Marshall Islands between 1946 and 1958. On one occasion—the fifteen-megaton "Bravo" shot on Bikini Atoll on 1 March 1954—radioactive fallout reached Marshallese natives on two other islands more than three-hundred miles away, contaminating them as well as American servicemen stationed in the area to be witnesses to the tests. Most weapons testing was shifted over to the continental United States in 1951. Thousands of American servicemen participated in atomic testing, marching to within nine-hundred yards of ground zero —the crater left by the atomic blast—within minutes after detonation.[2]

The purpose of these maneuvers was supposedly to determine whether troops would be adversely affected by conditions of nuclear warfare. A number of "stress tests" were designed to see how troops would respond to orders right after witnessing a nuclear blast. Would they still be able to dismantle a rifle? Could they throw a hand grenade and hit a prearranged target? Atomic Energy Commission scientists carefully planned these military exercises so they could gather data. They claimed that they needed this data to help train troops for nuclear warfare, that the military exercises were necessary for the "national defense." But the army's after-action report from the following November suggests that public relations was also a factor: the intent of the infantry troop test at Smoky was "to portray to the public the Army at its best, employing ROCID (pentomic)[3] organization in operations

1. See Howard I. Rosenberg, "The Guineapigs of Camp Desert Rock: Atomic 'Stress Tests' for Unwitting Soldiers," *Progressive*, June 1979, pp. 37–43. Some men were assigned to be "test subjects" by the Human Resources Research Organization (HumRRO). "The HumRRO team consisted of a group of . . . psychologists contracted by the Pentagon. . . ." These psychologists gave indoctrination examinations to make the men believe radiation was safe. Their questions included: How soon is it safe to walk through ground-zero (the crater resulting from the atomic blast)? The "correct" answer was "immediately afterward" (p. 39).

2. "Story of Nuclear Testing," *Atomic Veterans' Newsletter*, September-October 1979, pp. 2–3.

3. Rosenberg, "The Guineapigs of Camp Desert Rock," p. 38. "Pentomic" warfare refers to a five-unit system to disperse troops to make them less vulnerable to being wiped out in the event of nuclear attack.

under atomic warfare conditions."

The federal government estimates that 250,000 American soldiers, sailors, paratroopers, marines, and civilians were exposed to atomic weapons testing in the atmosphere. But according to the National Association of Atomic Veterans, "more than 400,000 people were involved in these ionizing radiation experiments for weapons" between 1946 and 1962. [4]

Initially the Atomic Energy Commission was in charge of the radiation safety program. They required that each serviceman participating in weapons testing wear a film badge to register the amount of radiation he was exposed to. The allowable radiation dosage was set at one rad for a thirteen-week period. [5] *(Research carried out by Dr. Irwin Bross and his staff at the Roswell Memorial Park Cancer Institute shows significant genetic damage at exposures of about one rad.)* [6] *Then, in 1952, the Department of Defense took charge of radiation safety procedures.* [7] *The maximum allowable radiation dose was increased from one rad to six rads over a thirteen-week period. Men were permitted to move closer to ground zero after the atomic blast.* [8] *Instead of requiring that each serviceman wear a film badge to register the amount of radiation he received, the DOD required only one film badge per platoon. "Complete exposure records were not kept because one time exposures were considered 'insignificant.'"* [9] *Even when film badges were kept, the radiation registered was all external—that is, they did not register the particles of radioactive plutonium that the men may have inhaled. For that reason the film badges were not really adequate instruments to*

4. "Story of Nuclear Testing," p. 2. The *New York Times* gives 400,000 as the estimate (see Patrick Huyghe and David Konigsberg, "Grim Legacy of Nuclear Testing," *New York Times Magazine*, 22 April 1979, p. 70), and the *Village Voice* gives 450,000 (John J Berger, "An Atomic Test Case: The Ordeal of Artie Duvall," *Village Voice*, 22 October 1979, p. 21).

5. "Story of Nuclear Testing," p. 2.

6. Irwin D. J. Bross, "Hazards to Persons Exposed to Ionizing Radiation (and to their children) from Dosage Currently Permitted by the Nuclear Regulatory Commission," in *Effect of Radiation on Human Health*, vol. 1, pp. 913–950.

7. A. O. Sulzberger, Jr., "Early Radiation Problems Laid to A-Bomb Program's Pace," *New York Times*, 20 June 1979, p. A–24.

8. Ibid. According to the Department of Defense, "some 80,000 servicemen viewed detonations from trenches as close as a mile from ground zero. . . . In a number of tests, troops marched toward ground zero shortly after the blast. . . ." Huyghe and Konigsberg, "Grim Legacy of Nuclear Testing," p. 70.

9. "Story of Nuclear Testing," p. 2.

measure radioactive contamination.

Camp Desert Rock was the home of fifty-eight thousand servicemen who were stationed in Nevada for varying periods of time during the years of atomic weapons testing. It is located sixty-five miles northwest of Las Vegas and surrounded by mountains. The nearby Nevada test site —Yucca Flats—saw ninety-three nuclear devices detonated in the atmosphere before the atmospheric test ban treaty of 1963.[10] Smoky—a forty-eight kiloton atomic bomb,[11] four times as powerful as the bomb that decimated Hiroshima—was one of the last shots in a series of atomic blasts set off during the summer of 1957 at Yucca Flats, Nevada. William H. Hodsden claims he was one of the servicemen present at Smoky.[12]

In 1977 the Department of Health, Education, and Welfare's Center for Disease Control (CDC) in Atlanta, Georgia, began to gather data on the servicemen who had been present at the 1957 Smoky test. In February 1979 the CDC reported that the leukemia rate among these servicemen was higher than would be expected in the general population. The expected leukemia cases in that same age population would be 3.5. But after twenty years—the latency period for cancer and leukemia is approximately twenty to thirty years—they found nine cases of leukemia, a surprisingly high number.[13]

Another serious effect of the bomb testing has shown up in the people of Saint George, Utah, and others subjected to radioactive fallout. Birth defects, childhood leukemias, and mental retardation have appeared at an increasingly alarming rate.[14] A United Nations committee suggested that bomb testing in the atmosphere up to 1958 alone caused something like twenty-five hundred to ten thousand

10. Fadiman, "The Downwind People," *Life,* June 1980, p. 32.

11. Smoky was supposed to be a forty-four kiloton blast, but it was actually forty-eight kilotons "which has not been revealed by some of our officials," according to Congressman Tim Lee Carter. Quoted in *Effect of Radiation on Human Health,* vol. 1., p. 68.

12. Dr. Glyn Caldwell of the Center for Disease Control, Atlanta, sets the figure of men present at Smoky at more than thirty-two hundred. Howard Rosenberg says, "At least 2,200 men were known to be present at Smoky. . . ." Rosenberg, "The Guineapigs of Camp Desert Rock," p. 38.

13. "Leukemia Among Persons Present at an Atmospheric Nuclear Test (Smoky)," *Morbidity and Mortality Weekly Report* 28 (10 August 1979): 361–362.

14. Fadiman, "The Downwind People," p. 32. See also J. L. Lyon, M. R. Klauber, J. W. Gardner, and K. S. Udall, "Childhood Leukemias Associated with Fallout from Nuclear Testing," *New England Journal of Medicine* 300 (1979): 397–402.

serious genetic effects.[15]

Did the military know that the servicemen and civilians who were exposed to radiation were being endangered? The military claims that it did not: "To our knowledge no one outside the test site has been hurt in six years of testing," an AEC public relations pamphlet stated back in 1957. "Only one person, a test participant, has been injured seriously as a result of 45 detonations. His was an eye injury from the flash of light received at a point relatively near ground zero inside the test site. Experience has proved the adequacy of the safeguards which govern Nevada test operations."[16]

But a transcript of an AEC meeting of December 1952 reveals that the Department of Defense planned upcoming nuclear tests with an awareness that soldiers "could be exposed to above-normal limits of radiation."[17] *According to AEC Commissioner Gordon Dean, "The AEC was not in a position to recommend that normal limits be observed."*[18] *Another former AEC commissioner, Eugene Zuckert, testified before a joint session of the Senate Judiciary Committee and Human Resources Health and Scientific Research Health Subcommittee in June 1979 that the "balance was allowed to tip to the military" when there was a conflict with the AEC's Division of Biology and Medicine. "They knew the implications," Zuckert said. "I don't think it was our responsibility to override them."*[19]

In the minutes from an AEC meeting on 14 November 1958, the commissioners report that while a "clean" atomic device—one with little radioactive fallout—could be developed, "there was a desire by the military for some degree of off-site radiation for troop training purposes."[20] *They* wanted *American servicemen to be irradiated.*[21]

15. Barry Commoner, *The Closing Circle* (New York, Bantam Books, 1974), pp. 45–62.

16. Fadiman, "The Downwind People," p. 36.

17. Sulzberger, "Early Radiation Problems," p. A–24. Senator Edward Kennedy presided over the 19 June 1979 hearings on the effects of low-level radiation. Hundreds of pages of recently declassified documents were made available by Senator Kennedy at these hearings. The Department of Defense "relaxed AEC radiation safety rules in order to make the tests more realistic. . . ." See also Note 3.

18. Sulzberger, "Early Radiation Problems," p. A-24.

19. Ibid.

20. Ibid.

21. The "Defense Department and the Atomic Energy Commission intentionally exposed about 450,000 civilian and military personnel in all services to atomic tests." Berger, "An Atomic Test Case," p. 21.

AEC scientists observed the Smoky blast from a distance of seven miles. They wore protective clothing and respirators. Howard Rosenberg asks the obvious question: if the AEC's own scientists were wearing protective clothing, why were "the soldiers permitted to maneuver through highly contaminated areas" without protective clothing?[22] Some of the atomic veterans now believe that they were guinea pigs in an experiment carried out by the U.S. military.

Servicemen who witnessed atomic weapons tests have had a hard time getting the Veterans Administration to admit that the radiation they were exposed to has had serious long-term health effects. The burden of proof is placed on the veteran. Not only must a serviceman like Hodsden "prove" that he was present at the test site, but he must also establish a cause-effect relationship between the radiation exposure he received at that particular test and the health effects which may not have shown up until many years afterward. Sometimes records are incomplete or missing; film badges have been lost, and they are often inaccurate.[23]

Since there is no absolute way to pinpoint radiation as the cause of cancer or other health effects, the Veterans Administration can continue to deny compensation to servicemen who developed their illnesses long after they left active duty. Only one of six hundred claims—that of Orville Kelly, a man exposed to twenty-two atomic blasts in the South Pacific—has been recognized to date. In his case, the cancer was called a "probable" effect of radiation.

Attorneys are not permitted to represent the Veterans Administration claimants unless their fees are less than ten dollars, according to a law protecting the United States government. This generally precludes legal counsel for atomic veterans.[24]

William H. Hodsden claims that he was one of the servicemen present at Smoky in 1957. His military records are incomplete, and the army maintains that he was never exposed to radiation—that he was at Fort Lee, Virginia, in the stockade during the Smoky test.

22. Rosenberg, "The Guineapigs of Camp Desert Rock," p. 42.

23. See Chapter 2, Bertell, p. 46 for a discussion on the importance of keeping records on public health.

24. Jo Thomas, "Stakes High as Senate Examines Cancer in Troops at Atom Tests," *New York Times*, 20 June 1979, p. A–1. This law—*Feres v. United States*, 340 US Code, 95 ed 152, 71 S Ct 153—was intended to protect the U.S. government during wartime, but it is being used now during peacetime. See Pat Broudy, "Letter to Orville Kelly," *Atomic Veterans' Newsletter*, Spring 1980, p. 19.

One third of the military records on GIs—records containing infor-mation critical to veterans attempting to win federal benefits for radia-tion exposure—were destroyed in a Saint Louis fire in 1973. Only four and a half million folders were salvaged of the twenty-two million folders stored on the sixth floor of the federal government storage building that went up in flames in 1973. U.S. attorneys investigating the blaze issued a report saying that the fire had been set, accidentally or deliberately. No charges were pressed. [25]

William H. Hodsden enlisted in the U.S. Army in 1955 at the age of nineteen, feeling he was ready to lay down his life for his country. He was stationed at Fort Lee, Virginia.

Late in 1955, Hodsden's company, the 496th Quarter Master Com-pany, participated in Exercise Sagebrush, a maneuver held in Louisiana. "It was a full-fledged war game—about two-hundred-fifty-thousand troops—army, navy, marine. You had everything. You had the full Infantry Division, the full Army Division. They dropped bombs. You fired real ammunition, and they used gas. We went back and forth fighting this war game for six months. Then they had to cut the maneu-ver short because they began to have a lot of injuries—some planes making mistakes and hitting the wrong targets. . . ."

One of these "mistakes" involved a personnel carrier. "A personnel carrier is like a tank, but it doesn't carry a gun. It opens up and you can put a squad of men in it. You can close it and run toward the enemy, let the ramp down, and come out and charge the enemy. Some of the guys decided, 'We're going to ride up in these personnel carriers, through the woods and tear down some trees.' But there were these guys bivouacking in the woods. They were lying up there on the hill on bivouac—asleep. Well, these other guys jump in the personnel carrier and run up the hill. Rrrrrrrrummmmmm! rrrrrrummmmmmm! Run right over and kill three to five guys on bivouac. Americans.

"It didn't change my patriotism much, but I began to see something was wrong. The army was supposed to protect *people.*"

In the mid-1950s the army, preoccupied with nuclear war, decided to

25. "Whatever Happened to . . . Those GI Records Lost in '73 Fire," *U.S. News & World Report,* 15 November 1976. In *Atomic Veterans' Newsletter,* September-October 1979, p. 3.

Leslie J. Freeman

William H. Hodsden at the National Citizens' Hearings for
Radiation Victims, Washington, D.C., 1980

develop the "pentomic army,"[26] which involved reducing the size of a
battalion, a division, and a company. The military claimed that to
prepare soldiers for atomic warfare, they needed to go through maneuvers, simulating a real atomic explosion. "They did these tests that didn't
involve nuclear weapons. They'd take maybe two or three thousand
pounds of TNT and about so many gallons of gasoline and a couple of
detonators and put it all down on the ground. Set them off. The gasoline
would go up in a big fireball. They'd wait sometimes late in the evening
when it was getting dark, and that gave it a beautiful effect—the effect

26. See Note 3, p. 173.

of an atomic bomb."

Combat soldiers were given orientation sessions about what to do during an atomic bomb attack. They were told to build a slit trench, cover all exposed parts of the body, and wear a gas mask. They were not told about protective clothing, goggles, Geiger counters, or "hot spots." Part of the training for atomic warfare involved public relations. "We'd do these little skits. They'd all sit off somewhere and watch us go through this exercise—dig a trench and lie down in it, and then WHAM! they'd say, 'Get up and go!' and we'd get up and charge toward ground zero. It was all to give the civil defense personnel and certain politicians a sense that the army was preparing itself in case we had to fight Russia. They filmed portions of these skits. That's what they were showing the civilian population. There was this program called 'This is the Army' and remember 'The Big Picture'? This was during the time they were building a whole lot of fallout shelters and storing them up with water and food. . . ."

The soldiers were told that the greatest danger from an atomic explosion was not radiation; it was the big fireball. "If that got hold of you, you were dead. You had to get away from the fireball. That's why you built the slit trench—so when the fireball came it would go past you, and maybe you'd survive."

In one orientation session Hodsden recalls asking, "What happens to you if you get radiated?" and being told not to think about it. "We're in charge of that. It's for us, you understand? You don't have to worry about that. What you've got to worry about is that big yellow fireball."

Between 1955 and 1957 Hodsden's company participated in a number of tactical drills simulating atomic warfare. During that time Hodsden got married and spent a good deal of time off-post. One day in 1957 when he returned to the post Hodsden was told he was going to be court-martialed for overstaying his pass. Hodsden claims he was only three hours late. Since court-martials almost always apply to felony offenses, Hodsden believes he was singled out for such a severe penalty because he is black.

He had not yet been court-martialed when he was told to report for a new set of orders. "It was during the second week of May. They took five of us—me, PFC Bennett, Private Kilmore, Specialist McDonald, and Sergeant Cooper—and they said, 'You're going to be on the maneuver Smoky.' They took five of us from the 496th Quarter Master Company, five guys from each of the other companies in that area, and they formed a composite company called the Quarter Master Petroleum Supply Company."

Hodsden told them that he was about to be court-martialed and might not be able to go on the maneuver. He was told not to worry about it. "We were given two slips of paper, and on them—I'll never forget this —it said that they wanted our permission for the FBI to run security checks on us. It also said, 'The United States government will be responsible for you while you are at the nuclear test site.' "

The soldiers were told not to discuss the nuclear test: "What we'd see at the test site we were to keep to ourselves—'Don't say too much about it. Just keep it under your hat.' "

On 25 May 1957, before leaving for the test site, Hodsden was court-martialed and sentenced to three months of hard labor in the stockade. One of his chores was to go around to all the barracks and pick up ash cans that weighed close to one hundred and fifty pounds. "I got so I could take an ash can, pick it up, and raise it over my head, and shake it into a dump truck. I did this for two or three months and my arms became so big and powerful I was like a weightlifter."

Hodsden claims he was released from the stockade on 18 August 1957. He asked his friends what had happened with the Smoky maneuver and was told that it had been postponed.[27] He recalls that he got his orders a few days later. "I remember standing in formation when they called the names out. I said to myself, 'Sounds like they're calling guys out to go on that maneuver.' They kept calling names and I remember thinking, 'Well, I just came out of the stockade. Probably won't be me. . . .' Then I remember hearing 'Private William H. Hodsden.' I walked up and they handed me these orders for Camp Desert Rock. Private William H. Hodsden RA 12471 TDY to Quarter Master Petroleum Supply Company. Will depart from Fort Lee on August 25 on orders to Camp Desert Rock, Nevada.' "

A week later five or six men from each company, about twenty-eight men all together, left the Fort Lee area and rode by bus to Nevada. They reached Camp Desert Rock on 27 August 1957.

---

27. Smoky was delayed two months because of severe weather during June and July at the test site.

"The sun, not the bomb, is your worst enemy at Camp Desert Rock."

> —*from a booklet given to atomic test participants at Camp Desert Rock. Thomas, "Stakes High as Senate Examines Cancer in Troops at Atom Tests," p. A-1.*

Camp Desert Rock: Arrival

Let me explain about Yucca Flats, Nevada. There are two or three camps. If you say, "I'm going to Camp Desert Rock," you're going to Camp Desert Rock as a permanent complement. They would take a single corps company and say, "You're going to Camp Desert Rock," and when you get there, you stay two, three, four, five months. If you come there on a maneuver and you're going to go back, then they put you up at Camp Murray or Camp Mercury.

We were assigned to Camp Murray. They have a big sign just before you get in there that says: "What you see here, what you hear here, and what is said here, leave it here!"

As soon as we got off the bus, army picture teams appeared and began to film the whole thing. Then these guys turned up.

"I am your instructor, your range instructor."

And there were other personnel—civil defense personnel, wearing the civil defense helmet and arm bands. There were marine personnel. And as we got off the bus, those pentomic teams were taking pictures.

I didn't have any thoughts about what was happening. Just the feeling of a show about to happen. There was a little bit of excitement. You feel that way when you see four or five guys with cameras slung across their shoulders running around and looking in your face.

The following day—the 28th—they put us in trucks and gave us a riding tour around Camp Desert Rock and the different base camps. They looked different than the ones in Camp Murray. These were half huts—quonset huts—and when the guys stayed there they named the huts different things like "Oasis Hilton." There were a lot of sand dunes around, and they gave us a tour of different areas. That was the 28th.

The 29th they took us to these museums in the desert. They have these different types of museums with different vehicles of all kinds. And captions like: THIS VEHICLE WAS BLOWN UP BY A FIFTEEN-KILOTON ATOMIC BOMB.

Here you're looking at a two-ton truck that's been melted down to the size of a garbage can. It was awesome. Here, this is a tank, a medium Patton tank, and it's been melted down! They had all these things that they had used before in testing to see what happens to them.

On the 30th was the 4.7-kiloton atomic device called "Franklin Prime." We were taken out to the desert and moved behind some sand dunes in a hilly area.

Two or three guys started getting jumpy—scared. Here comes a guy riding in a Jeep. Jumps out. Here comes the camera—eeeeeeeeee—. Some of the guys are posing. Here's an information officer, and he starts interviewing some of the guys. There were six of us.

"Soldier, how do you feel that you're about to witness an atomic bomb?"

The guy—he was jumping. Nervous, you know. "Man, I don't know."

"Out there," the officer says—because we were behind a sand dune —"out there in a few minutes, you're going to witness an atomic bomb. How do you feel?"

And the camera's going. He's got the microphone. And the guy's going "I—uh—uh—" and you can see him shaking—"I . . . feel pretty good."

So they get in the Jeep and go off.

The range instructor says, "When I give the word 'go' I want you guys to run up the side of this sand dune and stand on top and watch it."

So we're standing there behind the sane dune and he says, "Go!"

Never heard anything. Run up the top of the sand dune and look out. And we see a little flash, and a little trail of smoke in the air. I had to squint.

And I said, "What the hell is that?"

It was eight miles away, and it looked like a little campfire.

Some of the guys started laughing. "Where's the ball?"

Another one says, "There it is."

"That's not."

So when the guys start laughing in the group, this guy—this range officer—froze up a bit. "That was an atomic bomb," he says. "That was an *atomic bomb.*"

The guys say, "Aw, man, that ain't nothing."

And the range officer says, "That's all right. You guys are going to get yours tomorrow."

OTI-57-93   Nevada Test Organization   August 24, 1957

OFFICE OF TEST INFORMATION

1235 South Main Street
Las Vegas, Nevada

FOR IMMEDIATE RELEASE

CAMP DESERT ROCK, NEV.—Can a highly trained soldier think clearly and perform the duties of his fighting mission efficiently in the shadow of a nuclear bomb's mushroom cloud?

Two minutes after a blast with an explosive force of over 20,000 tons TNT, will his hands tremble as he kneels to field-strip and reassemble his rifle?

Will he obey promptly the orders of his commanding officer, or will he falter as a choking dust cloud whirls around him?

Will he move quickly to clear a mine field, or will he "gawk" at the eerie "snow cap" forming above his head?

For the first time since man learned to split the atom, the United States Army is prepared to find the answers to these and other unknowns concerning human behavior in nuclear warfare, in connection with the shot "Smoky" which will be detonated above Yucca Flat at the Nevada Test Site Wednesday, August 28.

—In *Effect of Radiation on Human Health,* vol. 1, pp. 62–63.

Smoky: 31 August 1957

The next morning at 4:00 they wake us up. "Everybody up! Let's go!" We ate breakfast. There were some pills in the middle of the table.

"Everybody has to take one of these pills." I think they were some kind of sulfa drug.

We were put on trucks. It was dark. We didn't know where we were going.

"Here we go!"

"Give me five guys off this truck!"

So we jump off.[28] We could just make out in the darkness this big damn bunker and a trench. Another truck pulled up.

"Give me five more guys. I want you right here!"

So they move five more guys off another truck. This is where these other guys I'd never seen before from the Twelfth Infantry appeared. I was the only black guy among the five from my company, but the five guys that got off the other truck were black.

The range officer—it was a different one this time, not the one who'd said, "You guys will get yours"—the range officer said, "I want to explain something to you. We're going to have to scale a pretty steep wall." This damn bunker we were inside of. "We're going to have to scale this little bit of concrete. See, there are some wires hanging down. I want you to be careful of them wires. Be very careful of them wires going up."

I kept looking in the dark, trying to see what the hell was up there. The bunker looked like it had a number on it . . . number 19? 9? Something like that in the concrete up near the top where the entrance of the trench was. It was very hard to see in the dark, but I kept looking, trying to make out something—where I was at, you know, what the heck was going on.

One of the guys from the other group that I'd never seen before was running around acting crazy, stupid, bothering everybody. A couple of the guys said, "Look, Sarge, tell this guy to cool it. We're kind of nervous as it is, and here we got to climb this steep wall to get to the top of the hill. Tell him to be cool."

So the sergeant said, "Okay, I want you to shut up. You're making everybody nervous."

The guy was tugging on people, tugging on his buddies and smiling, and kind of shaking.

"Cut it out!" the sergeant said. "You're making everybody nervous. Cut that crap out!" Then he turned to us. "When I say the word 'go!' I want you to go up that wall. Everybody got to be careful—" In other words we had to go so far up and then reach back and pull another guy

---

28. "It just so happened that when they got to our truck we were the last five guys so they had to bring up another five guys from another company and put us together to make us a squad"—Hodsden.

up. We had to make a chain going up there to get to the top. And it was dark, dark as hell.

"Go!"

You had to take your hands and boost the guy up on top of the side of concrete, and he had to go up, and then you came up, and there was a slant, a hill. You go up and then you were on top. I was one of the last guys to get on top. The whole area on top was lit with floodlights. It was dark down in the trench. You could look up and you couldn't see floodlights up on top. You got to the top of the hill and you make out the illumination of the floodlights on that hill.

It was flat and a little slanted, and the area beveled off. Out in front of us was a barrier. They'd chopped down trees and made a barrier in front of this area.

I kept squinting because when you turned around you were looking into these lights and you could hardly see. It looked like there was another bunker with very small slits in it—another concrete building.

"Somebody help that man," the sergeant said. "Somebody help that guy." I walked to the end of the hill and looked over, down back in the trench. There was a little ledge over the top of the trench, hanging out, and it was very high. I see this guy lying there—lying on top of this ledge. He had fallen over back into the trench on this ledge, and he was unconscious. Everybody's looking at him.

This black corporal says, "Somebody go down and get him."

Everybody's just standing there, looking. I was one of the last ones up, so I looked over the edge.

"Come here," the corporal says to me. "You got very powerful arms. You'll be able to shinny down on the ledge and grab him. Would you go get him?"

"Okay."

I took my helmet off and started to shinny over the edge. There was just enough room on that ledge where I could stand on it. I couldn't do any movement. The guy's slumped in the corner of the ledge, which is about four or five feet long. So what I did—I grabbed his field jacket in my left hand very hard, and I reached up so some of these guys could reach down to pull me up. I put my foot against the concrete, and they yanked me.

But my foot slipped, and I went *bam!*—flat against the side of the trench. So I was dangling with him in my hand, and they were holding me. The drop was maybe three, four stories, and I'm hanging there, with him in my hand. He's dead weight. This pain shot through me because now I'm being pulled both ways. That's a hell of a damn pain. Maybe he weighed a hundred fifty pounds or so, and I'm being stretched both ways.

So the corporal raises hell. "Let them back down!"

They ease me back down to the ledge, and I almost blacked out too.

Then the corporal said, "The hell with this!" and he reached over and grabbed my arm and lifted me, and I came across the top of the bunker with that guy on my arm, and that was it. I blacked out from the pain.

When they pulled me up across the top of the bunker, they grabbed the guy I'm holding and pulled him back up. He's still unconscious. I came back out of it pretty fast. I remember lying on the ground, waking up and shaking my head.

I got up, and the guys are still looking at him. I looked at him too. He was just lying there. Still in a daze, I opened up his field jacket. We took off his jacket. He was still unconscious, and we didn't know why. I took off my jacket and my other fatigue shirt and rolled them up and put them under his head. I checked his heartbeat, and then I gave him artificial respiration. I had no idea I was in radioactive terrain.

Then the loudspeaker came on. "All right, you guys. Get ready."

I picked up a field jacket and put it on.

"I want everybody lined up in single file," says the voice over the loudspeaker.

We all sat down on the ground in single file with our backs to ground zero. There was white powder on the ground and some black stuff. My head was hurting like hell, and my hip too. And my arm. I remember looking down at my field jacket and seeing the nameplate on the chest. When you look down at it, it looks backwards. Momentarily I thought it was my name because my name starts with H too. I see H-A-R-T. Hart. So the unconscious guy was Hart. Private Hart. I was wearing his field jacket now.

We wait and we wait.

"All right," the corporal says, "stand up." So we stand up. "Everybody turn around and take five steps forward. Okay, you guys on the right, be careful of that wire. Okay, turn around. Everybody down on one knee and cover your eyes."

I remember going down on my right knee. And the pain shot through

GIs witnessing Smoky, 31 August 1957

CIs witnessing Smoky, 31 August 1957

me again. I remember just saying "Whew!" and going limp while I was there, and then the sound.

It's an awesome sound. About three or four seconds later, the backs of my eyes began to light up. See, I had my hands covering my eyes and in the back the nerve started to light up. Then I could feel something —it passed through me. It stopped my heartbeat. When it passed through me, my heart went like this—*(he makes a fist—opens and closes it several times, then stops it suddenly).*

My knee started to hurt. To burn. I felt a warm sensation in my knee —a stinging and burning sensation going up inside my kneecap.

"All right. Everybody stand up."

So I stood up, and the guy, still unconscious, was behind us. We were facing away and he was behind us. We turned around and now he was in front of us. He was between me and the tower.

It hurt for me to move. My right hip hurt like hell.

A guy on my right said, "Man, do you feel that?"

The guy on my left goes "Yup."

Around the rectum it began to feel warm, very warm, and a pinprick sensation, and around the testes the same sensation.

The guy on my left says, "Man!" and he starts to jump. "Oh oh oh!" And he says, "Man, do you feel that?"

Then the strangest thing—this is the strangest—when you looked at the fireball, you'd hear the noise. If you looked up at it—it's weird— a gold yellowish color, and from the center—it's the weirdest thing I've ever seen as far as a fire—the center is like a swirl that's all them bright yellows and gold colors in swirls. And when I looked up at it, I became very aware of the noise. It sounded like about fifteen freight trains going by. Only louder—a deafening roar. So we grabbed our ears. When we became aware of the noise and we felt the pressure on our ears, we grabbed our heads.

I kept looking down at the guy, kept feeling that sensation. I looked back up again. Then my eyes began to sting. And then we felt the breeze —a hot wind blowing in our face and the smell of smoke, of burnt metal.

We stayed there, in that position. I looked up at the fireball and looked down there and see the guy lying on the ground. That's what I was doing. I kept checking him, looking at him. I looked back up at the fireball and kept looking down at him. Up at the fireball and down at him.

Then I felt something on my thigh. A burning sensation, and I looked down and saw a piece of dust—it was gray and it was on my right thigh. Stuck to it. That wind was blowing—that slight wind blowing. And that dust particle stuck there. Then I felt some sort of cut. It went into my leg and stopped at the back of my thigh and then burned again. I felt it on the inside. I looked back at my leg and the dust particle was gone! The strangest damn thing. The uniform wasn't burning. There was no hole down there. If it was a cinder, it would've burned a hole and burned the skin. But it wasn't that. It was just a piece of dust—a piece of ash that had cooled off already.

Smoky was exploded from a tower seven hundred feet in the air. When the fireball began to burn, it came down. It did not go up. It came down. And as it was coming down, pieces of the tower would become white hot and go *chewwww!* and shoot out from it. The fireball came down a little bit and *ccchhh! chhew!* and it came down a little more and you see part of that tower—maybe fifty- or sixty-feet sections—white hot.

Now the fireball is down here. It's smaller. And as it descends, it descends right on that damn tower, and so around it was white hot melting—you see white hot metal. It would fall off, and then you see it begin to cool. You look around ground zero and it begins to cool. When it cooled, it turned white. I'll never forget this. It was just as if it had snowed out in front of us and part of it had gotten dirty—little black smut on it. That's what was out in front of us.

Smoky was detonated at 5:30 in the morning. So by now it's beginning to get light and we can see a little bit in front of us. We're standing on top of a mound, and we're up over the desert floor, and about two thousand feet out there's another mound with the same type of thing —with a trench embedded in it, and guys sitting in there, holding their heads, bent over.

And the side of the hill—where you come out of the trench and go up the side, there were guys lying all over. And on the other side of it —between the trench and ground zero—guys were lined up in formation. I kept looking. And as it got lighter, you could see more.[29]

Then I heard someone yelling through a loudspeaker: "Goddamn! if you guys don't get your asses out of them damn trenches, you gonna go

29. "Our group was on the outskirts. We were maybe a little on the inside of a mile from ground zero. About five thousand feet away from the blast. Observers were all over —I think between two thousand and five thousand feet from ground zero"—Hodsden.

to Leavenworth!"

Then this guy in front—whoever he was—kept going back in the trenches and grabbing guys. "Get the hell out of there!"

And when he'd pull them up out of the trench and they'd get up on the side, he'd kick them in the ass. "Hew! git out of here!"

They'd run to the top and get in formation. Now when they came out of their trenches, they were about two thousand feet from ground zero. Then they started marching. They marched to the right of the tower, turned up toward ground zero, and went about one hundred yards through that ash.[30] Then the guy in the front, who's leading them out, saluted.

He saluted ground zero.

It's light now. We're still standing, looking. Then the loudspeaker comes on, and it says: "You have just witnessed one of the most powerful weapons in the world. And it belongs to one of the best damn armies in the world—the United States Army!"

The test was over.

Aftermath

We went off the side. They grabbed the guy who was unconscious and started dragging him through that damn dust. Something said to me something's wrong here, so I grab the guy and pick him up out of the dust. He had the dust all over him. Two guys grabbed him when we were going off the range, back down the side of the hill.

There was an area there that was square. They had logs around it and a hose—a faucet and a hose. You go in that area and hose your boots down. Come out and go off the hill, and there's a road down here, and this guy runs up to me.

30. Lieutenant Colonel Frank W. Keating was the commanding officer of the 12th Battle Group which sent troops to participate in the Smoky shot. In 1978 he testified at congressional hearings and was questioned by Congressman Tim Lee Carter: "Mr. Carter: 'How near to the ground zero did you get after the blast?' Colonel Keating: 'We went right in.' Mr. Carter: 'How close did you get to the site of the tower?' Colonel Keating: 'About 300 feet.' " *Effect of Radiation on Human Health*, vol. 1., pp. 162–163. Jack Russell Dann testified at the same hearings that his group "walked down to ground zero within about 200 or 300 yards." Ibid., p. 178.

"Hey, man, you all right? you all right?"

"Yeah, but my thigh hurts, and my hip hurts, and I'm sore."

He says, "Walk around! Walk around! See how it is."

So I walk around, and I got a slight limp. They put the other guy—he's still unconscious—in the army ambulance.

He comes back and says, "You sure it hurts?"

"Man, there was something on my right leg, and it's sore now."

He says, "Oh, don't worry about it. Walk around! Let me see how . . . oh, you're all right." And he jumps in the truck and goes off.

They put us in a truck, and this time we didn't go back to the decontamination unit. They take us to this area which is nothing but big bleachers in the desert. They put us in these bleachers and we sit there.

By and by the loudspeaker comes on. "All right, look out directly to your front!"

We hear planes off in the distance—maybe five miles or so. They look to me like C-119s. My neck is beginning to hurt—stiffening up. My leg's stiffening up. From our position we can see parachutes opening in the distance. They're streaming—you know how they do it? They come out and there's a boom, boom, boom—like that. And it seems to me that two guys come out and keep going.

My buddy was up on the next tier and I remember saying to him, "Man, what happened to them dudes, you know?"

He said, "They opened—their chutes opened."

We're sitting there watching what looks like paratroopers being dropped on the contaminated site.

Then they took us over to the decontamination unit. This time it's different from the day before because now they got something that when you go through it, a light comes on. They were scanning us or taking pictures.

"Take off all your clothes. Throw them in a basket." You never see them again. Kept the boots though.

You go through this area where you step down. This thing comes on you and you have to stand there. Then through another area and a shower. Then another shower and you come out, put new clothes on, and go on. Each area had a color code.

SMOKY, 5:30 A.M.

Seven miles away, thirty-one-year-old AEC scientist John Auxire and technician P. N. "Barney" Hensley watched the Smoky blast from the cab of their Army two-and-a-half ton truck. Their mission was to lead a convoy of AEC vehicles toward the test site and retrieve instruments that had been left at various distances from ground zero to record radiation levels. They were wearing white coveralls taped at the wrists and ankles, gloves, boots, goggles, and respirators.

Four minutes after the detonation, Hensley started the truck's engine and began leading the convoy toward ground zero at top speed. The men knew they would have only seconds to grab their instruments and get out before they were contaminated. As their truck reached a point four or five miles short of their goal, Auxire was alarmed to see his portable dosimeter recording dangerously high levels of radiation. He signaled Hensley to turn back and the men beat a hasty retreat. . . . Smoky stands out in Auxire's mind as the only shot where radiation levels were so high that AEC scientists couldn't retrieve their instruments for several days after the blast.

> —from Rosenberg, "The Guineapigs of Camp Desert Rock," p. 41.

The Sickness . . .

We went back to our area—back to Camp Murray—and like GIs do, we just hung around in the barracks, doing nothing. Go to eat, chowtime, come back, stick around, smoke, look, pick around looking at clothes, stuff like that. My neck was still hurting, still stiffening up.

My buddy said, "What's wrong?"

"I can't hardly turn my damn neck. And my leg is sore as hell too."

I remember some of these guys from the Airborne coming over to me about two hours after we were back in camp—guys from my company, the Composite Company.[31] I remember them coming to me and saying, "We heard what happened. Man, you know, we're kind of proud of you. We heard what happened in the rescue."

That's all they said. They smiled. They were from the 82nd Airborne.[32]

That was Saturday the 31st. Sunday I began to stiffen up more. I

31. The Composite Company was made up of servicemen from different companies. There were some "guys from Quarter Master Corps, some guys from the Twelfth Infantry, some guys from the 82nd Airborne. We were in this Composite Company when they put us all in trucks"—Hodsden.

32. There were 457 observers at Smoky in addition to participant troops. See "Exercise Desert Rock VII and VIII: Final Report of Operations," Annex E, Section V: Troop Tests (unclassified), 1957, in *Effect of Radiation on Human Health*, vol. 1, pp. 240–266.

began getting a little nervous. I went in and took another shower early Monday morning in the barracks, and it never dawned on me to look down at my leg. I just took a shower and put my things on.

One of my buddies said, "Man, let's go outside and get a smoke."

"Okay."

So we walked outside the barracks and sat up on one of the trucks. When I got up there, something burned me and I went *slap!* like that.

"What's wrong with you?"

"I don't know, man." Then I saw a little fluid—a little spot. I pull up my pants and look at it. Where I'd hit it, I'd bust a blister—like the size of a half-dollar. And I'll never forget—he said, "Man, you better tell somebody about that."

"I didn't—that's the first time I seen it."

"You better tell somebody about that," he says. "Come on!"

We run into the barracks.

"Hey, sarge, look at this here. He had a blister there!"

"Don't get excited, don't get excited!" said the sergeant.

I can't move. My neck's hurting, my heart's palpitating. I guess my eyes were big, too, because I was getting scared.

"Come on. We're going to take the three-quarter truck."

So we jump in the three-quarter and he takes me up to the infirmary. Those barracks are straight, and they have a little vestibule and a porch you come down out of. So you go up the steps on the porch and into the little vestibule. And they had a table there, and this guy is sitting there.

The guy with me says, "Hey, he's got a blister."

The guy sitting there gets up and runs out. I don't know where he goes. When he does that, two or three guys come to the door and look.

"Hey, what's wrong with you?"

When they peered out, their damn heads were huge, and their eyes had stretched and they were red. This white dude—he was swollen in the face, and his nostrils were big and you see blood running—

He said, "Look at this, man! What's wrong with you?"

"I got a blister."

He said, "Damn, we got to remember this shit!"

Another black guy came, and he said, "What's wrong?"

And their faces—I do not think they realized—but their faces looked so swollen that the cracks had turned red—the eyelids had separated in the corners and their noses—

"Man, we got to remember this!"

If you get sick like that, your memory goes. That's the hardest damn thing. There are things that happened there that I won't say because you get fuzzy and maybe you start hallucinating. I'll just say what I remember. . . .

The guy who was at the desk came back in. "You come with me." They put me in another barrack in the front of the area. They had it partitioned off and all the windows blackened out, and they took all my clothes off, set me in the bed with my legs crossed at the ankles. I was all naked. He used four or five pillows to prop me up. "Your leg is very swollen," he says. "Your hip and your leg is very swollen. We're doing this to keep it from hyperextending."

So I'm sitting there naked, and all of a sudden my right leg begins to swell. Then I start to get very nauseous, and then I was throwing up. I looked down. I was secreting—pissing. So he gives me a glass of water.

"See if you can keep this down."

Whew! it comes right back up again.

"Well, take it with this here." He gives me a pill with some water. The water comes up.[33] And this right leg is swelling. Then it starts hurting in the groin and all up in the back of my spine, then my neck, and I become very weak.

If you ever get sick like that, I swear to God you get so weak your mind goes. You just go out. Eventually you come around and you get a little bit of your senses back, and you're still secreting, pissing, throwing up. You're not gagging—see, you got nausea, and if you take anything, it comes right back up, but you're not cramping in your stomach.

My leg was swollen and I would look at it. The orderly who was with me all the time wouldn't come up close to me. When he handed me the medicine he'd reach over—"here you go"—and go back real fast.

This other guy would come and hand things in from the door. He had something—a box maybe—and he'd point it at me and then go back. Now it seems to me that he had a technician's jacket on or something,

33. The classic symptoms of radiation sickness include vomiting and diarrhea, bodily fatigue and fever. "The sickness due to . . . fallout radiation may lead to a more protracted sequence of symptoms [other than those who suffer fatal exposures] . . . persons with only minor radiation injuries will exhibit the same symptoms as those with fatal injuries. . . ." Fred Charles Iklé, *The Social Impact of Bomb Destruction* (Norman, Oklahoma: University of Oklahoma Press, 1958), pp. 21–22.

but I'm not sure. I do remember that every once in a while a machine was turned on. It sounded like a camera whining. Whenever this happened, the lights would get a little brighter and that whining sound would come on. During the next four or five days this went on—the light came on, and I would hear that whining. This went on one, two, three, four, five days, five nights. Sitting naked. Feet crossed. Swollen. And blacking out. Getting very weak. You lose all control.

I remember after about five or six days trying to get on my side and saying, "Man, look, I got to lie down. My back is killing me!"

"You can't lie down! You can't lie down!"

I remember going to my side to get off that damn leg, and when I leaned to the side the pain hit me and I blacked out again. I woke up again and I'm still propped up.

On the eighth or ninth day the pain began to subside—the pain in my groin—and my leg started to go down. I still had the weakness and tiredness, but I was gaining more control of myself. They let me put my clothes back on.

"All right. You can get up and walk around a little bit, but you can't go outside." I remember that. "We can't let you out in the sunlight. We can't let you out in daylight."

I was in a little cubicle they had partitioned off.

I remember saying, "Damn! I want to go outside!" But I go back and lie down and get weak again and very tired. That was Sunday. Monday. Tuesday.

Then on Wednesday a guy came in and said, "I want to talk to you." "Yeah?"

"The guys want to talk to you, but we won't let them do it. The commander of the post has ordered them not to come and talk to you."

"What the hell's going on?"

"We had orders not to do it," he said.

"I don't know," I said. "I don't really like that."

But Friday the guys came over. I guess they had traced me to where the hell I was.

"Hey!" They were outside. "We want to talk to you! Hey, can you come out?"

Here comes this same guy again. "You can't go out there!"

So I asked the orderly—he was with me all the time—"Can I go outside?"

"I don't care."

This other guy says, "You can't go outside! Now that's a direct order from the commander. You can't go out there!"

I pushed him away and went outside the door. The sun wasn't shining. It was evening. Kind of overcast. I see these guys—they are the black guys from the 12th Infantry. I recognized the corporal who'd asked me to get the guy on the ledge.

"We wanted to thank you for what you did," one of the guys said. These guys looked drawn. Dark circles under their eyes. They looked sick. "We heard you injured your hip and your groin."

"Yeah."

"We got to remember this here."

"Yeah."

I remember the corporal. He said, "I'll tell you what. If you ever need any help on this—if anything ever comes of this—" he didn't know I had the blister, and I didn't say anything to him because they'd told me to keep my mouth shut. These guys thought I was in there for the injury, see, the injury to my hip. So the corporal said, "If you ever need any help, you try and get in contact with me. You can remember my name —Kelly—kelly green—" and he smiled—"you know, the Irish—" and he smiled again. Kelly's an Irish name, but he was a black guy—"You can remember my name—the Irish, the kelly green."

The guy I had lifted up—Hart—comes over. "Man, I want to thank you a lot for what you did."

"Well, you all right now?"

"Yeah," he said. "I'm all right. I'll be all right."

These guys looked very drawn. They looked like they'd been at Desert Rock a real long time.

Return to Fort Lee: September 1957

I went back inside. That was a Friday. Saturday they let me go back to the barracks of my company, my buddies. That same guy—that instructor from Franklin Prime who'd said, "You guys will get yours!" —that guy came into the barracks and said he wanted to talk to me.

"The post commander has said that you are not to say anything once you leave here—you understand? You are supposed to keep your mouth shut about the burn. You could be in a lot of trouble. . . . You are to keep your mouth shut—" and he mentioned a colonel, and said this colonel was the post commander.

That Monday they put us on trains back to Fort Lee. We got to Fort Lee around the middle of September. I remember coming into the company area and some of my black buddies coming up to me.

"Hey, man, where you been at?"

"Well—" I wanted to tell them, "Hey, man, you know what happened to me—" But the threat was there. Keep your mouth shut. So I got nervous, kind of excited. "Man, let me tell you something," I said. "I just witnessed two atomic bombs."

"Man, why don't you just cut that crap out. They don't let black people see no damn atomic bombs!"

"What's wrong with you?" says another one. "Why you up here telling us that damn lie?"

"No, man," I said, "that's where I been at."

"No, they don't do that. They don't do that. They don't let nobody see no damn atomic—specially black people. Man, you crazy?"

One of the guys—he was a big old dude—I'll never forget—he said, "I'm gonna punch you in your damn mouth!"

"Wait a minute now. I seen them atomic bombs."

We huddled together in the barracks off in the corner.

He said, "Man, get the hell out of here, goddammit! I'll jump on your ass. Stop telling them damn lies. Where you been at?"

"Okay," I said, and I walked away from them and came down the steps.

And he yelled after me, "Man, why the hell don't you stop damn lying!"

"Well, if that's what you—"

And this sergeant—Sergeant Cooper—walked by and heard. "Come here," he said.

Sergeant Cooper was white. He was a good dude. He was like a father to us. We were between ages twenty and twenty-three. He was a little bit up in age, and he was a staff sergeant. He had time and rank. When we was out there in the desert, a lot of times he'd helped out. You know —"Hey, man, sarge, what's going to happen?" If you're scared, you know, you could feel secure with him.

So he said, "Come here. I want to tell you something. You don't have to argue with them. You know where you been. You just cool it. I thought you had more sense than that."

That's what he said. Real calm. "I thought you had more sense than that."

I said, "You're right." So I didn't say anything more about it.

Discharge

One day I was called into the Orderly Room, and this colonel says, "We've got a follow-up on you. You've been recommended for a medal. Do you know a lieutenant so and so and sergeant so and so?"

I didn't. I recognized the name Kelly and Simmons and the guys, but I didn't recognize the officers he was talking about.

Then he said, "You can't accept this medal because it would involve a lot of investigation. This is a top-secret project, and if you know what's good for you, you'll keep your mouth shut about that blister."

So I didn't get a medal. . . .

I began to get very weak in the legs, and my muscles would start twitching. It would start in my knees—very slight. And the muscles in my legs got so tired I couldn't stand up. I'd have these stupors. Here I was back at Fort Lee doing these various duties.

"All right," the sergeant would say. "Come on, let's go. Today we're going to wash down trucks." Crap like that.

I'd say, "Okay."

"Private Hodsden? I want you to go with so and so."

While I'm going there, I begin having these damn stupors—this weakness. I had to sit down. He'd see me sitting down. "I thought I told you to go somewhere!" So the sergeant started getting on my ass. Not Sergeant Cooper. Him and Bennett and Kilmore got sick and disappeared for a few days. They put them in bed like they had a cold or something—put them in the dispensary for two days or so.

Then I broke out with some infections on my right leg.

Then they got on me. "You can't do nothing. There's something wrong." They didn't say there was something wrong with *me.* They said there was something wrong with my *personality.* "You don't want to work. You don't want to do your job. You got a personality disorder.[34] You got a character defect."

The army was saying that. My sergeant! Because I was having these damn stupors. Getting weak all the time when I walked around.

Then my father wrote the company commander. He wanted to know what was wrong with me. They sent a letter back in January 1958. Your son "has been doing a fine job here in the company. He seems well adjusted and accepts his responsibilities in a soldierly manner."[35] January 1958!

The last week of February they call me before a board and they're saying, "You can't do the job," and so on.

I said, "Something's wrong with me. I can't get settled."

They gave me a less than honorable discharge a week later, which was March 8, 1958—after my full tour of duty!

I felt really hurt to be released out of the army like that. Before I went in I was, you know, I was the black John Wayne in patriotism. That's what I felt. I can't explain what it means when they hand you something that says you are released from the army other than honorable.

The stupors increased. I began to withdraw from people. The swellings continued. The stupors continued. I was hospitalized and they diagnosed me as a schizophrenic.[36] I stayed in the hospital with treat-

---

34. "A personality disorder is not a disease or injury within the meaning of applicable legislation providing compensation benefits." Board of Veterans Appeals, "In the Appeal of William H. Hodsden, Findings and Decision," C-21 641 736, Washington, D.C., 29 November 1978, p. 7.

35. Captain George J. Nawrocki, Jr., captain of 496th Quartermaster Company to Mr. Leslie Hodsden, 9 January 1958.

36. Hodsden was hospitalized at the Harlem Valley State Hospital in New York from 1960 to 1965. Diagnosis, according to the army, was "schizophrenia-paranoid type." (U.S. Department of Health, Education, and Welfare, Social Security Administration, Bureau of Hearings and Appeals, "Hearing Decision in the Case of William H. Hodsden," 8 July 1975, p. 6.) Hodsden states that he was first hospitalized at Jacobi Hospital in 1959, then full time at the Bronx Mental Hospital. "I became very ill and spent five years in the psychiatric hospital. . . ." (Army Discharge Review Board, "Proceedings in the Case of William H. Hodsden," Department of the Army, Washington, D.C., 16 July 1974, p. 10.) The medical records of this time are missing. "The request for these records was returned with a notation that records are only kept 10 years. . . ." (Board of Veterans Appeals, "Findings and Decision," p. 6.)

ment. I had malfunction of the blood. The stupors and swellings kept on.

While I was in the hospital I had nightmares. I kept getting sick—one thing after another. I lost weight, I had infections. I couldn't stand loud noises. . . . In 1961, while I was a patient at Harlem Valley, I filed a claim with the Veterans Administration and the Department of the Army saying my illness was maybe due to exposure to atomic radiation. Those letters are now lost. . . . I got back a letter when they disallowed my claim, saying, "The United States doesn't use troops in nuclear testing."

I continued to have problems with swellings in my neck and legs, but now tumors were developing. I had one tumor removed from my right thigh, and the biopsy was scarred tissue—"burnt scar tissue." It was in the same area that I had had the blister before.[37]

I had to have treatments for my back, my neck, and then a tumor developed in my neck and it began to affect my eyes. I had blurred vision. I began having more nightmares—sometimes about the Smoky test. . . . I was scared. They put me on thorazine and gave me group therapy. . . .

After two years my wife divorced me. And then, while I was convalescing, I met another girl. She was a nurse from Asheville, North Carolina. She was there for a rest for two months. She told me, "If you're nervous, Asheville's a good place to go to. It's up in the mountains. You can probably find a good job there." When I left the hospital I married her and relocated there.

From 1958 through June of last year I've had to have psychiatric treatment and medication and hospitalizations. All the time taking treatments, wearing a back brace. Sometimes I had to take off and go to the hospital for traction, for evaluation. They gave me all kinds of therapy—assertiveness all the way back to compensative behavior.

---

37. "The earliest postservice medical evidence of record is a report from the J. [Jacobi] Hospital indicating that the veteran was seen there in September 1958, complaining of bilateral knee joint pain and swelling. . . ." (Board of Veterans Appeals, "Findings and Decision," p. 3.) There is also a record that a tumor was removed from Hodsden's right thigh in 1966. (Ibid., p. 4.)

North Carolina

I have four kids. The first are twins. They have defects—minimal brain dysfunction. Skin sores. Skin pigmentation. Red blood disorders. The third and fourth are the same. The same—all four. My son Mark is anemic. . . .

I went back to college—two years of technical college—and began to work with young people as a juvenile cottage parent. I was good at it. I worked four years doing that. I supervised a program in the center in the neighborhood. We had tutoring in the evenings. But I was having trouble working. . . .

In 1974 I started to fight my case as being injustice to the veteran. There was a hearing and I won my rank back and my honorable discharge. I changed from a private doctor to the Veterans Administration doctors because now I could get free treatment.

But in 1975 my condition worsened to the point that I could not do any work. I applied to the VA at least eight times from 1974 to the present time for "service-connected injuries." They've turned me down. They say I can't prove I was at the Smoky test site.[38] They say my problems are emotional.

DEPARTMENT OF HEALTH, EDUCATION, AND WELFARE. HEARING DECISION CLAIM FOR DISABILITY INSURANCE BENEFITS—WILLIAM H. HODSDEN

The real problem here is claimant's mental health. . . .

He was easily distracted from his work and he did not demonstrate any degree of tolerance for work in the unit. The shortcoming appeared to be more emotional than physical. . . .

---

38. The army claims Hodsden was court-martialed on 26 August 1957 and sentenced to two months' confinement in the stockade and was released 18 September 1957, and that he could not have been present at the nuclear test Smoky (Board of Appeals, "Findings and Decision", p. 6). Hodsden believes that there has been an elaborate "coverup." "The Pentagon released the names of Smoky participants, but not of all the observers . . ."—Hodsden.

See *Effect of Radiation on Human Health*, vol. 1, p. 288. The chairman of the committee on Long Term Medical Effects of Operation Desert Rock, Dr. Lawrence R. Stromberg, says, ". . . all participants in the nuclear weapons program were not issued film badges" and there was a failure to keep complete records. "Corroborative information to

On July 24, 1973 the claimant was evaluated by Dr. Robert S. Byron who limits his practice to psychiatry. . . . Dr. Byron found claimant to be cooperative and attentive, neat and clean in personal habits. His thoughts were free flowing, spontaneous and coherent, and connected logically. The speed of thinking was normal. Mental trend was one of ambivalence and contained a rather deep underlying sense of doubt and, indeed of futility. . . . There was no psychotic ideation. . . .

Dr. Byron diagnoses him as schizophrenia, paranoid type, in remission. . . .

He wears a back brace and testified that he cannot lift 25 pounds without pain. . . . He takes 5 mgs of Valium four times a day and Darvon. . . . He also said that he had a tumor of the cervical spine which caused visible swelling, pain in the right arm which runs down his back and which causes some distortion in his hearing. He also had black out type symptoms. . . .

Claimant himself felt he was physically unable to hold down part time employment although the doctor felt that this would be possible if he consistently took his medication. . . .

From all reports and medical evaluations, I conclude that his physical condition does not prevent him from engaging in substantial gainful activity, possibly including heavy work. He has been observed playing volleyball, baseball. . . . He recently painted his apartment which demonstrates an ability to work. However, the question is whether his emotional condition is such that he can work on a sustained basis. On balance it would appear that he is able to, and is suited to. . . . Under these circumstances I find the claimant is not disabled within the meaning of the Social Security Act.

DECISION

It is the decision of the administrative law judge that, based on the application filed January 4, 1973, the claimant is not entitled to a period of disability.

Robert D. Hoffman
administrative law judge
8 July 1975

---

establish the participation of some individuals will be difficult to obtain, and it is unlikely that all individuals who participated will ever be obtained." See Ibid., p. 202–208 for a detailed description of the obstacles encountered in trying to obtain official records on these nuclear tests.

Afterword

"Nuclear testing, by and large, has been one of the safest things that was ever done."

> —Robert Newman, Nevada test site manager, quoted in Berger, "The Ordeal of Artie Duvall," p. 23.

"No one has ever been crippled, killed, or severely maimed in a nuclear weapons test. Show me an industrial program with a better safety record."

> —Gordon Jacks, former army colonel, eighteen-year veteran of atomic testing, quoted in Berger, "The Ordeal of Artie Duvall," p. 23.

"People have got to learn to live with the facts of life, and part of the facts of life are fallout."

> —W. F. Libby, AEC commissioner, minutes from AEC meeting, 23 February 1955, quoted in Fadiman, "The Downwind People," p. 38.

CHAPTER 8

David Pyles, Lab Technician

"The motto of the management was 'Cover your ass.' And this really bugged me."

It is October, early evening. We are sitting in a small, dimly lit restaurant in downtown Buffalo, New York, drinking beer and talking about West Valley, the nuclear reprocessing plant located about thirty miles southeast of here. Dave Pyles worked in the plant as a lab technician and then lab shift supervisor from 1967 to 1972, when he resigned. He is a tall thirty-five year old, with a full, thick auburn beard. In his red- and green-checkered flannel shirt, he looks like the outdoorsman he is.

Pyles liked working at West Valley—he liked learning nuclear chemistry. It was the science that attracted him, for he had wanted to study chemistry from the time he was in high school. His family didn't have the money to send him through college.

Even though he enjoyed the work, Pyles started locking horns with Nuclear Fuel Services, the company that operated West Valley. "The place was insane, really insane. It was the worst-run place. . . ." Part of the problem was that no one seemed to have any authority or technical expertise. All the management people were "down in Rockville, Maryland, to sweet-talk the AEC."

West Valley is currently shut down. It was closed in 1976 when Nuclear Fuel Services said it could not afford to operate in the face of "changing regulations." But "they couldn't afford to operate with any regulations," Pyles says. "They bungled everything."

David Pyles

West Valley is a product of the government's campaign to make atomic energy look "peaceful." In the late 1950s the Atomic Energy Commission actively encouraged private industry to enter the nuclear field, by offering private industry its nuclear weapons technology on reprocessing. The W. R. Grace-Davison Chemical Company took advantage of this offer and set up a subsidiary company, Nuclear Fuel Services, Inc. (NFS) to construct and operate the first commercial reprocessing plant in the United States. The AEC issued a construction permit to NFS in 1963 and an operating license in 1966, and sweetened the deal by guaranteeing two years' worth of fuel to reprocess. But NFS did not make a profit during the entire time that the plant was on line —from 1967 to 1972. In fact, NFS lost "millions of dollars," according to Pyles. In 1969, when Grace-Davison could no longer use NFS as a tax write-off, it sold NFS to Getty Oil Company, which is the current owner.

Like many others, Pyles believed the work he was doing was helping people. "We were going to make the electric rates cheaper. Advance the cause of nuclear power." It took time, but eventually he started putting the pieces together. West Valley was not exactly what it was supposed to be.

Pyles started slowly. First he wrote letters complaining about the conditions. Then he joined forces with a friend in the plant. "We were the unofficial plant organizers. . . . " When he became lab shift supervisor, he refused to send his men into unsafe working areas. He protested by taking his men to work in the lunchroom instead of staying in an irradiated area. After he quit, he became active in an environmental group and worked to close the plant down permanently.

Now he works on a Sierra Club Radioactive Waste Campaign publication, Waste Paper, to inform the public about West Valley. "It doesn't get the publicity it deserves. . . . "

From West Virginia to West Valley

Pyles was born 1943 in Moundsville, West Virginia, in coal mining country. "It's down the lovely, scenic Ohio Valley, where you can't see the sky on sunny days because of the crud in the air. I'm used to crud. I've lived with crud all my life." Pyles's father worked as a turret lathe *operator and could not afford to support his son's education much beyond high school. More than anything Pyles wanted to be a chemist. For two years he managed to attend college and get some training as a lab technician. When the money ran out, Pyles had to look for a job. "There aren't many jobs in the northern part of West Virginia, unless you want to work in the coal mines, which I didn't. Unless you want to run a turret lathe, which I didn't. I'd heard that there are a lot of light chemical kinds of industries in Rochester, New York, so I went up there looking for a job, knowing that these kinds of industries needed technicians."*

First he found a job as a lab technician working for Strausenberg Laboratories, a pharmaceutical company in Rochester, New York. Next he worked in a research lab for the Rochester Button Company—"the world's biggest button company." Pyles didn't like living in Rochester. "I wanted to live in the country, but my wife, Helen—she was from West Virginia too—liked living in the city. 'Look,' I said, 'I really hate living in the city. I want to get out of the city. I want to move.' 'I'll make a deal with you,' she said. 'If you can find a job in the country, out of the city, that'll pay us enough money to live on, I'll happily move with you.'"

For eight or nine months Pyles flipped through want ads. Then he stumbled across an add for Nuclear Fuel Services. In 1967 NFS was looking for technicians with two years of college and some actual hands-on lab experience to work at its West Valley nuclear reprocessing plant, thirty-three miles southeast of Buffalo, New York. Pyles went out for an interview. "So I went out and got the story: 'Nuclear power—it's the new industry, you know, the wave of the future. Nuclear power is this wonderful thing.' It sounded good to me, so I took the job and we made the big move out to the country."

Pyles started working at West Valley in 1967.

Inside West Valley

The first time I walked into the plant was sort of interesting. Going to the lab, you'd walk up a flight of stairs, down a hallway, up three more stairs, through a door, around a hallway, down ten more stairs, on around

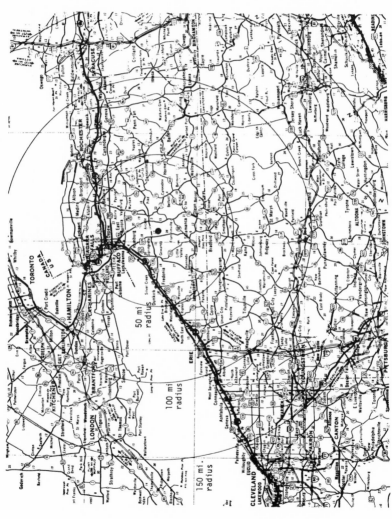

Location of Western New York Nuclear Service Center, West Valley "Environmental Report, Nuclear Fuel Services, Inc. Reprocessing Plant, West Valley, New York, as revised, 1975"

this big cell area where all this process[1] was going on inside, and then back up another flight of stairs. It was up and down. It was very strange, this layout, you know, because the whole thing was designed for the comfort of the equipment rather than the employees.

They built the whole building to minimize the distance for pumping material from one part of the process to the other. In the center of the building there are all these big concrete cells with all your chemical equipment in them that did extraction—the piping, pumps, all this stuff —in big concrete cells to shield the radiation. Around the outside of these cells were all your operating rooms—the labs, the Health and Safety Department. These were basically peripheral. It was like you walked in, and you became part of the machine.

On the ceilings all the conduits were open for the electrical stuff. All the stairs were open steel, big steel risers, attached to walls. You went up and down and zigzagged around. It's very hard for me to describe the feeling of that building.

The building was alive. It made noise. All the air for the building came in one place, and it all went out the stack. The first place it went into was the control room, the cleanest area, and then it was directed down through the laboratory areas. The laboratory areas were a little dirtier than the control room, of course, because we were handling samples.[2] Then it went into some of these other operating hallways and into the process cells.[3] This was all done just by having increasingly negative pressure on these other cells, until finally the air went in through the dirtiest process cells, and then it was all directed through a big duct—which happened to run right under the lab that I worked in—through a big scrubber[4] and out the stack. Well, the air made a lot of noise going through the building—the constant flow of this hiss, rumble of air. It was strange, but you got used to it.

1. *process:* the separation of plutonium and uranium from waste or fission products, and then the separation of uranium from plutonium.

2. *samples:* the laboratory handled *hot samples*—radioactive materials in liquid form: plutonium, uranium, and fission products. There were also *chemical samples*—the chemicals going into the plant's process to cause the separations.

3. *process cells:* shielded areas of the plant where highly radioactive material—spent nuclear fuel—was handled in large quantities as part of the plant's process.

4. *scrubber:* an area where water was sprayed through a stream of air, washing the radioactive particles out of the air before the air was released to the environment.

When a process was running, it made its own special little noises that you could hear all around. All those processes were behind thick walls. There were no definite distinct hissings and bumpings and thumpings or things like that—but just its own little rumble that it had. When the process was operating, it was like the plant was alive. It sat there and just sort of vibrated and rumbled.

I remember a couple of power outages, ventilation outages where the ventilation quit. The way the system worked was air wasn't blown into the plant, but rather air was sucked out of it.[5] Something would happen and the big fans that suck the air would shut down. All of a sudden you didn't have this noise any more. It was the strangest feeling to be in this building when it was quiet, because it was never quiet in there. And you didn't realize it wasn't quiet until all this ventilation noise quit. Also the building had no windows. That's something else. You're always working under artificial light.

A couple of times the power went off completely, and the emergency system didn't kick in the way it was supposed to. The lights went out. The ventilation went off. The whole process shut down. It was the strangest feeling in the world. I don't know if you've ever been any place that's totally black. If you had your hand against your nose, you couldn't see it.

Now, what we had to do in a situation like that is get the hell out of there, and you didn't know which direction you were going. We always kept our flashlights in these cabinets, which was really silly, because when the lights went out, you couldn't find the cabinet. It only happened to me once, being stuck in the dark with no flashlight, because after it happened once, then the first priority of the day forever after that was to go into the toolbox when your shift came on and get the flashlight out and park it on the shift supervisor's desk so it was somewhere you could find it.

With normal lighting we had it down. We could get out of the building in about thirty seconds if the evacuation alarms went off— which they did periodically for drills and so on. And it normally took about ten minutes to walk up and down to get out of there.

We were totally dependent on this crazy plant—this thing we were inside of. We had these open-faced fume hoods that we worked with

5. This was so that air contaminated with radioactive particles including plutonium was not inhaled by workers.

that were very contaminated inside. They were just basically big steel boxes with glass doors on them, sort of boxes stuck on the wall. You could close the door part way and stand outside the box and still work under it by sticking your arms through the opening. The idea is the boxes suck air in, so that any kind of experiment you're doing—working with toxic fumes or whatever, or in this case the radioactive contamination and so on—the contaminated air is always moving away from you. So you didn't have to worry about it as long as the air was sucking into them. But when the fans went off, the ventilation backed up and started blowing out of these hoods.

So the first thing that would happen when the ventilation went off is that you ran around, closing all these hoods up, sealing them with duct tape. Duct tape is this silver-looking tape a couple of inches wide. Labs all over the world are held together with duct tape. So we closed these hoods, taped them shut with duct tape.[6] The object of taping them up before we left—taping the doors shut—was that if you didn't tape them shut before you left the lab, when you came back you'd have to spend the next three days de-conning[7] the lab because of all this junk that blew out of the hoods all over the floor.

So you took this chance. I guess I felt it was a bit better to take a chance of breathing a little plutonium than cleaning the lab up later. Now that I think about it—I never thought about it in quite this light before—it seems like a pretty stupid thing to do.

Tension . . . Practical Jokes

Technicians at West Valley worked rotating shifts seven days a week. They had days off, but these usually did not coincide with weekends. Often they worked nights and slept days. This schedule made it difficult for workers at the plant to spend time with their families or to have much social life.

You do a lot of things to release the tension, very childish kinds of things. This was 1967, so I was twenty-four. The average age of the people in the plant, including all the supervision, the management, was

---

6. Taping the hoods shut required between two and three minutes, during which time air contaminated with plutonium could be breathed by workers.

7. *de-conning:* decontaminating.

twenty-six. Everybody was really young. Even the management people were fairly young. They were in their middle thirties. Working with a bunch of guys about the same age, you can have a lot of fun, play a lot of practical jokes.

For example, we found out that you could call into the PA system of the plant from outside the plant. We had all these people that we put up to calling into the plant, making their little announcements from outside to all the employees inside—girls calling in, whispering sweet nothings over the PA system.

We used to periodically firebomb the john when somebody was in it. You take acetone, which is a pretty flammable solvent, and saturate paper towels with it, and roll a lot of paper towels very loosely around the outside. You go into the john, and you light the outside paper towels with a match and roll it under the stall door while somebody's sitting in there. And before they can put it out, this six-foot ball of flame jumps up in front of them while they're on the toilet. It just lasts for a couple of seconds.

We used to have water fights in the plant. You get these nice wash bottles full of water that you can squirt around at each other. You couldn't hurt this building. It was great, you know. It was all stone, all concrete, like a pigpen. Once, a chemical operator who wasn't too well versed in how things were laid out in the lab decided he was going to get in this water fight. And he grabbed this innocuous looking bottle, wash bottle of stuff, and it happened to be full of sulfuric acid. Sulfuric acid will eat your skin off very quickly and make very bad burns. He didn't squirt anybody with it. But we did get ourselves into a state of panic periodically.

The control room of the plant was forty feet long. And there was nothing in it except a couple of desks in the middle and control panels around the walls. The control-room operators—in fits of boredom—used to race in the office chairs across the control room. And the plant had this tank of boron poison[8] that could be dumped into a dissolver[9] to stop

8. *boron:* a neutron absorber that absorbs neutrons to keep them from hitting uranium atoms. It is used to stop an uncontrolled release of neutrons.
9. *dissolver:* where the spent nuclear fuel is put after it is chopped up. Here is where nitric acid is added to dissolve the fuel. The dissolver contains uranium, plutonium, and fission products. It is a liquid process.

a reaction in case of criticality.[10] The boron was controlled by a button on the control panel. Once the boron is in the stuff, the uranium in this dissolver is useless. Amidst one of the races I remember somebody couldn't stop his chair quite soon enough and slammed into the control panel and dumped the boron into the dissolver and, you know, destroyed a million and a half dollars worth of uranium.

"We are launching a unique operation here today which I regard with pride as a symbol of imagination and foresight. . . ."

—*Governor Nelson A. Rockefeller at the groundbreaking ceremony at West Valley, 13 June 1963. Quoted in Richard Severo, "Too Hot to Handle,"* New York Times Magazine, *10 April 1977, p. 15.*

Continuous Air Monitor

It was insane. We had all these alarms. We had a continuous air monitor in the hall, outside the lab. A continuous air monitor—CAM —has two alarms on it. One's a level that says, "It's up. You can work in here for maybe forty hours before you get your maximum radiation exposure." It's nothing to panic about, but just a warning that there's particulate[11] in the air, that it's building up, that something should be done about it.

And then there's another alarm level that means "Get out of the area."

Well, the no-panic alarm went off all the time. The first couple of times we evacuated everybody from the lab and pulled an air sample. We never found anything in the air. The thing malfunctioned for a year and a half. It would just go off. Finally, we didn't even leave any more. It went off and we'd say, "Oh, it's just the CAM going off."

And we had these other basic monitoring instruments. They were

10. *criticality:* an uncontrolled nuclear reaction.
11. *particulate:* radioactive particles.

called "Cutie Pies." There were fifteen of them in the plant. The Health and Safety Department was required to have at least one all the time in its office. We were required to have at least one all the time in our lab, and there had to be at least one at all times in the control room.

We had one electronics technician who did all the repair work—and he had them all in his office! All but one were down for repairs. This guy had so much work to do. He complained he wanted another technician. He wanted some help. And they just wouldn't give him any. Finally the guy had a nervous breakdown and left. He was off for three months recuperating. When he came back, they still didn't have anybody to help him. Not only that, they had three months more work piled up for him to do. He worked for a while, but then he left again.

Using Temporary Workers

When Nuclear Fuel Services couldn't give their permanent employees any more radiation exposure, they would haul in temporary employees. Kids. A lot of them were as young as sixteen or seventeen and were lying about their age—they weren't supposed to work here if they were under eighteen. Nuclear Fuel Services paid them $3.85 an hour in 1970 and guaranteed them half a day's pay.

These guys sat in the lunchroom until they were called to do a little cleanup job. The health and safety technician would come and get them. They would suit them up in their coveralls, their plastic gloves and suits and so on, and send them in. They were told, "Scrub that bolt, turn that nut—whatever, until we tell you to come out."

The health and safety technician knew how much radiation exposure was in the area, so he timed these guys and signaled them to come out whenever their time was up. They were told nothing about radiation hazards.

I used to talk to the kids a lot in the lunchroom. I'd tell them to go home, that they were crazy to go in there.

"Here you are, getting three months' worth of radiation exposure in three or four minutes."

"We need the money," they said. "It's nice money. Where else can we go where we can work for five minutes and get paid for four hours?"

Some of them were from Buffalo, but most were just kids from the area. There are very few families right now in the three or four towns that surround the Nuclear Fuel Services' site that didn't have somebody who worked at the plant as a temporary employee at one time or another.

Temporary workers—also called "jumpers"—are frequently brought into a nuclear plant when there is a shutdown for routine maintenance or refueling. Consolidated Edison, for example, had to bring 1,700 welders into Indian Point-1 during one pipe failure because each worker could only work a few minutes before receiving his maximum radiation dose for a three-to six-month period.[12] At West Valley there were 180 full-time employees and 1,400 part-time employees between 1967 and 1972. The temporary workers were mostly teenagers bused in from manpower programs in nearby Buffalo. They were "not informed of the hazards of their work, nor given safety training, but were placed in highly contaminated areas which regular plant employees could not afford to work in without using up their yearly permissible dosage."[13] The temporary workers received as much as three thousand millirems in fifteen minutes. "One guy would go in, turn a screw a quarter of a turn, then rush out. It was the most callous use of human beings since the slave trade."[14] Leukemia, spontaneous abortions, and birth defects have occurred in the families of these temporary nuclear workers.[15]

Security: Tools, Tanks, Plutonium

People used to take a lot of tools home from the plant. There was a warehouse outside it, loaded with tools. Nuclear Fuel Services figured it was cheaper to throw away hand tools, wrenches, screw drivers, and the like after you'd done a hot[16] job with them, than it was to de-con

12. Helen Caldicott, *Nuclear Madness: What You Can Do* (Brookline, Massachusetts, Autumn Press, 1978), p. 49.

13. *Honicker vs. Hendrie: A Lawsuit to End Atomic Power* (Summertown, Tennessee: The Book Publishing Company, 1978), p. 88.

14. Dr. Irwin D. J. Bross, Roswell Memorial Park Cancer Institute, quoted in *Honicker vs. Hendrie*, p. 88.

15. Robert Gillette, "Transient Nuclear Workers: A Special Case for Standards," *Science,* October 1974, pp. 125–127.

16. *hot:* radioactive.

the tools and use them again. So a lot of people came to have a hot tool box. They would go in, do a job, and keep de-conning their hot tools, using them over and over again. Then they'd check new tools out of the warehouse and take them home.

A few people—one person in particular—used to take anything out of the plant. He didn't care where they came from. He took them and sold them at a local farm auction. So somewhere around western New York there must be a lot of hot tools being used.

Plant security was zero. One of my friends had a little farm, and wanted to get into cheese making. To make cheese you need all stainless steel equipment. So he went to one of the maintenance men and said, "Hey, you know, there's some nice quarter-inch steel down in the maintenance shop. Why don't you weld me up a tank this size by this size by this size?" Which the maintenance man did. But my friend didn't know how to get it into his car, because this tank was big as a bed, huge. So he called the security guard and he said, "Hey, I've got this tank down here. How about bringing a pickup truck down and loading it on there, and put it on my car for me?"

So the guard did! I can only remember twice when they looked in lunchboxes to see what people were taking out of the plant. They could have saved forty thousand dollars a year on tools by checking lunchboxes.

Supervisory personnel drove in the plant and parked inside. Others parked outside. They only checked the trunks of the supervisors' cars and basically they opened the trunk and closed it, never looked in. You could take out tons of stuff.

We used to talk about what it would be like to steal plutonium. Easy. The plutonium we had was in liquid form, and we could've put it in a stainless steel thermos bottle and walked right out of the plant with it. You could've taken a little bit every day for however long, and nobody would've found it.

It would be easy because it was real clean. Most of the radiation from plutonium is alpha radiation. You can shield alpha radiation with a piece of paper. As long as it's external to your body, as long as you don't get it inside you, alpha radiation doesn't hurt you. You can even handle plutonium, hold it in your hands. You might want to wear gloves, so you don't contaminate your fingers and lick them later. But you've got how many layers of dead skin on the outside of your body—seven, ten layers of dead skin—which is plenty of shielding for this radiation. We used to talk about it, plot how we would take it out, what container we would use, which guard would be on security when we did it—that sort of thing. You could carry the stuff out in a thermos. Drive to the Canadian border and take it across. The only people they check are people that look long-haired and weird. Even if they did check you, you'd say, "I've got a thermos full of coffee in my car." Big deal. You could smuggle it out as anything. You could smuggle it out in a shipment of something else, because they don't check for radiation.

In order for a lot of plutonium to get moved out of the United States, there might have to be an agreement between some pretty powerful people. A multinational corporation says to some country that wants the bomb, "I'll get it for you." Then these corporate people say, "Okay, we have some friends at a plutonium handling company who can do the work. They can repackage plutonium, rehandle the material, even line a briefcase with it. So you don't have to worry about some sloppy person contaminating half the world and leaving a trail. Our friends will package it up very neatly. They'll handle it very well."

In fact, there was a lot of plutonium missing from Nuclear Fuel Services at West Valley. About four thousand grams—eight pounds. It takes only ten pounds to make an atomic bomb. It makes me nervous thinking about it. A lot of people could have made a lot of money off of Nuclear Fuel Services. In fact, I believe a lot of people did.

Learning How It Works

During my first two years at West Valley I really enjoyed learning all the chemistry involved in nuclear things. I learned how to analyze the various chemicals used in reprocessing. Our job was to take samples, analyze what was in them, and let the Operations Department know whether the plant was running right or not. "Yes, indeed, the uranium is separating from the plutonium." Or, "Half the plutonium is coming over into what should be all uranium"—or whatever.

"If You Don't Like It Here . . . "

The nuclear fuel cycle involves mining uranium and enriching it so that it is fissionable in nuclear reactors. The enriched uranium is formed into small pellets which are then placed into twelve-to-fourteen-foot long metal fuel rods which are packed into the center or "core" of a nuclear reactor where fission takes place. The nuclei of uranium-235 atoms split apart into fragments or fission products, releasing heat which is then used to produce electricity. As these uranium-235 atoms split apart, the fuel rods get used up or "spent." Every year a nuclear reactor must be closed down so that a third of these spent fuel rods can be replaced. The spent fuel is intensely radioactive. A few seconds of exposure without shielding would be lethal. These spent fuel rods still contain some fissionable uranium as well as some plutonium. A reprocessing plant is designed to retrieve the usable portion of uranium and plutonium left in spent fuel rods. A chemical process is used first to separate the waste products from the uranium and plutonium, and then the uranium and plutonium from each other. This is a difficult and dangerous operation because of the intense radiation. Workers at West Valley found it hard to avoid contamination.

One time the lunchroom got contaminated.[17] This is before I was a lab supervisor. I forget who was in charge of cleaning up the lunchroom, but it wasn't lab people, I know that. The de-con consists of washing down the walls and the fronts of the vending machines, and even washing out the microwave oven we used to heat things in. But nowhere did the de-con have anything to do with taking the stuff that was in the vending machines out and throwing it away. I mean, there's a pretty good chance that this contamination would get in the vending machines, right?

One guy in the plant—I forget the kid's name—was a lab person. "I'll put up with a lot around here," he said, "but the first time I have to put shoe covers on at the gate, I'm going to quit."

It's one thing to put shoe covers on inside the building, you know, to keep from tracking things around, but he really didn't think the stuff should be out on the lawn. We all took it as a joke until we had an

---

17. The lunchroom was contaminated on 11 June 1968. Gyorgy, *No Nukes,* p. 51.

incident where a filter in the air system blew out the stack.[18] Very strange. It just blew out. A bunch of us were sitting in the lunchroom —in June—and all of a sudden it looked like snow was coming down, just in front of the lunchroom. All these little pieces of paper from the filter. Luckily the wind wasn't blowing too hard, so it stayed on the plant site. The filter paper was pretty radioactive. It had been filtering all the radioactive dust from inside the hot cells,[19] all the blast air going out.

Soon we had guys out there with brooms—with Geiger counters on the bottoms of broom handles and little nails on the bottoms of broom handles, like the park paper-picker-uppers, you know, checking around. If the Geiger counter indicated that they were looking at something hot, they stabbed it with a nail and stuck it in the bag. You know, you're cleaning up the yard at this point.

Well, this kid with the thing about the shoes comes into work, and we're issuing shoe covers at the gate. He put on his shoe covers, and walked in, but instead of going into the locker room like he ordinarily would have, he went around the corner, then upstairs to the laboratory, the analytical department, and told the guy he could take the job and shove it up his ass. Then he went back down, went back out the gate, took off his shoe covers, went home, and we never saw him again.

If workers at West Valley complained about working conditions in the plant, they were told, "If you don't like how it's run here, quit. Go someplace else." They were told that five other workers were waiting to take their job because it paid so well. In 1971 NFS was paying technicians about eleven thousand a year. Pyles thought this was pretty good pay. Nevertheless, he did complain. "I complained to my supervisor, to various management people, and even to the plant manager, if things really bugged me. I wrote letters to whoever I thought was in charge of things."

Quite a few people shared his concern, but they were reluctant to

18. This was a HEPA Filter (High Efficiency Particulate Air Filter) which was sucked into an exhaust fan and out the stack, spewing shredded radioactive material around. See *Honicker vs. Hendrie*, p. 88.

19. *hot cell:* an area approximately six feet by six feet, and seven feet high, in which highly radioactive plutonium, uranium, and fission products could be handled remotely by manipulators. They are heavily shielded areas where contaminated materials are handled. The lab had hot cells.

criticize how things were being done because they didn't want to lose their jobs. "The operators[20] didn't want to complain because they were right out of high school. The training they had at West Valley wouldn't earn them any money anywhere else, so they were sort of stuck in their jobs." The operators worked in the Operations Department and usually made less money than the lab technicians. Most of them were local people who did not want to move out of the area. "The lab people on the other hand were mostly imported people. My friend Ralph and I— the "dynamic duo" as far as complaining went—were the unofficial plant organizers—definitely complainers."

"They Left Certain Safety Equipment Out of West Valley . . . "

We had reason to complain. When the plant was built, very good technology existed for remote decontamination of hot cells. They'd used the remote decontamination method in Hanford.[21] And they were using it in the reprocessing plant at La Hague in France which was being built at the same time as West Valley.

The Nuclear Fuel Services plant at West Valley was designed like the plant at Hanford. The basic design was the same—the dissolvers and the columns where the actual separations took place and the process equipment were about the same. But in Hanford they had remote decontamination equipment. All their radioactive areas—process cells, hot cells, analytical cells—could be *remotely* decontaminated. But at West Valley *people* had to go in to do the decontamination. The employees would get all this extra radiation exposure that they wouldn't need to get if the remote operating equipment had been in there.

Remote de-con equipment had been designed into NFS at West Valley.[22] I saw the blueprints. But Nuclear Fuel Services got by without putting this equipment into the plant. And because of that, NFS gave their employees twice the radiation exposure of any other reprocessing plant in the world.

20. *operators:* the chemical operators did the actual process work. Most were high school graduates under twenty-five years of age.

21. *Hanford:* U.S. military reservation at Hanford, Washington.

22. Nuclear Fuel Services, Inc. (NFS) operated West Valley. The Bechtel Corporation designed the plant. Bechtel dominates the nuclear engineering and construction industry.

It is boasted by the nuclear industry that because spent fuel is so highly radioactive, all work in a reprocessing plant is done by remote control behind heavy shielding. But the Department of Energy acknowledged in a 1978 study that Nuclear Fuel Services, West Valley, did not have the equipment needed for remote decontamination of many areas. "Dismantlement was not a consideration during the design of this plant," the report says, "and provisions were not included for remote decontamination of many areas. As a result, it may be impossible to decontaminate some of the cell areas without exposing workers to excessive radiation."[23]

Working with Radioactive Samples

The hot cells in our lab were about six feet by six feet and seven or eight feet high. They had a window to look through the front of them, two manipulators sticking inside of them that copied the movements of your hands on the inside through the wall, and a big pan that we worked on. When you're using clumsy manipulators to draw a little bit of liquid up to a little line in a pipette and trying to see six feet away, you definitely lose a lot of accuracy.

So we didn't like to run samples[24] in the hot cells. We much preferred to run them in the lab. But first we had to check them with monitoring instruments to see how radioactive they were. If they were above a certain limit—and that limit varied at the whim of the person, how much of a hurry he was in—they couldn't be brought out of the hot cell. If they were within a limit, one that you set, then you could carry them in, and run them in the hood in the lab.

We had a system for bringing samples out of these hot cells to monitor and check on them. You had this transfer drawer which slides on a big screw next to one of the hot cells. If you followed standard operating procedure, you cranked this drawer, which was very heavy, all the way to the front to bring out the sample. It took—I'll never forget

23. U.S. Department of Energy, *Western New York Nuclear Service Center Study: Final Report for Public Comment*, TID-28905-1, Washington, D.C., November 1978, p. 27.
24. *Samples:* see note 2, p. 211.

how many—180 turns on this crank from front to back. Then you put a plastic bag in the drawer, cranked it all the way back, reached in with the manipulators, picked up the sample, dropped it in the plastic bag, put the bag back in the drawer, cranked the drawer back out again— and this was *before* you could even monitor it, to see if it was low enough in radiation to bring it out.

We had a system to save time. Air flowed into the cells, which meant you had great air flow in there. Since all we were doing was putting in a plastic bag, we would crack open the door and let the air suck the plastic bag into the cell. Then we would catch the bag with the manipulator—which was a *very* difficult thing to do. It took a lot of practice to catch anything with one of those stupid manipulators, be- cause the plastic bags were moving pretty fast when they shot back through there. Then we'd load the sample in the bag, and reach around and monitor the radiation level. This took about a minute and a half as opposed to ten minutes.

This system caused trouble because a lot of times we missed with the plastic bags. The air would suck the plastic bags over and down under the pan that we worked on. Besides the plastic bags, there were also needles[25] that got dropped under this pan.

Unannounced Inspection

Manny—my supervisor—and I were working in the lab one day when we were told the hot cells had to be cleaned. There was going to be an "unannounced inspection" the next day.

Manny said, "My supervisor told me to clean the cells. I'm going to go in and do it."

The procedure always called for two people to make an entry into a hot cell, one person to be there in case the other one has trouble. But

25. *needles:* "hypodermiclike needles which were used to transfer plutonium samples from one bottle to another. When these needles got dull and had to be replaced, they were sometimes changed in the same hot cell where the lab technicians ran their samples. Every now and then one of the needles was accidentally dropped underneath the pan where the technicians worked. These needles were among the most radioactive instru- ments in the plant. Many things ended up falling down underneath this pan, so the hot cell had to be cleaned out periodically"—Pyles.

there were only two of us working in the lab, and we had a lot of samples coming in, so both of us couldn't do it. Manny was going to go in and do it by himself. There was also a state law that said if anybody's working in a lab, two people must be there in the lab in case one gets in trouble. So we were breaking two state laws by him going into the hot cells while I stayed in the lab. Anyway, Manny insisted. Between the back of the hot cells and where I was there was a PA sort of thing.

"Turn it up loud," Manny said. "If I have any trouble, I'll yell, and you can get in there."

Of course, I wasn't suited up to go in, but I would've probably gone in anyway. I made sure he brought me an extra air mask, and I would've gone in in my regular coveralls and air mask. He was all suited up, in his four pairs of coveralls, all his gloves and booties, and I was wearing one pair of coveralls, which is what we normally wore in the lab.

So he went back to do the job, and I was merrily running samples. He'd only been in there for about ten minutes when he came out, staring at his hand. I looked at his hand. It was all bloody! Inside one of the gloves. He still had the inside glove on. He pulled off his glove.

"I ran a damn needle through my finger."

He'd been scooping up all the plastic bags and cleaning the area under the pan when he jammed one of those needles through his finger.

So we did the routine thing that we were supposed to do in this case. Take a piece of filter paper, smear some of the blood on the filter paper and count it, or take it to the Health and Safety Department to count it to see if there's radioactive material being washed out of this puncture. So we did that. Took it to health and safety. And in the meantime— because we never really trusted health and safety's numbers—we counted another smear on our instruments upstairs. And they matched up, basically, saying there was nothing wrong. It was fine.

So Manny gave up on cleaning the cell for the day. After the flak I'd given him about him not going in, he certainly wasn't going to ask me to go in. He took a shower, got back into his normal work clothes, and we ran samples for two or three hours until lunch. Outside the lunch-room was a hand and foot counter. You stick your hands or the soles of your feet in and check for radiation. Manny got about four feet from this hand and foot counter and it went off. The hand counters went off. The foot counters went off. You know, everything went off!

Well, it was quite obvious that there was something in Manny's finger. This was the only place that he could have gotten that much radiation. So all hell broke loose. I panicked and rushed Manny up to the Health and Safety Department. I got one of the health and safety technicians. He called the health and safety manager. In the meantime, they set up the chest counter where you lie down and this instrument counts radiation coming off your body. The idea of using a chest counter is, if you got blood contamination it'll be pumping through your heart, so the chest counter will pick it up.

Manny is on the chest counter, and the head of the Health and Safety Department is there. He calls the company doctor to come. Meanwhile we send two operators into the hot cell to find the needle. I don't know why we wanted it. All part of the panic, right?

So everybody was there. To do the chest count, they also have to have somebody else there, someone roughly the same size.[26] Manny was a pretty small guy, and the only person we could find who was close to Manny's size was the security guard. So we called him to come up for a chest count, and he locks the chain on the gate, brings his keys with him, and stretches out on the table next to Manny. The company doctor is outside. He wants to get in.

"This is Dr. Rothschild. Somebody let me in," he calls in on the phone outside. He has this German accent. "I'm out here. I've been waiting out here ten minutes! There's nobody here to let me in!"

The health and safety technician has a problem. He says, "Well, you can't send the guard down. He's on the chest counter. We're doing this background. The background can change any minute if we stop and start over again."

The guard, of course, following the great standard operating procedure, has refused to give the health and safety technician his keys to unlock the gate for the doctor.

"I can't give this guy my keys. I can't."

By now the doctor's been waiting outside for twenty minutes.

We always kept a pair of bolt cutters around, and the doctor found the bolt cutters, cut the chain locking the gate, and let himself in.

---

26. To do a chest count you need to know how many counts are coming from the source being counted and how many are coming from sources other than the one being counted. You place an object of approximately the same volume and density on the counting machine. The background radiation count is then subtracted from the gross sample count.

That upset the guard. When Rothschild finally gets up there, he decides there is definitely something in Manny's finger because if you get a Geiger counter four feet away from it, the Geiger goes crazy. He decides he's going to cut the thing out.

They pack Manny up and take him to the hospital. And they take an instrument called a Class Master with them, which is a Geiger counter kind of thing, except that it's a big sort of plug-in model Geiger counter. It's got a five- by seven-inch speaker in the top of it to make the clicking noise, and a needle on the front that spans about a foot across the front of this dial. It's a really big needle. And they're going to use this as they cut away at Manny's finger to check and make sure that they're getting the radioactive stuff out—check each little piece that they take out.

We have always been told that the health and safety and the local hospital's people[27] are well trained to take care of emergencies, because this is the place you're supposed to go. And if somebody is exposed to radiation, we have these big rules. You get different color tags for people's toes, depending on whether they're contaminated or not—you know, if they're dead or unconscious. Red tags, green tags, and yellow tags to put on people's toes. They were heading out, and I was harassing Manny about getting the right colored tag for his toe. Then I went back to the lab to run samples.

Later I found out how they took him over. Plug in this Class Master. Get it all set. Start cutting away. And the emergency staff is all there ready to help. Until they get the first piece of hot flesh out of Manny's finger.

This Class Master went off. And this thing is loud. It's like having a radio turned up too loud when it goes off. You hear this horrendous clicking.

And everybody left. The whole emergency room staff just walked right out of the room. They refused to stay in there. Except for the doctor and the head of Health and Safety Department who worked on Manny's finger and cut out this thing.

We did find the needle, finally. And the thing was so hot, we couldn't read it on any of the instruments we had. We had to get what we called a "pig," basically a gallon paint can with a little half-pint paint can inside, with lead around, and a big lead plug in the top that you could

27. Bertrand Chaffee Hospital in Springville, New York.

put things into and shield this radiation. We put the needle in the pig and brought it out. Still we had no instruments in the plant that could read it. A couple of monitors would read fifty rems an hour. And this was somewhere well beyond fifty rems an hour. We didn't normally handle anything over three rems. Anything at fifty rems, we didn't need anything to read—because when it was that hot, we left it where it was and got away.

We did scrape a little of this stuff off the needle on the outside, and we know that most of the stuff on the needle was plutonium, plus the mixed fission products that gave it all the high gamma radiation. There was also a lot of alpha radiation, which was plutonium.

Manny's got plutonium lodged in his bones. What he's got is radiation coming from inside his body—internal exposure from the stuff that washed off this needle, a very intense dose to his blood and to his bones. Because of this material, he will forever get radiation from internal sources, from this plutonium floating around inside him.

I mean, this wasn't much of a cut on Manny's finger. It wasn't like the door had slammed shut and chopped his foot off, or something like that. It was just a little nick, a little needle puncture. We hadn't thought about how easy it was for somebody to get hurt really badly in there. Manny was twenty-six.

It was things like that that led me to wonder whether I should continue working at West Valley. The whole thing was insane, you know.[28]

"Fears of accidents in the reprocessing plants have little foundation. The careful control required to maintain the efficiency of the process minimizes the probability of an accident."

> —William P. Bebbington, "The Reprocessing of Nuclear Fuels," Scientific American, *December 1976, p. 110.*

---

28. This incident occurred on 14 April 1968. Inspection records say "the wound was surgically laid open and the tissue excised." According to the *New York Times* no records were kept after the incident as to where the worker went or what the state is of his current health. Severo, "Too Hot to Handle," p. 18.

There are several types of radiation. Gamma radiation is a very high energy form of electromagnetic energy emitted by many radioactive substances including cesium-137 and iodine-131. It is extremely penetrating; gamma rays can travel hundreds of feet in the air and pass through anything except heavy lead shielding. X-rays are very similar to gamma rays except lower in energy. Beta radiation consists of very high energy electrons emitted by radioactive substances such as cesium-137 and iodine-131 as well as substances that do not emit gamma such as strontium-90. The beta particles are much less penetrating than gamma or X-ray but produce more damage in a smaller space. Alpha radiation is emitted by radioactive substances such as plutonium-239 and uranium-235. Alpha particles are the least penetrating and cannot pass through paper or human skin. It is important to realize, however, that the range of the particle is not the crucial factor once the radioactive substance has been ingested or inhaled since this brings the source of radiation into intimate contact with the vulnerable tissue. For example, when substances which release alpha particles are taken into the body, they intensely irradiate the cells in their immediate vicinity and are extremely carcinogenic.

Becoming a Lab Shift Supervisor: 1970

I became a laboratory shift supervisor a year and a half before I left. A man above me was the lab supervisor, and his basic role was to make sure the shift crew got its work done, to coordinate the work, and split it in some equitable way among the four shifts.

Right away I got into situations like him coming down and saying, "The hot cells have to be cleaned tonight." The same situation Manny was in when he punctured his finger. "The hot cells have to be cleaned. Somebody's got to do it. There's going to be an inspection. You get them cleaned at all costs."

I couldn't have my guys do that. I couldn't put myself or any of my people in that situation. But this was the routine. "This gets done at all costs."

The first time they asked me to do a job like that, it was a drain pipe with a leak in it under one of our fume hoods. The fume hoods had to be cleaned out, and I was told to have one of my guys do it. We didn't have any provisions for supplied air[29] close to the lab, so I was hunting around for air lines that I could run from down the hall somewhere to get supplied air into this guy, so he could work under the hood and not have to breathe the contamination in there.

We had the whole side of the lab shut off because of this leaky pipe. We had taken the equipment that was normally there and moved it to the hoods on the other side. So this made it very crowded and very difficult to run samples.

Ed, my supervisor, was saying, "You don't have time to futz around with this air business."

So I told him, "Look, if he's going to go in there, he's going in with supplied air or else I'm not sending him in."

I mean, I'm getting all this about wasting my time getting supplied air for this guy when "All he's got to do is clean out the area under the hood!" Had it been a room he had to walk into, he would've had to wear four pairs of coveralls, supplied air, seventeen dozen pairs of gloves. But just because he only had to stick his head in, I was told we didn't need to take these precautions.

"Well," he said, "you'd better send him in."

I told him I wasn't sending anybody in. He could clean it himself. Which he did. He went in there with a canister mask, without supplied air, and cleaned it. The filters in a canister mask aren't very good. A lot of very fine particles get through them. It took him half an hour to clean up. He had to take up a bunch of shelves, so a plumber could get in there and repair the leak.

Ed was the kind of guy that would do it. He wouldn't send anybody any place he wouldn't go himself, but he was such a blithering idiot that he'd go anywhere himself.

The Children

Nuclear workers whose jobs involve contact with radioactive materials are required to check themselves for contamination on the way out of the plant. This is to prevent contamination being carried outside the nuclear facility. For this reason hand and foot counters were stationed

---

29. *supplied air:* clean air brought in for a worker in a contaminated area.

*at the door of West Valley, but these instruments measured only beta
and gamma radiation, not alpha. Plutonium is an alpha emitter. "The
instrument we had to measure alpha radiation never worked quite right,
so about half the time we just skipped it."*

*One day Pyles left the plant after a four-to-midnight shift and went
home. Helen was a nurse, working nights, and she had left their two
children, aged one and two, with a babysitter. When Pyles arrived home,
the children were in bed. He sent the babysitter home and went to sleep.*

About three o'clock in the morning I got a call. They had found an
alpha contamination all over the lab. They thought I might come in and
have myself checked out.

"You know, it's three o'clock in the morning," I told them. "I got
kids home in bed. You can't get a babysitter now. You can't go off and
leave little kids in bed. Send the health and safety technician here."

After a big argument a health and safety technician did come out, to
check me with a monitoring instrument, and he found plutonium
smeared on the inside of my arm. We go scrub it off my arm, down my
bathroom sink, down the drain. And we start checking out other things.
At this point it was on my robe, because I'd put my bathrobe on, it was
on my bedsheets, on my pillow. I always sleep with my arm under the
pillow.

The thing that got me thinking more about it than anything was my
luck—I was really lucky that I hadn't handled my kids. They could bury
my robe and my bedsheets, you know. I didn't want to bury my kids.
All I'd done was *looked* in their room. If they'd been up—had it been
a day shift—I'd have been playing with them for a while. I would've had
it all over them.

"The Main Reason I Left" . . . the Vent Duct

A vent duct ran under our lab, and this vent duct was probably the
main reason I left there finally. This duct was the last place the air passed
along in the whole plant before it went through the scrubbers that
scrubbed out most of the radioactive dust and then through the filters
and out the stack. A lot of the dust settled out in this duct, and it got
very hot. I didn't know this vent duct ran right under our lab.

Everyday we did a survey of the lab to check radiation levels. We went around with a radiation monitor. Aimed the thing, and if there was a hot spot, we'd clean it up. If it was a spill, we'd scrub it up with paper towels, gloves, whatever. Take the material and throw it in the waste box, and it would go off to low-level-waste burial grounds every day.

One day the lab technician on my shift says, "Hey, look at this. This is hot."

It was down along the front of the fume hood areas. First thing we did was run a piece of rope across that side of the lab, so nobody would wander back in there. If there's a spill, it could be tracked all over the place. We don't know what it is. We think, Okay, there's something hot in there. A leak. So we roped off the lab.

A crew of technicians went down and changed clothes. Basically, what you wear when you make an entry into a hot cell and what you wear normally is about the same thing. You just wear more of it. We normally worked in blue coveralls. We made entries in two or three pairs of white coveralls. The only reason they were a different color was so they could tell them apart when it came to laundry. So then the technicians came back up and started digging around in the cabinets. Opened up the doors, kneeled down, checked out the area with the radiation monitor. There wasn't a whole lot of radiation exposure. We had a lot of solvents and things stored under the cabinets. They started pulling out bottles. There was a shelf under there, so they had to take out a bunch of screws and take this panel off underneath to see the floor. We were looking for a leak, maybe a drain leak.

I was just doing paper work while they were trying to find the hot spot. It was no big deal. Just a routine hot spot. They did a very thorough smear survey. You take a piece of filter paper and you smear it across an area. Then, if it's contaminated, this will pick up on the paper, and you can take it and put it in the counter. So they smeared every surface —the whole area. There was no smearable radiation, no spills. And the monitor was reading twenty-five millirems. Which is enough that there should have been some counts. It had to be coming through the floor.

So I went downstairs with the radiation monitor, to the floor below, right under our lab. And we could read it then, coming down through the ceiling. We didn't have to look real far because somebody in the Operations Department had already posted it as a Radiation Area. Nobody had told us about it, and nobody had come upstairs to check it out from up above. Something was between the concrete ceiling of the floor above and the concrete floor of the lab.

So I went to my supervisor. "You know, there is something in there. It's hot. It's certainly not in the lab. It's shining both ways.[30] It's down in the lower extraction aisle"—which was the name of the aisle below us. He went down and checked the blueprints to see what ran between these two floors, and came back and said, "It's the vent duct."

It happened to be at the end of the shift, near shift-change time. So there was the next shift supervisor and me and my supervisor. We got into this long discussion of what to do about this vent duct and how to protect ourselves from it. A first suggestion was to put some lead on the floor. He was happy with that idea—you know, to put lead on the floor.

"That's a good idea," I said, "but don't you think the duct should be cleaned?"

Here it is shining down below where people have to work, shining up above where people have to work.

"Yeah, it seems like a reasonable idea," he said. "I should check it out."

But it was an evening shift, and nobody was around to check it. Midnight shift was coming on. So my supervisor said the next day he would deal with it. There was nothing he or any of us could do to clean it. The idea was to play the chain of command routine and go to the analytical manager who would go to the production manager and the plant manager. Deal with it from on high. And you know, nothing came back for two or three weeks. Meanwhile we were getting twenty-five to thirty millirems shining up through the floor.

Cleaning the vent duct wouldn't have been very complex. Basically they would've had to shut the plant down to get the air pressure out of this duct, and then open some panels to get to the duct—get up above it—then take hoses and just flush it out with water. But it would have taken a long time because once the plant shuts down, it is very difficult to start up again. It's like having a very old car. As long as you keep it running, it's all right. But don't dare turn it off because it might take you hours to get it started again. Getting the process lined out and operating right wasted a whole length of time. Plutonium would be where uranium's supposed to be. Uranium where waste products are

30. *Shining both ways:* giving off radiation in both directions.

supposed to be. And this was the whole logic. That it took twenty-four hours. That the plant had to be shut down for twenty-four hours. Twelve hours to de-con the pipe and twelve hours to start it up again, cycle the material back through the plant again to get it where it belongs. They just didn't want to do that.

So they said, "You know, it costs us a couple of thousand dollars an hour to have this plant shut down. We don't want to spent forty-eight thousand dollars to clean this duct."

That came back down from the plant manager. So we put lead on the floor. Maybe it was just a piece of something hot that would eventually blow away. But it never did. These sheets of lead were very soft metal. You could bend them. They were an eighth of an inch thick, so we just laid them down on the floor. We took our glorious duct tape that we used for everything. Taped down all the corners. Took hammers and pounded all the corners down so you didn't have them sticking up, and taped all these edges.

So now we were walking around on lead, which isn't the greatest thing in the world. You're not only getting radiation exposure, but you're also kicking lead dust into the air when you walk around on it and getting lead poisoning. We started writing letters to the managers saying, "You've got to get something done." I got the other shift supervisors writing letters. That way they were on record. Put it on their daily reports.

Now only four or five millirems were coming up. Not a whole lot. Enough that our feet were probably getting four or five millirems. The lead cut it pretty well down. Finally the radiation came back up again. We took the survey and one day it was twenty-five. Next day we got a reading of thirty-two. Next day maybe we only got twenty-two. But the average was going up. Very slowly building. We kept writing letters and nothing ever got done. It was always the same story. "If you don't like it, quit."

We put more lead down. First we put down an eighth of an inch. Then we added more to that, then more. All the time, of course, this duct was getting hotter.

One day we had one hundred millirems an hour coming up through the lab floor! Now, you know, the legal limit is five rems a year. This means if you work forty hours a week at one hundred millirems an hour, you get four-fifths of your annual radiation exposure in a *week*.

So I went to the lab manager and said, "Look, we're not going to stay in the lab. I'll have my guys run samples, but I'm not going to have them do anything else in there."

The lab manager looked at me like he had never had anybody come to him and say, "I refuse to go where you tell me to go."

We moved to the lunchroom. That didn't help much but it did get us more lead, which took the radiation back down. Then we went back to the lab for a while. By now we had almost three-quarters of an inch of lead on the floor. That's a lot of weight, even spread over the whole floor of the lab. We were really worried the floor wouldn't hold the lead if we kept putting it down.

And we also started telling our boss, that if we put it any deeper, we wouldn't be able to get the doors of our cabinets open. We told him the benches were getting too low, that we had to get down on our knees to work. We were just giving him all these insane sob stories.

But it kept getting hotter. I decided we couldn't stay in the lab. We were getting too much radiation exposure. It had been reading in a range of one hundred millirems an hour for months!

I was the first lab supervisor to move my crew out of the lab. The other lab supervisors followed. We were in the lab only when we had samples to run. We'd do all our paperwork and everything else in the lunchroom. Of course, we got flak.

Our answer was, "Clean the vent duct, we won't hang out in the lunchroom."

And the company always said, "We can't. We'd have to shut the plant down. It costs a lot of money to clean the duct, you know."

We complained about it for a year.

In March of 1972 Nuclear Fuel Servies announced a routine shutdown. Nobody knew that this was going to be their shutdown for expansion of the plant, or any extended shutdown, except the management. So we started getting on them again.

"The plant's shut down. Now let's clean the vent duct. We'd like to be able to work in the lab again. We're losing all our friends that are operators because we have to spend all our time in the lunchroom, and they won't even talk to us any more because they think we don't do anything except sit there drinking coffee all day."

So June rolled around. That's when I quit. June 2, 1972.

It was still reading one hundred millirems an hour through the lab floors. It was two months, three months. We'd been complaining about it for a year and a half.

I left because of this radiation exposure. The first year I worked there I got two rems radiation exposure. Second year I worked there I got two rems. Third year I got four. But the last year I worked there I got seven! It was just ridiculous. I was definitely better at handling my samples. I could run samples, get them out of the way quicker—the extra radiation exposure wasn't from the samples I was handling.

So I handed in my resignation. I told them, due to the increasing radiation hazard I felt compelled to submit my resignation.

The last I heard about the vent duct was a couple of years later, when I was poring over old AEC reports. I discovered that in December that same year—1972—the AEC cited Nuclear Fuel Services for having the vent duct under the shift office in the lab. It was still reading over one hundred millirems an hour.[31]

The company had been shut down for nine months and they still hadn't spent the twenty-four hours it took to clean this thing up.

Discovering the Lie: It's Plutonium, Not Power

You work in a place, the place is small enough. You talk to managers. You find out what's going on. One person gets half the story. Another person gets half the story, and you just start putting it all together. I put some more of it together later, after I left West Valley.

When I took the job, they told me what I would be doing. "What the plant does is reprocess[32] spent fuel[33] from nuclear power reactors. The whole idea is, of course, to stretch the amount of uranium, to be able to use it longer, for electricity. If you don't reprocess uranium, you can't use it again. You would waste 80 percent of the uranium that goes

31. "Interim Safety Evaluation I, Nuclear Fuel Services, Inc., and NYS Energy Research and Development Authority, Western New York Service Center," Docket No. 50-201, August 1977, Table 3-2. Radiation levels in support areas, October 1976, were reading 150 millirems in the vent duct near the spectrographic lab where Pyles worked. In *Western New York Nuclear Service Center Study: Companion Report,* TID-28905-2, Washington, D.C., November 1978, pp. 3–9.

32. *reprocess:* spent fuel arrives, is cut up into small pieces, and dissolved in nitric acid, so that uranium and plutonium (the fissionable materials) can be removed and used again. The only reprocessing plants in commercial operation at this time are the large French plant in La Hague and a small plant in Windscale, England. Gyorgy, *No Nukes,* p. 50.

33. *spent fuel:* each spent fuel rod contains about .6 percent plutonium and .8 percent usable uranium-235. Nuclear fuel rods are used up, or "spent," when about two-thirds of the uranium-235 atoms are gone.

into a reactor if you didn't reprocess it. It would have to be tossed away."

They laid out these nice beautiful diagrams of the fuel cycle. "This place fits here. This is what it does. West Valley is a commercial reprocessing plant for the nuclear power industry. It's going to make your electric rates cheaper. It's going to help nuclear power." And that would have been a good explanation, had the plant been operating on mostly commercial fuel.[34]

Although this place was touted as a commercial plant, we knew that a lot of the stuff coming in—the spent nuclear fuel—was from a government reactor in Hanford, Washington. We were told that this was an experimental reactor for nuclear power—NPR—and that NPR stood for National Power Reactor. Everybody knows how much money the federal government puts into commercial nuclear power, so that wasn't hard to believe.

Some time after I left there, I learned what the NPR really was. NPR didn't stand for National Power Reactor. It stood for National Production Reactor, and it was designed to produce a maximum amount of plutonium. National Production Reactor was a weapons reactor which produced plutonium for bombs.[35]

Which meant that almost all of what we were doing at West Valley was for the weapons industry!

They took the uranium from West Valley to the enrichment plant,[36] and stored it there. They told us that we were reprocessing the uranium

34. During the six years it operated, Nuclear Fuel Services reprocessed 640 tons of spent fuel—379 tons from Hanford National Production Reactor, 100 tons from government-owned experimental reactors, and the remainder from electric utility companies (Con Edison's Indian Point, Commonwealth Edison's Dresden-1, Consumers Power's Big Rock Point, Yankee Rowe, and PG & E's Humboldt Bay). Hanford is the government's nuclear military reservation located in Richland, Washington. See Gene I. Rochlin et al., "West Valley: Remnant of the AEC," *Bulletin of the Atomic Scientists,* January 1978, p. 23.

35. NPR was AEC owned and operated "primarily for the production of plutonium for the military weapons program." Rochlin, "West Valley: Remnant of the AEC," p. 21. See the table supplied by Nuclear Fuel Services on p. 239.

36. *enrichment plant:* Natural uranium contains about .7 percent uranium-235 and about 99 percent uranium 238. Standard reactors require fuel that is between 2 to 4 percent U-235. A single plant at Oak Ridge, Tennessee, requires more electricity for this process than is required for Nashville, Knoxville, and Chattanooga combined, including both industrial and residential uses. There are three enrichment plants in the U.S.—Oak Ridge, Tennessee; Paducah, Kentucky, and Portsmouth, Ohio. They are all government owned. Union Carbide operates the plants at Oak Ridge and Paducah. Goodyear Atomic operates the plant at Paducah.

and sending it to the enrichment plant so the uranium could be used
to fuel nuclear reactors again and again. But when they started to run
it in the enrichment plant, it didn't work.[37] All of our spent fuel had
this contaminating fission product—technetium-99—in it, and our reprocessing didn't take it out. The enrichment plant got contaminated
by the technetium. It gummed up the works. None of the spent fuel
reprocessed at West Valley could be used in a power reactor again
because of this technetium-99.[38] Which means that West Valley was
basically useless for uranium recycling, its ostensible purpose. We were
never told the plutonium we were separating would be used for bombs.
A lot of us wouldn't have worked in a weapons place, and I think the
company knew that. I think in order to keep their employees, they made
a corporate decision not to tell people exactly what West Valley was.
There was definitely a concerted effort to keep us from knowing this was
a weapons plant. I'm calling West Valley a weapons plant because that's
what it was when it operated. We were separating plutonium for bombs.

---

*More than 60 percent of the spent fuel was supplied by the N-
plutonium production reactor (NPR) at Hanford, a military facility in
Washington.*[39] *"Some of the recovered plutonium went back to Hanford, apparently for the manufacture of bombs and other military purposes—a detail that would have come as a surprise to those New Yorkers
who took pride in what they saw as the state's pioneering role in the
peaceful use of the atom."*[40]

---

37. The enrichment plant that was contaminated with techetium-99 was in Portsmouth, Ohio. It is also important to note that no uranium from a commercial reprocessing
plant has been successfully reclaimed. See Bebbington, "The Reprocessing of Nuclear
Fuels," pp. 99–110.

38. The NRC has proposed a solution for the "large amount of scrap metal contaminated with Tc-99 [technetium] and low-enriched uranium" at the U.S. enrichment
plants. Scrap metal contaminated with this radioactive material could be used as smelted
scrap for "any number of consumer or capital equipment products such as automobiles,
appliances, furniture, utensils, personal items and coins." This would be especially advan-
tageous, according to the NRC, because "radioactive waste bural costs would be avoided
and new metal would not have to be produced." See U.S. Nuclear Regulatory Commission, "NRC Proposes Licensing Requirement Exemption for Contaminated Smelted
Alloys," News Release, Washington, D.C., 29 October 1980.

39. See Rochlin, "West Valley: Remnant of the AEC," pp. 18, 23.

40. See Severo, "Too Hot to Handle," p. 16.

Summary of Fuel Processed at West Valley

Reactor	Commencement date	uranium (metric tons)	Total plutonium (kilograms)	Average megawatt-days per metric ton of uranium
NPR[a]	4-22-66	19.7	1.7	75
NPR	5-20-66	28.8	2.3	75
NPR	7-15-66	46.7	50.9	1,287
Dresden-1	11-12-66	50.0	191.0	8,500
Yankee Rowe	6-07-67	49.8	185.1	11,200
NPR	9-02-67	26.6	52.6	2,700
NPR	12-02-67	26.1	47.4	2,700
NPR	1-06-68	42.4	75.4	2,700
NPR	5-05-68	38.8	79.1	2,850
NPR	6-29-68	55.3	115.7	2,870
Indian Point-1	11-15-68	special case - 16 metric tons		uranium + thorium
NPR	2-13-69	48.9	102.5	2,850
Yankee Rowe	5-14-69	19.6	176.0	20,500
NPR	8-16-69	30.3	—	unirradiated
Dresden-1	10-01-69	21.5	104.6	10,900
Indian Point-1	11-23-69	15.6	107.6	15,794
Yankee Rowe	6-02-70	9.3	95.6	24,381
Pathfinder[b]	8-14-70	9.6	7.1	2,231[c]
Big Rock Point	11-26-70	18.4	72.8	9,212
Indian Point-1	1-11-71	7.6	68.1	23,455
NPR	2-25-71	15.8	25.4	2,868
Bonus Superheater[d]	4-15-71	1.7	0.9	1,552
Bonus Boiler[d]	4-18-71	2.4	4.0	3,230
Humboldt Bay	5-02-71	20.8	87.2	10,466
Yankee Rowe	7-16-71	9.5	95.7	23,653
CVTR[e]	10-04-71	3.5	11.6	9,783
Big Rock Point	11-30-71	5.8	27.9	13,567
SEFOR[f]	12-12-71	—	95.5	—

Nuclear Fuel Services. Inc.

a. N-plutonium production reactor at Hanford. Wash. b. Pathfinder was an experimental commercial power reactor (58.5-megawatt electrical ater reactor with nuclear superheat) operated by Northern States Power Co. at Sioux Falls. South Dakota, from 1964-67. c. Only irradiated fuel ed d. Bonus Superheater and Bonus Boiler were parts of an experimental reactor (16.5-megawatt electrical boiling water reactor with nuclear eat) operated by the Puerto Rico Water Resource Authority and the AEC at Punta Higuera, PR. from 1964-68. e. CVTR (Carolina-Virginia Tube r) was a heavy water pressure tube reactor (17 MWe) operated by the Carolina-Virginia Nuclear Power Associates at Parr. South Carolina, from . f. SEFOR (Southwest Experimental Fast Oxide Reactor) was an experimental reactor for testing liquid metal fast breeder reactor fuel ed by the Southwest Atomic Energy Association (GE-AEC-FRG) at Strickler, Arkansas. from 1969-72.

mary of fuel processed at West Valley   SOURCE: *Nuclear Fuel Services,*
from the BULLETIN OF ATOMIC SCIENTISTS

Helping to Close West Valley

Soon after leaving I got involved with a group that had intervened in the relicensing hearing of West Valley. NFS was going to expand the plant and I didn't think their management could possibly run a larger plant right, because they didn't care about their employees at all. I wanted to see safety devices in there that would limit radiation exposure to employees. At the same time, I was trying to keep them from getting their license, period. I didn't want to see the plant operate at all. We were lucky on that one.

Late in 1975 and early 1976 several of us decided that in order to have another group in the fight, we would organize a Friends of the Earth[41] in Buffalo. A geologist from Buffalo State College came and joined the group.

I started talking to him: "I seem to remember reading something about an earthquake fault in Zoar Valley." Zoar Valley is just a big gorge that Cattaraugus Creek flows through.

He said the fault shouldn't be hard to find. So a bunch of us decided to look for this thing. A couple of housewives and students and this geologist and me went down the creek in canoes and we did find a shift in the rock—a little shift about three and a half miles from the plant. It was a foot and a half wide. We took pictures of it, made duplicate copies of them, and sent them off to the Nuclear Regulatory Commission.

It worked. Within two months the Nuclear Regulatory Commission was considering NFS under their new earthquake criteria.[42] Nuclear Fuel Services would have to completely rebuild the plant if they were to operate again under the new criteria. They figured it would cost them six hundred million dollars. They said they couldn't afford it, and they shut down.

41. *Friends of the Earth:* a national environmental action group.

42. "The fact is that between 1840 and 1967 there were 13 earthquakes, with epicenters within 100 miles of the N. F. S. plant, carrying intensities of 5 or higher on the Modified Mercalli scale. The Batelle Pacific Northwest Laboratory, under contract to the U.S. Government, conducted a study in 1976 and concluded that the West Valley site could have an earthquake with an intensity of nearly 8 once every 750 years or so." Severo, "Too Hot to Handle," p. 16. An earthquake of this magnitude could cause an accident that released radioactivity from the spent fuel storage pools. Such an accident could devastate hundreds of square miles surrounding West Valley.

West Valley Plutonium

Plutonium, one of the deadliest, carcinogenic substances known to man, remains radioactive for more than 24,000 years.

ESTIMATED COMPOSITION OF CONTENTS OF WASTE STORAGE TANK 8D2, WEST VALLEY:

Plutonium—35 kilograms

> —*U.S. Department of Energy,* Western New York Nuclear Service Center Study: Companion Report, *p. 3–26.*

"The design life of the high level waste storage tanks is 50 years. . . ."

> —*U.S. Department of Energy,* Western New York Nuclear Service Center Study: Final Report for Public Comment, *p. 4.*

"There are no indications that the tanks at Nuclear Fuel Services have ever leaked. . . ."

> —*Ibid., p. 4.*

"Recently a small hole was discovered in a catch-pan lying beneath the underground tank holding the liquid waste. . . ."

> —*Steven R. Weisman, "U.S. and New York Agree on Disposing of Nuclear Wastes,"* New York Times, *21 March 1979, p. B-2.*

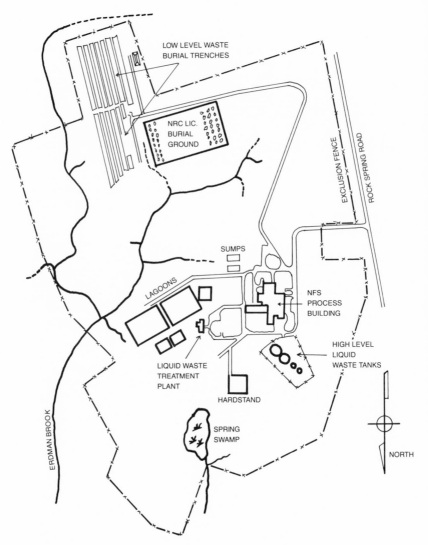

LOW LEVEL WASTE
BURIAL TRENCHES

NRC LIC.
BURIAL
GROUND

EXCLUSION FENCE

ROCK SPRING ROAD

SUMPS

LAGOONS

NFS
PROCESS
BUILDING

HIGH LEVEL
LIQUID
WASTE TANKS

LIQUID WASTE
TREATMENT
PLANT

HARDSTAND

ERDMAN BROOK

SPRING
SWAMP

NORTH

Radioactive accumulations at West Valley   *U.S. Department of Energy, TID–28905–2*

From Peter M. Skinner et al., DECOMMISSIONING CRITERIA FOR THE NUCLEAR FUEL SERVICES REPROCESSING CENTER, WEST VALLEY, NEW YORK, *August 1978,* p. 31.

Postscript

When Nuclear Fuel Services closed down permanently (October 1976), they left behind six hundred thousand gallons of high-level radioactive waste and two million cubic feet of low-level waste. A 1977 U.S. Congress Committee on Government Operations reported that the problem of what to do with this waste was "gargantuan" and might cost as much as six or seven hundred million dollars. No one knows what to do with this waste. Both high- and low-level forms contain substantial quantities of deadly plutonium. "Because of the probable high concentration of plutonium in this sludge at West Valley, some experts fear that it may go 'critical,' initiating a reaction similar to a meltdown and releasing tons of deadly radioactive materials into the biosphere. If the six hundred thousand gallons of high-level waste stored at West Valley were to be dispersed in this way, the resulting radiation could devastate Buffalo and surrounding towns."[43]

The wastes at West Valley contain materials that will be radioactive for tens of thousands of years. Some of the buried radioactive wastes have been leaking into Cattaraugus Creek, which flows into Lake Erie, the source of Buffalo's drinking water.[44] It is also known that the tanks in which these wastes are buried were designed to last up to fifty years, even through their contents will be radioactive for much longer than that.

The original contract signed by New York State and Nuclear Fuel Services charges the state with final responsibility for containing and disposing of these wastes. Local citizens are afraid that New York State will agree to make West Valley a national site for the burial of radioactive wastes in exchange for the federal government agreeing to pay for the costs of dealing with the wastes left by NRC. They call this "blackmail."[45]

43. Caldicott, *Nuclear Madness*, p. 59.

44. "Traces of radioactive tritium were found in Buttermilk Creek which empties into the Cattaraugus Creek. The Cattaraugus Creek empties into Lake Erie. . . . So far, the amount of radioactive material in the water supply is small, but environmentalists are worried that it will increase. . . ." Richard Beer and Peter Biskind, "West Valley: The Tombstone of Nuclear Power?" *Seven Days*, 29 March 1977, p. 6.

45. U.S. Department of Energy, *Western New York Nuclear Service Center Study: Companion Report*, p. 1–13.

William Oldham, general manager of Nuclear Fuel Services, felt that much of the criticism directed against the company had been unfair. He suggested that Dr. Bernard Cohen, a nuclear physicist from the University of Pittsburgh, evaluate Nuclear Fuel Services in terms of radioactive waste, contamination of water and milk, and overall safety.[46] Dr. Cohen concluded that evidence suggesting contamination of water and milk and a higher incidence of infant mortality was statistically without any basis. According to Richard Severo of the New York Times, Cohen also affirmed his belief that "plutonium is so safe that 'I am willing to eat eight tenths of a gram of it before a public audience.' Dr. Cohen also said he would be willing to eat a smaller amount of strontium-90."[47]

46. Severo, "Too Hot to Handle," p. 19.

47. Ibid., p. 19. Dr. Cohen has written of the "blessings of nuclear energy," and man's need to "get over his unreasonable fears." Among these blessings, Cohen mentions "radiation sterilization or pasteurization" widely used for medical equipment, which is now "beginning to be used for food preservation as a substitute for refrigeration." See Bernard L. Cohen, "Promises vs. Fears of Nuclear Energy," *News World*, 4 September 1978, p. 11A. Cohen believes eating nuclear wastes poses no serious danger: "In fact, one can calculate that after 600 years, a person would have to ingest approximately half a pound of the buried waste to incur a 50% chance of suffering a lethal cancer." Bernard L. Cohen, "The Disposal of Radioactive Wastes from Fission Reactors," *Scientific American*, June 1977, pp. 21–31.

CHAPTER 9

Tom Martin, Millwright
Richard Ostrowski, Welder
Dale G. Bridenbaugh, Engineer
Gregory C. Minor, Engineer
Richard B. Hubbard, Engineer

TOM MARTIN, MILLWRIGHT

"The nuclear industry was born, nurtured and developed with public safety in mind."

—James R. Schott, Cincinnati Gas & Electric (CG & E), station superintendent, Wm. Zimmer Nuclear Power Station.[1]

Tom Martin worked as a millwright on the control rods of the Wm. Zimmer Nuclear Power Station, a General Electric plant under construction outside Cincinnati, during the latter part of 1977. Millwrights measure machine parts very precisely—down to thousandths of inches. They make sure very fine parts, like pumps and valves, are lined up exactly. His job at Zimmer was to measure the control rods for straight-

1. James R. Schott, " 'Working at Zimmer Will Be Safer than Driving to It,' " *Cincinnati Post,* 9 August 1979, p. 9.
Wm. Zimmer Nuclear Power Station is operated by the Cincinnati Gas & Electric Electric Company. It is located in Moscow, Ohio, a small town near Cincinnati. By the time Martin worked in the reactor in 1977, CG & E had already spent about $850 million on the construction of the plant. The Zimmer reactor is a GE boiling water reactor (BWR) with a Mark II containment design, the same containment design used in the Shoreham reactor. See Chapter 5.

Tom Martin

ness, thickness, and roughness.

The control rods in a nuclear reactor absorb neutrons in order to control the nuclear fissioning of uranium atoms. To start a nuclear reaction, the control rods are lifted out of the reactor core. When a nuclear reaction is in danger of going out of control, the control rods are inserted into the core to slow down the fissioning process. Without proper functioning of the control rods, a nuclear plant is in constant danger of having an accident of catastrophic proportions.

From his first day at Zimmer, Martin found things wrong with the control rods. They were not as straight as they should be; they were too thick in certain places; and the seals—which are supposed to keep radioactive water from leaking out—were rougher than the specifications called for. What was even more disturbing was that when the rods were being installed, they hit the sides of the control rod tubes and started vibrating. He could hear them bouncing around. When they did not fit into the tubes as they were supposed to, they were clamped and forced into place. Control rods are pliable, and so Martin was concerned that forcing them would result in bending them and damaging what are critical components of the plant. They might get stuck when they were really needed, which could result in a runaway reaction and a disastrous core meltdown.

Martin told the Cincinnati Gas & Electric project engineer that the rods should be taken out and rechecked. The engineer said he'd look into it. Some time later Martin and the two other millwrights working on the control rods were approached by one of their supervisors. "I don't know who it was," he said, "but somebody told the project engineer that there are things wrong with the construction of this plant." No one said a word. He went on to say that he had been told by his supervisor to tell the crew that whether something was wrong or not, they should keep quiet about it.

Martin was shocked. Here he had made it known to his superiors that something was wrong with the control rods, and instead of something being done about correcting the problem, all Martin was getting back was "keep quiet." The control rods had to operate properly just to shut the plant down for maintenance. And everyone knew what would happen if the rods didn't function smoothly in an emergency. . . .

His crew was still working on the control rods when the general foreman came over. "Get your tools," he said. "All three of you are laid off."

Martin believes all of the millwrights were fired because one of them had mentioned defects in the control rods. The crew did not blame Martin for speaking up, because, like him, they thought Zimmer was "the worst-run job they'd ever worked on."

Martin decided to call the Nuclear Regulatory Commission. "I thought there should be somebody in the NRC who's concerned about the potentially dangerous situation at the plant. . . ." The NRC sent someone out to see about the control rods, but after looking at some of them, the man from the NRC said he didn't see anything that would affect the safe operating of the plant.

When Martin learned that public hearings were going to be held on the licensing of the Zimmer plant, he knew he had to go. . . .

The Licensing Hearings for Zimmer Nuclear

I don't work all year. I might be off six months and not earn a penny. It's from job to job, and when you have a chance to make the money, you want to make it. I was working at Ford, and with overtime I was making a thousand dollars a week. That's the most I might hit the whole year. And I took three weeks off for this hearing. The reason that I went to the hearings is I just had this false ideal that if people knew the way this plant was built—if they knew what I knew from being there—they would stop it from going into operation.

I talked to several other millwrights, other workers there, who say they know things are wrong with the plant, but they didn't want to go through what I went through—missing three weeks of work going down to the hearings and being badgered about six hours a day. You know, they were trying to break me down. When you have a good attorney trying to break you down for six hours a day, it's a little nerve-racking.

First of all they ask me if I'd had training on the job. I told them no. Then they came at me with these papers they had which said we had training to do this work and they tried to say I was perjuring myself. Okay, what came out after hours of badgering me was that you can't "train" somebody to do something they already know how to do. They didn't train me. They told me to run a slide gauge up this thing and if it stuck in place use a micrometer and find out how many thousandths it is. See, that's what I do for a living. They said they'd given us a half hour of training. I mean they didn't talk to us for no half hour, and they considered this "training." It's just, they were trying to break me down, saying that I was lying.

Then they brought some pictures of a control rod that didn't look at all like a control rod and wanted me to find the seal on it. Okay, I couldn't find the seal because I couldn't tell anything from the picture, and they was trying to imply that I didn't know where the seal was and didn't know how to use a preparatory gauge. It was funny because they finally called a Cincinnati Gas & Electric witness who pointed out where the seal was, and at the end it came out—after about two days of cross-examination—their own witness came out and said I knew exactly what point I was supposed to be looking at because he'd shown it to me himself. It's just that they were trying to break me down.

I thought the purpose of the hearing was to find out if there was something wrong with the plant, but the way they set it up, people that knew something couldn't get it across. Anybody who was either for or against nuclear power had the opportunity to get up and say what he felt. There were all together fifty or a hundred people who got up and said what they felt about it, but none of that was taken into consideration because they weren't under oath, so that wasn't supposed to sway their judgment[2] at all in licensing the plant.

I was under oath and I was the only witness on the control rods. But my lawyers were just out of law school. They tried, but they didn't have the experience of the NRC lawyers. The utility lawyer asked me questions about the control rods, and I tried to get my lawyers to elaborate on it, but their questions were thrown out of court. Compared to the NRC and CG & E lawyers, our lawyers seemed to be working in the blind. I wanted them to rephrase questions to try to get to the heart of the matter. I tried to give them some questions when I was sitting at the bench with them, but most of the time I was on the stand, and I couldn't talk to the lawyers.

I sat on one chair by myself away from the lawyers. Now all the utility witnesses sat right behind their lawyers, conferring with each other during the time they were cross-examined. They could talk to their lawyers, but I couldn't. I didn't think this was quite fair—the utility

2. The judgment of the Atomic Safety and Licensing Board of the Nuclear Regulatory Commission.

lawyers talking to their witnesses during the examination.

The way court procedures go, you can expand on something for so long, but once you change to something else you can't go back to it. So after the break came, a particular issue could not be brought up again.

I figured I had to try to tell them what I'd seen, but I didn't have an opportunity to tell them very much at all. The attorney for the NRC kept reminding me, "You can't say anything unless it concerns the control rods." Numerous times he kept telling me it was a game—you got to play by the rules. I didn't like the game they were playing. Seems like the NRC lawyers are just for the utility company.

I had a lot of people tell me that I should back off, that I could get myself into a lot of trouble—repercussions from the union and stuff. But I'm not the type of person most people would threaten, you know. Most people know that a threat wouldn't have an effect on me anyway. I'd still have gone to the hearings. I knew there was stuff wrong with the plant, and I had to do my best to bring out as much as I could. I would've liked to bring out a lot more, but you got to try to do what you can. I didn't accomplish what I'd liked to, but still I had to do it.

I never got real threats. Never had phone calls or anything, saying, "You back off or we're going to blow you away." Nothing like that. Just a lot of people saying, "You work too hard. You're liable to get into trouble."

And then it was funny—the radiator of my car had all kinds of problems. I hadn't had that type of problem before. Not before the hearings or after. It just happened right at the hearings. Every time I went to the hearings, you know, there was something else wrong with the radiator. It was overheating. I'd repair it, and then next day the radiator was just eaten up. It was like it had acid in it or something— I don't know—it just seems funny to me that when the hearings were going on I had all these problems.

"And the Control Rods at Zimmer . . ."

The job wasn't done, but they laid us off. They got new people in there, but as far as dealing with the control rods, millwrights didn't do it. Quality Control inspectors did it—which they weren't supposed to do. After the way the control rods were beating and banging into the control rod tubes, they were probably in worse condition the second time than they were the first. They definitely didn't want any millwright to know that they were like that. I can't think of any other reason why millwrights didn't do it because it was our job.

Comments on Wm. Zimmer Nuclear Power Station

"I made arrangements to have the welders tested by Gladstone Laboratories in order to obtain the certifications. Every welder failed his tests miserably. When we examined the reasons for these failures, we found that none of our welders had ever had any training in the area of 'Quality' welding . . . all Zimmer welds were made by uncertified welders using the old production weld process. These welds are of marginal quality, principally in that they lack fusion, which is the key to strength in a quality weld. This problem has now been compounded in that CG & E has greatly overloaded these cable trays. . . . The NRC never tested the welds on the Vertical Fittings which are the critical welds. Instead, they tested welds which are not critical. . . ."

> —*Edwin Hofstadter, sworn affidavit, 8 June 1979, former manager of Industrial Engineering at Husky Products, a supplier of electrical cable trays to Zimmer.*

"As much as 80% of the cable trays throughout the plant are overloaded beyond National Electrical Code Specifications of volume per tray. These trays are filled to as much as 150% of capacity in some cases . . . [and] will cause breakdown of cables if the heat generated is of a sufficient level. . . . Control devices are in many instances of very poor quality, and sometimes unreliable. . . ."

> —*Donald Blanch, sworn affidavit, 26 June 1979, general foreman for Westinghouse Electrical Corporation at Zimmer, supervising installation of cable trays.*

(After meeting with officials of the federal government and CG & E, Blanch decided not to testify at Zimmer's licensing hearings and retracted his affidavit, saying "they'll take care of the problems." Acknowledging he had received threatening phone calls after making his charges against Zimmer, Blanch denied threats had influenced his decision not to testify. See Douglas Starr, "Worker Alters Zimmer Stand," Cincinnati Post, 26 July 1979, p. 15.)

"CG & E did not provide total independent *inspection of critical component assemblies, and the detail parts making up these assemblies, for those items purchased directly from vendors by the owner, CG & E. Since the health, and even the lives, of tens of thousands of people depend upon the proper functioning of these components, I resigned in February 1976 and made public my concerns. The lack of independent verification of the quality of those components violates all recognized standards which are applied nationwide to components affecting public safety."*

—Victor C. Griffin, sworn affadavit, 3 June 1979, former supplier quality assurance engineer for Kaiser Engineers at Zimmer.

"This job is very screwed up [speaking of the piping in the plant]. This is a common problem, but Zimmer seems to be the worst case."

—Isa T. Yin, inspector for the Nuclear Regulatory Commission, quoted in Douglas Starr, "Zimmer Opening May be Delayed," Cincinnati Post, 15 February 1979, p. 1.

"Zimmer is just too far along to change plans."

—*Jack Curry, executive secretary of
the Cincinnati Electrical Association, quoted in Jim Greenfield and
Bob Elkins, "Life Styles Shape
Moscow's Views at NRC Hearing,"*
Cincinnati Enquirer, *23 May 1979,
p. B-3.*

*"Among the morning limited appearance speakers was Jeannine Ho-
nicker, the Nashville woman who has gone to federal court to try to shut
down nuclear plants all over the country. Facing the ASLB [Atomic
Safety and Licensing Board], Honicker thundered, "What portion of
the Constitution gives you the authority to license random, premeditated murder?"*

*"ASLB Chairman Bechloefer replied, 'I'm afraid we don't answer
questions.'"*

—*quoted in Jim Greenfield, " 'Cutting Corners' Called Top Concern
At Zimmer,"* Cincinnati Enquirer,
20 June 1979, p. C-1.

RICHARD OSTROWSKI, WELDER

*A man in his late twenties, Ostrowski works for Consolidated Edi-
son. He has done a few jobs at Indian Point[3] and is familiar with their
"spiel about how safe radiation is." The health physicists are required*

---

3. Indian Point Station, Units 2 and 3, is operating in Buchanan, New York, twenty-
six miles from New York City. Indian Point Station, Unit 1, was started up in 1962 and
is now shut down.

Richard Ostrowski

by NRC regulations to inform workers about the hazards of their work: "They'd tell us how it's more dangerous to drive up to Indian Point than to work there. That's a big one. Smoking, of course, is worse for you. There's a risk working there, but it's worth taking. The benefits exceed the risks—and the benefits are the money you could make up there."

For many years welders worked at Indian Point on a voluntary basis.[4] But in 1978, after several workers were injured, the men started saying they didn't want to go there. The union told Ostrowski, who was a shop steward, that if enough men didn't volunteer, men would be required to work at Indian Point or they would lose their jobs. Ostrowski—not an opponent of nuclear power—believed that the men should not be forced to work at a job that they felt endangered their health. He himself did not want to work at Indian Point. He had worked there one time too many:

I'll give you a specific example. The second time I went up to Indian Point I didn't really want to go. But I figured, well, maybe the last time was just an extreme situation. So I went.

I was working a stainless steel job on some duct, and it was in a "hot" area—a contaminated area—but it wasn't terribly "hot." All of a sudden these alarms started going off. I wasn't qualified to work in there alone because I was only carrying what they call a blue badge. A blue badge doesn't allow you to walk into a contaminated area without someone who's wearing a yellow badge. Now the yellow badge people are supposed to be better trained than you.

So I was working in there and these alarms started going off. I asked the man I was working with what the alarms were about.

And he said, "Oh, don't worry about it. It's gas."

And I said, "Well, what kind of gas?"

And he said, "Krypton gas"—something I didn't know about—and not to worry. "It'll pass in a few minutes."

"What do you mean it'll *pass* in a few minutes?" I said. "Is it radioactive? Is it contaminated or isn't it?"

4. See Robert Gillette, "Transient Nuclear Workers: A Special Case for Standards," *Science,* 11 October 1974, for a discussion of union welders used at Indian Point, pp. 125–127.

"Yeah," he said. "But don't worry about it. It's only a very small amount, so it won't hurt you. Anyway, by the time we leave the area, the gas will have passed, and we'd just have to come right back in."

That's when I put down my shield and my handle and went out of the place. And I never went back there.

You go up to Indian Point and you see all this stuff going on—like guys leaving their badges in the lockers. One particular foreman was "burnt out" and what he did was borrow another foreman's badge so he could go back in there. And that's what they did. The men were very lax in their safety precautions and procedures. The foremen were just as bad, if not worse. They would let you do whatever you wanted to do. If you went up to them and said, "This isn't safe," they said, "Well, what're you breaking *my* balls for?"

They wouldn't make an issue of it. And the men didn't make an issue of it either. So the foremen just overlooked everything. The supervisors overlooked everything. To me it just wasn't worth working with people like that.

The men were afraid to work there. They'd heard about these two guys who'd been working in a supposedly "cold"—uncontaminated—area of the plant. One of them had been told he was going to work in the reactor and to go get suited up—that means get dressed in protective clothing. So he was on his way into the so-called white room—this is where you change your clothes and put on the white coveralls and shoe coverings they give you. Usually on the way out of the place you check yourself for contamination. They've got Geiger counters and hand meters and foot meters.

On his way *into* the place this guy set off all the alarms!

And he wasn't supposed to have been near any contamination whatsoever. So then they had to trace everything. They traced his job back and found that the job he was working—and approximately eighty other men were working—for the last three weeks was contaminated. And there had been no protection given to any of these men. They hadn't even *known* they were working where it was contaminated!

For three weeks they all could've been bringing stuff home. If they brought their work clothes home—washed them in their machines—well, their families could have been—

The men had all heard about this. Now they were afraid. They didn't think they should be forced to work up there.

There was one particular meeting when Ostrowski realized that the union wasn't going to support the workers. . . .

Up to this point my union was telling me that nobody would be forced to go up there—that it's a voluntary situation. Now I'm sitting here in this meeting, and my superintendant says, "I'm surprised that you weren't informed that you have to go up to Indian Point."

"What do you mean I *have* to go up there?" I said. I looked at my co-chairman to come to my aid, because I was taken aback completely. I thought he'd say, "That's right, you don't have to go up to Indian Point." But he just sat there.

I left the meeting with my co-chairman and we went into another office. He looked totally perplexed.

"What's going on?" I asked him.

He looked at me and shook his head. "I don't know. I can't believe my union's been lying to me all this time."

"Something's not right here," I said.

"The union's doing their job," he said.

And that was it. The welders were told if they refused to work at Indian Point they would be suspended indefinitely.

I thought that was wrong. You can't do that—force a person to work up there, to do something that could be dangerous to himself and to someone else. Let's face it—if I have to work up at Indian Point, and the guy I'm working with is scared to death, how can I trust the man? I got to rely on him if something goes wrong. Both of us got to take care of each other. But the union stood there with their finger up their rear end, not saying anything.

Ostrowski decided to get the men more information. He went to the SHAD Alliance and asked if someone who had done firsthand research on the health effects of low-level radiation could come speak to the Edison workers.

Dr. Thomas Najarian came—the man who studied the Portsmouth shipyard workers—who overhauled the nuclear submarines.[5] When the meeting was held in New York, the union handed out leaflets saying that I was trying to close Indian Point!

5. See Gyorgy, *No Nukes,* p. 194, for a discussion of Dr. Thomas Najarian's research.

All I was trying to do was give men who might be forced to work up there the information from the other side. We'd been told there were no problems with radiation, and I knew many scientists were saying that wasn't true.

Because of this meeting I was brought up on charges. They said I was "doing willful harm to the union and its members." They said I was "collaborating with a group called the SHAD Alliance."

I was suspended from my union shop steward position for fourteen months.[6] That's the Utility Workers Union of America, Local 1–2.

DALE G. BRIDENBAUGH, ENGINEER

Born during the depression in 1931 on a farm in South Dakota which had no running water or electricity, Bridenbaugh went to work in 1953 for the world's largest electrical and technical company—General Electric. From 1953 to 1976 he worked on everything from turbines to nuclear reactors. In 1958, when General Electric was building the world's first commercial boiling water reactor, Bridenbaugh was assigned to supervise the installation of the turbine. Shortly after Dresden Unit I went into service,[7] things in the reactor "began to fall apart. Valves weren't working, heat exchangers were leaking, the control rods were warping and bending and cracking. . . ."[8]

6. Ostrowski and other union members sued the union for violations of rights under Section 101 (a) (2) of the Labor Management Reporting and Disclosure Act (LMRDA). On 17 March 1980 Federal Court Judge Constance Baker Motley granted a preliminary injunction ordering Ostrowski's reinstatement as shop steward, pending the conclusion of litigation. Judge Motley ruled that, like all union members, shop stewards are entitled to the protection of the free speech and assembly provisions of the LMRDA.

7. Dresden Nuclear Power Station, Unit I went on line in 1960. It is operated by the Commonwealth Edison Company and located in Morris, Illinois, outside Chicago.

8. See Peter Faulkner, *The Silent Bomb* (New York: Vintage Books, 1977), pp. 288–289, for a discussion of some of the problems of Dresden-I in 1960.

Dale G. Bridenbaugh

After supervising the start-up of Dresden-I, Bridenbaugh was asked to stay on and remedy all the things that were going wrong. "Nobody knew what to do when things didn't work. The designers really didn't understand what they were dealing with. They had thought about how to install it, how to operate it, but not what to do when it didn't work. . . . We had to figure that out. . . . We did a lot of strange things at Dresden. . . ."

I had this guy Pete who worked for me—Pete Rumondi. Pete was a laborer, the sort of guy you have to have on construction projects. You tell him to do some impossible thing, and he would figure out how to do it. He would hound people until he got someone to do what was required. He was a very determined person.

One of the things I asked Pete to do one time—and he really thought this was funny—was get rid of a whole bunch of contaminated pipe insulation. There had been a leak, and it had gotten wet and contaminated with radioactive water. It had been stored outside—this was wintertime in Illinois—and the water had frozen. We thought it had dried off, but it hadn't actually.

We were going to put this insulation in boxes and ship it off to a burial site to get rid of it. So we brought it into the building to load it. We put it in a box, and of course it thawed out and started to leak out the bottom.

What were we going to do with this?

Then I had an idea. We had a big box—four by four by eight feet long, made out of four-by-eight sheets of plywood, and we were going to ship all this crap out, and we didn't want it to leak out on the truck. It's now illegal to ship liquid radioactive waste because it might leak.

So I went up to Pete. "Here's what we're going to do," I said. "You get inside this box and completely line it with Kotex."

So he got inside one of those boxes with a great big carton full of Kotex and a stapling gun, and he completely lined the inside of the box with Kotex.

Pete thought that was the craziest damn job he'd ever gotten involved in.

Why did you use Kotex? "It's one of the most expendable materials used in a nuclear power plant. We used it for things you wouldn't believe. . . ." Where did you get it? "We bought it by the truck-load, almost by the railroad-car-full. What keeps a nuclear plant running is lots of Kotex, lots of masking tape, and lots of plastic bags."

Most workers at Dresden really didn't understand about radiation. We told them not to worry. "We're going to take care of you." A few people got nervous even so. I remember one pipefitter's notion shortly after the plant went into operation. Everybody at the plant had to wear film badges to monitor exposure. This pipefitter somehow had gotten the impression that his film badge was like a radiation shield, that if he wore it, all of the radiation coming at him would be sucked into that film badge, and it would protect him from being exposed.

The guys were told, "Always leave your film badge at the gate. There's a guard at the gate. Don't take it home." That was because we were afraid they'd lose it. Then we wouldn't have a record of what they were exposed to. He somehow got the idea that he shouldn't take it home because it had sucked in all this radiation, and so it was a dangerous thing.

So one night he forgot to leave his badge at the gate, and he wore it home. He woke up in the middle of the night, and he thought of that radiation badge sitting in his pants in the bedroom there, and he began to worry about his wife and kids. Maybe that radiation would leak out of the badge and harm them.

And so he got up in the middle of the night and went out in the backyard and dug a hole and buried it.

Radiation Limit

Bridenbaugh worked at Dresden Unit I from 1958 to 1963, and in the last year or so of that time he became the site manager of General Electric's operations.

At first Dresden wasn't very radioactive, and we were very cautious. We limited exposure to fifty millirems per day.[9] Then the plant got

9. Federal regulations limit radiation exposure to no more than 3,000 millirems per calendar quarter, or 5 rems (a rem = 1000 millirems) per year. This exposure limit is the subject of much debate. Scientists like Sternglass and Gofman claim it is much too high and causes thousands of cases of cancer every year; nuclear proponents claim that it has not been demonstrated conclusively to cause cancer and therefore is acceptable.

more and more radioactive, and we said, "Well, jeez, we've got to go to a hundred per day." Then it got more radioactive and the jobs got tougher, and we said, "Well, jeez, for this one we can go to five hundred per day." Then it got a little "hotter"—several hundred millirems an hour—and on this one we brought in construction workers from other jobs. "Well, we'll run these guys up to fifteen hundred or two thousand on the weekend because they're not going to work in a radioactive area on this other job they're doing. . . ."

You know, over a time you begin to realize that the basis for setting the exposure limit—a lot of it—is what is necessary to get the job done. It's not any real scientific basis.[10]

In 1960, shortly after start-up, the control rods at Dresden-I were found to be defective.[11] They had extensive cracks in them after only a minimal amount of irradiation. They had to be completely replaced after only about six months of operation. The only question was how.

We had to get rid of this whole bunch of control rods that were no good, and they were highly radioactive. An engineer from San Jose[12] was given the responsibility for figuring out how to do that. So he designed this big cask that we were going to load the rods into under about thirty feet of water. We put this big cask down in the pool of water where the control rods were sitting, and we took the lid off. We moved the rods into the cask with long-handled poles. Then we put the lid back on, and we pulled the cask up out of the water.

When we got it out of the water it was so damn radioactive it set off every alarm in the place. "Uh-oh, I guess we underdesigned the cask," he said.

What the hell were we going to do with this thing? So we put it back down underwater. The guy from San Jose decided that what he wanted was to pull the cask almost up to the surface of the fuel pool and pump

10. "There was no science in setting the 5 rem level; there was no science in setting the 50 rem level. These were arbitrary values as you have heard. They do not indicate safety"—Dr. Irwin Bross, Roswell Park Memorial Cancer Institute, in *Radiation Standards and Public Health*, p. 30.

11. Dale G. Bridenbaugh, Richard B. Hubbard, and Gregory C. Minor, "Testimony," in Faulkner, *The Silent Bomb*, pp. 288–289.

12. San Jose, California, is where General Electric has its Nuclear Energy Division.

this cask full of concrete while it was hanging there.

Then I said, "Hey, we're not going to do that. You know that's crazy. It just won't work."

If you started that, you'd dump concrete into the pool, and pretty soon you'd get the whole pool full of concrete, plug up all the drains, and just make a god-awful mess.

Eventually what we did was clear everybody out of that end of the plant. We built a wall of fifty-five gallon drums, and filled them with water. We pulled the cask up out of the pool and set it down behind the barrels full of water which acted as shielding. Then we had a truck bring a load of steel plate in. We hung the steel plate all over this cask and welded it on until we got enough steel welded on the outside of it to bring the radiation down to a reasonable level.

Spent Fuel

Nuclear fuel is made up of enriched uranium shaped into small pellets about an inch long. These pellets are sealed into slender metal rods between ten and fourteen feet in length. There are about forty thousand in the reactor core gathered into fuel bundles, and they must be constantly cooled if they are not to overheat and melt. After a nuclear reactor has been in operation, the fuel becomes more and more radioactive. This is because after the fissionable uranium (U-235) atoms split, they leave highly radioactive by-products, such as strontium and cesium and others, in addition to generating plutonium from another uranium isotope. Used fuel is called "spent fuel." When this spent fuel is removed from the core, it is so radioactive that it has to be cooled off in on-site storage pools for four to six months. Approximately one quarter of the nuclear fuel must be replaced each year.

One day I got a call from the manager of customer service in San Jose. "Here's what we want you to do," he said. "We want a sample of the fuel to examine in the RML.[13] We are shipping you a cask so that you can take a fuel bundle, cut it up, and ship a section of rod back to California for examination."

13. *RML:* remote materials (handling) laboratory.

They wanted to see what the uranium looked like after it had operated for a while.

I said, "Fine, uh, how are we going to do it?"

"Well, Leo is designing this machine which is a power-operated hacksaw that you're going to put down underwater in the fuel pool. And you will—underwater—put this fuel bundle on this table and cut it up. We're not sure when you cut it up, though, how much radioactive gas will be released. So you'll have to monitor it as you go."

"Okay, fine."

I got off the telephone and I thought, Jesus, I hope they know what they're doing.

You can't just take spent fuel and cut it up. It is intensely radioactive. It is so radioactive that if you had it out of the fuel pool and walked in the same room with it, you'd receive a lethal dose in a couple of seconds!

We wanted to cut up—oh—I think four or five different sections of it—about a foot long—and put it in a lead cask and ship it back to California. The physical act of cutting it up was quite a problem. What we did was take a very long pole and take the casting nuts off of the fuel assembly. Then we pulled the rod out of the fuel bundle and laid it down on this long table under water and clamped it. We moved the power hacksaw into position and started sawing through it. All this took place under about ten to thirty feet of water.

It's different than working in a high spot and being afraid of falling. I've done a lot of that, too, in construction work. At least when you're working on something high, you either fall or you don't fall, and if you fall, you're dead, and if you don't fall, you're all right. But when you're working with something radioactive, you can be overexposed and not even know it.

I could see the fuel giving off this blue glow down underneath the water. It was eerie. It was down there, not doing anything. Just sitting there, glowing at me. . . .

GE's Manager of "Nuclear Complaints" Around the World

In 1966 Bridenbaugh was promoted manager of General Electric's Nuclear "Complaint Department." "That meant I was responsible for the broken-down nuclear reactors GE had placed into service all over the world." He traveled overseas to plants in Japan, Germany, Italy, Switzerland, Spain, and India. "I had responsibility for two reactors we'd sold to India. We were having a lot of trouble with them. The generator broke down. A transformer failed. The fuel was defective. I had to arrange to ship sixty tons of equipment by air from Chicago to India."[14] When Bridenbaugh went to India, he saw the Tarapur plant for himself. "That was quite an education. . . ."

We had to ship these nuclear instruments (in-core detectors) that were forty feet long. After arriving in the Tarapur train station, they had to be transported from there to the plant which was about eight miles away. But they didn't have a truck long enough to carry these things. My site manager and his foreman went out to a nearby farm and got two farmers to tie two ox-carts together and haul these goddamn things from the train station by ox-cart. One of the guys who was working for me got kicked in the leg by an ox. Damned near broke his leg.

To see this reactor sitting out in the boondocks in India, sixty miles from Bombay, was just—the idea of keeping that plant properly maintained in those conditions was incredible.

And on top of that anybody who is educated in India is taught not to get his hands dirty. So you have to bring in all of the farmers and fishermen to do the dirty work. Because there is a class separation between the educated people and the farmers, they hardly talk to each other. So it's a mess, that's what it is. It is just an impossible place to run something as demanding as a nuclear power plant.

Half a mile from the Tarapur plant in India, the Indian government was building a fuel reprocessing plant. Then in 1974 the Indians set off an atomic bomb. It made quite an impression on me when I learned that their bomb was made out of material that came from their theoretically "peaceful" program. That's what the whole program is about—you operate the "peaceful" atom to produce electricity. You generate about five hundred pounds of plutonium in that "peaceful" reactor. Then

14. The Tarapur Atomic Power Station (TAPS) is located on the western coast of India. It supplies power to the city of Bombay. Completed in 1969, it was the first atomic plant to go into operation in the Third World. The fuel which General Electric supplied was defective and caused "widespread contamination." See Anil Agarwil, "Nuclear Power in the Third World," *Nature*, June 1969, p. 469.

people take the spent fuel out of the reactor and reprocess it and get plutonium. That's weapons grade material. You can make nuclear bombs out of it. That's what they did in India.

Go to India and see the poverty. They put all this money and effort into building a nuclear power plant. Then they build a reprocessing plant right next door. Now they have the bomb.

GE's Manager of Nuclear Reactor Performance

He was one of the most respected engineers in the nuclear field—an owner's group of sixteen U.S. utility companies issued a joint letter praising Dale G. Bridenbaugh's exemplary performance working for GE. He had a secure management position, making $36,000 a year. Then, after almost twenty-three years with GE, he walked out.

I could no longer justify what I was doing. I was not assessing the safety of plants—I was doing whatever I could to make sure they kept operating.

There was a serious deficiency in nineteen of GE's U.S. plants.[15] I broke the latest news to my boss: "The computer run says that if the design basis accident occurs, the whole damn thing might collapse or jump off its foundation."

He said, "That can't be." He just refused to believe it. Meaning—if that's true, we've got to shut them down. So obviously that can't be true. "We've got to do whatever we can to keep those plants from being shut down," he said. "If we have to shut down all nineteen of those plants because of such a basic screw-up in the design, it could mean the end of the nuclear business for GE! It could mean the end of the commercial nuclear program in the United States!"

I met with the utilities to discuss what we would tell the Nuclear Regulatory Commission. I told them we should say, "We've got a problem. As soon as we can, we'll shut the plants down and modify

15. *serious deficiency:* a computer analysis predicted that in the event of an accident, a swell of water would be thrown up violently because of the pressure that would be released. Since the plants were not built to withstand this violent swell, the containment could be breached and deadly radioactive material in the plant could be released into the atmosphere.

them." But one after another those sons of bitches refused to do that. They were afraid. They all said, "I don't have the authority to make that commitment for the utility."

I remember at two o'clock in the morning in Holiday Inn saying, "Look, it doesn't make a goddamn bit of difference whether you have the authority or not! We have to do this." I made this impassioned speech to them: "We've got to quit screwing around with this thing and go to the NRC tomorrow and say, 'We know it's a bad design. We don't know if it will withstand an accident—but we're going to commit ourselves to correcting it just as fast as is humanly possible.'"

But no. One after another these bastards said, "I can't make that commitment."

I was trying to get them to see that they were going to have to spend millions of dollars. They were going to have to make hardware changes. If they didn't do that, they might get a disastrous core meltdown. It was obvious to me. And they were still operating with the mentality that somehow we were going to pull a computer-run out of our ass and make it go away.

So at two in the morning I called my boss in San Jose. "We've been telling the utilities they have to face up to this deficiency in the system," I said. "I told them we aren't going to analyze it away. But they're waffling on it. We need to tell them, 'Look, if you don't commit yourselves to making these changes, GE cannot support the continued operation of these plants.'"

My boss said, "Well, it can't be that bad."

"We should tell the NRC that we won't support continued operation of those plants unless they make those changes!"

"Don't rush into anything, Dale. I don't think we can take such a hard line."

And I said, "Oh, shit."

He said, "The information is too preliminary, too sketchy. I don't think we can do that at this time."

Bridenbaugh submitted his resignation less than two weeks later on 2 February 1976. Two other GE management-level engineers, Richard B. Hubbard and Gregory C. Minor, submitted their resignations at the same time. The Joint Committee on Atomic Energy promptly invited the three GE engineers to testify in Washington, D.C., on the safety

*problems that led them to resign. Asked about meeting with the Joint
Committee on Atomic Energy, one of the engineers, Gregory Minor,
said "It was the closest I've ever come to experiencing a witch hunt."* [16]

GREGORY C. MINOR, ENGINEER

*Gregory C. Minor attended the University of California, Berkeley,
where he received a degree in electrical engineering. He wanted to be
"involved in a new research and development area," to "rise up the
ladder and achieve," to have "good company backing" and be "respected." He looked particularly at the company name and interviewed
at General Electric, Westinghouse, Du Pont, Proctor and Gamble. He
chose General Electric. It was 1959. Minor was twenty-one, and he had
a wife and a newborn baby.*

Hanford, Washington

They couldn't fit me in at San Jose, so they said, "We have one other
West Coast location that we can put you in, [17] and that's Hanford,
Washington."

I thought, that's all right. Washington's a beautiful state—too much
rain—but they have gorgeous trees and streams and rivers. I could enjoy
that.

So my wife and I loaded up our 1950 blue Ford two-door coupe
pulling a trailer and started out for Washington. We went north
through Oregon—God, it was beautiful!—up to Portland and turned
east and up the Columbia River. The trees got smaller and less dense
and then there were no trees at all, and pretty soon no bushes even, no

16. From an interview with Gregory C. Minor, 22 August 1979.
17. GE had an engineering training program which rotated engineers from site to site
for two years.

Gregory C. Minor

jackrabbits, nothing. That's where Hanford, Washington, is—out in the desert.

Hanford, Washington, is a huge military reservation built during World War II for the manufacture of plutonium for the Manhattan Project—the secret two billion dollar effort to develop the first atomic bomb (1942–1945). At that time Hanford's plutonium production was directed by Du Pont. In 1959, when Minor worked there, the Hanford facility—still a government operation for the production of plutonium —was being operated by the General Electric Corporation for the AEC.

We lived in the last house next to the desert on Catskill Road. You looked out our front window and you saw a road that looked like any normal suburban road leading down toward the river. On the other side were cliffs that created a big bend in the river, and on top of the cliffs is where they had the NIKE missiles. Every so often the sirens would go off in the town, and you'd actually see the NIKE missiles rise up out of the silos and point toward the heavens. . . .

One morning a little bottle appeared on our doorstep. Every doorstep had them. We didn't know what the little bottles were for. My wife asked the neighbors.

"What is it?"

"Oh, well, that's for your urine sample."

Suddenly it dawned on me that radiation doesn't just hit your hand and bounce off. It doesn't just go through you and out, but radioactive material can get *into* you and *stay* in you and pass through your entire system. But I didn't worry about that very much at the time. . . .

Each morning I'd get on the bus—these were AEC buses—and go the twenty or thirty miles out into the desert. A security guard would get on the bus at the gate before you entered the reservation—the total fenced area where the reactors were—and he'd walk through the bus and look everybody over. You had to have your badge on. Then he'd get off. And when you got out to the area—fifteen or twenty miles later—a guard would get on again. Every so often he'd make you open up your lunchbox and he'd look through it to see if you had anything in there.

We'd drive across the reservation, and along the way we'd pass the "200 Areas." The 200 Areas are what they call the Waste Separation Area—the plutonium separation buildings where they take the fuel that comes out of the reactors and separate out the plutonium. That's what the whole facility was for—all of Hanford, Washington, was only to make plutonium for bombs. There was no electrical generation. No productive use. It made plutonium and that's all it did.

The 100 Area reactors created the plutonium for the 200 Areas. People didn't talk about the 200 Areas—where they actually separated the plutonium. You didn't hear a lot about the processes. We were kept quite separate. . . . I worked in the 100 Areas—the reactor areas—that were located along the river every few miles. I did some design development work on the 100 D-R reactor and was maintenance engineer on the K-east reactor. When you worked in the 100 K-east area, all you knew was what K-east would do, and when you were in the 200 Area, all you knew about was the 200 Area.

To make the plutonium, the uranium fuel was formed into aluminum-covered slugs, and these were stacked in long horizontal tubes in the reactor. The reactors were operated until a certain quantity of plutonium was created—not a lot, just a fraction of the uranium becomes plutonium. I watched the men putting on the white uniforms, the hoods and masks and gloves, saw them getting up on the special refueling racks to refuel the reactor to get the spent fuel. They'd push in a new slug with a big long rod—push it through these long tubes—and the spent one would automatically fall out the other side—like weenies out of a tube—fall out into the spent fuel pool.

Every once in a while I'd see the train car come in with a big lead cask to haul away the spent fuel from the reactor for the 200 Area so they could reprocess it for plutonium. There they treated it chemically by remote processes to separate out the plutonium from all the uranium and crap. That's the stuff—the wastes, the leftovers—that's what wound up in the tanks and caused the famous Hanford leaks.

The Hanford Leaks

About fifty million gallons of high-level super-hot wastes are currently being stored at the Hanford site. These wastes are leftovers from the AEC's weapons program of the 1940s—leftovers from reprocessing spent fuel for plutonium in the production of nuclear weapons. They are stored in tanks supposed to last for fifty years. This is considered "tempo-

rary" storage, since the wastes will be deadly for more than 24,000 years.
No permanent waste solution has been found. By the year 1970 eleven
tanks at Hanford had begun to leak. . . .

To store this highly radioactive liquid, they built large steel tanks in
the ground, and they put monitoring stations on them, so that they'd
know when the liquid level was changing in case there was a leak. They
had a lot of these tanks—several of them quite full—and they'd monitor
them every day. And sure enough, they kept monitoring them and kept
monitoring them, and long after I left they discovered that they had
been leaking for quite some time.[18]

The guy who'd been monitoring them had been recording the fact
that the liquid level was going down. To him it was just a reading he
took everyday. He wasn't translating that into any "problem."

When they discovered the stuff was really leaking,[19] they didn't know
what to do. The only thing they could do was build another tank and
transfer the fluid out of there and then try to find out where the leaks
were in the first one and maybe patch them. But it's a terribly radioactive goop they've got in there. You can't get in and fix it. You can't send
a diver down to the bottom to patch up anything so terribly radioactive.

So they finally built new tanks and transferred the fluid. Meanwhile
they lost thousands and thousands of gallons underground![20]

The Atomic Energy Commission says that the radioactivity was all
contained[21]—that since it's a low rainfall area, the stuff won't sink very
deep down. They have profiles to show how deep they think it is now.

18. The worst leak was discovered on 8 June 1973. Tank 10-6T, built in 1944, had leaked
about 115,000 gallons of highly radioactive liquid wastes. When the leak was discovered,
it was "draining the tank by some 2500 gallons a day. It had leaked for 51 days. . . ." The
115,000 gallons of waste contained 14,000 curies of strontium-90, 40,000 curies of cesium-
137, and 4 curies of plutonium. Gyorgy *No Nukes,* pp. 58–61. See also Robert Gillette,
"Radiation Spill at Hanford: The Anatomy of an Accident," *Science,* August 1973, p. 728.

19. On 8 June 1973 Atlantic-Richfield (ARCO) discovered that 115,000 gallons of
intensely radioactive wastes had leaked.

20. A government report in 1972 revealed that there was enough plutonium in the soil
of the Hanford cribs (i.e., trenches) to conceivably cause a nuclear chain reaction which
could leak to a low-grade nuclear explosion. See Gyorgy, *No Nukes,* pp. 58–61.

21. The AEC admitted that 11 out of 151 containers at Hanford had developed leaks
between 1944 and 1970. See McKinley Olson, *Unacceptable Risk* (New York: Bantam
Books, 1976), p. 164.

They show the groundwater down beneath it. They say it will just stop where it is now. But you can't prove that it will stop there. If any of that stuff gets down to the groundwater, it would pollute the groundwater with cesium, strontium—everything. It's a pretty huge basin that feeds the Columbia River. That river is just ten miles away from where the stuff spilled—and that river goes past Portland and a lot of other places before it goes on out to the ocean.

"Abnormally high concentrations of accumulated radioactivity have already been found in water plants, fish, and wild fowl in the river."[22]

Once radioactivity escapes into the environment it can get into the food chain. A cow grazing on radioactive grass gets the radioactivity in its milk; fish that eat radioactive plantlife build up concentrations of radioactivity much higher than the miniscule amount which seemed to escape. Strontium-90 goes from grass into dairy products, such as milk and cheese. Once it is absorbed into the human body, strontium-90— which resembles calcium—gets into the bone and radiates the cells there. This internal exposure can be deadly—causing bone cancer and many other problems.

Advocate of Nuclear Power

General Electric offered Minor a permanent position at Hanford, but he decided to leave there after only eight months. "I knew I didn't want to stay at Hanford. I didn't like the area or the end-product of the work. I didn't want a career as a supplier for the bomb builders." Minor went back to school and got a master's degree and advanced engineering training at GE. By the time he finished his degree in 1966, he had a house and three children, and he was working in General Electric's Nuclear Energy Division in San Jose. Here Minor learned the company line on nuclear power.

22. Ibid., p. 165.

Besides learning the technical goings on at GE, I kept abreast of changes by taking courses, reading "Nuke Week" [Nucleonics Week] —the trade publication that everybody in the industry reads. You read what the "bad guys" say and what the "good guys" say, and during that time the "bad guys"—Dan Ford and Henry Kendall[23]—were really giving hell to this industry, and the "good guys"—Westinghouse and General Electric—were trying to make power for this country. There were "education sessions" periodically to update managers on what was going on in GE and the industry. Usually this was done in the form of a management seminar where we went off to a location in Santa Cruz or Monterey Bay and sat at a motel out there and spent—oh—two days getting pumped up, talking about the progress we made in the last year, and where we're going, and how many reactors we're going to sell, and how many utilities we're working on.

They'd say, "These guys are likely to buy. These are less likely. These are maybes."

And so you plot the forecast—the number of reactors per year you expect to sell in the future. Believe me, when the first oil embargo hit in 1973–74, I looked at this forecast and said, "By God! I'm in the right place!" Because reactor sales were just going bananas! All the utilities were jumping in, buying reactors. I really felt secure. We could put reactors everywhere!

When people asked me about reactors, I always gave them the "standard pitch"—just like a Barbie doll. Pull the chain under my neck and I give you twenty canned words on what's good about nuclear power:

What's good about nuclear power?

It's going to save you from the oil crisis. It's the future source of energy. It's clean, safe, and cheap.

What about radioactive waste?

Don't worry. That's not GE's problem. That's the government's problem. The government's going to take care of that.

How much waste is there?

If you take the volume of radioactive waste over a forty-year lifetime

---

23. See Ford and Kendall, *An Assessment of the Emergency Core Cooling Systems Rulemaking Hearing.* Ford and Kendall listed about twenty points about the ECCS that showed it wouldn't work properly. These hearings resulted in Ralph Nader joining the opponents of nuclear power, convinced that reactor safety was a myth.

of a nuclear reactor and divide it up among everybody in the United States—two hundred million people—it turns out to be the equivalent of no more than one aspirin-size tablet per person.

What's in the tablet?

Strontium, cesium, plutonium—all the leftovers from spent fuel.

What about accidents?

You don't have accidents. You don't even have incidents—because you have your safety systems. You will never have a serious accident because we build redundant systems into everything. If one system fails, we have backup systems. . . .

Safety

One day out of the blue Dale Bridenbaugh said to me, "Have you ever given any thought to your part in creating this nuclear legacy?"

I thought—"nuclear legacy"—that sounded like a positive thing. Then I looked at his face and realized he meant a legacy of waste and that sort of thing.

"Oh, not me," I told him, "because I'm designing safety systems. I'm in design and safety, and we're working to make nuclear energy safe. If it weren't for me, it wouldn't be as safe—because I'm concerned about that. And I'm doing a good job."

Then in 1975 the Browns Ferry fire happened.[24] I had been in the group that made some of the fundamental drawings used to build Browns Ferry. We'd written in special requirements for separation of the electrical cables for safety. We had routed them in metal trays two or three feet apart, so even if something happened to one set of cables, the others would still function.

This was a brand new requirement. Browns Ferry was the first plant we built this way. I thought this was the best plant we had designed.

One day in 1975 somebody comes up to me and tells me they had a fire at Browns Ferry. It had wiped out the emergency core cooling

24. Browns Ferry Nuclear Power Plant is near Decatur, Alabama and operated by the Tennessee Valley Authority (TVA). Started up in 1973, it had the greatest number of "events" reported that year. Two years later in 1975 the fire there was one of the most serious accidents to date. Browns Ferry was a GE design. The electrical cables burned for more than six hours.

system. I just couldn't believe that. I didn't want to believe it. But the data kept coming back from Browns Ferry—yes, that was what had happened. . . .

Minor learned that two technicians, working below the control room of Reactor Units 1 and 2, had been checking for air leaks in the cable-spreading room—the room where electrical cables that control both reactors are located. They were doing a routine job—trying to seal air leaks by packing insulating material around the cables—and checking their work as they often did, with a candle held near the cable. If the flame flickered, that meant there was still an air leak to plug. What the technicians did not consider, however, was that the electrical cables had been sealed with flammable polyurethane foam. When one of them held a candle too close to this material, the flame was sucked horizontally inward and the insulating material burst into flame. They tried to beat the flame out with a flashlight but were unsuccessful. The fire spread to the cables and then to the reactor building itself.

A series of horrifying events followed.[25] Confusion about which emergency phone number to dial for the fire alarm delayed sounding the alarm. A shift engineer tried the carbon dioxide fire extinguisher and found that it was covered by a nonremovable plate. When the alarm was finally sounded, the operators in the plant's control room did not shut down the two reactors, but kept them running. By now, the fire was raging out of control and smoke was filling the control room. Control was lost over reactor relief valves and none of the normal or emergency low-pressure pumps were working. The fire chief arrived, but he was not permitted to use water to put out the fire because he was told it was an electrical fire, which was not true. "The problem was to cool the hot wires to prevent recurring combustion," the Athens fire chief explained later.[26] Sixteen hundred cables were damaged, many of them connected to safety devices. With the emergency core cooling system disabled and the core close to being uncovered, the chance of a meltdown was frighteningly real. For seven hours the Browns Ferry fire was precari-

25. See David Dinsmore Comey, "The Incident at Brown's Ferry" in Faulkner, *The Silent Bomb*, pp. 3–32. Details of the Browns Ferry fire were not made public until David Comey made a formal legal request to the NRC.

26. Faulkner, *The Silent Bomb*, p. 11.

ously out of control. When the decision was finally made to put the fire out with water, the firefighters found the nozzle would not stay on the hose. Finally, the day was saved when someone hooked up an auxiliary pump and managed to force water into the reactor. This prevented the core from being uncovered.[27]

That accident just really pulled the rug out from under me. One GE guy said to me, "You know, this is a really serious thing," and I said, "I can't even believe this happened." Then this other guy said, "Thank goodness everything worked!"

They were carefully building up a "non-accident" theory—sure, all the emergency systems were gone, but we didn't melt any fuel, we didn't kill anybody—it was a "non-accident."[28] But to me it was a disaster! All the safety systems were gone! All of our backup systems gone! I felt we were very, very lucky that we hadn't had a major catastrophe. It made me worry about the rest of our GE plants—because I knew that this was the one we had done a "good" job on. We had designed the Browns Ferry plant to be the *best.*

From that point on, all the problems of reactors and the rest of the nuclear fuel cycle took on a new meaning for me.

Shortly after the Browns Ferry fire, Minor decided to leave General Electric. He had worked for the company for seventeen years—since 1959—and he had a secure management position. He was afraid he might have trouble ever finding another job, but he could no longer justify working for the nuclear industry. One of the final blows to his faith in nuclear power came as a result of a public relations expert from GE coming out to a Creative Initiative Foundation gathering, where he addressed a group of people who were curious about nuclear energy, particularly because it had become a subject of much controversy in the mid-70s. Creative Initiative Foundation (CIF) was a group that Greg

27. See Ralph Nader and John Abbotts, *The Menace of Atomic Energy*, (New York: W.W. Norton & Company, 1977), pp. 94–96.

28. The NRC and TVA stated that no significant radiation had been released during the fire, although radiation monitoring instruments were knocked out by the fire and no samples were taken for hours after the fire began. Air sampling was not initiated in the direct area of the reactor and downwind of the reactor for almost ten hours after the fire started. See Faulkner, *The Silent Bomb*, p. 13.

Minor, Dale Bridenbaugh, and Richard Hubbard all belonged to, as did their wives. Meetings of CIF were designed to bring people together and enhance understanding. "It's a personal development organization, the idea being that everybody has more potential than he's using. They have seminars and lectures. . . ." Minor and Bridenbaugh had invited a health physicist out to CIF, a man who was in the public relations business and made presentations for GE on a regular basis.

We invited this guy to CIF because we wanted to influence the organization, make them see what was good about nuclear power. The people who were there—about two dozen or so—asked him about reactor safety, and he gave them all the standard answers. He did what GE trained him to do. Showed slides and talked. "What's a reactor? How does it work? You know, the rod goes here, this is how the reaction works, this boils the water, steam turns the generator and turns on your lights." Then he told them about all the work GE was doing to test emergency systems and he made all the standard comparisons—like when you fly to Denver or live in Denver, you are exposed to more radiation than when you live next door to a nuclear plant. Because Denver is a mile high, and you go a mile up when you fly, and you receive a certain dose from cosmic rays. He wanted to compare a plant running perfectly, that never had an unplanned release of radioactivity, to flying across the U.S. or living in Denver. He didn't want to allow for the fact that there could be an accident. Someone asked him about an accident, and he said, "We've got the fuel rods, we've got the pressure vessel, we've got the containment. We've got all these redundant emergency systems so there won't be any accident."

At one point this public relations guy asked for a drink of water and somebody gave him a glass of water and he said, "Gee, I wish this was vodka or gin." You could tell he felt a little hassled by that point. Then someone asked him about plutonium. "What is the real danger of plutonium? How toxic is it?"

"Plutonium's dangerous," the public relations guy said, "but there's also enough water in Lake Tahoe to drown everybody in the state of California, if you could put it into their lungs. Well, plutonium has the same problem. You mustn't get it in everybody's lungs."

People were stunned. They wanted to know how many milligrams of plutonium in the lungs would cause cancer and with what probability.[29] Instead, this guy was telling them about drowning in Lake Tahoe water.

"Maybe I misjudged this group," he said, at the end of his presentation. "I thought this was just going to be the normal church group, where you give them the story about nuclear power and they go away feeling secure." It was clear he felt he'd been through the wringer. The people at CIF happened to be far more tuned-in to the issue than he expected. I didn't feel too good about the whole thing. I had never really heard his pitch before. In the back of my mind I'd thought there must be other people at GE who were just burgeoning with answers to all the questions these people were asking. They must be in all the halls and buildings—all you had to do was go and unlock the right door.

Minor, Bridenbaugh, and Hubbard, all GE management level nuclear engineers, decided not only to leave GE simultaneously, but to make their resignations a public event. Having each made the personal decision to quit, they decided that the three of them resigning together could have more meaning, more impact. They picked 2 February 1976 as the date they would resign.

Sometime in January 1976 I heard that an NRC person was going to resign in protest. Initially I had no idea who it was. Then I heard someone mention Bob Pollard's[30] name. I'd only met Pollard a couple of times—once when he came to San Jose to review details of a GE reactor control system that my group had designed. I'd really been impressed by how quickly he grasped things, how he persevered and

29. For a full explanation, see John W. Gofman, "The Cancer Hazard from Inhaled Plutonium" (San Francisco: Committee for Nuclear Responsibility, 14 May 1975).

30. After six years with the NRC, Robert D. Pollard resigned in January 1976. Before leaving the NRC, Pollard submitted a report on reactor safety at Con Ed's Indian Point, Units 1 and 2, twenty-six miles north of New York City, stating that Indian Point was "an accident waiting to happen" and that the "unresolved safety problems are so fundamental to the basic evaluation of reactor safety that it is not possible to conclude on a technical basis that operation of any nuclear reactor is safe enough to provide reasonable assurance of adequate protection for the public health and safety." See Robert D. Pollard to William A. Anders (chairman, U.S. Nuclear Regulatory Commission), second enclosure, "Report On the Nuclear Regulatory Commission Reactor Safety Review Process," 6 February 1976. See also testimony of Robert D. Pollard before the Joint Committee on Atomic Energy, 18 February 1976, in Faulkner, *The Silent Bomb*, Appendix B, pp. 315–319.

didn't let us off the hook with superficial answers. At the time I'd thought maybe we should hire him, he's so thorough. When I heard *he* was about to leave—this man I really respected—leave the Nuclear Regulatory Commission, I felt a tremendous uplift. My decision was verified. Here was a totally independent person that I trusted making the same decision.

The night we were leaving, this guy from the NRC came around. My wife, Pat, answered the door. The man said they wanted us to come to Washington to talk to the NRC. "We would like to have a chance to hear your views and share your safety concerns. We're here to regulate the safety of nuclear power, the safety of the public."

So we went to Washington, D.C.—the three of us and our lawyer—and met with Anders, chairman of the NRC at the time, and he had about eight other commissioners and lawyers with him. We told them of our concerns. We were really naive. After we met with the NRC, the Joint Committee on Atomic Energy asked us to testify. The whole thing with the NRC had really been a preview for them so that they could marshal their arguments against us for the Joint Committee. We decided that if we were going to go before the Joint Committee, we needed to put together some solid testimony. We locked ourselves in my dining room and spent a week building an outline, deciding what to include, what to leave out, dividing up the work, and starting to write. We spent days getting it typed and edited—days with all of us working on it. We got seventy-some pages of testimony together for the Joint Committee.[31]

The Joint Committee hearing rooms were also used for the nuclear navy room, where they evaluate submarine designs and God knows what else. When we walked in, I saw a small room with the Joint Committee spread around with the senators on one side and the representatives on the other, and all the TV cameras lined up against one wall. It was packed, jam-packed. All the GE executives were sitting in one row—all the top bosses were there—all the way to the top. My boss wasn't there, and Dale's wasn't, Dick's wasn't, but all these top executives were there.

We had decided that I would be the spokesman for the group. As soon as I started reading the testimony, it became clear that we were not

31. Bridenbaugh, Hubbard, and Minor, "Testimony," in *Investigation of Charges Relating to Nuclear Reactor Safety*, vol. 1. Also in Faulkner, *The Silent Bomb*, Appendix A, pp. 280–314.

going to be allowed to read it. First they said they didn't have enough copies of it to go around. Then McCormack started breaking in on us. He's the representative from the state of Washington, from the Hanford area. He interrupted us repeatedly, clearly mouthing things from the nuclear industry. He brought up affidavits from people from GE that implied that the three of us leaving like this was a conspiracy. He made it sound like we had been brainwashed. It was even suggested that we had been paid off.[32, 33]

A Note about the Hearings

The experience of the three GE engineers before the Joint Committee on Atomic Energy illustrates what happens to dissenters who were once a part of the nuclear industry. Having spent days gathering together everything they knew that might have a bearing on public health and safety, the men were put on the defensive and made to feel that they were the accused. When Minor concluded his introductory comments, saying, "We could no longer rationalize the fact that our daily labor would result in a radioactive legacy for our children and our grandchildren for thousands of years to come," he was interrupted by Senator Pastore.

"If what you say is true, how do you account for the fact there hasn't been one fatality or one serious injury in all the time we have been engaged in the development of nuclear power? How do you account for that if everything you say is true? How do you account for that?"[34]

32. The chairman brought up the suggestion that the GE engineers might have been paid off: "I hope we don't go too far afield on this. Here are three men who have developed tremendous seniority with the company. They have given up their jobs. I don't know whether they have done it as a sacrifice or for an emolument . . ."—Chairman Pastore in *Investigation of Charges Relating to Nuclear Reactor Safety*, vol. 1., p. 42.

33. McCormack suggested that the GE engineers had been exploited: "Mr. Chairman, my whole point is this. There have been serious suggestions made about the resignations by these gentlemen, that they have been pressured into these resignations . . . that they are being exploited by the political organization that is running the antinuclear petition in California"—Representative McCormack. Ibid, p. 42.

34. This is a position often taken by the nuclear industry—to try to prove the inherent safety of nuclear power by stating that there have been no fatalities during the history of reactor operation. Accidents that are not mentioned include: the SL-1, a small test reactor at Idaho Falls was being repaired on 3 January 1961 when the reactor went out of control and killed three men, impaling one of them on the ceiling of the reactor building.

Hubbard pointed out that such a statement ignored deaths due to radiation put into the environment.

"You knew that when you started," Pastore retorted.

"We are not here to argue whether or not deaths have occurred in the past," Bridenbaugh said. "What I specifically am here to present are my deep concerns about the technical flaws that I see developing in the program and the vast potential this has for future deaths and consequences to the total public."

Pastore persisted: "Are these defects you speak of correctable?"

"Many of them are correctable, yes, sir," Bridenbaugh said.

"Are they correctable to the point of making it safe?"

"In my opinion, they are not."

"Why?" Pastore demanded.

"Because we have no way of minimizing, or getting to a reasonable low enough level, the human error, the oversights, and the generic problems that are inherent in the program," Bridenbaugh returned.

"In other words," Pastore said, "what you are actually saying is we should never have started on this in the first place, is that correct?"

"At least we are going too fast," Minor said.

The technique in the hearings was to draw the men out, then to catch them in a position where whatever they said compromised their stand and resulted in making the Joint Committee and the nuclear industry look well-intentioned—even innocent. The aim is to discredit the men's motivation in appearing at the hearings—and thus to deflect attention away from the real issue:

"Mr. Bridenbaugh," Representative McCormack began, "there have been a number of statements to this committee and to the press that your decision or the decision of the CIF members to resign from the General Electric Company, from their jobs, was a calculated program orchestrated to obtain the maximum possible public effect, that this program was set out in a meeting in February 1975 . . . that the discussion of resignation as a political tool was discussed at a CIF meeting and that the decision was made that resignation should be held off and then orchestrated in such a way to maintain a maximum political impact."

Here the ground had shifted. The technical concern which led these men to leave their management-level positions was not being evaluated; instead it was their motivation which was being questioned. McCormack did not stop with implication, however. A moment later he said,

"I have here a written statement by Lynn Gillette, who is also an employee of General Electric, also a member of CIF—"

Hubbard interrupted. "He is not an employee of General Electric, I don't believe."

"If you don't know him I am surprised you know he is not a member of General Electric," McCormack replied, and proceeded to read from a CIF meeting held in January 1975, at which one of the CIF leaders purportedly said, *'God did not create plutonium and therefore it is evil.'* Then McCormack turned to the GE engineers: *"Do you agree with the statement made by a leader of CIF . . . that God did not create plutonium and therefore it is evil?"*[35]

Pastore interceded for the engineers at this point, but the bait had already accomplished its aim. McCormack left in the record the suggestion that the GE engineers had somehow been manipulated into resigning from GE, and that their concern about nuclear safety was merely a public relations stunt. The experience of the GE engineers before the Joint Committee illustrates the tactics the nuclear industry and its champions in government use to deflect attention away from the very real deficiencies and dangers of nuclear power.

RICHARD B. HUBBARD, ENGINEER

Richard B. Hubbard's parents were divorced when he was two, and he was raised by his mother and grandparents. They lived in a small, conservative town in Ohio. "I can remember my grandfather nearly having a heart seizure in 1948 when Truman beat Dewey." Hubbard's mother worked as a librarian in the local high school. The family did

35. *Investigation of Charges Relating to Nuclear Power Safety,* hearings of the Joint Committee on Atomic Energy of the U.S. Congress, 94th Congress, vol. 1. (Washington, D.C.: U.S. Government Printing Office, 1976), pp. 7–47. See also Gail Sheehy, "California's Impossible Nuclear Decision: A Reporter's Personal Search for an Answer," *New West,* 7 June 1976, pp. 51–58.

Richard B. Hubbard

not have a lot of money. "As a boy I remember I always wanted an electric train, but I never had one. I liked to operate the controls, to see the lights come on. . . ."

He chose electrical engineering at the University of Arizona. "It suddenly dawned on me in my second year of college that I was going to have to earn a living. Having no father or a family with a business to go into, I really had to think about that. It was 1957 and they needed engineers everywhere. So I said, 'I'll become an engineer.' "

Right out of college in 1960 Hubbard went to work for General Electric on their three-year technical marketing training program for engineers. First he worked in advertising and marketing for appliance controls, like range timers, then designed automatic test equipment for auto-pilots on the F-105 jets, and later worked in the checkout and start-up of one of the first automated steel mills in Detroit. "The constant thread was controls—something to control how a process worked."

Then, in 1964, Hubbard was offered a job in GE's Nuclear Divison in San Jose. . . .

That really excited me. The nuclear industry looked like a chance to do something really positive. I didn't want to work in an industry where people had been doing it for years and years—I'd never get ahead that way—and I didn't want to work in weapons or missiles, although that was pretty glamorous at the time. No, I didn't want to get into the military industries. My father was a retired colonel—he'd spent his whole life after the divorce in the military.

I wanted a new business that was going to grow a great deal—and where I could really make a contribution. So in August of 1964 I came to San Jose.

First Impression

The first day I was at work they took me out to where GE has radiation laboratories and test reactors in a place called Vallecitos, about twenty miles from San Jose, and they gave me a tour of the place. They took me from room to room and "counted" my hands and "counted" my feet—you know, seeing my radiation level—all the time telling me how safe it was. They took me to where they had the radiation cells which had remote manipulators in walls a couple of feet thick that you look through since you can't get in there and touch anything. You do everything with these remote manipulators—like hands—and they had me work them. This went on for three hours.

When we were all through, the man who'd taken me around said, "Well, Dick, what did you think about that?" He was very proud.

"You know," I said, "I wouldn't bring a customer here. All I've heard for three hours is all the things you're doing to make these nuclear facilities safe, and the impression I get—rather than how safe it is—is how dangerous it must be."

That was my first impression, but I didn't think about that again for a number of years.

The Nuclear Airplane

When I started out in the nuclear business, GE was completing some work on the nuclear airplane. It was going to be an airplane that would fly around forever—like the nuclear submarine, it would have a nuclear reactor as its power source. GE was having all sorts of problems with it, however, because the radiation was so high that we needed more lead shielding.

Lead is very, very heavy. The more lead you need for shielding, the bigger the reactor you need to overcome the weight of the lead. So we were in a constant dilemma. We talked about building some prototypes and testing them at an airfield up in Idaho—because the question had come up: Where could you land one of these things?

Looking back now, fifteen years later, you laugh. "Who would really think of having a nuclear airplane!" But that was something GE spent a lot of money on—it was a very well funded government program.

Moving Up in Management

In 1965, after five years with GE, I was made a manager for the first time. I thought, I'm out of college five years and I already have the title "Manager." I have people working for me. I'm starting to make it. The plan is working. By 1969 I had ten people working for me—and one of those was actually a manager. Then I got another promotion to where

I had twenty engineers working for me and three managers reporting to me. Then in 1971 the plant manager came to me and said, "Dick, you've been critical of the quality of the reactor equipment we're building"— things didn't work when they got out to the construction site—"How would you like to manage the quality group?"

That meant I would manage one hundred and fifty people and it would be another promotion! So in 1971 I became manager of the quality assurance in the manufacturing part of the Nuclear Division.

Hubbard spent more and more time in production meetings, coordinating schedules and budgets, and in staff meetings, getting briefed on all of GE's problems. He was part of "the inner circle" in management. Then in 1975 he concluded that GE had "lots of problems. Things were not turning out the way that all of us had hoped they would."

Rather than figure out how much money GE was going to make on nuclear power, we were talking about how we could minimize our losses. In that period of 1975 GE reactor sales were almost nil. You couldn't *give* away reactors around the world.

I remember one weekly staff meeting where we started asking, "Where are we going to sell our next plant?"

And the general manager said, "Well, the three leading candidates are Israel, Egypt, and South Africa."

"Israel and Egypt and South Africa have had a certain amount of violence," I remember someone saying, "a certain probability of war. Is it really a good idea to be selling nuclear reactors to these people? Surely they can make bombs out of the spent fuel."

And the answer he gave was, "That's not GE's responsibility. That's the country's foreign policy." That was the overall theme—it's not our responsibility. . . .

Things weren't turning out to be cheap or clean or safe. "We had lots of little accidents like Browns Ferry. . . ."

I remember sitting in a staff meeting when the Browns Ferry fire was reported to us. GE had built that equipment, and we thought it was safer and better than anything we had ever done. It incorporated all the new regulatory changes.

Maybe the outside world had the view that the Browns Ferry plant was always under control, but I got a different picture of how close we had come to an accident, with the lights off in the control room, smoke pouring in and everybody running around with masks on—gas masks— running around in the dark. I could picture the chaos and it was really scary. We were coming a lot closer to a big accident than the public was being told.

I remember another time when we were working on one problem and we discovered a whole bunch of other problems. There was a vibration inside the reactor core and these forty-foot neutron sensors were going back and forth because of the water flowing through.[36] The whole core of the reactor was shaking and fuel channels were cracking. Then we found that GE engineers had not calculated some of the core cooling system rates correctly and that probably the water wouldn't fill back up and flood the core as fast as we thought if there was an accident. That meant we didn't have the margin of safety we thought we had.

I'll never forget the response of the top GE management. The man in charge—one of the vice-presidents—said, "It's important when you look under a rock—the angle that you look." And what he meant by that was—look just straight under the rock. If you have to get an answer to a question, look, find the answer, but for God's sake, don't look all around and find other problems!

So over the years the margin of safety kept eroding. . . .

Questions

In California in the 1970s there were lots of questions about nuclear power. In 1975 people were going from door to door—including very good friends of mine—getting petitions to put the questions on the ballot. I would talk to them and tell them, "You really shouldn't be doing this. You don't understand." And they would say, "Tell me about it," and they started asking me questions, like: Could nuclear waste be stored? Would emergency systems work? Were there evacuation plans for the nuclear plants? And was there adequate insurance? Lots and lots

36. Neutron sensors measure the number of neutrons in the core—i.e., the power level of the reactor.

of questions about nuclear power.

It forced me to get out of my narrow area of technical management responsbility and look for answers. First I went to the Public Relations Department of GE and said, "What do you have? How do I answer questions like that? Give me the word. What do I say?"

They gave me the standard answers which I then gave my friends: "Safety?—No member of the public has ever died as the result of an accident from a commercial nuclear plant. Waste?—That's not a big problem. A big thousand megawatt nuclear power plant makes just an aspirin tablet a year of high-level radioactive waste for each member of the public. Surely we can store an aspirin tablet! Look how many train-loads of waste a coal plant makes and all those coal miners that die— you know, nuclear is much safer. At the end of the year, all the waste from a commercial nuclear plant would just fill one telephone booth. That's hardly *any* waste!"

There was a lady who lived across the street from me and she said, "Dick, you haven't really answered the waste question."

"Well, it's not our responsibility anyway," I told her. "It's the government's responsibility. The government is responsible for waste disposal and they really need to get on with solving the problem! It's not a technical problem, it's a political problem—let the politicians decide."

That didn't satisfy my friends. So I started reading and looking at what the industry experts were saying. I found out that there really were no answers to a number of problems—like waste disposal. I had always accepted the idea that you could put the waste in geologic formations, such as salt, but salt storage turns out not to be a good idea. It would be a little like putting something hot on top of snow in Alaska—the waste from a nuclear plant is still both radioactively hot and also thermally hot for a number of years. It could start sinking. It could sink right through the salt and you don't know quite where it would end up. It could get into the water system and then get distributed quite widely —and the important fact about nuclear wastes is that they're very toxic for a very, very long time, so you really want to keep them away from people.

That's why the GE public relations man talked about the aspirin tablet when I asked him about waste disposal. He didn't talk about *time* —that some of the waste is radioactive for half a million years—or how little of it would be enough to kill someone. He only talked about

volume. The same kind of thing was true when he talked about safety
—the standard line is very carefully worded: "No member of the public
has ever died"—which means that plant workers don't count—"as a
result of an accident at a commercial nuclear plant." You have to say
"commercial" because people have been killed at government facilities.
. . . And the government only talks about immediate deaths, not the
latent effects which cause cancers and genetic mutations for generations.

I started branching out and reading about other controversial topics
and thinking about the relationship of weapons and nuclear power. The
more research I did, the more I thought we were not seeing the total
impact of what we were doing and that we were underestimating the
real risks. I concluded that an accident was likely to happen—that the
probability was high and that the public had really not been told all the
facts.

Leaving GE

I thought of leaving the company, but I liked working there. When
I walked into a party at night, I had status. I was a manager at GE. I
had my own private parking spot there. I was earning a great deal of
money—around forty-two thousand dollars. Having come from a background without a lot of money, I felt that if you had money, you had
freedom.

So my first plan was to ask GE to simply send me to another plant.
But most GE plants were back east and I knew I didn't want to go back
there, so I ruled that out. Then I thought I could write up a résumé and
look for a job in the Bay Area. I even went so far as to get a book on
how to write résumés. But then I thought some more about it and I said
to myself, "What's really needed is for me to speak out on what I know."

I went to the friends of mine who'd been involved in putting the
nuclear issue before the public and I said, "Would it be of some use if
I spoke out?" and they said, "Yes."

*Going public in criticism of the company was tantamount to heresy.
"I knew that people who speak out become virtually unemployable in
big industry. . . . It's all right to be critical when you're within the
company, but once I became an 'outsider' there would be an absolute
fence."*

He decided to resign publicly with Dale Bridenbaugh and Gregory Minor, two other GE engineers. . . .

The day before we resigned we met with newspaper people at the San Francisco airport. I remember being very nervous and walking into that room with the reporters from the *New York Times,* the *LA Times,* and the *San Francisco Chronicle* sitting there with their backs against the glass and the sun shining so you couldn't really see their faces.

The first thing I heard was just this voice: "I'm glad you made it, because the last time that I was in a room like this, the person never appeared."

It was David Burnham of the *New York Times* who had waited for Karen Silkwood in the motel in Tulsa, Oklahoma. She never came. She was killed on her way to talk to him.

As soon as we resigned I called up the person I'd worked with for a number of years. "I'm sorry I couldn't tell you before we resigned," I said. "I really wanted to, but there was no way I could."

I could feel we were not communicating, that already there was a wall between us.

Finally he said, "You know, I never had a friend who threatened my job."

I thought about that and I said, "Well, it's not me who's threatening your job. What's threatening your job is the truth. If what I said is true, you *should* feel threatened."

The next day we flew down to Los Angeles and had a press conference at the Los Angeles Press Club. I'd never been to a press conference let alone participated in one. I was so nervous that I couldn't eat.

We were sitting at a table during the press conference, answering questions, and all of a sudden over at the side I saw the GE public relations man from San Jose. He was the man I'd written articles with, the man who'd published things for me. We'd worked together for years.

Now we were on opposite sides.

I guess what I'd say to a person who's making a decision about whether to leave or not is that the roughest part is making the decision.

I have three children and at the time I left GE they were fourteen, twelve, and ten. I remember telling them I was leaving. My oldest son's reaction was, "Go get them, Dad!"

My daughter, who was twelve, said, "My friends aren't going to like me."

And my third child—the youngest—said, "Am I still going to be able to take piano lessons?"

You can talk to your children forever about values, but if you don't live those values, they'll never pick them up.

Afterword by
Helen Caldicott, M.D.

Nuclear power involves radiation at every stage of the fuel cycle from mining uranium fuel to radioactive waste disposal. As a physician I know that no amount of radiation is safe. I have worked with children with leukemia. I have had to break the news to their parents and look into their faces. When a radioactive substance is inhaled or ingested, radioactive particles are released. These particles may lodge in the tissues of the body and irradiate surrounding cells. Strontium, for example, is tasteless and odorless. The body cannot distinguish it from calcium, so it is deposited in the bones and irradiates bone or blood-forming cells. In every cell there is a gene that controls the rate of cell division. If this gene is hit by a radioactive particle emitted from the strontium atom, it can be damaged or destroyed. This is called ionizing radiation—that is, the electrical charge of the atoms and molecules in the normal cell is altered. The cell may not show the effects of ionizing radiation immediately. It may sit quietly for five to fifty years and then go berserk and produce billions of similarly damaged cells. This uncontrolled growth is called cancer, and it can probably be initiated by one radioactive particle hitting one gene in one cell.

Ever since the Manhattan Project there has been secrecy about radiation and health effects of nuclear weapons and nuclear war. In 1953 President Eisenhower told the Atomic Energy Commission (AEC) to

293

keep the public confused[1] about radioactive fallout. About the same time, Eisenhower went before the UN and talked about "atoms for peace" and the AEC continued to stockpile nuclear weapons. People don't understand that the commercial nuclear power program is just window dressing for the military—for weapons; and until recently the whole industry was classified under the secrecy umbrella of the Pentagon. Not until the Freedom of Information Act were people able to obtain information about nuclear power plants. Because these plants were designed and built for the production of weapons, it was a technology the military has not wanted people to understand.

Nuclear reactors were originally designed to produce plutonium for bombs. Until 1975 I had never heard of plutonium. When I learned about it, it made my hair stand on end.

Plutonium is a terribly carcinogenic substance. It comes from uranium. When uranium atoms split, they produce radioactive fission products and by-products: one of these is plutonium—a highly fissionable[2] substance that remains radioactive for more than half a million years. When exposed to air, plutonium ignites, forming very fine particles—like talcum powder—that are completely invisible. A single one of these particles could give you lung cancer. Hypothetically, if you could take one pound of plutonium and could put a speck of it in the lungs of every human being, you would kill every man, woman, and child on earth—not immediately, but later, from lung cancer. In one year a nuclear reactor produces four hundred to five hundred pounds of plutonium! John Gofman[3] says that if only 0.01 percent of the plutonium that is to be handled to the year 2000 should leak—which would be a remark-

1. "In May 1953, when the public was complaining increasingly of the dangers of nuclear testing, the Atomic Energy Commission issued a memo saying that the commission press releases and speeches should not use the words 'thermonuclear,' 'fusion' and 'hydrogen.' The memo asserted the President [Eisenhower] says 'Keep them [the public] confused as to fission and fusion.' " Judith Randal, "Charge Ike Misled Public on N-tests," *Daily News*, 20 April 1979, p. 10.

2. Because plutonium is so unstable, it splits or "fissions" easily. It breaks down into other elements that are also unstable—or "radioactive"—i.e., these atoms emit particles as they decay. Radiation refers to the rays that are given off as the atoms split or break down. According to Karl Grossman, plutonium is "the most toxic substance in the universe." Karl Grossman, *Cover Up: What You Are Not Supposed to Know About Nuclear Power* (New York: The Permanent Press, 1980), p. 13.

3. The bio-physicist who worked with plutonium on the Manhattan Project to build the first A-bomb and later left the nuclear industry. See Chapter 4.

ably small amount, something the industry has never achieved—it would cause an extra twenty-five million cases of cancer in the American population in the next fifty years!

Now there is a plan to progress to breeder technology.[4] In a breeder reactor one hundred tons of plutonium is placed in a reactor core. The plutonium core is surrounded by a blanket of uranium-238, and since the plutonium is naturally fissionable, it starts to fission, producing fission products that are made in an ordinary reactor. During this process neutrons are released which are captured by the blanket of uranium-238, which is then converted to plutonium. During this fission reaction, heat, electricity, and fission products (radioactive waste) are produced—but most important, more plutonium is generated than is used.

There are two worrying aspects about this process. One, the plutonium core could explode in a nuclear reaction, releasing massive quantities of plutonium to the environment. Two, the breeder reactor is cooled by liquid sodium—a very volatile substance. If liquid sodium is exposed to air, it ignites or explodes. This means that *no* cracks can ever occur in the piping system. It is ludicrous to assume a breeder can be operated safely.

But a breeder does produce more plutonium than you put into it—and plutonium is the fuel for nuclear weapons. Even though the military has its own reactors for plutonium production, there is a plutonium shortage now, and they're going to need a lot of plutonium for all the weapons planned for the future—the neutron bomb,[5] Trident missiles,[6]

---

4. The nuclear energy companies are optimistic that with breeder reactors they can realize huge profits. They claim that breeders are needed because they "will run out of affordable fuel without them. Uranium prices have skyrocketed in recent years. . . ." Creg Darby, "Beware the 'Fast Flux': Industry is Readying a New Kind of Nuke," *Progressive*, September 1980, p. 24.

5. A high-radiation bomb that destroys living things but leaves property intact. The neutron bomb is made out of plutonium.

6. The largest submarines ever built. The Trident I missile will carry eight 100-kiloton nuclear warheads. The Trident II missile will carry fourteen 150-kiloton MARVs ("Maneuverable Reentry Vehicles") that can adjust their course at the end of a flight to hit their target very accurately). According to Robert Aldridge, a former Lockheed missile designer, the Trident submarine is "leading the U.S. into a first-strike posture" against the Soviet Union—i.e., the ability to knock out the enemy's nuclear system so retaliation is impossible. Mitchel Kling, "Book Review: *The Counterforce Syndrome* by Robert C. Aldridge," *PSR Newsletter*, August 1980, p. 5.

and the MX missiles.[7] Also, the plutonium will continue to be cycled in the breeder system, producing an endless supply of electricity—a utilities' dream! Once the MX missiles are built, and the Russians respond in kind—which they will—within ten to twenty years there will be enough weapons to create lethal fallout for every human being on earth within weeks.

The military-industrial complex is, within the definition of clinical psychiatry, not mentally healthy. There is a split between the reality of what they are doing and their affect, or understanding of reality. They are mixing all the ingredients to make a cake, putting it in the oven, and hoping to God they don't get a finished cake—which is nuclear war. This is basically psychotic behavior.

According to a former computer analyst at the Pentagon, the World Wide Military Command and Control System (Wimex), which has to sort out all the data coming in before the decision is made about nuclear war, breaks down about every thirty-five minutes.[8] There is so much

7. Huge intercontinental missiles that are transported on roadways covering a rectangular area of more than forty-five thousand square miles. The MX system is made up of two hundred "clusters," each with twenty-three shelters strung out along six-by-ten-mile elliptical roadways. Along each of these roadways a Transporter-Erector-Launcher moves, hauling a missile with ten independently targeted nuclear warheads. Each of these vehicles, weighing five hundred tons, stops at every one of the twenty-three shelters along its loop. At one of these shelters it secretly leaves its missile and its launcher. Once empty, each vehicle continues around its loop. Thus missiles are distributed secretly in only two hundred of the forty-six hundred shelters. This system is supposed to make attack by the Soviets virtually untargetable. Senator William Proxmire (D-Wis.) estimates that the real cost of the MX program is one hundred billion dollars. Erica Schoenberger and Amy K. Glasmeier, "Selling the MX: The Air Force Asks Nevada to Move Over," *Progressive*, May 1980, pp. 16–21. Also Tristram Coffin, "The MX, America's 100 Billion Dollar 'Edsel,'" *Washington Spectator and Between the Lines*, 15 October 1980, pp. 1–3.

8. Wimex is a network of thirty-five computers, the primary warning system that controls U.S. military forces throughout the world. Wimex is the President's own crisis computer network. "John Bradley, the former chief test engineer on the computer network, says it is so unreliable that senior military officials have learnt to mistrust it. He estimates that there are 10 false alerts for every one that the Press is told of. . . . The system fails, on average, once every 35 minutes. . . . Bradley's statements are supported by the former supreme allied commander in Europe, General Alexander Haig. In November 1976 Haig sent a memorandum to the joint chiefs of staff in Washington which said that Wimex 'is generally considered to be inefficient and approaching obsolescence. . . .' According to the General Accounting Office . . . things began to go wrong as early as 1973. . . . By March 1976, the system was incapable of working for more than an hour at a stretch without breaking down. . . ." David Blundy and John Bierman, "The Computer that Keeps Declaring War," *Times* (London), 22 June 1980, p. 8.

information coming in from all around the world that no human mind can contain it all. Therefore the signal to begin a nuclear war would be given by a computer—but a computer that does not function properly. Their problem in the Pentagon is that the computer may not work fast enough for the U.S. to press her button and annihilate Russia during the nine minutes it takes the Russian submarine-launched missiles to reach American missile silos. The Pentagon doesn't have a problem about America being destroyed—because they think it will happen—and so do I—but they worry about their ability to destroy the "aggressor."

In nine minutes do you have an aggressor?

That's how they think in the Pentagon.

Recently we had presidential candidate Jerry Brown and George Kistiakowsky, the man who was in charge of the Explosives Division in the Manhattan Project, at our house to discuss the arms race. Kistiakowsky is eighty now, an old man and sick. As he was leaving I said, "George, do you think we'll survive?"

He looked down at me and said, "Well, I'll survive my natural life-span. You won't."

Many people at MIT who are or who have been involved in making weapons agree. Three computer mistakes between November 1979 and June 1980 put us within minutes of nuclear war. Within two to three years "launch on warning" will be developed by the Pentagon.[9] If they decide to deploy this system, American missiles will be launched within three minutes after an American reconnaissance satellite detects an irregularity in Russia. There will be no human input.

Every town and city in the USA with a population of 25,000 or more is targeted with a nuclear weapon. This is also true for every major city in the USSR, China, Europe, and England. Not many people will

9. "Launch on warning" is a term used by the military to explain a technique for launching missiles under attack before the missiles are actually hit. Instead of waiting for the actual attack, missiles are launched when there is a warning of attack. President Carter's secretary of defense, Harold Brown, has "warned the Soviets that the United States is capable of launching on warning and may well do so if we think we are under attack." Robert Thaxton, "Directive Fifty-Nine: Carter's New 'Deterrence' Doctrine Moves Us Closer to the Holocaust," *Progressive*, October 1980, pp. 36–37. In the *Wall Street Journal*, the secretary of defense is quoted as saying that "launch under attack" is a "bad idea" because we might not be able to respond in time. "We can't be certain we would be able to do that [launch under attack]. That is why we shouldn't depend on it." Kenneth H. Bacon and Thomas J. Bray, "An Interview with Harold Brown," *Wall Street Journal*, 1 July 1980, p. 22.

survive nuclear war. Even if you happened to be far enough away from a targeted area not to be immediately vaporized, and you got yourself into a fallout shelter and didn't come out for two weeks so you wouldn't die from the intense fallout, when you did come out there would be nothing to eat or drink. Within a few weeks you would probably be deathly ill. It is predicted that after a full-scale nuclear war 90 percent of the American population would be dead within thirty days. It is possible that only cockroaches and other insects, which are 400,000 times more resistent to radiation than man is, would survive. Truly the living would envy the dead. If only 10 percent of the American and Russian weapons stockpiles were to be used, sufficient ozone would be destroyed in the atmosphere to blind every organism on earth.

Given the obvious insanity of nuclear war, you might ask why, when we have enough bombs to kill the Russians forty times over, do we still continue to make or recycle three to ten hydrogen bombs every single day?

Because the weapons industry makes a lot of money. Over half the scientists in this country work in the military-industrial complex. Almost every big industry is involved in it. General Electric, Union Carbide, Westinghouse make parts for hydrogen bombs. Even Singer Sewing Machines makes parts for missiles. Sylvania has just received a contract to make parts for the MX missile. More than fifty cents out of every federal tax dollar we pay goes to the military-industrial complex.

This money is draining into weapons instead of into consumer areas to keep this country truly strong. The main cause of inflation in America is the military-industrial complex—the sacred cow that is never touched. Instead, they cut the budget for health care, for old people, for Head-start—and they make more bombs to annihilate us all.

There are thirty-five countries that now have the capability of producing nuclear weapons because this country and other countries have sold them nuclear reactors. Since many of these reactors produce about five hundred pounds of plutonium a year, most of these countries could theoretically make about fifty atomic bombs in a single year.

We have to become educated. We must teach each other about the facts of radiation and nuclear war. The more people learn, the more they will say, "I won't put up with this." We need Paul Reveres riding through the streets warning everyone. We have to stop this industry and this insane arms race.

It is starting to happen. People are demonstrating at Trident plants, at Portsmouth Naval Shipyards—at many places. I used to have to work hard to get audiences to listen. Now I don't have to. People want to know. When they first hear the truth about nuclear power and nuclear war, they are shocked and depressed. Then they turn to action and feel better. I can see it happening. I know what we are capable of. The power of people speaking out in one voice is remarkable.

August 1980

Bibliography

CHRONOLOGY OF EVENTS IN THE HISTORY OF NUCLEAR POWER

Brown, Anthony Cave, and Charles B. MacDonald. *The Secret History of the Atomic Bomb.* New York: Dell Publishing Company, 1977.

Divine, Robert A. *Blowing on the Wind: The Nuclear Test Ban Debate 1954–1960.* New York: Oxford University Press, 1978.

Epstein, William. *The Last Chance: Nuclear Proliferation and Arms Control.* New York: Collier Macmillan, 1976.

Fuller, John G. *We Almost Lost Detroit.* New York: Ballantine Books, 1976.

Gyorgy, Anna, and Friends. *No Nukes: Everyone's Guide to Nuclear Power.* Boston: South End Press, 1979.

Novick, Sheldon. *The Electric War: The Fight Over Nuclear Power.* San Francisco: Sierra Club Books, 1976.

Reader, Mark; Ronald Hardert; and Gerald L. Moulton. *Atom's Eve: Ending the Nuclear Age.* New York: McGraw-Hill Book Company, 1980.

Schneir, Walter and Miriam. *Invitation to an Inquest: Reopening the Rosenberg "Atom Spy" Case.* Baltimore: Penguin Books, 1973.

Sternglass, Ernest J. *Low-Level Radiation.* New York: Ballantine Books, 1972.

ONE. JAMES PIRES

Bertell, Rosalie. "Testimony before the Nuclear Regulatory Commission in the Matter of Boston Edison Company et al., Pilgrim Nuclear Power Station Unit 2." Docket No. 50–471. Cambridge, Massachusetts, 19 April 1977.

Franklin, Ben A. "Atom Plants Are Hiring Stand-Ins To Spare Aides the Radiation Risk." *New York Times,* 16 July 1979.

"Highest N-Radiation at Pilgrim-1 Admitted." *Brockton Enterprise,* 13 March 1979.

Hott, Larry. "Pilgrim Nuke Owners Sued." *Clamshell Alliance News,* September-October 1979.

Kerr, Frank. "Most Serious of Pilgrim II Setbacks Seen as Cutback in Edison Rate Hike." *Brockton Enterprise,* 30 March 1978.

Paige, Connie. "Burning Out Workers at Pilgrim 1." *Real Paper,* 3 March 1979.

Raber, Martha. "Pilgrim I Accident 'Coverup' Charged." *Brockton Enterprise,* 30 March 1978.

Rosenthal, Robert J. "His Massive Dose of Radiation Called 'Time Bomb' by Wife." *Boston Globe,* 30 April 1979.

U.S. Nuclear Regulatory Commission, Office of Inspection and Enforcement, Region I. Report No. 50–293/77–31, Docket No. 50–293. Washington, D.C., 12 January 1978. Includes: "Inspection Summary"; "Event Description"; "Boston Edison Company Enforcement History Relating to Radiation Protection 5-12-76 to 11-30-77." License No. DPR-35, Docket No. 50-293.

———— to Boston Edison Company. Docket No. 50-293. Washington, D.C., 8 March 1978. Includes: Appendix A: "Notice of Violation"; Appendix B: "Notice of Proposed Imposition of Civil Penalties"; Appendix C: "Boston Edison Company Enforcement History Relating to Radiation Protection 5-12-76 to 11-30-77: Noncompliance Items."

Two. Rosalie Bertell

Anderson, Robert E., M.D.; Tsutomu Yamamoto, M.D.; and Todd W. Thorslund, B.S. "Aging in Hiroshima and Nagasaki Bomb Survivors: Soluble-Insoluble Collagen Ratio." Hiroshima, Nagasaki, Japan: American Bomb Casualty Commission, 1972. Technical Report No. 11-72. A paper based on this report was published in the *Journal of Gerontology* 29 (1974): 153–159.

Bertell, Rosalie to H. David Maillie, director of Health Physics, University of Rochester Medical School, 3 April 1980.

————. "Measurable Health Effects of Diagnostic X-ray Exposure." In *Effect of Radiation on Human Health: Radiation Health Effects of Medical and Diagnostic X-Rays.* Vol. 2. Hearings before the Subcommittee on Health and the Environment of the Committee of Interstate and Foreign Commerce of the House of Representatives. Serial No. 95-180. Washington, D.C., 11 July 1978.

————. "More About Nuclear Suicide." *Nuclear Opponents,* May–June 1975.

————. "New Structures for Growth." Invited address, World Future Studies Conference: Science and Technology and the Future, Berlin, East Germany, 8–10 May 1979.

————. "The Nuclear Crossroads." La Veta, Colorado: Environmental Action Reprint Service, 29 April 1978.

————. "Nuclear Power: Colossal Experiment on Human Beings." Syracuse, New York: Syracuse Peace Council, 11 March 1977.

————. "Nuclear Suicide." *America* 131 (1974).

————. "The Nuclear Worker and Ionizing Radiation." *American Industrial Hygiene Association Journal* 40 (1979): 395–401.

————. "Radiation Exposure and Human Species Survival." *Issue Papers: Working Docu-*

ments of 10 March 1980 Public Meeting. Vol. 1. Bethesda, Maryland: Committee on Federal Research into the Biological Effects of Ionizing Radiation, National Institutes of Health, 1980.

———. "Written Testimony on the Hazards of Low Level Radiation." Subcommittee on Energy and the Environment of the Committee on Interior and Insular Affairs of the U.S. House of Representatives, Washington, D.C., 6 August 1975.

———. "X-ray Exposure and Premature Aging." *Journal of Surgical Oncology* 9 (1977): 379–391.

Bertell, Rosalie, and Dr. Irwin D. J. Bross. *Proceedings of a Congressional Seminar on Low Level Ionizing Radiation.* Report No. 79–767–0. Washington, D.C.: U.S. Government Printing Office, 1976.

Bross, Irwin D. J. "A Report on the Action of the Two Federal Agencies, ERDA and NCI, in Terminating Funding for Two Major Studies of the Health Hazards Produced by Low Levels of Ionizing Radiation," 5 July 1977. In *Effect of Radiation on Human Health: Health Effects of Ionizing Radiation.* Vol. 1. Hearings before the Subcommittee on Health and the Environment of the Committee on Interstate and Foreign Commerce of the U.S. House of Representatives. Serial No. 95–179. Washington, D.C., 24, 25, 26 January and 8, 9, 14, 28 February 1978.

——— to Rosalie Bertell, on the activities of Dr. Sidney Marks, 13 April 1978.

——— to John O. Pastore, chairman, Joint Committee on Atomic Energy (JCAE), U.S. Congress, 6 October 1975.

———. "Low Level Ionizing Radiation is Hazardous to Health: A Coverup and its Consequences." In *Effect of Radiation on Human Health.* Vol. 1. 8 February 1978.

———. "Major Strategic Mistakes in the Management of the Conquest of Cancer Program by the NCI." Testimony to the Subcommittee on Intergovernmental Relations and Human Resources of the Committee on Government Operations of the U.S. House of Representatives, Washington, D.C., 14 June 1977.

Bross, Irwin D. J., and N. Natarajan. "Genetic Damage from Diagnostic Radiation." *Journal of the American Medical Association* 237 (May 1977): 2399–2401.

———. "Leukemia from Low Level Radiation." *New England Journal of Medicine* 287 (1972): 107–110.

———. "Risk of Leukemia in Susceptible Children Exposed to Preconception, in Utero, and Postnatal Radiation." *Preventive Medicine* 3 (1974): 361–369.

Brownstein, Ron. "A $1,000,000,000 Energy Boondoggle." *Critical Mass Journal,* June 1980.

Chowka, Peter Barry. "A Tale of Nuclear Tyranny." *New Age,* August 1980, pp. 26–35, 68.

Court-Brown, W. M., M.B., and Richard Doll, M.D. "Mortality from Cancer and Other Causes after Radiotherapy for Anklylosing Spondylitis." *British Medical Journal* (1965): 1327–1332.

Durkin, John A., U.S. Senate, to James R. Schlesinger, secretary of the Department of Energy (DOE), 27 January 1978.

Effect of Radiation on Human Health: Health Effects of Ionizing Radiation. Vol. 1. Hearings before the Subcommittee on Health and the Environment of the Committee on Interstate and Foreign Commerce of the U.S. House of Representatives. Serial No.

95–179. Washington, D.C., 24, 25, 26 January and 8, 9, 14, 28 February 1978.

Effect of Radiation on Human Health: Radiation Health Effects of Medical and Diagnostic X-Rays. Vol. 2. Hearings before the Subcommittee on Health and the Environment of the Committee on Interstate and Foreign Commerce of the U.S. House of Representatives. Serial No. 95–180. Washington, D.C., 11, 12, 13, and 14 July 1978.

Graham, S.; M. L. Levin; A. Lilienfeld, et al. "Methodological Problems and Designs of Tri-State Leukemia Survey." *Annals of the New York Academy of Science* 107 (1963): 557–569.

Gyorgy, Anna, and Friends. *No Nukes: Everyone's Guide to Nuclear Power.* Boston: South End Press, 1979.

Liverman, James L., director, Division of Biomedical and Environmental Research, Energy Research and Development Administration (ERDA), to Sister Rosalie Bertell, senior cancer researcher, 24 June 1975.

———, acting assistant secretary for environment, DOE, to John A. Durkin, U.S. Senate, 20 March 1978.

———, director, Division of Biomedical and Environmental Research, ERDA, to George F. Murphy, Jr., executive director, Joint Committee on Atomic Energy (JCAE), U.S. Congress, 17 September 1975.

Mancuso, Thomas F.; Alice Stewart; and George Kneale. "Radiation Exposures of Hanford Workers Dying from Cancer and Other Causes." *Health Physics* 33 (1977): 369–384.

Pastore, John O., chairman, JCAE, U.S. Congress, to Emma Sacco, 22 September 1975.

Radiation Standards and Public Health. Proceedings of a second congressional seminar on low-level ionizing radiation. Washington, D.C.: Congressional Research Service, Library of Congress, 10 February 1978.

Report to the Nuclear Regulatory Commission from the Staff Panel on the Commission's Determination of an Extraordinary Nuclear Occurrence. NUREG-0637. Washington, D.C.: U.S. Government Printing Office, 1980.

Rotblat, J. "The Puzzle of Absent Effects." *New Scientist* 75 (1975): 475.

Seltser, Raymond, and Philip E. Sartwell. "The Influence of Occupational Exposure to Radiation on the Mortality of American Radiologists and Other Medical Specialists." *American Journal of Epidemiology* 81 (1965): 2.

"$20 Billion Voted for Nuclear Fusion." *New York Times,* 26 August 1980.

U.S. Department of Energy DOE/NASA Satellite Power System Concept Development and Evaluation Program. "Some Questions and Answers about the Satellite Power System." DOE/ER–0049/1. Washington, D.C., January 1980.

THREE. ERNEST J. STERNGLASS

Arakawa, E. T. "Radiation Dosimetry in Hiroshima and Nagasaki Atomic Bomb Survivors." *New England Journal of Medicine* 263 (1960): 488–493.

"Cancer from Nuclear Sub Work." *Clamshell Alliance News,* March-April 1978.

Clark, Herbert M. "The Occurrence of an Unusually High-level Radioactive Rainout in the Area of Troy, New York." *Science,* 7 May 1954.

Curry, Bill. "A-Test Officials Feared Outcry After Health Study." *Washington Post,* 14 April 1979.

"The Danger of Radiation at Portsmouth Shipyard." *Boston Globe,* 19 February 1978.

DeGroot, Morris H. "Statistical Studies of the Effect of Low Level Radiation from Nuclear Reactors on Human Health." In *Proceedings of Sixth Berkeley Symposium on Mathematical Statistics and Probability,* edited by J. Neyman. Berkeley: University of California Press, 1971.

Effect of Radiation on Human Health: Health Effects of Ionizing Radiation. Vol. 1. Hearings before the Subcommittee on Health and the Environment of the Committee on Interstate and Foreign Commerce of the U.S. House of Representatives. Serial No. 95-179. Washington, D.C., 24, 25, 26 January and 8, 9, 14, 28 February 1978.

Environmental Effects of Producing Electric Power. Hearings before the Joint Committee on Atomic Energy, 91st Congress. Part I, October–November 1969. Part II, January–February 1970.

Finch, Dr. S., et al. *Preliminary Findings.* New Haven: Yale University Study, sponsored by the Atomic Bomb Casualty Commission, 1966.

Finkel, Miriam P., and Birute O. Biskis. "Pathologic Consequences of Radiostrontium Administered to Fetal and Infant Dogs." In *Radiation Biology of the Fetal and Juvenile Mammal, Proceedings of the Ninth Annual Hanford Biology Symposium at Richland, Washington, 5–8 May 1969,* edited by Melvin R. Sikov and D. Dennis Mahlum. CONF-690501. Springfield, Virginia: Clearinghouse for Federal Scientific and Technical Information, 1969.

Griffiths, Joel. "Backgrounding the Controversy." *Beaver County (Pa.) Times,* 7 June 1974.

———. "State Panel Questions Radiation Safety." *Beaver County (Pa.) Times,* 7 June 1974.

Hollingsworth, J. W. "Delayed Effects in Survivors of the Atomic Bombings: A Summary of the Findings of the Atomic Bomb Casualty Commission, 1947–1959." *New England Journal of Medicine* 263 (1960): 481–487.

Honicker vs. Hendrie: A Lawsuit to End Atomic Power. Summertown, Tennessee: The Book Publishing Company, 1978.

Kahn, Herman. *On Thermonuclear War.* Princeton, New Jersey: Princeton University Press, 1960.

Kissinger, Henry. *Nuclear Weapons and Foreign Policy.* New York: Harper & Brothers, 1957.

Lade, James H. "Effect of 1953 Fallout in Troy, New York, upon Milk and Children's Thyroids." *Science,* 9 November 1962.

Lapp, Ralph E. "Nevada Test Fallout." *Science,* 25 October 1963.

Lyon, J. L.; M. R. Klauber; J. W. Gardner; and K. S. Udall. "Childhood Leukemias Associated with Fallout from Nuclear Testing." *New England Journal of Medicine* 300 (1979): 397–402.

MacMahon, Brian. "Prenatal X-Ray Exposure and Childhood Cancer." *Journal of National Cancer Institute* 28 (1962): 1173–1191.

Mancuso, Thomas F.; Alice Stewart; and George Kneale. "Radiation Exposures of Hanford Workers Dying From Various Causes." *Health Physics* 33 (1977): 369–384.

Martell, E. A. "Actinides for the Environment and their Uptake by Man." Boulder, Colorado: National Center for Atmospheric Research (NCAR), 1975.

————. "Iodine-131 Fallout from Underground Tests II." *Science*, 25 June 1965.

Mayo, Anna. "Bombing Out: Physicist Suggests Link Between A-Tests and SAT Scores." *Voice*, 3 September 1979.

Najarian, Thomas, and Theodore Colton. "Mortality from Leukemia and Cancer in Shipyard Nuclear Workers." *Lancet* (1978): 1018–1020.

National Academy of Sciences. "The Effects on Populations of Exposure to Low Levels of Ionizing Radiation." Report of the Advisory Commission on the Biological Effects of Ionizing Radiation (BEIR Report). Washington, D.C., November 1972.

Nuclear Explosives in Peacetime. Denver, Colorado: Scientists' Institute for Public Information, 1977.

Pauling, Linus. *No More War*. New York: Dodd, Mead & Company, 1958.

Pawlick, Thomas. "The Silent Toll." *Harrowsmith*, June 1980, pp. 33–49.

Pollock, Richard. "Business as Usual in Pennsylvania: 1971 Radiation Scare Fails to Bring Action." *Critical Mass Journal*, December 1979.

Robertson, James, and John Lewallen, eds. *The Grass Roots Primer*. San Francisco: Sierra Book Club, 1975, pp. 125–135.

Sanders, R. *Project Plowshare: The Development of the Peaceful Uses of Nuclear Explosives*. Washington, D.C.: Public Affairs Press, 1962.

Schneir, Walter and Miriam. *Invitation to an Inquest: Reopening the Rosenberg "Atom Spy" Case*. Baltimore: Penguin Books, 1973.

Seaborg, Glenn T., and William R. Corliss. *Man and Atom: Building a New World through Nuclear Technology*. New York: Dutton & Company, 1971.

"Shippingport Nuclear Power Station: Alleged Health Effects." Report to Governor Milton Shapp of Pennsylvania, 1974.

Sternglass, Ernest J. "Cancer Mortality Changes around Nuclear Facilities in Connecticut." In *Radiation Standards and Public Health*. Proceedings of a second congressional seminar on low-level ionizing radiation. Washington, D.C.: Congressional Research Service, Library of Congress, 10 February 1978.

————. "Cancer: Relation of Prenatal Radiation to Development of the Disease in Childhood." *Science*, 7 June 1963.

————. "Can the Infants Survive?" *Bulletin of the Atomic Scientists*, June 1969.

————. "The Death of All Children." *Esquire*, September 1969.

————. "Environmental Radiation and Human Health." In *Proceedings of the Sixth Berkeley Symposium on Mathematical Statistics and Probability*, edited by J. Neyman. Berkeley: University of California Press, 1971.

————. "Infant Mortality and Nuclear Tests." *Bulletin of the Atomic Scientists*, April 1969.

————. "Infant Mortality Changes Associated with Nuclear Waste Discharges from Research Reactors into the Upper Ohio River Watershed." Presented at the AEC Rulemaking Hearings on proposed amendments to 10CFR50. Washington, D.C., 15 February 1972.

————. *Low-Level Radiation*. New York: Ballantine Books, 1972.

————. "Radioactive Waste Discharges from the Shippingport Nuclear Power Station and Changes in Cancer Mortality." Written testimony for hearings on Shippingport Atomic Power Station, Governor Milton J. Shapp Commission, 8 May 1973.

———. "The Role of Indirect Radiation Effects on Cell Membranes in Immune Response and Evidence for Low Level Radiation Effects on the Human Embryo and Fetus." In *Radiation Biology of the Fetal and Juvenile Mammal, Proceedings of the Ninth Annual Hanford Biology Symposium at Richland, Washington, 5–8 May 1969,* edited by Melvin R. Sikov and D. Dennis Mahlum. CONF-690501. Springfield, Virginia: Clearinghouse for Federal Scientific and Technical Information, 1969.

———. "Safety Data on Shippingport Nuclear Plant Questioned." News Release, "Environment Pittsburgh," Pittsburgh, 3 January 1973.

———. "Significance of Radiation Monitoring Results for the Shippingport Nuclear Reactor." Report to Governor Milton J. Shapp, 21 January 1973.

———. "Strontium-90 Levels in the Milk and Diet Near Connecticut Nuclear Power Plants." Report to Congressman C. J. Dodd and Representative John Anderson, 27 October 1977.

Stewart, Alice, and George W. Kneale. "Radiation Dose Effects in Relation to Obstetric X-Rays and Childhood Cancers." *Lancet* (June 1970): 1185–1187.

Stewart, Alice; Josefine Webb; and David Hewitt. "A Survey of Childhood Malignancies." *British Medical Journal* (June 1958): 1495–1508.

Swift, M. N., and C. L. Posser. "The Excretion, Retention, Distribution and Clinical Effects of Strontium-89 in the Dog." USAEC Report CH-3843. Argonne National Laboratory, 1947.

Teller, Edward, et al. *Constructive Uses of Nuclear Explosives.* New York: McGraw-Hill, 1968.

United Nations. "Radiation-induced Chromosome Aberrations in Human Cells." *Report of the United Nations Scientific Committee on the Effects of Radiation.* Annex C, Supplement No. 13 (A/7613). New York, 1969.

U.S. Arms Control and Disarmament Agency. "PNE (Peaceful Nuclear Explosion) Activity Projections for Arms Control Planning." Vol 1. Submitted by Gulf Universities Research Consortium, Galveston, Texas. Contract No. ACDA/PAB-253. Washington, D.C., 10 April 1975.

U.S. Atomic Energy Commission. "Engineering with Nuclear Explosives—Proceedings of the Third Plowshare Symposium." TID-7695. 1964.

U.S. Congress. Hearings of the Joint Committee on Atomic Energy, Special Subcommittee on Radiation: (a) May 1957 hearings on fallout; (b) May 1959 hearings on fallout; (c) June 1959 hearings on the biological and environmental effects of nuclear war; (d) June 1962 hearings on fallout; (e) June 1963 hearings on fallout; (f) August 1963 hearings on fallout; (g) June 1965 hearings on federal radiation council protective action guides. Washington, D.C.: U.S. Government Printing Office.

U.S. Department of Health, Education, and Welfare, Bureau of Radiological Health. "An Estimate of Radiation Doses Received by Individuals Living in the Vicinity of a Nuclear Fuel Reprocessing Plant in 1968." BRH/NERHL-70-1, HEW-PAS, EHS. Rockville, Maryland, May 1970.

———. "Radioactive Waste Discharges to the Environment from Nuclear Power Facilities." BRH-DER 70-2. Rockville, Maryland, March 1970.

————. "Radiological Surveillance Studies at a Boiling Water Nuclear Power Station." BRH-DER 70-1. Rockville, Maryland, March 1970.

FOUR. JOHN W. GOFMAN

Fadiman, Anne. "The Downwind People: A Thousand Americans Sue for Damage Brought on by Atomic Fallout." *Life*, June 1980, pp. 32–40.

"Fast-Breeder Reactor Backed—Jolt for U.S." *San Francisco Chronicle*, 26 February 1980.

Ford, Daniel F., and Henry F. Kendall. *An Assessment of the Emergency Core Cooling Systems Rulemaking Hearing.* San Francisco: Friends of the Earth/Union of Concerned Scientists, 1974.

Gerber, C. R.; R. Hamburger; and E. W. S. Hull. *Plowshare.* Washington, D.C.: Atomic Energy Commission, Understanding the Atom Series, 1967.

Gofman, John W. "The Cancer and Leukemia Consequence of Medical X-Rays." *Osteopathic Annuals*, November 1975.

————. "The Cancer Hazard from Inhaled Plutonium." CNR Report 1975-IR. San Francisco: Committee for Nuclear Responsibility (CNR), 14 May 1975.

————. "Estimated Production of Human Lung Cancers by Plutonium from Worldwide Test Fallout." San Francisco: CNR, 10 July 1975.

————. "Federal Radiation Council Guidelines for Radiation Exposure of the Population at Large—Protection or Disaster?" Testimony presented to the Senate Committee on Public Works, 18 November 1969. In *Environmental Effects of Producing Electric Power.* Hearings before the Joint Committee on Atomic Energy (JCAE), 91st Congress. Part I, October–November 1969.

————. "The Fission-Product Equivalence between Nuclear Reactors and Nuclear Weapons." *Senate Congressional Record, Proceedings and Debates of the 92nd Congress, 1st Session.* Vol. 117. Washington, D.C., 8 July 1971.

————. *"Irrevy," An Irreverent, Illustrated View of Nuclear Power.* San Francisco: CNR, 1979.

————. "Low Dose Radiation, Chromosomes, and Cancer." Presented at the Institute for Electrical, Electronic Engineers (IEEE) Nuclear Science Symposium. San Francisco, 29 October 1969.

————. "The Question of Radiation Causation of Cancer in Hanford Workers." *Health Physics* 37 (1979): 617–639.

Gofman, John W., and Arthur R. Tamplin. "Epidemiologic Studies of Carcinogenesis by Ionizing Radiation." In *Proceedings of the Sixth Berkeley Symposium on Mathematical Statistics and Probability*, edited by J. Neyman. Berkeley: University of California Press, 1971.

————. *Poisoned Power: The Case Against Nuclear Power Plants.* Emmaus, Pennsylvania: Rodale Press, 1971.

————. *Population Control through Nuclear Pollution.* Chicago: Nelson-Hall Company, 1970.

Mayo, Anna. "John Gofman: An American Dissenter." *Village Voice*, 7 May 1979.

National Academy of Sciences. "The Effects on Populations of Exposure to Low Levels of Ionizing Radiation." Report of the Advisory Committee on the Biological Effects of Ionizing Radiation (BEIR Report), November 1972.

Pauling, Linus. *No More War.* New York: Dodd, Mead & Company, 1958.

Seaborg, Glenn T., and William R. Corliss. *Man and Atom: Building a New World through Nuclear Technology.* New York: E. P. Dutton Company, 1971.

Segi, M.; M. Kurihara; and T. Matsuyama. *Cancer Mortality in Japan, 1899–1962.* Sendai, Japan: Department of Public Health, Tohoku University School of Medicine, 1965.

Shutdown! Nuclear Power on Trial. [Testimony of Dr. John W. Gofman and Dr. Ernest J. Sternglass.] Summertown, Tennessee: The Book Publishing Company, 1979.

Sternglass, Ernest J. "The Death of All Children." *Esquire,* September 1969.

———. *Low-Level Radiation.* New York: Ballantine Books, 1972.

Stewart, Alice; Josefine Webb; and David Hewitt. "A Survey of Childhood Malignancies." *British Medical Journal* (June 1958): 1495–1508.

Stewart, Alice, and George W. Kneale. "Radiation Dose Effects in Relation to Obstetric X-Rays and Childhood Cancers." *Lancet* (June 1970): 1185–1188.

Teller, Edward, et al. *Constructive Uses of Nuclear Explosives.* New York: McGraw-Hill, 1968.

Thaxton, Robert. "Directive Fifty-Nine: Carter's New 'Deterrence' Doctrine Moves Us Closer to the Holocaust." *Progressive,* October 1980, pp. 36–37.

Underground Uses of Nuclear Energy. Hearings before the Subcommittee on Air and Water Pollution of the Committee on Public Works of the U.S. Senate, 91st Congress, 1st Session, on S. 3042, Part I, 18–20 November 1969. Includes testimony of John W. Gofman: "A Proposal for at Least a Ten-Fold Reduction in the Federal Radiation Council Guidelines for Radiation Exposure to the Population-at-Large: Supportive Evidence." Presented to the JCAE, 28 January 1970; "IRCP [International Committee on Radiation Protection] Publication 14 vs. the Gofman-Tamplin Report." Supplement to Gofman testimony, 28 January 1970.

Underground Uses of Nuclear Energy. Hearings before the Subcommittee on Air and Water Pollution of the Committee on Public Works of the U.S. Senate, 91st Congress, 2nd Session, on S. 3042, Part II, 5 August 1970. Includes testimony of John W. Gofman: "16,000 Cancer Deaths from FRC Guideline Radiation (Gofman-Tamplin) vs. 160 Cancer Deaths from FRC Guideline Radiation (Dr. John Storer): A Refutation of the Storer Analysis." Testimony to the JCAE, 9 February 1970.

FIVE. JOHN EVERETT

Bridenbaugh, Dale G.; Richard B. Hubbard; and Gregory C. Minor. "Testimony." In *Investigation of Charges Relating to Nuclear Reactor Safety.* Hearings of the Joint Committee on Atomic Energy of the U.S. Congress, 94th Congress. Vol. 1. Washington, D.C.: U.S. Government Printing Office, 1976.

Burnham, David. "Gulf Aides Admit Cartel Increased Price of Uranium." *New York Times,* 17 June 1977.

Cassidy, J. "Says He Failed Test, Toiled at A-Plant." *Daily News,* 7 December 1979.

Cerra, Frances. "L.I. Union Agent Ousts Son Over Atom Plant Testimony." *New York Times,* 7 December 1979.

———. "U.S. Studies Charges of Poor Work at L.I. Atom Plant." *New York Times,* 15 December 1979.

Everett, John. "Testimony from the People of the State of New York v. Matthew J. Chachere, Defendant." Hauppauge District Court of Suffolk County, 6 December 1979.

Freeman, Leslie, and Daniel Pisello. "Big Money—Nuclear Plans Behind Squeeze at Mohawk Nation." *Akwesasne Notes,* Summer 1980.

Fresco, Robert. "NRC Probes Shoreham Construction." *Newsday,* 15 December 1979.

———. "Shoreham: Delays and Rising Costs." *Newsday,* 4 April 1979.

Fried, Joseph P. "Ex-Union Aide Loses Court Bid to Regain Post." *New York Times,* 12 January 1980.

Giller, Susan. "Shoreham Witness Sues to Regain Job." *Newsday,* 28 December 1979.

Gillette, Robert. "Nuclear Safety (I): The Roots of Dissent." *Science,* September 1972.

Gofman, John W. *"Irrevy,"* An Irreverent, Illustrated View of Nuclear Power. San Francisco: Committee for Nuclear Responsibility, 1979.

Greenfield, Jim. " 'Cutting Corners' Called Top Concern at Zimmer." *Cincinnati Enquirer,* 20 June 1979.

Grossman, Karl. *Cover Up: What You Are Not Supposed to Know About Nuclear Power.* New York: Permanent Press, 1980.

———. "Shoring Up Shoreham: Long Island's Nuclear Interlock Has Big Plans, Leaky Pipes." *Seven Days,* 26 October 1979.

Gyorgy, Anna, and Friends. *No Nukes: Everyone's Guide to Nuclear Power.* Boston: South End Press, 1979.

Hull, A. P. "Background Radiation Levels at Brookhaven National Laboratory." Report submitted at the licensing hearings, Shoreham nuclear plant. Docket No. 50-322. 15 May 1970.

Jacobs, Gloria. "Inside the Nuclear Industry's Heart: Construction Workers Talk about the Monster They're Building at Shoreham." *Seven Days,* 26 October 1979.

Jaffe, Susan. "New York City: We're Surrounded." *Village Voice,* 7 May 1979.

———. "Repression: The New Nuclear Danger." *Village Voice,* 31 March 1980.

Lane, Robert. "Sues Dad Over N-Plant 'Blackball'." *Daily News,* 28 December 1979.

Lawrence, Steve. "Shoreham: The First $2 Billion Plant?" *Daily News,* 12 February 1980.

Miller, Keith (consultant, Advanced Code Review Group) to Stan Fabic, NRC, Washington, D.C., 7 May 1976. In Gyorgy, *No Nukes,* pp. 116–117.

"PSI Explains Its Side of Marble Hill Dispute." *Cincinnati Enquirer,* 20 July 1979.

Radiation Standards and Public Health. Proceedings of a second congressional seminar on low-level ionizing radiation. Washington, D.C.: Congressional Research Service, Library of Congress, 10 February 1978.

Selvin, Barbara. "Nuke Consultants Defend Role to Be Played." *Suffolk Life,* 3 September 1980.

U.S. Atomic Energy Commission. "Reactor Safety Study: An Assessment of Accident Risks in U.S. Commercial Nuclear Plants." (WASH-1400), Summary Report. Washington, D.C., August 1974.

Wick, Steve. "Fail-Safe Improved at N-Plant: LILCO." *Newsday,* 8 December 1979.
———. "N-Plant Witness Fired for Testifying." *Newsday,* 7 December 1979.
"Zimmer Nuclear Plant A New Threat to American Electric Power System." *Together.* Castlewood, Virginia: Coalition of American Electric Consumers, June 1980.

SIX. URANIUM MINERS AND THEIR WIDOWS

Ambler, Marjane. "Study of Radioactive Homes 'Lost' for 8 Years." *High Country News,* 25 January 1980.
Archer, V. E.; J. D. Gillan; and J. K. Wagoner. "Respiratory Disease Mortality Among Uranium Miners." *Annals of New York Academy of Sciences* 271 (1976): 280–293.
Archer, V. E.; J. K. Wagoner; and F. E. Lundin. "Lung Cancer Among Uranium Miners in the United States." *Health Physics* 25 (1973): 351–371.
Barry, Tom. "Bury My Lungs at Red Rock: Uranium Mining Brings a New Peril to the Reservation." *Progressive,* February 1979, pp. 25–28.
———. "Land Rights, Not Uranium Miners." *Akwesasne Notes,* Summer 1979.
Carter, Luther J. "Uranium Mill Tailings: Congress Addresses a Long-Neglected Problem." *Science,* 13 October 1978.
Comey, David Dinsmore. "The Legacy of Uranium Tailings." *Bulletin of the Atomic Scientists,* September 1975.
Committee on Mining and the Environment. "Uranium Mining and Milling." Gold Hill, Colorado: Information Series #3, 1979.
Cox, Jack. "Casualties Mounting From U-Rush of '49." *Denver Post,* 2 September 1979.
———. "Effects of Radiation on Early Miners Comes to Light." *Denver Post,* 3 September 1979.
———. "Insurance Claims Can Take Four Years." *Denver Post,* 6 September 1979.
———. "Lifeline Question of a Miner." *Denver Post,* 5 September 1979.
———. "Studies Show Radon Guidelines May Be Weak." *Denver Post,* 4 September 1979.
Fadiman, Anne. "The Downwind People: A Thousand Americans Sue for Damages Brought on by Atomic Fallout." *Life,* June 1980, pp. 32–40.
Federal Radiation Council. "Guidance for the Control of Radiation Hazards in Uranium Mining." Staff Report No. 8, revised. September 1967.
"The Four Corners Today: The Black Hills Tomorrow?" *Black Hills Paha Sapa Report,* August 1979.
Garrity, Michael. "The Pending Energy Wars: America's Final Act of Genocide, Part I." *Akwesasne Notes,* Winter 1979.
———. "The Pending Energy Wars: America's Final Act of Genocide, Part II." *Akwesasne Notes,* Early Spring 1980.
Gilinsky, Victor. "Remarks by Victor Gilinsky" (commissioner, U.S. Nuclear Regulatory Commission), presented at the Pacific Southwest Minerals and Energy Conference, Anaheim, California, 2 May 1978.
Ivins, Molly. "Dam Break Investigated: Radiation of Spill Easing." *New York Times,* 28 July 1979.

————. "100 Navajo Families Sue on Radioactive Waste Spill." *New York Times*, 15 August 1980.

Kaufmann, R. F.; G. G. Eadie; and C. R. Russell. "Effects of Uranium Mining and Milling on Groundwater in the Grants Mineral Belt, New Mexico." Unnumbered report. Las Vegas: Office of Radiation Programs, U.S. Environmental Protection Agency, undated [discussion closed 1 February 1977].

LaDuke, Winona. "The History of Uranium Mining: Who Are These Companies and Where Did They Come From?" *Black Hills Paha Sapa Report*, July 1979.

————. "Shades of Big Mountain." *Akwesasne Notes*, Early Spring, 1980.

Lyon, J. L.; M. R. Klauber; J. W. Gardner; and K. S. Udall. "Childhood Leukemias Associated with Fallout from Nuclear Testing." *New England Journal of Medicine* 300 (1979): 397–402.

Madsden, Reed. "Cancer Deaths Linked to Uranium Mining." *Deseret News*, 4 June 1979.

————. "Miners Didn't Fear Radon." *Deseret News*, 5 June 1979.

Mayo, Anna. "The Nuclear State in Ascendency." *Village Voice*, 22 October 1980.

Metzger, Peter H. "Dear Sir: Your Home is Built on Radioactive Uranium Waste." *New York Times Magazine*, 31 October 1971.

Moelaert, John. "Uranium Miner Speaks: This Dust is Making Me Sick." (From the Energy File) *Saskatoon Sun*, 5 April 1979.

National Academy of Sciences. "Rehabilitation Potential of Western Coal Lands" (1974). Excerpts in *Black Hills Paha Sapa Report*, August 1979.

National Citizens' Hearings for Radiation Victims. "Testimony of the Radiation Victims." Washington, D.C.: Environmental Policy Center, 12 April 1980.

"The Native American Connection." *Up Against the Wall Street Journal*, 29 October 1979.

"The Navajo Nation: Relocation Threatens 6,000 Navajos." *Akwesasne Notes*, Summer 1979.

Oswald, Sherry, and Colleen Ragan. "Brafford Family Leaves Home." *Black Hills Paha Sapa Report*, August 1979.

Pinsky, Mark Alan. "New Mexico Spill Ruins a River: The Worst Radiation Accident in History Gets Little Attention." *Critical Mass Journal*, December 1979.

Pohl, Robert O. "Health Effects of Radon-222 from Uranium Mining." *Search*, August 1979, p. 345.

Preusch, Deb, and Tom Barry. *People and Energy in the Southwest.* [Slideshow and Script.] Albuquerque, New Mexico: New Mexico People and Energy Research Project, 1979.

Public Interest Research Group (PIRG). "PIRG Urges Federal Action to Warn New Mexico Uranium Workers of Radioactive Drinking Water." Press Release. 17 August 1979.

"Report to the Nuclear Regulatory Commission from the Staff Panel on the Commission's Determination of an Extraordinary Nuclear Occurrence." NUREG-0637. Washington, D.C.: U.S. Government Printing Office, 1980.

Schwartz, Loretta. "Uranium Deaths at Crown Point." *Ms.*, October 1979.

Schuey, Chris. "The Widows of Red Rock." *Scottsdale Daily Progress, Saturday Maga-*

zine, Part I, 2 June 1979. Part II, 9 June 1979.

Shipp, E. R. "Hunt for Uranium Upsets 2 Rustic Towns in New Jersey." *New York Times,* 23 August 1980.

Simpson, Craig. "Native People Oppose Uranium Mining in New Mexico." *WIN,* 20 July 1978, pp. 8–10.

Smith, R. "Radon Emissions: Open Pit Uranium Mines Said to be Big Contributor." *Nucleonics Week,* 25 May 1978, p. 21.

Strain, Peggy. "Radiation Found in Colorado Water Supply." *Washington Post,* 14 July 1979.

"Tailings Dam Break: 100 Million Gallons." *Black Hills Paha Sapa Report,* August 1979.

Taylor, Lynda, and Judy Luis-Melius. "Health and Radiation." Albuquerque, New Mexico: Southwest Research and Information Center, 1979.

Tessier, Denise. "Uranium Gas Causes Lung Cancer, UNM Group Told." *Albuquerque Journal,* 11 March 1980.

Wagoner, Joseph. "Uranium Mining and Milling: The Human Costs." Presented at the University of New Mexico Medical School, Albuquerque, New Mexico, 10 March 1980.

Wagoner, Joseph K., et al. "Radiation as the Cause of Lung Cancer Among Uranium Miners." *New England Journal of Medicine* 273 (1965): 181.

"Water . . . A Question of Survival: The Expanding American Desert." *Black Hills Paha Sapa Report,* August 1979.

U.S. Department of Agriculture, Forest Service. "Draft Environmental Statement for Homestake Mining Company's Pitch Project." USDA-FS-R2-DES (ADM) FY-78-03. Grand Mesa, Uncompahgre and Gunnison National Forests, 1978.

U.S. Environmental Protection Agency. "Environmental Analysis of the Uranium Fuel Cycle." Report EPA-520/9-73-003-B. Washington, D.C., 1973.

——. "Interim National Drinking Water Regulations." 40FR34324, (b) para. 141.26. Washington, D.C., 6 July 1976.

——. "Interim Primary Drinking Water Regulations—Proposed Maximum Containment Levels for Radioactivity." 40FRI 58. Washington, D.C., 1975, pp. 34323–34324.

——. "Part IV—Supplementary Analysis: 1976." EPA Office of Radiation Programs, Washington, D.C., July 1976.

U.S. Joint Committee on Atomic Energy, U.S. Congress. Hearings on Radiation Exposure of Uranium Miners, Parts I and II. Washington, D.C., 1967.

SEVEN. WILLIAM H. HODSDEN

Anderson, Donald H. "Letter to Orville Kelly." *Atomic Veterans' Newsletter,* Spring 1980, pp. 14–15.

Army Discharge Review Board. "Proceedings in the Case of William H. Hodsden." Department of the Army, Washington, D.C., 16 July 1974.

"A-Tests May Have Exposed 300,000." *Washington Post,* 11 February 1978.

Berger, John J. "An Atomic Test Case: The Ordeal of Artie Duvall." *Voice,* 22 October 1979.

Board of Veterans' Appeals. "In the Appeal of William H. Hodsden, Findings and

Decision." C-21 641 736, Docket No. 77-38 251. Washington, D.C., 29 November 1978.

Bross, Irwin, D. J. "Hazards to Persons Exposed to Ionizing Radiation (and to their children) from Dosage Currently Permitted by the Nuclear Regulatory Commission." In *Effect of Radiation on Human Health: Health Effects of Ionizing Radiation.* Vol. 1. Hearings before the Subcommittee on Health and the Environment of the Committee on Interstate and Foreign Commerce of the U.S. House of Representatives. Serial No. 95-179. Washington, D.C., 24, 25, 26 January and 8, 9, 14, 28 February 1978, pp. 913–950.

Broudy, Pat. "Letter to Orville Kelly." *Atomic Veterans' Newsletter,* Spring 1980, pp. 18–19.

Commoner, Barry. *The Closing Circle.* New York: Bantam Books, 1974.

Cooper, Nancy. "The Paul Cooper Story." *Atomic Veterans' Newsletter,* Spring 1980, pp. 10–11.

Dann, Russell Jack. "Letter to the Editor." *Atomic Veterans Newsletter,* November-December 1979, p. 9.

Effect of Radiation on Human Health: Health Effects of Ionizing Radiation. Vol. 1. Hearings before the Subcommittee on Health and the Environment of the Committee on Interstate and Foreign Commerce of the U.S. House of Representatives. Serial No. 95-179. Washington, D.C., 24, 25, 26 January and 8, 9, 14, 28 February 1978.

"Exercise Desert Rock VII and VIII: Final Report of Operations." Annex-E, Staff of Headquarters, U.S. Sixth Army. In *Effect of Radiation on Human Health,* Vol. 1, pp. 241–266.

Fadiman, Anne. "The Downwind People: A Thousand Americans Sue for Damage Brought on by Atomic Fallout." *Life,* June 1980, pp. 32–40.

Herbers, John. "Atomic Issue Shifts to Political Arena." *New York Times,* 5 July 1979.

Hines, William. "Ailing Veteran of A-Tests Wins Struggle for Disability Benefits." *Washington Post,* 28 November 1979.

Huyghe, Patrick, and David Konigsberg. "Grim Legacy of Nuclear Testing" *New York Times Magazine,* 22 April 1979.

Iklé, Fred Charles. *The Social Impact of Bomb Destruction.* Norman, Oklahoma: University of Oklahoma Press, 1958.

Jackovitch, Karen G., and Mark Sennet. "The Children of John Wayne, Susan Hayward and Dick Powell Fear that Fallout Killed Their Parents." *People,* 10 November 1980, pp. 42–47.

Leary, Robyn. "More Fallout from the Atom: A Participant in Operation Hardtack, Orville Kelly Was Subjected to 22 Nuclear Explosions. Twenty Years Later, He Developed Widespread Cancer." *Figaro,* 21 January 1980, pp. 13–14.

"Leukemia Among Persons Present at an Atmospheric Nuclear Test (Smoky)." *Morbidity and Mortality Weekly Report* 28 (10 August 1979): 361–362.

Lyon, J. L.; M. R. Klauber; J. W. Gardner; and K. S. Udall. "Childhood Leukemias Associated with Fallout from Nuclear Testing." *New England Journal of Medicine* 300 (1979): 397–402.

Lyons, Richard D. "Public Fears Over Nuclear Hazards Are Increasing." *New York Times,* 1 July 1979.

National Citizens' Hearings for Radiation Victims. "Report of the Commission." Washington, D.C.: Environmental Policy Center, April 1980.

Nawrocki, George J. (captain of 496th Quartermaster Company), to Mr. Leslie Hodsden, 9 January 1958.

Osborne, Clyde. "Area Men Saw A-Blasts." *Asheville Citizen*, 2 March 1978.

Peterson, Charles. "20 Years Ago, Were You There at Yucca Flats, Nev., Atomic Blast?" *Parade*, 19 June 1977.

Pinkus, W. "Use of Troops in Nuclear Tests Probed." *New York Post*, 24 January 1978.

Randal, Smith. "Charge Ike Misled Public on N-Tests." *Daily News*, 20 April 1979.

Rosenberg, Howard I. *Atomic Soldiers: American Victims of Nuclear Experiments.* Boston: Beacon Press, 1980.

————. "The Guineapigs of Camp Desert Rock: Atomic 'Stress Tests' for Unwitting Soldiers." *Progressive*, June 1979, pp. 37–43.

"Story of Nuclear Testing." *Atomic Veterans' Newsletter*, September–October 1979, pp. 2–3.

Sulzberger, A. O., Jr. "Early Radiation Safety Problems Laid to A-Bomb Program's Pace." *New York Times*, 20 June 1979.

Thomas, Jo. "Stakes High as Senate Examines Cancer in Troops at Atom Tests." *New York Times*, 20 June 1979.

Uhl, Michael, and Tod Ensign. *G. I. Guinea Pigs: How the Pentagon Exposed Our Troops to Dangers More Deadly than War.* New York: Playboy Press, 1980.

U.S. Department of Commerce. "PLUMBBOB On-Site Safety Report." No. OTO-57-2. Springfield, Virginia: National Technical Information Services (NTIS).

U.S. Department of Health, Education, and Welfare. Social Security Administration, Bureau of Hearings and Appeals. "Hearing Decision in the Case of William H. Hodsden." 8 July 1975.

"Veteran Exposed to Atomic Tests is Given Benefits: Cancer Was Found Long After He Left the Army." *New York Times*, 27 November 1979.

"Whatever Happened to . . . Those GI Records Lost in '73 Fire." *U.S. News & World Report*, 15 November 1976. In *Atomic Veterans' Newsletter*, September-October 1979, p. 3.

EIGHT. DAVID PYLES

Bebbington, William P. "The Reprocessing of Nuclear Fuels." *Scientific American*, December 1976, pp. 99–110.

Beer, Richard, and Peter Biskind. "West Valley: The Tombstone of Nuclear Power?" *Seven Days*, 29 March 1977, pp. 3–6.

Caldicott, Helen. *Nuclear Madness: What You Can Do.* Brookline, Massachusetts: Autumn Books, 1978.

Cohen, Bernard L. "The Disposal of Radioactive Wastes from Fission Reactors." *Scientific American*, June 1977, pp. 21–31.

————. "Promises vs. Fears of Nuclear Energy." *News World*, 4 September 1978.

Daly, J. C., et al. "Iodine-129 Levels in Milk and Water Near a Nuclear Fuel Reprocessing Plant." *Health Physics* 26 (1974): 333–342.

Duckworth, James P. "High Level Radioactive Waste Management Program at Nuclear Fuel Services." In *High Level Radioactive Waste Management*, edited by Milton H. Campbell. Energy Research Abstracts, ERA 39320. (Also in *Advanced Chemical Series* 153 (1976): 72–83.)

Faulkner, Peter. *The Silent Bomb: A Guide to the Nuclear Energy Controversy.* New York: Vintage Books, 1977.

Gillette, Robert. "Nuclear Fuel Reprocessing: General Electric's Balky Plant Poses Shortage." *Science,* 30 August 1974.

———. "Plutonium (I): Questions of Health in a New Industry." *Science,* 20 September 1974.

———. "Transient Nuclear Workers: A Special Case for Standards." *Science,* 11 October 1974.

Gyorgy, Anna, and Friends. *No Nukes: Everyone's Guide to Nuclear Power.* Boston: South End Press, 1979.

Honicker vs. Hendrie: A Lawsuit to End Atomic Power. Summertown, Tennessee: The Book Publishing Company, 1978.

"Hospital Treats West Valley Nuclear Center Worker for Radiation Poisoning." *Courier Express,* 23 September 1967.

Magno, Paul R.; Thomas C. Reavey; and John C. Apidianakis. "Iodine-129 in the Environment Around a Nuclear Fuel Reprocessing Plant." Washington, D.C.: EPA Office of Radiation Programs, Field Operation Division, U.S. Environmental Protection Agency, 1972.

Nader, Ralph, and John Abbotts. *The Menace of Atomic Energy.* New York: W. W. Norton & Company, 1977.

"Nuclear Waste Burial at West Valley a Failure, but Not Hazard." *Buffalo Evening News,* 9 February 1977.

"Radiation Monitoring at West Valley Processing Plant, October-December 1970." Docket No. 50201-61. *Nuclear Science Abstracts* 25: 13080.

Resnikoff, Marvin. "Expensive Enrichment." *Environment,* July-August 1975, pp. 28–35.

Rhodes, Suzanne. "Barnwell: Achilles Heel of Nuclear Power." In *Southern Exposure, Tower of Babel: A Special Report on the Nuclear Industry,* Winter 1979.

Rochlin, Gene I.; Margery Held; Barbara G. Kaplan; and Lewis Kruger. "West Valley: Remnant of the AEC." *Bulletin of the Atomic Scientists,* January 1978.

Severo, Richard. "Angry Buffalo Residents on Hearing on Atomic Waste." *New York Times,* 14 January 1979.

———. "Too Hot to Handle." *New York Times Magazine,* 10 April 1977.

Skinner, Peter N., et al. "Decommissioning Criteria for the Nuclear Fuel Services' Reprocessing Center, West Valley, New York. The Report by the West Valley Decontamination and Decommissioning Task Group." Report to the Subcommittee on Conservation, Energy and Natural Resources of the House Committee on Government Operations on Issues Related to the Closing of the NFS Inc. Reprocessing Plant at West Valley, New York. GAO Report EMD-77-27 at 2. Washington, D.C.: U.S. General Accounting Office, 1978.

"Spent Fuel Accident Devastating. Can Millions Be Evacuated?" *Waste Paper,* August-September 1979.

Terpilak, M. S., and B. L. Jorgensen. "Environmental Radiation Effects in Nuclear

Facilities in New York State in Radiation Data and Reports." U.S. Environmental Protection Agency, July 1974.

U.S. Department of Energy. *Western New York Nuclear Service Center Study: Final Report for Public Comment.* TID-28905-1. Washington, D.C., November 1978.

————. *Western New York Nuclear Service Center Study: Companion Report.* TID-28905-2. Washington, D.C., November 1978.

————. "Low Level Radiation: Biological Interactions, Risks, and Benefits—A Bibliography." TID-3373. Washington, D.C., September 1978.

U.S. Department of Health, Education, and Welfare. "Estimate of Radiation Doses Received by Individuals Living in the Vicinity of a Nuclear Fuel Reprocessing Plant in 1968." Bureau of Radiological Health/NERHL 70-1, HEW-PAS, ESH. May 1970.

U.S. Nuclear Regulatory Commission. "NRC Proposes Licensing Requirement Exemption for Contaminated Smelted Alloys." News Release. Washington, D.C., 29 October 1980.

"Uranium Returned to AEC from NPR Failed Fuel Assemblies." Docket No. 50201-119. *Nuclear Science Abstracts* 26: 30919.

"Ventilation System Performance for January–June 1972 in West Valley Processing Plant, head-end." *Nuclear Science Abstracts* 26: 50437.

Weisman, Steven R. "U.S. and N.Y. Agree on Disposing of Nuclear Wastes." *New York Times,* 21 March 1979.

"West Valley and the Nuclear Waste Dilemma. 12th Report by Committee on Government Operations Together with Additions and Dissenting Views." Report No. 95-755, Union Calendar No. 394. 95th Congress, 1st Session, 26 October 1977.

"West Valley Nuclear Leakage is Cited." *Courier Express,* 29 April 1978.

NINE. TOM MARTIN ET AL.

Agarwal, Anil. "Nuclear Power in the Third World." *Nature,* June 1979, pp. 468–470.

Blanch, Donald. Sworn Affidavit, 26 June 1976.

Bridenbaugh, Dale G. "Spent Fuel Disposal Costs." Report prepared for the National Resources Defense Council. Washington, D.C., 31 August 1978.

Bridenbaugh, Dale G.; Richard B. Hubbard; and Gregory C. Minor. "Testimony." In *Investigation of Charges Relating to Nuclear Reactor Safety.* Hearings of the Joint Committee on Atomic Energy of the U.S. Congress, 94th Congress. Vol. 1. Washington, D.C.: U.S. Government Printing Office, 1976.

Burnham, David. "Indian Point Decision Is Termed 'Charade'." *New York Times,* 17 February 1980.

————. "Safety an Issue at Indian Point." *New York Times,* 22 September 1974.

————. "Three Engineers Quit G.E. Reactor Division and Volunteer in Antinuclear Movement." *New York Times,* 3 February 1976.

Caldicott, Helen. *Nuclear Madness: What You Can Do.* Brookline, Massachusetts: Autumn Press, 1978.

Comey, David Dinsmore. "The Incident at Browns Ferry." In Peter Faulkner, *The Silent Bomb.*

Bibliography

317

Faulkner, Peter. *The Silent Bomb: A Guide to the Nuclear Power Controversy.* New York: Vintage Books, 1977.

Ford, Daniel F., and Henry F. Kendall. *An Assessment of the Emergency Core Cooling Systems Rulemaking Hearing.* San Francisco: Friends of the Earth/Union of Concerned Scientists, 1974.

Gerber, C. G.; R. Hamburger; and E. W. S. Hull. *Plowshare.* Washington, D.C.: U.S. Atomic Energy Commission, Understanding the Atom Series, 1967.

Gillette, Robert. "Radiation Spill at Hanford: The Anatomy of an Accident." *Science,* August 1973.

———. "Transient Nuclear Workers: A Special Case for Standards." *Science,* 11 October 1974.

Gofman, John W. "The Cancer Hazard from Inhaled Plutonium." CNR Report 1975-IR. San Francisco: Committee for Nuclear Responsibility, 14 May 1975.

Greenfield, Jim. "After Slow Start, Latest Testimony Bolsters Zimmer's Foes." *Cincinnati Enquirer,* 1 July 1979.

———. " 'Cutting Corners' Called Top Concern At Zimmer." *Cincinnati Enquirer,* 20 June 1979.

———. "New Doubts Raised About Zimmer Welding." *Cincinnati Enquirer,* 30 June 1979.

———. "Witness Levels Charges Against Zimmer Supplier." *Cincinnati Enquirer,* 23 June 1979.

Greenfield, Jim, and Bob Elkins. "Life Styles Shape Moscow's Views at NRC Hearing." *Cincinnati Enquirer,* 23 May 1979.

Griffin, Victor C. Sworn Affidavit, 3 June 1979.

Gyorgy, Anna, and Friends. *No Nukes: Everyone's Guide to Nuclear Power.* Boston: South End Press, 1979.

"Hanford Comes Through Again: New Leak in April." *Not Man Apart,* Mid-May 1975.

Hofstadter, Edwin. Sworn Affidavit, 8 June 1979.

Holland, Gail Bernice. "3 Nuclear Dissidents Find Niche in N-Power." *San Francisco Examiner,* 15 August 1978.

Investigation of Charges Relating to Nuclear Reactor Safety. Hearings of the Joint Committee on Atomic Energy of the U.S. Congress, 94th Congress. Vol. 1. Washington, D.C.: U.S. Government Printing Office, 1976.

Jaffe, Susan. "Slow Death at Indian Point." *Village Voice,* 24 December 1979.

———. "The Tyranny of the Working Class." *Village Voice,* 8 October 1979.

Kaufman, Ben L. "Ex-Zimmer Inspector's Claims Called 'Hogwash'." *Cincinnati Enquirer,* 16 August 1979.

———. "3 More Zimmer Challengers To Get Federal Airing." *Cincinnati Enquirer,* 8 August 1979.

Keenen, Thomas D., to Dr. Roy Beaton, Nuclear Energy Systems Division, General Electric, 30 December 1975.

Kemp, Jo. "NRC Inspects Zimmer; Poor Workmanship Charged." *Community Journal,* 23 October 1979.

Kendall, Henry W., and Lawrence S. Tye. *Browns Ferry: The Regulatory Failure.* Washington, D.C.: Union of Concerned Scientists, 10 June 1976.

Liebau, Ron. "How Fast Can 25,000 Leave Zimmer?" *Valley Post,* 2 October 1980.
———. "Nuts and Bolts of Zimmer Construction." *Valley Post,* 26 May 1979.
Mancuso, Thomas F.; Alice Stewart; and George Kneale. "Radiation Exposure of Hanford Workers Dying from Cancer and Other Causes." *Health Physics* 33 (1977): 369–385.
Mayer, Vicky Anderson, and Nancy Flaherty. "What We Learned Has Frightened Us." *Cincinnati Post,* 9 August 1979.
McNutt, Randy. "Nuclear Plant Threat to Youth, Expert Says." *Cincinnati Enquirer,* 26 October 1979.
Milham, Samuel, Jr., M.D. "Increased Cancer Mortality Among Male Employees of the Atomic Energy Commission Hanford, Washington, Facility." In *Effect of Radiation on Human Health: Health Effects of Ionizing Radiation.* Vol. 1. Hearings before the Subcommittee on Health and the Environment of the Committee on Interstate and Foreign Commerce of the U.S. House of Representatives. Serial No. 95–179. Washington, D.C., 24, 25, 25 January and 8, 9, 14, 28 February 1978.
Nader, Ralph, and John Abbotts. *The Menace of Atomic Energy.* New York: W. W. Norton & Company, 1977.
Najarian, Thomas, and Theodore Colton. "Mortality from Leukemia and Cancer in Shipyard Nuclear Workers." *Lancet* (1978): 1018–1020.
Olson, McKinley. *Unacceptable Risk.* New York: Bantam Books, 1976.
Pollard, Robert D., to William A. Anders (chairman, U.S. Nuclear Regulatory Commission), second enclosure: "Report On the Nuclear Regulatory Commission Reactor Safety Review Process," 6 February 1976.
Radiation Standards and Public Health. Proceedings of a second congressional seminar on low-level ionizing radiation. Washington, D.C.: Congressional Research Service, Library of Congress, 10 February 1978.
Randall, Nan. "What If . . . ?" *New York,* 16 April 1979.
Schott, James R. " 'Working at Zimmer Will Be Safer than Driving to It'." *Cincinnati Post,* 9 August 1979.
Sheehy, Gail. "California's Impossible Nuclear Decision: A Reporter's Personal Search for an Answer." *New West,* 7 June 1976.
Smothers, Ronald. "Con Ed Welders Fear A-Plant Job, But Company Says Work or Quit." *New York Times,* 24 March 1978.
Starr, Douglas. "The Cast Before Zimmer Licensing Court." *Cincinnati Post,* 7 August 1979.
———. "CG & E Asks Workers to Divulge Zimmer Faults." *Cincinnati Post,* 9 August 1979.
———. "CG & E Challenges Worker's View that Zimmer's Reactor Seals Faulty." *Cincinnati Post,* 9 August 1979.
———. "CG & E Continues to Fire Away at Anti-Zimmer Plant Witness." *Cincinnati Post,* 27 June 1979.
———. "Memos Cast Doubt on Zimmer Welds." *Cincinnati Post,* 29 June 1979.
———. "Welds Remain Zimmer Issue." *Cincinnati Post,* 28 June 1979.
———. "Worker Alters Zimmer Stand." *Cincinnati Post,* 26 July 1979.
———. "Zimmer Opening May Be Delayed." *Cincinnati Post,* 15 February 1979.
———. "Zimmer Plant Hearings Focus on Safety of Nearby Pupils." *Cincinnati Post,* 20 June 1979.

U.S. Nuclear Regulatory Commission. "Licensing Hearings of the Atomic Safety and Licensing Board (ASLB) on the Wm. Zimmer Nuclear Power Plant." Docket No. 50-358. Washington, D.C., 7–9 August 1979.
———. Office of Inspection and Enforcement, Region III to Mr. Donn D. Rosenblum, Public Utilities Commission from James G. Keppler, director, Region III, 31 July 1979. Docket No. 50-358. Enclosures: "Inspection Summary, 27–28 February 1979, 1–2, 19–23 March 1979, and 9–11 April 1979. Including Section 10: "Control Rod Blades Inspection." IE Inspection Report No. 50-358/79-06.
"Zimmer Nuclear Plant A New Threat to American Electric Power System." *Together*, Castlewood, Virginia [Coalition of American Electric Consumers], June 1980.

AFTERWORD

Bacon, Kenneth H., and Thomas J. Bray. "An Interview with Harold Brown." *Wall Street Journal*, 1 July 1980.
Blundy, David, and John Bierman. "The Computer That Keeps Declaring War." *Times* (London), 22 June 1980.
Caldicott, Helen. *Nuclear Madness: What You Can Do*. Brookline, Massachusetts: Autumn Press, 1978.
Coffin, Tristram. "The MX, America's 100 Billion Dollar 'Edsel.' " *Washington Spectator and Between the Lines*, 15 October 1980.
Darby, Creg. "Beware the 'Fast Flux': Industry is Readying a New Kind of Nuke." *Progressive*, September 1980, pp. 24–27.
Grossman, Karl. *Cover Up: What You Are Not Supposed to Know About Nuclear Power*. New York: Permanent Press, 1980.
Kling, Mitchel. "Book Review: *The Counterforce Syndrome* by Robert C. Aldridge." *PSR Newsletter*, August 1980.
Randal, Judith. "Charge Ike Misled Public on N-tests." *Daily News*, 20 April 1979.
Schoenberger, Erica, and Amy K. Glasmeier. "Selling the MX: The Air Force Asks Nevada to Move Over." *Progressive*, May 1980, pp. 16–21.
Thaxton, Robert. "Directive Fifty-Nine: Carter's New 'Deterrence' Doctrine Moves Us Closer to the Holocaust." *Progressive*, October 1980, pp. 36–37.

Index

abortions, spontaneous, 44, 217
Abraham, Karl, 136
aging, premature, 45
    diagnostic X-rays and, 28–29
    leukemia and, 28–29
    low-level radiation and, 29–30
airplanes, nuclear, 286
ALARA principle ("as low as reasonably achievable"), 125
Aldridge, Robert, 295n
alpha radiation, 218–19, 228, 231
    defined, 229
America, 38
American Association for the Advancement of Science (AAAS), 97, 98
American College of Radiology, 43
Anaconda, 141, 165
Anders, William A., 280
Andes, John, 159
Andognini, Carl, 20
antiballistic missiles (ABM), 93, 94
Archer, Victor, 141, 142, 144
Argonne National Laboratory, xvii, 50, 168
"as low as reasonably achievable" (ALARA principle), 125
Atomic Bomb Casualty Commission, 37, 38, 42, 62n
atomic bombs, 47
    "Atoms for Peace," xviii, 158
    Einstein's views on, 57–58
    fuels for, 81, 82–83
    India's development of, 265–66
    peaceful use of, xviii, 63–69
    radiation dosage standards and, 31–32, 37–38, 42n

survivors of, 37, 38, 62
    see also atomic tests; Manhattan Project; nuclear weapons; Plowshare Program
Atomic Energy Act (1946), xvii, xviii, 140
Atomic Energy Commission (AEC), xvii, 72n, 75, 81n, 86, 87–88, 97, 99, 208, 270
    bomb tests and, 173, 174, 176–77, 194
    dissenting scientists opposed by, 52, 73, 102, 106, 107
    dissolution of, 39n, 103–4
    Plowshare Program of, 67n, 68–69, 76, 91–92
    public deceived by, 81, 88–91, 93–95, 126n, 168–69, 170n, 203n, 293–94
    safe threshold of radiation and, 95–96
    studies sponsored by, 50n, 62n, 63n, 101, 127, 236
    uranium mining and, 140, 167
    waste disposal and, 271–73
    weapons program of, 64n, 271, 294
Atomic Safety and Licensing Board (ASLB), 253
atomic tests, 90–91, 169
    atmospheric, xvii, 61, 87n, 173, 175–76
    Chinese, 73
    compensation for exposure to, 171, 177
    film badges worn in, 174–75
    infant mortality and, 61, 92–95
    leukemia and, 175
    stress tests and, 173
    underground, xx, xxi, 66n, 68
    U.S. servicemen exposed to, 158, 169, 171–205

atomic tests *(continued)*
   see also atomic bombs; Nevada test site;
      Smoky
Auxire, John, 194

Babcock, George, 118, 134n
Barker Nuclear Power Station, 33–35,
   158
Battelle Pacific Northwest Laboratories,
   40–41
Beaver Valley-1, 71, 72
Bebbington, William P., 228
Bechtel Corp., xxvi, 1, 4, 222n
Begay, Kee, 142–44
Bell Aircraft, 22, 24–25, 26
bentonite, defined, 158n
   described, 161
Bertell, Rosalie, 22–49
   background of, 22–26
   Congress in retaliation against, 38–40
   in highway accident, xxv, 48–49
   on inadequacies of radiation standards,
      31–32
   leukemia rates studied by, 26–29
   nonprofit research organization formed
      by, 44
   nuclear industry in retaliation against,
      35–37
   nuclear power plant opposed by, 33–37
   on premature aging among radiation
      workers, xxiv, 29–31
   see also Tri-State Leukemia Survey
beta radiation, defined, 229
Bettis Laboratory, 59
Beverly, Bob, 142
Biggs, Max, 87
Big Rock nuclear power plant, 34–35
Biological Effects of Ionizing Radiation
   (BEIR) Report, 103
birth defects, 50, 175, 217
Blanch, Donald, 251–52
bombs, *see* atomic bombs; atomic tests; hydrogen bombs; nuclear weapons
Booboor, Jeff, 126
boron, described, 214n
Boston Edison, 1n
   fined for negligence, 14
   lawsuit against, 3, 15–17
   on Pires and Fitts case, 20, 21
   see also Pilgrim Nuclear Power Station
      Unit I

Bradley, John, 296n
Bravo, 173
breakdowns:
   cost of, 6n
   defined, 4n, 5n
breeder reactors, xix, xx, xxi, xxv, xxvii,
   108–10, 295–96
Bridenbaugh, Dale, 129, 135, 258–68, 275,
   278
   at Dresden, 258–63
   in GE Nuclear "Complaint Depart-
      ment," 264–66
   at JCAE hearings, 267–68, 280–83
   resignation of, xxiii, 266–68, 279, 281n,
      282–83, 291
British Columbia Medical Association, 47
Brookhaven National Laboratory, 132–33
Bross, Irwin, 36, 40n, 43, 174, 217n
Brown, Harold, 297n
Brown, Jerry, 297
Browns Ferry Nuclear Power Plant, xxiii,
   275–77, 287–88
Bruce, June, 122
Buechley, Robert W., 141–42
Bulletin of the Atomic Scientists, 93, 94
Bureau of Indian Affairs (BIA), 155, 156,
   157, 158
Bureau of Radiological Health, 69–70
   Division of Environmental Radiation of,
      70n
Burnham, David, 291
burning out workers, defined, 5

Camp Desert Rock, 175, 181, 182–83, 198
cancer, 38, 170
   described, 293
   diagnostic X-rays and, 60, 95n
   fallout and, 61
   low-level radiation and, 41, 95–96
   among radiation workers, 69, 85, 101,
      261n
   radio-iodine treatment and, ix, 78–80
   rate in U.S., xxvi
   see also leukemia
cancer, breast, 80
   detection of, 43
cancer, lung, 294
   breeder reactors and, 108, 109
   smoking and, 141–42
   among uranium miners, 101, 140, 141–
      42, 143, 144, 168

carbon-14, 88n
Carter, Jimmy, xviii, 297n
Carter, Tim Lee, 41n, 192n
Center for Disease Control (CDC), 175
cesium-137, 84, 110, 229, 263
Chachere, Matthew, 121n, 133, 134
chemical samples, defined, 211n
chest counts, defined, 226n
Cincinnati Gas & Electric Co. (CG & E), 245n
   see also Zimmer, Wm., Nuclear Power Station
Citizens' Energy Project, 48n
Clinch River Breeder Reactor, xxvii, 108
coal gasification, defined, 156
Cohen, Bernard, 244
Columbia Gas System, 63n, 64
Commonwealth Edison Co., 258n
   see also Dresden Nuclear Power Station
Congress, U.S., 108
   see also Joint Committee on Atomic Energy
Conoco, 141, 162, 165
Consolidated Edison, 217, 237n, 253
   see also Indian Point Station
continuous air monitors (CAM), 215
control rods, function of, 247
cores, defined, 220
Creative Initiative Foundation (CIF), 277–79, 282–83
criticality, defined, 215n
Crouse Nuclear Energy Services, 3
curies, defined, 70n
Curry, Jack, 253
cyclotrons, 82

Dann, Jack Russell, 192n
Dean, Gordon, 176
"Death of all Children, The," 93
de-conning, defined, 213n
DeGroot, Morris, 70–71, 72
Denver Post, 142
Department of Defense, U.S., 149, 174, 176
Department of Energy, U.S. (DOE), xxiii, 32n, 41n, 42n, 106, 223
   as front for weapons industry, 47–48
Department of the Interior, U.S., 63n
dissolvers, defined, 214n
DNA (Dinebeiina Nahiilna Be Agaditahe), 150

double doses, defined, 6n
Drake, Gerald, 34–35
Dresden Nuclear Power Station, xix, xx, xxi, xxii, 70, 70n, 258–63
   faulty control rods at, 262–63
   radiation limits at, 261–62
   workers uninformed at, 260–61
Duquesne Light Company, 72, 73
Durkin, John, 41n

Einstein, Albert, xv, xviii, 54–58
   atomic bomb as viewed by, 57–58
Eisenhower, Dwight D., xviii, 87n, 293–94
electrons, 55–56
Emergency Core Cooling System (ECCS), 104, 274n
Energy Research and Development Association (ERDA), xxii, 39, 40–42, 104
enrichment plants, 237–238
   see also Oak Ridge Lab
Environmental Impact Statements, defined, 161n
Environmental Protection Agency (EPA), 32n, 75, 141, 163
Erwin, Tenn., nuclear fuel plant, 29–31
Esquire, 93
Everett, James, 115–17, 118, 130, 133–34
Everett, John, 115–36
   in antinuclear demonstrations, 115, 130–32
   at Brookhaven Lab, 132–33
   as carpenter at Shoreham, 118–24, 126
   on quitting Shoreham, 129–30
   on release of radioactive water, 124–25
   in trial, 133–35
   union harassment of, 115–17, 133–34
"extraordinary" events, defined, 158–59
Exxon Minerals, xxiv, 159

Fabic, Stan, 127
fallout, 52, 61, 62, 76, 93
   radiation sickness from, 196n
fallout shelters, 60
fetal deaths, 44, 61, 217
film badges, 174–75, 203n, 261
Finch, Robert, 103
Fitts, Ralph, 14n, 169
   illness of, 16n
   overexposure of, xxiv, 3, 7, 9, 10, 11, 12, 19, 20
fluoroscopy, 59

food chain, radioactivity and, 273
Ford, Daniel F., xxii, 103–4, 274
Foster, John, 87–89, 91, 92
"Franklin Prime," 183–84, 198
Freedom of Information Act, 294
Friends of the Earth, 240
fuel processing:
  enrichment in, 238
  for Manhattan Project, 84–85, 270
  reprocessing in, 220, 236n
  for weapons industry, 52, 76–77, 237–
    38, 265–66, 294
  see also plutonium; uranium; specific
    plants
fuel rods, described, 263
fusion, 47

gamma radiation, defined, 229
General Electric Co. (GE), 136, 156n,
    245, 298
  defective reactors built by, 128, 129,
    264–65, 266–68, 288
  executives at, 258–92
  high-level resignations from, 267–68,
    279–83, 290–92
  official public relations line of, 273–75,
    278, 289–90
  poor sales record of, 287
genetic damage, 44–45, 60–61, 110–11
Geological Survey, U.S., 162
Getty Oil Co., 208
Gillette, Lynn, 283
Global Education Associates, 44
Gmuca, Joe, 157
Gofman, John W., ix, 78–114, 261n
  AEC coverup and, 89–91
  in atomic bomb research, 82–85
  funding cut for, 104–7
  harassment of, 96–102
  Livermore Medical Department organ-
    ized by, 86–89
  low-level radiation, xxi
  nuclear power opposed by, 103, 107,
    108–12, 294–95
  on sociopolitical aspects of nuclear weap-
    ons, 112–14
Goodyear Atomic, 237n
Grace-Davison, W. R., Chemical Co., xxi,
    208
Griffin, Victor C., 252

Grossman, Karl, 136, 294n
Gulf Minerals, 165

Haig, Alexander, 296n
Hanford Engineer Works, xvi, 222,
    268–73
  accidents, xxiii
  background, 270
  National Production Reactor (NPR),
    237, 238
  nuclear workers, xxi
  plutonium made at, 270–71
  waste leakage at, xxii, 271–73, 272n
Health Research Group, Nader's, 5n, 135
Hensley, P. N. "Barney," 194
Hiroshima, atomic bomb dropped on, xvi,
    85, 175
  survivors of, 37, 38, 62
Hodsden, William H., 169, 171–205
  children of, 203
  disability benefits denied to, 203–5
  illness of, 194–98, 200–202
  at Smoky, 171, 177, 180–81, 184–94,
    203n
  in war games, 178–80
Hofstadter, Edwin, 251
Holzer, Fred, 66n
Honicker, Jeannine, 253
hot, defined, 217
hot cells, defined, 221n
hot samples, defined, 211n
Hubbard, Richard, 135, 278, 283–92
  background of, 283–84
  in GE nuclear division, 284–90
  at JCAE hearings, 267–68, 280–83
  resignation of, xxiii, 267–68, 279, 281n,
    282–83, 290–92
Human Resources Research Organization
    (HumRRO), 173n
Husen, LaVerne, 141
hydrogen bombs, 47
  "peaceful" use of, 91–92

Idaho Falls test reactor, xx, 281n
Indian Point Station, 253–58
  lax safety procedures at, xxiii, 255–56
  Unit 1, xx, 217, 253n, 279n
  Unit 2, xxvi, 253n, 279n
  Unit 3, 253n
infant mortality, 170

infant mortality *(continued)*
  bomb tests and, 61, 92–95
  near nuclear power plants, 70–71, 72, 74
Institute for Electrical, Electronic Engineers (IEEE), meeting of, 95–96, 97, 103n
International Commission on Radiological Protection (ICRP), 32n, 167
International Exhibition of the Peaceful Atom, 60
iodine-131, 73, 229
ionizing radiation, defined, 293

Jablon, Seymour, 42–43
Jacks, Gordon, 205
Joint Committee on Atomic Energy (JCAE), 70n
  Bertell and, 39, 40n, 41n
  GE executives and, xxiii, 266–67, 280–83
  Gofman and, 100–102
jumpers, defined, 217

Kahn, Herman, 60
Keating, Frank W., 192n
Kelly, Orville, 169, 177
Kendall, Henry W., xxii, 103–4, 274
Kennedy, Edward, 176n
Kerr-McGee Nuclear Corporation, xviii, xxii, xxiv, 141, 142, 149, 164n, 165
Khrushchev, Nikita, 87n
kidneys, radioactive materials and damage to, 30
Kissinger, Henry, 60–61
Kistiakowsky, George, 297
Knapp, Harold, 90–91
Kneale, George, xxi, 42n, 95n
krypton gas, 255–56
Kunkler, J. L., 162n

Labor Management Reporting and Disclosure Act (LMRDA), 258n
Lapp, Ralph E., 14n
lasers, 48
"launch on warning," defined, 297n
Lawrence, Ernest, 84, 86
Lawrence Livermore National Lab, xxv, xxvi, 64, 67, 86–89, 93, 98–99
Lawrence Radiation Laboratory, 64n, 84–85, 86

leukemia, 38, 74
  age and susceptibility to, 28
  data available on, 26–27
  diagnostic X-rays and, 27–29, 39, 60, 95n
  fallout and, 52, 61, 62, 64
  premature aging and, 28–29
  among radiation workers, 15, 85, 217
  see also Bertell, Rosalie; radiation dose standards
Levin, David, 106–7
Levy, Paul, 135
Libby, W. F., 205
lipoproteins, defined, 86
Liverman, James, 39, 40, 41n–42n
Livermore Lab, *see* Lawrence Livermore National Lab
Lofton, John, 63–64
Long Island Lighting Co. (LILCO), 115, 117, 119, 122, 126, 128, 129, 135–36
  see also Shoreham nuclear power plant
Los Alamos Scientific Laboratory, xvi, 84, 86, 168
loss of coolant accidents (LOCA), 121
Lynch, Tom, 156

McCarthy, Bob, 11, 13
McCormack, Mike, 281, 282–83
McGuire, Paul, 20
McNamara, Robert S., 92
Maillie, H. David, 31
mammography, 43
Mancuso, Thomas, xxi, 41, 60
Manhattan Project, xvi, 57, 83–85, 140, 293, 294n, 297
  establishment of, 57n
  plutonium produced for, 84–85, 270
Marble Hill nuclear power plant, 123n
Marks, Sidney, 40–42
MARK II, 129
Martin, Tom, 245–51
  faulty control rods discovered by, 247–48
  at licensing hearings for Zimmer, 248–50
Mazzocchi, Tony, 168
meltdowns, 74, 121, 126–27
mental retardation, 175
MHB Technical Associates, 135–36

microwaves, 48
milksheds, defined, 87n
Miller, Keith, 127
milliroentgen, defined, 4n
Millstone Nuclear Power Station, xxii, 75–76
Ministry of Concern for Public Health, 44
Minor, Gregory, 129, 135, 267–83
  in GE Nuclear Energy Division, 273–77
  at Hanford, 268–73
  at JCAE hearings, 267–68, 280–83
  resignation of, xxiii, 267–68, 277, 279, 281n, 282–83, 291
Mobil, 141, 162, 165
Morgan, Karl Z., 32, 72n
Motley, Constance Baker, 258n
Murphy, George F., Jr., 40n
Museler, William, 122n
Muskie, Edmund S., 96, 97, 100, 103
MX missiles, xxvii, 296, 298

Nader, Ralph, 5n, 103, 135, 274n
Nagasaki, atomic bomb dropped on, xvii, 81, 85
  survivors of, 37, 38, 62
Nahkai, John Smith, 144, 145–46
Nahkai, Pearl, 144–46
Najarian, Thomas, 69n, 257
NASA, 59
National Academy of Sciences, 5n, 32n, 62n, 103
National Association of Atomic Veterans, 169, 174
National Cancer Institute (NCI), xxvi, 41n, 42–43, 105, 106–7
National Citizens' Hearings on Radiation Victims, 137, 171
National Commission on Radiological Protection, 167
National Council on Radiation Protection and Measurements, 32
National Environmental Policy Act (NEPA; 1969), 161n, 163
National Institute of Occupational Safety and Health (NIOSH), 141
National Research Council, 32n
"National Sacrifice Areas," 149
natural gas, underground bomb-testing and, 63–69
Nautilus, 59, 69n

Navajo lands:
  acquisition of, 157–58
  allotment of, 157n
  cultural ties to, 160–61
  mining plans disregarded on, 162–63
  open mining pits on, 146, 147–48, 161
  uranium mining on, 137–67
  uranium tailings exposed on, 144, 146, 149, 164, 165
  water contamination on, 144, 163–64, 166–67
  water shortage on, 144, 162–63
  see also uranium miners
Nevada test site, xviii, xxi, 184
  see also Camp Desert Rock, Yucca Flats, Smoky
neutron bombs, 295
neutrons, 83, 214n, 247
neutron sensors, defined, 288n
Newman, Robert, 205
New York State Electric & Gas Company (NYSEG), 33n, 129
New York Times, 166, 291
Niagara Mohawk Power Co., 158
Nixon, Richard M., 75, 107
Nuclear Fuel Services, Inc. (NFS), xx, xxi, 29n, 206, 208, 209, 222n, 243
  see also West Valley reprocessing plant
nuclear power plants, 69–77, 103, 107
  fatalities in, 281n
  infant mortality near, 70–71, 72, 74
  as licensed murder, 111–12
  military linked to, 52, 76–77, 265–66, 294
  perfect containment in, 110–11
  politics and regulation of, 75
  probability of disaster in, 127, 279
  radioactive releases from, 69–76
  radioactive water discharged by, 124–25
  shoddy construction of, 123n
  temporary workers at, 217
  thermal pollution from, 125–26
  see also specific plants
nuclear reactors:
  breeder, 108–10, 295–96
  foreign policy and sale of, 287
  life expectancy of, 128n

Nuclear Regulatory Commission (NRC), 127, 238n, 255, 266–67, 277n, 279–80
  coolant water regulated by, 125
  establishment of, 39n, 75, 104
  exposure standards set by, 5n, 32n
  nuclear facilities closed by, 31, 123n, 240
  Pilgrim I investigated by, 13–14, 19–20
  Shoreham inspected by, 122, 136
  Site Survey of (1975), 136n
  Three Mile Island investigated by, ix, 32
  Zimmer and, 248, 249, 250, 251
"Nuclear Suicide" (Bertell), 38
Nuclear Utilities Services Corporation (NUS), 72, 73
nuclear warfare, 296–99
  computers and initiation of, 296–97
  survival in, 60–61, 297–98
  U.S. servicemen prepared for, 158, 169, 171–205
  see also atomic bombs; nuclear weapons
nuclear wastes, xix, 238n, 241, 243–44, 271–73, 274–75, 289
nuclear weapons:
  deterrence policy vs. first-strike capability and, 113–14
  in future, 48, 295–96
  "peaceful" use of, 63–69, 91–92
  sociopolitical aspects of, 112–14
  see also atomic bombs; nuclear warfare; weapons industry; MX missiles, Trident missiles

Oak Ridge Lab, xvi, 25, 41n, 237n
Oldham, William, 244
on time, defined, 76n
Oppenheimer, J. Robert, xvii, xviii, 84, 86n
Ostrowski, Richard, 169, 253–58
  at Indian Point, 254–56
  union pressures on, 255, 257–58
Oyster Creek nuclear power plant, 125–26

pacemakers, plutonium, 76
Palanquin, 66n
Panama Canal, nuclear bombs and rebuilding of, 67, 91–92
particle physics, 55–56
particulate, defined, 215n

Pastore, John O., 39, 40n, 281–82, 283
Pauling, Linus, 61, 88n, 112
"peaceful" atom, 60, 294
  see also Plowshare Program; Project Ketch
pentomic warfare, 179
  defined, 173n
Peshlakai, Elsie, 150–66
  childhood of, 151–53
Phillips, Bill, 142
Phillips Petroleum, 162, 165
photoelectric effect, 54
photons (light waves), 54, 56
Pierce, Hank, 65–66
Pilgrim Nuclear Power Station Unit I, xxi, 1–13
  coverup attempted at, 11–12, 13
  NRC investigation of, 13–14, 18–19
  overexposure of workers at, xxiv, 3, 7–11, 18–19
  radiation dosages at, 1n, 5–6
  workers' orientation at, 3–4
  see also Boston Edison
Pires, James, 1–21, 169
  in lawsuit, 3, 15–17
  laying off of, 12–13
  overdose received by, xxiv, 3, 7–11
Pittsburgh Post Gazette, 63, 65–66
Plowshare Program, xxi, 66n, 67, 68–69, 76, 91–92
plutonium, 80–81, 83n, 244
  alpha emitter, 228, 229
  contamination, xix, xxi, 212n, 213n, 220, 228
  in breeder reactors, 108–9, 295–96
  experiments with, xvi
  as fuel in nuclear weapons, 81, 83–85, 219, 270–71, 295–96, 298
  hazards of, 108, 109, 110, 218, 241, 278, 294–95
  in power plant processes, 211n, 220, 263
  stealing of, 218–19
Pollard, Robert D., xxiii, 279–80
pollution, thermal, 125–26
positrons, 55–56
potassium-40, 82n
premature births, 70
Price Anderson Act, xix, 158–59
process cells, defined, 211n
Project Gasbuggy, 66n, 68

Project Ketch, xxi, 63–67, 158
Project Rio Blanco, 68
Project Rulison, 68
Proxmire, William, 296n
Public Health Service, U.S., 32n, 46–47,
    70, 80, 102, 168
Pyles, David, 169, 206–44
    background of, 208–9
    on plutonium being carried home,
        230–31
    relicensing of West Valley opposed by,
        240
    resignation of, 235–36
    at West Valley, 206–8, 209–38

quantum theory, 56

radiation, types of, 229
radiation dosage standards, 4–6, 31–32,
    110, 262n
    atomic bomb data as basis for, 31–32,
        37–38, 42n
    at bomb tests, 174
    calendar quarters in computation of, 5–6
    federal regulations for, 4n, 5n, 31–32,
        261n
    increases in, 32n
    as recommendations vs. laws, 32n
    safe threshold and, 95–96, 100
    in water, 163
Radiation Effects Research Foundation
    (RERF), 38n
    see also Atomic Bomb Casualty Com-
    mission
radiation sickness:
    Smoky and, 194–98
    symptoms of, 196n
radioactive tracers, defined, 82n
radioactivity, artificial, defined, 81n
radioactivity, natural, defined, 81n
radio-iodine, xxi, 84
    bomb tests and, 87–88, 90
    in thyroid treatment, ix, 78–81
radium, 140
"radon daughters," 140
radon gases, 109n, 140, 164n
rad-waste areas, defined, 7n
Rasmussen Report, xxii, xxiv, 127
rectennas, 48n
remote decontamination equipment,
    222–23

rems (roentgen equivalent man), defined,
    6n
reprocessing plants, 228, 236, 271
    defined, 220, 236n
    see also Hanford Engineer Works; West
    Valley reprocessing plant
Robinson, Paul, 159–60, 166
Rockefeller, Nelson A., 215
Rockwell International, 42n
Rocky Flats Nuclear Weapons Facility,
    xvii, xix, xxi, xxiv, 25, 31, 42n
Rogers, Paul, 42n
Roosevelt, Franklin D., xv, xvi, 57
Rosenberg, Howard, 177
Rumondi, Pete, 260

Sacco, Emma, 40n
San Francisco Chronicle, 96, 108–9,
    291
satellites, 48, 59
Schlesinger, James R., xxiii, 41n
Schott, James R., 245
Schwartz, Arthur, 117
Science, 52, 164n
scrubbers, defined, 211n
Seaborg, Glenn, 69, 81–82, 83, 91, 99
Seeger, Pete, 134
Seegmiller, Pratt, 147
Severo, Richard, 240n, 244
SHAD Alliance, 257, 258
Shippingport Atomic Power Station, xviii,
    xxi, 64n, 70, 71–74, 75
    leakage of radioactive gases at, 71–72
    zero-release claims of, 71–73
Shoreham nuclear power plant, xxiv, 115–
    36, 245n
    construction defects at, 115, 117, 120–
        24, 126, 136
    construction payroll padded at, 119–20
    cost of, 128n
    demonstration at, 115, 130–32
    evacuation plans for, 126–27
    reactor design at, 128–29, 135–36, 245
Silkwood, Karen, xxii, xxiv, 291
Singer Sewing Machines, 298
Smith, Paul B., 163–64
smoking, 141–42
Smoky, xix, 171, 180–81, 184–94, 203n
    AEC scientists at, 177, 194
    detonation of, 190–91
    power of, 175

Smoky *(continued)*
  radiation sickness after, 194–98
  as stress test, 173–74
sodium, liquid, 109, 295
solar power, 130
solar-powered satellite system (SPS), 48
spent fuel, 220, 236n, 263–64
Standard Oil of Ohio (Sohio), 159
start-ups, defined, 7n
Sternglass, Ernest J., 50–77
  atomic bomb opposed by, xxi, 60–61, 63–67
  background of, 52–54
  Low-Level Radiation, xxii
  on bomb tests and infant mortality, 61, 92–93, 94
  Einstein and, 54–58
  on military and nuclear reactors, 76–77
  on safety of nuclear reactors, 69–72, 74–77, 261n
Stewart, Alice, xix, xxi, 42n, 60, 95n
Storer, J., 41n
Strain, Peggy, 164
Stromberg, Lawrence R., 203n
strontium-90, xix, 73, 84, 88n, 110, 229, 244n, 263, 273
  hazards of, 293
submarines, nuclear, 59, 69, 286
supplied air, defined, 230n
Szilard, Leo, xv, 57n

Tamplin, Arthur, xxi, 93–96, 97–98, 99, 100, 102, 103, 106, 107
Tarapur Atomic Power Station (TAPS), xxi, 265–66
Tay Sachs disease, 58–59
technetium-99, 238
Teller, Edward, xvii, 57n, 67, 86n, 93
Tennessee Valley Authority (TVA), 168, 275n, 277n
test-ban treaty, xx, 87n, 92, 175
thermal pollution, 125–26
thermoluminescent detector devices (TLD), 11n
thorium, 82, 83n
Three Mile Island, ix, xxiv, 32, 47, 64, 74, 110, 158–59
  evacuation from, 170
TLD reading rooms, defined, 11n
TLDs (thermoluminescent detector devices), 11n

Trident missiles, 295
Tri-State Leukemia Survey, xx, 26–27, 39
  data collected in, 26–27
  funding cut for, 40–44
  interpretation of, 27, 39
  see also Bertell, Rosalie
Tullabee, 69n

Union Carbide, xvi, 39, 40, 142, 237n, 298
Union of Concerned Scientists, 103–4
United Nations, xix, 44, 175–76
United Nuclear Corporation, xxiv, 141, 155, 157, 159, 160, 165, 166–67
uranium, 271, 294, 295n
  extraction and refining of, 140
  hazards of, 108–9
  in power plant processes, 211n, 220, 236–38, 247, 263
  water contaminated by, 140, 141, 144, 163–64
uranium miners, 109, 167
  compensation for, 149
  lung cancer among, 101, 140, 141–42, 143, 144, 168
  Navajos as, 141–50, 160
uranium nitrate, plutonium produced from, 84–85
uranium tailings, 144, 146, 149, 164n
  defined, 140–41
uranium-233, 82–83
uranium-235, 82, 83n, 220, 229, 236n, 263
uranium-238, 108
urine, blood in, 30
Utah International, 141, 156

Vanadium, 141
Veterans Administration, 169, 171, 177, 202, 203

Wagoner, Joseph, 142
Wahl, Arthur, 83
Waltz Mills reactor, xx, 74
weapons industry, 296
  DOE as front for, 47–48
  nuclear power program linked to, 52, 76–77, 265–66, 294
  profit motive in, 298
  reprocessing plants and, 237–38
  secrecy in, 25
  see also atomic bombs; nuclear weapons
Weaver, Charles, 70n

Weidenmann, Fran, 20
Weisman, Steven R., 241
Western Nuclear, 165
Westinghouse, 59–60, 64n, 71, 108, 298
West Valley reprocessing plant, xx, xxi, xxiv, 29n, 31, 206–8, 209–24
  accident at, 225–28
  air monitored at, 215–16
  closing of, xxii, 240, 243
  contaminated vent duct at, 231–36
  earthquakes and, 240
  fuel processed at, summarized, 239
  layout of, 209–11
  lunchroom contaminated at, 220–21
  power outages at, 212–13
  practical jokes at, 213–15
  safety equipment lacking in, 222–23
  samples monitored at, 223–24
  security at, 217–19
  temporary workers at, 216–17
  waste disposal at, 241, 243–44
  weapons industry and, 237–38
  workers' complaints at, 221–22
Western New York Nuclear Service Center. *See* West Valley
Wigner, Eugene, 57n

Windscale reprocessing plant, xix, 236n
World Wide Military Command and Control System (Wimex), 296–97

X-rays, 229
  skin disorders treated with, 53
X-rays, diagnostic:
  on babies and fetuses, xxi, 58, 60, 95n
  fluoroscopy as, 59
  leukemia linked to, 27–29, 39
  mammography as, 43
  premature aging and, 28–29
  radiation standards compared to, 31, 32

Yazzie, Clifford, 147, 149
Yazzie, Fannie, 147–49
yellowcake, defined, 140
Yin, Isa T., 252
Yucca Flats, 175, 182, 184

Zimmer, Wm., Nuclear Power Station, 123n, 245–53
  faulty construction at, 251–52
  faulty control rods at, 247–48, 250–51
  licensing hearings for, 248–50, 251–53
Zuckert, Eugene, 176